Java Deep Learning Projects

Implement 10 real-world deep learning applications using
Deeplearning4j and open source APIs

Md. Rezaul Karim

BIRMINGHAM - MUMBAI

Java Deep Learning Projects

Commissioning Editor: Sunith Shetty
Acquisition Editor: Tushar Gupta
Content Development Editor: Karan Thakkar
Technical Editor: Dinesh Pawar
Copy Editor: Vikrant Phadkay
Project Coordinator: Nidhi Joshi
Proofreader: Safis Editing
Indexer: Rekha Nair
Graphics: Tania Dutta
Production Coordinator: Arvindkumar Gupta

First published: June 2018

Production reference: 1280618

Published by Packt Publishing Ltd.
Livery Place
35 Livery Street
Birmingham
B3 2PB, UK.

ISBN 978-1-78899-745-4

www.packtpub.com

`mapt.io`

Mapt is an online digital library that gives you full access to over 5,000 books and videos, as well as industry leading tools to help you plan your personal development and advance your career. For more information, please visit our website.

Why subscribe?

- Spend less time learning and more time coding with practical eBooks and Videos from over 4,000 industry professionals

- Improve your learning with Skill Plans built especially for you

- Get a free eBook or video every month

- Mapt is fully searchable

- Copy and paste, print, and bookmark content

PacktPub.com

Did you know that Packt offers eBook versions of every book published, with PDF and ePub files available? You can upgrade to the eBook version at `www.PacktPub.com` and as a print book customer, you are entitled to a discount on the eBook copy. Get in touch with us at `service@packtpub.com` for more details.

At `www.PacktPub.com`, you can also read a collection of free technical articles, sign up for a range of free newsletters, and receive exclusive discounts and offers on Packt books and eBooks.

Contributors

About the author

Md. Rezaul Karim is a Research Scientist at Fraunhofer FIT, Germany. He is also a PhD candidate at RWTH Aachen University, Germany. Before joining FIT, he was a Researcher at Insight Centre for Data Analytics, Ireland. Before that, he was a Lead Engineer at Samsung Electronics, Korea.

He has 9 years of R&D experience in Java, Scala, Python, and R. He has hands-on experience in Spark, Zeppelin, Hadoop, Keras, scikit-learn, TensorFlow, Deeplearning4j, and H2O. He has published several research papers in top-ranked journals/conferences focusing on bioinformatics and deep learning.

About the reviewer

Joao Bosco Jares is a Software Engineer with 12 years of experience in machine learning, Semantic Web and IoT. Previously, he was a Software Engineer at IBM Watson, Insight Centre for Data Analytics, Brazilian Northeast Bank, and Bank of Amazonia, Brazil.

He has an MSc and a BSc in computer science, and a data science postgraduate degree. He is also an IBM Jazz RTC Certified Professional, Oracle Certified Master Java EE 6 Enterprise Architect, and Sun Java Certified Programmer.

Packt is searching for authors like you

If you're interested in becoming an author for Packt, please visit authors.packtpub.com and apply today. We have worked with thousands of developers and tech professionals, just like you, to help them share their insight with the global tech community. You can make a general application, apply for a specific hot topic that we are recruiting an author for, or submit your own idea.

Table of Contents

Preface

The continued growth in data, coupled with the need to make increasingly complex decisions against that data, is creating massive hurdles that prevent organizations from deriving insights in a timely manner using traditional analytical approaches.

To find meaningful values and insights, deep learning evolved, which is a branch of machine learning algorithms based on learning multiple levels of abstraction. Neural networks, being at the core of deep learning, are used in predictive analytics, computer vision, natural language processing, time series forecasting, and performing a myriad of other complex tasks.

Until date, most DL books available are written in Python. However, this book is conceived for developers, data scientists, machine learning practitioners, and deep learning enthusiasts who want to build powerful, robust, and accurate predictive models with the power of Deeplearning4j (a JVM-based DL framework), combining other open source Java APIs.

Throughout the book, you will learn how to develop practical applications for AI systems using feedforward neural networks, convolutional neural networks, recurrent neural networks, autoencoders, and factorization machines. Additionally, you will learn how to attain your deep learning programming on GPU in a distributed way.

After finishing the book, you will be familiar with machine learning techniques, in particular, the use of Java for deep learning, and will be ready to apply your knowledge in research or commercial projects. In summary, this book is not meant to be read cover to cover. You can jump to a chapter that looks like something you are trying to accomplish or one that simply ignites your interest.

Happy reading!

Who this book is for

Developers, data scientists, machine learning practitioners, and deep learning enthusiasts who wish to learn how to develop real-life deep learning projects by harnessing the power of JVM-based Deeplearning4j (DL4J), Spark, RankSys, and other open source libraries will find this book extremely useful. A sound understanding of Java is needed. Nevertheless, some basic prior experience of Spark, DL4J, and Maven-based project management will be useful to pick up the concepts quicker.

What this book covers

Chapter 1, *Getting Started with Deep Learning*, explains some basic concepts of machine learning and artificial neural networks as the core of deep learning. It then briefly discusses existing and emerging neural network architectures. Next, it covers various features of deep learning frameworks and libraries. Then it shows how to solve Titanic survival prediction using a Spark-based Multilayer Perceptron (MLP). Finally, it discusses some frequent questions related to this projects and general DL area.

Chapter 2, *Cancer Types Prediction Using Recurrent Type Networks*, demonstrates how to develop a DL application for cancer type classification from a very-high-dimensional gene expression dataset. First, it performs necessary feature engineering such that the dataset can feed into a Long Short-Term Memory (LSTM) network. Finally, it discusses some frequent questions related to this project and DL4J hyperparameters/nets tuning.

Chapter 3, *Multi-Label Image Classification Using Convolutional Neural Networks*, demonstrates how to develop an end-to-end project for handling the multi-label image classification problem using CNN on top of the DL4J framework on real Yelp image datasets. It discusses how to tune hyperparameters for better classification results.

Chapter 4, *Sentiment Analysis Using Word2Vec and the LSTM Network*, shows how to develop a hands-on deep learning project that classifies review texts as either positive or negative sentiments. A large-scale movie review dataset will be used to train the LSTM model, and Word2Vec will be used as the neural embedding. Finally, it shows sample predictions for other review datasets.

Chapter 5, *Transfer Learning for Image Classification*, demonstrates how to develop an end-to-end project to solve dog versus cat image classification using a pre-trained VGG-16 model. We wrap up everything in a Java JFrame and JPanel application to make the overall pipeline understandable for making sample object detection.

Chapter 6, *Real-Time Object Detection Using YOLO, JavaCV, and DL4J*, shows how to develop an end-to-end project that will detect objects from video frames when the video clips play continuously. The pre-trained YOLO v2 model will be used as transfer learning and JavaCV API for video frame handling on top of DL4J.

Chapter 7, *Stock Price Prediction Using the LSTM Network*, demonstrates how to develop a real-life plain stock open, close, low, high, or volume price prediction using LSTM on top of the DL4J framework. Time series generated from a real-life stock dataset will be used to train the LSTM model, which will be used to predict the price only 1 day ahead at a time step.

Chapter 8, *Distributed Deep Learning on Cloud – Video Classification Using Convolutional LSTM Network,* shows how to develop an end-to-end project that accurately classifies a large collection of video clips (for example, UCF101) using a combined CNN and LSTM network on top of DL4J. The training is carried out on Amazon EC2 GPU compute cluster. Eventually, this end-to-end project can be treated as a primer for human activity recognition from video or so.

Chapter 9, Playing *GridWorld Game Using Deep Reinforcement Learning,* is all about designing a machine learning system driven by criticisms and rewards. It then shows how to develop a GridWorld game using DL4J, RL4J, and neural QLearning that acts as the Q function.

Chapter 10, *Developing Movie Recommendation Systems Using Factorization Machines,* is about developing a sample project using factorization machines to predict both the rating and ranking of movies. It then discusses some theoretical background of recommendation systems using matrix factorization and collaborative filtering, before diving the project implementation using RankSys-library-based FMs.

Chapter 11, *Discussion, Current Trends, and Outlook,* wraps up everything by discussing the completed projects and some abstract takeaways. Then it provides some improvement suggestions. Additionally, it covers some extension guidelines for other real-life deep learning projects.

To get the most out of this book

All the examples have been implemented using Deeplearning4j with some open source libraries in Java. To be more specific, the following API/tools are required:

- Java/JDK version 1.8
- Spark version 2.3.0
- Spark csv_2.11 version 1.3.0
- ND4j backend version nd4j-cuda-9.0-platform for GPU, otherwise nd4j-native
- ND4j version >=1.0.0-alpha
- DL4j version >=1.0.0-alpha
- Datavec version >=1.0.0-alpha
- Arbiter version >=1.0.0-alpha
- Logback version 1.2.3
- JavaCV platform version 1.4.1

- HTTP Client version 4.3.5
- Jfreechart 1.0.13
- Jcodec 0.2.3
- Eclipse Mars or Luna (latest) or Intellij IDEA
- Maven Eclipse plugin (2.9 or higher)
- Maven compiler plugin for Eclipse (2.3.2 or higher)
- Maven assembly plugin for Eclipse (2.4.1 or higher)

Regarding operating system: Linux distributions are preferable (including Debian, Ubuntu, Fedora, RHEL, CentOS). To be more specific, for example, for Ubuntu it is recommended to have a 14.04 (LTS) 64-bit (or later) complete installation or VMWare player 12 or Virtual box. You can run Spark jobs on Windows (XP/7/8/10) or Mac OS X (10.4.7+).

Regarding hardware configuration: A machine or server having core i5 processor, about 100 GB disk space, and at least 16 GB RAM. In addition, an Nvidia GPU driver has to be installed with CUDA and CuDNN configured if you want to perform the training on GPU. Enough storage for running heavy jobs is needed (depending on the dataset size you will be handling), preferably at least 50 GB of free disk storage (for standalone and for SQL warehouse).

Download the example code files

You can download the example code files for this book from your account at `www.packtpub.com`. If you purchased this book elsewhere, you can visit `www.packtpub.com/support` and register to have the files emailed directly to you.

You can download the code files by following these steps:

1. Log in or register at `www.packtpub.com`.
2. Select the **SUPPORT** tab.
3. Click on **Code Downloads & Errata**.
4. Enter the name of the book in the **Search** box and follow the onscreen instructions.

Once the file is downloaded, please make sure that you unzip or extract the folder using the latest version of:

- WinRAR/7-Zip for Windows
- Zipeg/iZip/UnRarX for Mac
- 7-Zip/PeaZip for Linux

The code bundle for the book is also hosted on GitHub at `https://github.com/PacktPublishing/Java-Deep-Learning-Projects`. In case there's an update to the code, it will be updated on the existing GitHub repository.

We also have other code bundles from our rich catalog of books and videos available at `https://github.com/PacktPublishing/`. Check them out!

Download the color images

We also provide a PDF file that has color images of the screenshots/diagrams used in this book. You can download it here: `https://www.packtpub.com/sites/default/files/downloads/JavaDeepLearningProjects_ColorImages.pdf`.

Conventions used

There are a number of text conventions used throughout this book.

`CodeInText`: Indicates code words in text, database table names, folder names, filenames, file extensions, pathnames, dummy URLs, user input, and Twitter handles. Here is an example: "Then, I unzipped and copied each `.csv` file into a folder called `label`."

A block of code is set as follows:

```
<properties>
  <project.build.sourceEncoding>UTF-8</project.build.sourceEncoding>
  <java.version>1.8</java.version>
</properties>
```

When we wish to draw your attention to a particular part of a code block, the relevant lines or items are set in bold:

```
<properties>
  <project.build.sourceEncoding>UTF-8</project.build.sourceEncoding>
  <java.version>1.8</java.version>
</properties>
```

Bold: Indicates a new term, an important word, or words that you see onscreen. For example, words in menus or dialog boxes appear in the text like this. Here is an example: "We then read and process images into **PhotoID** | **Vector map**"

 Warnings or important notes appear like this.

 Tips and tricks appear like this.

Get in touch

Feedback from our readers is always welcome.

General feedback: Email `feedback@packtpub.com` and mention the book title in the subject of your message. If you have questions about any aspect of this book, please email us at `questions@packtpub.com`.

Errata: Although we have taken every care to ensure the accuracy of our content, mistakes do happen. If you have found a mistake in this book, we would be grateful if you would report this to us. Please visit `www.packtpub.com/submit-errata`, selecting your book, clicking on the Errata Submission Form link, and entering the details.

Piracy: If you come across any illegal copies of our works in any form on the Internet, we would be grateful if you would provide us with the location address or website name. Please contact us at `copyright@packtpub.com` with a link to the material.

If you are interested in becoming an author: If there is a topic that you have expertise in and you are interested in either writing or contributing to a book, please visit `authors.packtpub.com`.

Reviews

Please leave a review. Once you have read and used this book, why not leave a review on the site that you purchased it from? Potential readers can then see and use your unbiased opinion to make purchase decisions, we at Packt can understand what you think about our products, and our authors can see your feedback on their book. Thank you!

For more information about Packt, please visit `packtpub.com`.

1
Getting Started with Deep Learning

In this chapter, we will explain some basic concepts of **Machine Learning** (**ML**) and **Deep Learning (DL)** that will be used in all subsequent chapters. We will start with a brief introduction to ML. Then we will move on to DL, which is one of the emerging branches of ML.

We will briefly discuss some of the most well-known and widely used neural network architectures. Next, we will look at various features of deep learning frameworks and libraries. Then we will see how to prepare a programming environment, before moving on to coding with some open source, deep learning libraries such as **DeepLearning4J (DL4J)**.

Then we will solve a very famous ML problem: the Titanic survival prediction. For this, we will use an Apache Spark-based **Multilayer Perceptron** (**MLP**) classifier to solve this problem. Finally, we'll see some frequently asked questions that will help us generalize our basic understanding of DL. Briefly, the following topics will be covered:

- A soft introduction to ML
- Artificial Neural Networks (ANNs)
- Deep neural network architectures
- Deep learning frameworks
- Deep learning from disasters—Titanic survival prediction using MLP
- Frequently asked questions (FAQ)

A soft introduction to ML

ML approaches are based on a set of statistical and mathematical algorithms in order to carry out tasks such as classification, regression analysis, concept learning, predictive modeling, clustering, and mining of useful patterns. Thus, with the use of ML, we aim at improving the learning experience such that it becomes automatic. Consequently, we may not need complete human interactions, or at least we can reduce the level of such interactions as much as possible.

Working principles of ML algorithms

We now refer to a famous definition of ML by Tom M. Mitchell (*Machine Learning, Tom Mitchell, McGraw Hill*), where he explained what learning really means from a computer science perspective:

> *"A computer program is said to learn from experience E with respect to some class of tasks T and performance measure P, if its performance at tasks in T, as measured by P, improves with experience E."*

Based on this definition, we can conclude that a computer program or machine can do the following:

- Learn from data and histories
- Improve with experience
- Iteratively enhance a model that can be used to predict outcomes of questions

Since they are at the core of predictive analytics, almost every ML algorithm we use can be treated as an optimization problem. This is about finding parameters that minimize an objective function, for example, a weighted sum of two terms like a cost function and regularization. Typically, an objective function has two components:

- A regularizer, which controls the complexity of the model
- The loss, which measures the error of the model on the training data.

On the other hand, the regularization parameter defines the trade-off between minimizing the training error and the model's complexity in an effort to avoid overfitting problems. Now, if both of these components are convex, then their sum is also convex; it is non-convex otherwise. More elaborately, when using an ML algorithm, the goal is to obtain the best hyperparameters of a function that return the minimum error when making predictions. Therefore, using a convex optimization technique, we can minimize the function until it converges towards the minimum error.

Given that a problem is convex, it is usually easier to analyze the asymptotic behavior of the algorithm, which shows how fast it converges as the model observes more and more training data. The challenge of ML is to allow training a model so that it can recognize complex patterns and make decisions not only in an automated way but also as intelligently as possible. The entire learning process requires input datasets that can be split (or are already provided) into three types, outlined as follows:

- **A training set** is the knowledge base coming from historical or live data used to fit the parameters of the ML algorithm. During the training phase, the ML model utilizes the training set to find optimal weights of the network and reach the objective function by minimizing the training error. Here, the **back-prop rule** (or another more advanced optimizer with a proper updater; we'll see this later on) is used to train the model, but all the hyperparameters are need to be set before the learning process starts.
- **A validation set** is a set of examples used to tune the parameters of an ML model. It ensures that the model is trained well and generalizes towards avoiding overfitting. Some ML practitioners refer to it as a **development set** or **dev set** as well.
- **A test set** is used for evaluating the performance of the trained model on unseen data. This step is also referred to as **model inferencing**. After assessing the final model on the test set (that is, when we're fully satisfied with the model's performance), we do not have to tune the model any further but the trained model can be deployed in a production-ready environment.

A common practice is splitting the input data (after necessary pre-processing and feature engineering) into 60% for training, 10% for validation, and 20% for testing, but it really depends on use cases. Also, sometimes we need to perform up-sampling or down-sampling on the data based on the availability and quality of the datasets.

Moreover, the learning theory uses mathematical tools that derive from probability theory and information theory. Three learning paradigms will be briefly discussed:

- Supervised learning
- Unsupervised learning
- Reinforcement learning

The following diagram summarizes the three types of learning, along with the problems they address:

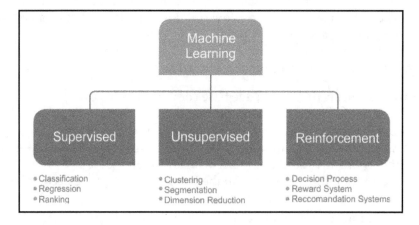

Types of learning and related problems

Supervised learning

Supervised learning is the simplest and most well-known automatic learning task. It is based on a number of pre-defined examples, in which the category to which each of the inputs should belong is already known. *Figure 2* shows a typical workflow of supervised learning.

An actor (for example, an ML practitioner, data scientist, data engineer, ML engineer, and so on) performs **Extraction Transformation Load** (**ETL**) and the necessary feature engineering (including feature extraction, selection, and so on) to get the appropriate data having features and labels. Then he does the following:

1. Splits the data into training, development, and test sets
2. Uses the training set to train an ML model

3. The validation set is used to validate the training against the overfitting problem and regularization
4. He then evaluates the model's performance on the test set (that is unseen data)
5. If the performance is not satisfactory, he can perform additional tuning to get the best model based on hyperparameter optimization
6. Finally, he deploys the best model in a production-ready environment

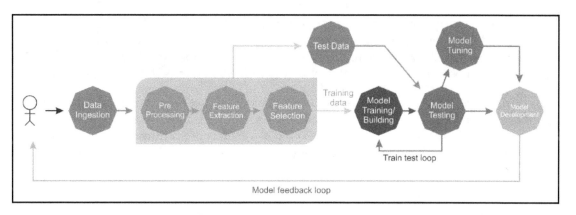

Supervised learning in action

In the overall life cycle, there might be many actors involved (for example, a data engineer, data scientist, or ML engineer) to perform each step independently or collaboratively.

The supervised learning context includes **classification** and **regression** tasks; classification is used to predict which class a data point is part of (**discrete value**), while regression is used to predict **continuous values**. In other words, a classification task is used to predict the label of the class attribute, while a regression task is used to make a numeric prediction of the class attribute.

In the context of supervised learning, **unbalanced data** refers to classification problems where we have unequal instances for different classes. For example, if we have a classification task for only two classes, **balanced data** would mean 50% pre-classified examples for each of the classes.

If the input dataset is a little unbalanced (for example, 60% data points for one class and 40% for the other class), the learning process will require for the input dataset to be split randomly into three sets, with 50% for the training set, 20% for the validation set, and the remaining 30% for the testing set.

Unsupervised learning

In **unsupervised learning,** an input set is supplied to the system during the training phase. In contrast with supervised learning, the input objects are not labeled with their class. For classification, we assumed that we are given a training dataset of correctly labeled data. Unfortunately, we do not always have that advantage when we collect data in the real world.

For example, let's say you have a large collection of totally legal, not pirated, MP3 files in a crowded and massive folder on your hard drive. In such a case, how could we possibly group songs together if we do not have direct access to their metadata? One possible approach could be to mix various ML techniques, but clustering is often the best solution.

Now, what if you can build a clustering predictive model that helps automatically group together similar songs and organize them into your favorite categories, such as *country, rap, rock,* and so on? In short, unsupervised learning algorithms are commonly used in clustering problems. The following diagram gives us an idea of a clustering technique applied to solve this kind of problem:

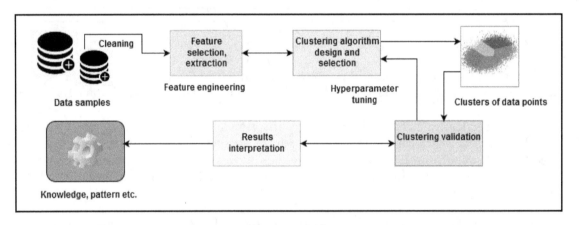

Clustering techniques – an example of unsupervised learning

Although the data points are not labeled, we can still do the necessary feature engineering and grouping of a set of objects in such a way that objects in the same group (called a **cluster**) are brought together. This is not easy for a human. Rather, a standard approach is to define a similarity measure between two objects and then look for any cluster of objects that are more similar to each other than they are to the objects in the other clusters. Once we've done the clustering of the data points (that is, MP3 files) and the validation is completed, we know the pattern of the data (that is, what type of MP3 files fall in which group).

Reinforcement learning

Reinforcement learning is an artificial intelligence approach that focuses on the learning of the system through its interactions with the environment. In reinforcement learning, the system's parameters are adapted based on the feedback obtained from the environment, which in turn provides feedback on the decisions made by the system. The following diagram shows a person making decisions in order to arrive at their destination.

Let's take an example of the route you take from home to work. In this case, you take the same route to work every day. However, out of the blue, one day you get curious and decide to try a different route with a view to finding the shortest path. This dilemma of trying out new routes or sticking to the best-known route is an example of **exploration versus exploitation**:

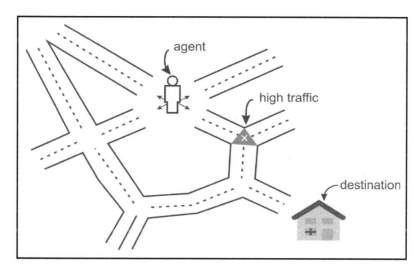

An agent always tries to reach the destination

We can take a look at one more example in terms of a system modeling a chess player. In order to improve its performance, the system utilizes the result of its previous moves; such a system is said to be a system learning with reinforcement.

Putting ML tasks altogether

We have seen the basic working principles of ML algorithms. Then we have seen what the basic ML tasks are and how they formulate domain-specific problems. Now let's take a look at how can we summarize ML tasks and some applications in the following diagram:

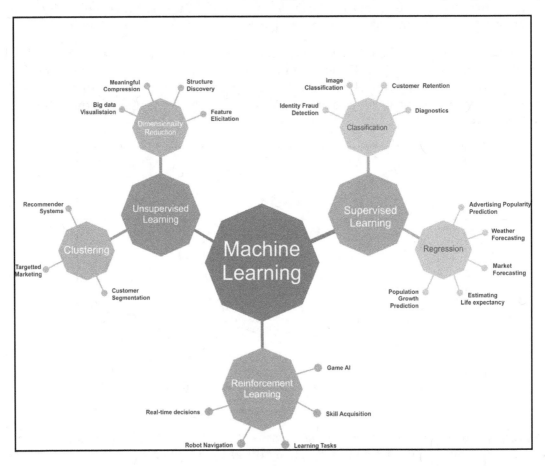

ML tasks and some use cases from different application domains

However, the preceding figure lists only a few use cases and applications using different ML tasks. In practice, ML is used in numerous use cases and applications. We will try to cover a few of those throughout this book.

Delving into deep learning

Simple ML methods that were used in normal-size data analysis are not effective anymore and should be substituted by more robust ML methods. Although classical ML techniques allow researchers to identify groups or clusters of related variables, the accuracy and effectiveness of these methods diminish with large and high-dimensional datasets.

Here comes deep learning, which is one of the most important developments in artificial intelligence in the last few years. Deep learning is a branch of ML based on a set of algorithms that attempt to model high-level abstractions in data.

How did DL take ML into next level?

In short, deep learning algorithms are mostly a set of ANNs that can make better representations of large-scale datasets, in order to build models that learn these representations very extensively. Nowadays it's not limited to ANNs, but there have been really many theoretical advances and software and hardware improvements that were necessary for us to get to this day. In this regard, Ian Goodfellow et al. (Deep Learning, MIT Press, 2016) defined deep learning as follows:

> *"Deep learning is a particular kind of machine learning that achieves great power and flexibility by learning to represent the world as a nested hierarchy of concepts, with each concept defined in relation to simpler concepts, and more abstract representations computed in terms of less abstract ones."*

Let's take an example; suppose we want to develop a predictive analytics model, such as an animal recognizer, where our system has to resolve two problems:

- To classify whether an image represents a cat or a dog
- To cluster images of dogs and cats.

If we solve the first problem using a typical ML method, we must define the facial features (ears, eyes, whiskers, and so on) and write a method to identify which features (typically nonlinear) are more important when classifying a particular animal.

However, at the same time, we cannot address the second problem because classical ML algorithms for clustering images (such as **k-means**) cannot handle nonlinear features. Deep learning algorithms will take these two problems one step further and the most important features will be extracted automatically after determining which features are the most important for classification or clustering.

In contrast, when using a classical ML algorithm, we would have to provide the features manually. In summary, the deep learning workflow would be as follows:

- A deep learning algorithm would first identify the edges that are most relevant when clustering cats or dogs. It would then try to find various combinations of shapes and edges hierarchically. This step is called ETL.
- After several iterations, hierarchical identification of complex concepts and features is carried out. Then, based on the identified features, the DL algorithm automatically decides which of these features are most significant (statistically) to classify the animal. This step is feature extraction.
- Finally, it takes out the label column and performs unsupervised training using **AutoEncoders** (**AEs**) to extract the latent features to be redistributed to k-means for clustering.
- Then the clustering assignment hardening loss (CAH loss) and reconstruction loss are jointly optimized towards optimal clustering assignment. Deep Embedding Clustering (see more at `https://arxiv.org/pdf/1511.06335.pdf`) is an example of such an approach. We will discuss deep learning-based clustering approaches in `Chapter 11`, *Discussion, Current Trends, and Outlook.*

Up to this point, we have seen that deep learning systems are able to recognize what an image represents. A computer does not see an image as we see it because it only knows the position of each pixel and its color. Using deep learning techniques, the image is divided into various layers of analysis.

At a lower level, the software analyzes, for example, a grid of a few pixels with the task of detecting a type of color or various nuances. If it finds something, it informs the next level, which at this point checks whether or not that given color belongs to a larger form, such as a line. The process continues to the upper levels until you understand what is shown in the image. The following diagram shows what we have discussed in the case of an image classification system:

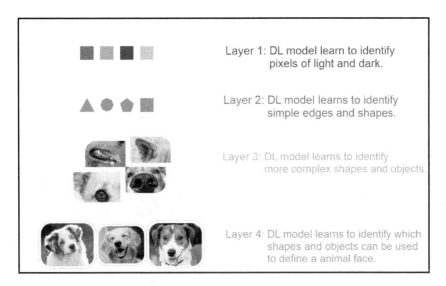

Layer 1: DL model learn to identify pixels of light and dark.

Layer 2: DL model learns to identify simple edges and shapes.

Layer 3: DL model learns to identify more complex shapes and objects.

Layer 4: DL model learns to identify which shapes and objects can be used to define a animal face.

A deep learning system at work on a dog versus cat classification problem

More precisely, the preceding image classifier can be built layer by layer, as follows:

- **Layer 1**: The algorithm starts identifying the dark and light pixels from the raw images
- **Layer 2**: The algorithm then identifies edges and shapes
- **Layer 3**: It then learns more complex shapes and objects
- **Layer 4**: The algorithm then learns which objects define a human face

Although this is a very simple classifier, software capable of doing these types of things is now widespread and is found in systems for recognizing faces, or in those for searching by an image on Google, for example. These pieces of software are based on deep learning algorithms.

On the contrary, by using a linear ML algorithm, we cannot build such applications since these algorithms are incapable of handling nonlinear image features. Also, using ML approaches, we typically handle a few hyperparameters only. However, when neural networks are brought to the party, things become too complex. In each layer, there are millions or even billions of hyperparameters to tune, so much that the cost function becomes non-convex.

Another reason is that activation functions used in hidden layers are nonlinear, so the cost is non-convex. We will discuss this phenomenon in more detail in later chapters but let's take a quick look at ANNs.

Artificial Neural Networks

ANNs work on the concept of deep learning. They represent the human nervous system in how the nervous system consists of a number of neurons that communicate with each other using axons.

Biological neurons

The working principles of ANNs are inspired by how a human brain works, depicted in *Figure 7*. The receptors receive the stimuli either internally or from the external world; then they pass the information into the biological *neurons* for further processing. There are a number of dendrites, in addition to another long extension called the **axon**.

Towards its extremity, there are minuscule structures called **synaptic terminals,** used to connect one neuron to the dendrites of other neurons. Biological neurons receive short electrical impulses called **signals** from other neurons, and in response, they trigger their own signals:

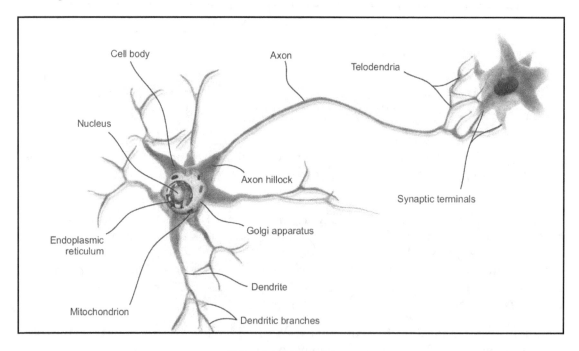

Working principle of biological neurons

We can thus summarize that the neuron comprises a cell body (also known as the soma), one or more **dendrites** for receiving signals from other neurons, and an **axon** for carrying out the signals generated by the neurons.

A neuron is in an active state when it is sending signals to other neurons. However, when it is receiving signals from other neurons, it is in an inactive state. In an idle state, a neuron accumulates all the signals received before reaching a certain activation threshold. This whole thing motivated researchers to introduce an ANN.

A brief history of ANNs

Inspired by the working principles of biological neurons, Warren McCulloch and Walter Pitts proposed the first artificial neuron model in 1943 in terms of a computational model of nervous activity. This simple model of a biological neuron, also known as an **artificial neuron (AN),** has one or more binary (on/off) inputs and one output only.

An AN simply activates its output when more than a certain number of its inputs are active. For example, here we see a few ANNs that perform various logical operations. In this example, we assume that a neuron is activated only when at least two of its inputs are active:

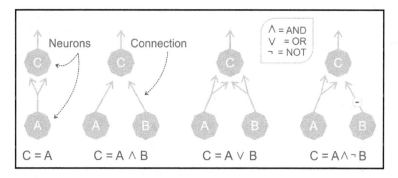

ANNs performing simple logical computations

The example sounds too trivial, but even with such a simplified model, it is possible to build a network of ANs. Nevertheless, these networks can be combined to compute complex logical expressions too. This simplified model inspired John von Neumann, Marvin Minsky, Frank Rosenblatt, and many others to come up with another model called a **perceptron** back in 1957.

The perceptron is one of the simplest ANN architectures we've seen in the last 60 years. It is based on a slightly different AN called a **Linear Threshold Unit** (**LTU**). The only difference is that the inputs and outputs are now numbers instead of binary on/off values. Each input connection is associated with a weight. The LTU computes a weighted sum of its inputs, then applies a step function (which resembles the action of an activation function) to that sum, and outputs the result:

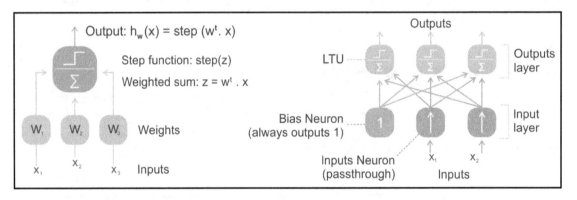

The left-side figure represents an LTU and the right-side figure shows a perceptron

One of the downsides of a perceptron is that its decision boundary is linear. Therefore, they are incapable of learning complex patterns. They are also incapable of solving some simple problems like **Exclusive OR** (**XOR**). However, later on, the limitations of perceptrons were somewhat eliminated by stacking multiple perceptrons, called MLP.

How does an ANN learn?

Based on the concept of biological neurons, the term and the idea of ANs arose. Similarly to biological neurons, the artificial neuron consists of the following:

- One or more incoming connections that aggregate signals from neurons
- One or more output connections for carrying the signal to the other neurons
- An **activation function**, which determines the numerical value of the output signal

The learning process of a neural network is configured as an *iterative process* of *optimization* of the *weights* (see more in the next section). The weights are updated in each epoch. Once the training starts, the aim is to generate predictions by minimizing the loss function. The performance of the network is then evaluated on the test set.

Now we know the simple concept of an artificial neuron. However, generating only some artificial signals is not enough to learn a complex task. Albeit, a commonly used supervised learning algorithm is the backpropagation algorithm, which is very commonly used to train a complex ANN.

ANNs and the backpropagation algorithm

The backpropagation algorithm aims to minimize the error between the current and the desired output. Since the network is feedforward, the activation flow always proceeds forward from the input units to the output units.

The gradient of the cost function is backpropagated and the network weights get updated; the overall method can be applied to any number of hidden layers recursively. In such a method, the incorporation between two phases is important. In short, the basic steps of the training procedure are as follows:

1. Initialize the network with some random (or more advanced XAVIER) weights
2. For all training cases, follow the steps of forward and backward passes as outlined next

Forward and backward passes

In the forward pass, a number of operations are performed to obtain some predictions or scores. In such an operation, a graph is created, connecting all dependent operations in a top-to-bottom fashion. Then the network's error is computed, which is the difference between the predicted output and the actual output.

On the other hand, the backward pass is involved mainly with mathematical operations, such as creating derivatives for all differential operations (that is auto-differentiation methods), top to bottom (for example, measuring the loss function to update the network weights), for all the operations in the graph, and then using them in chain rule.

In this pass, for all layers starting with the output layer back to the input layer, it shows the network layer's output with the correct input (error function). Then it adapts the weights in the current layer to minimize the error function. This is backpropagation's optimization step. By the way, there are two types of auto-differentiation methods:

1. **Reverse mode**: Derivation of a single output with respect to all inputs
2. **Forward mode**: Derivation of all outputs with respect to one input

The backpropagation algorithm processes the information in such a way that the network decreases the global error during the learning iterations; however, this does not guarantee that the global minimum is reached. The presence of hidden units and the nonlinearity of the output function mean that the behavior of the error is very complex and has many local minimas.

This backpropagation step is typically performed thousands or millions of times, using many training batches, until the model parameters converge to values that minimize the cost function. The training process ends when the error on the validation set begins to increase, because this could mark the beginning of a phase overfitting.

Weights and biases

Besides the state of a neuron, synaptic weight is considered, which influences the connection within the network. Each weight has a numerical value indicated by W_{ij}, which is the synaptic weight connecting neuron i to neuron j.

Synaptic weight: This concept evolved from biology and refers to the strength or amplitude of a connection between two nodes, corresponding in biology to the amount of influence the firing of one neuron has on another.

For each neuron (also known as, unit) i, an input vector can be defined by $x_i = (x_1, x_2,...x_n)$ and a weight vector can be defined by $w_i = (w_{i1}, w_{i2},...w_{in})$. Now, depending on the position of a neuron, the weights and the output function determine the behavior of an individual neuron. Then during forward propagation, each unit in the hidden layer gets the following signal:

$$net_i = \sum_j W_{ij} X_j \dots\dots\dots\dots (a)$$

Nevertheless, among the weights, there is also a special type of weight called *bias* unit b. Technically, bias units aren't connected to any previous layer, so they don't have true activity. But still, the bias b value allows the neural network to shift the activation function to the left or right. Now, taking the bias unit into consideration, the modified network output can be formulated as follows:

$$net_i = \sum_j W_{ij} X_j + b_i \dots\dots\dots\dots (b)$$

The preceding equation signifies that each hidden unit gets the sum of inputs multiplied by the corresponding weight—summing junction. Then the resultant in the summing junction is passed through the activation function, which squashes the output as depicted in the following figure:

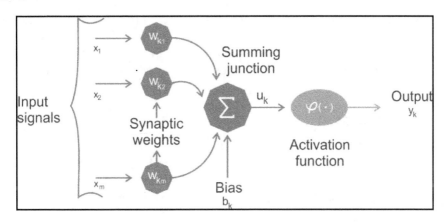

Artificial neuron model

Now, a tricky question: how do we initialize the weights? Well, if we initialize all weights to the same value (for example, 0 or 1), each hidden neuron will get exactly the same signal. Let's try to break it down:

- If all weights are initialized to 1, then each unit gets a signal equal to the sum of the inputs
- If all weights are 0, which is even worse, every neuron in a hidden layer will get zero signal

For network weight initialization, Xavier initialization is nowadays used widely. It is similar to random initialization but often turns out to work much better since it can automatically determine the scale of initialization based on the number of input and output neurons.

Interested readers should refer to this publication for detailed info: Xavier Glorot and Yoshua Bengio, *Understanding the difficulty of training deep feedforward neural networks*: proceedings of the 13th international conference on **Artificial Intelligence and Statistics (AISTATS)** 2010, Chia Laguna Resort, Sardinia, Italy; Volume 9 of JMLR: W&CP.

You may be wondering whether you can get rid of random initialization while training a regular DNN (for example, MLP or DBN). Well, recently, some researchers have been talking about random orthogonal matrix initializations that perform better than just any random initialization for training DNNs.

When it comes to initializing the biases, we can initialize them to be zero. But setting the biases to a small constant value such as 0.01 for all biases ensures that all **Rectified Linear Unit** (**ReLU**) units can propagate some gradient. However, it neither performs well nor shows consistent improvement. Therefore, sticking with zero is recommended.

Weight optimization

Before the training starts, the network parameters are set randomly. Then to optimize the network weights, an iterative algorithm called **Gradient Descent** (**GD**) is used. Using GD optimization, our network computes the cost gradient based on the training set. Then, through an iterative process, the gradient G of the error function E is computed.

In following graph, gradient **G** of error function **E** provides the direction in which the error function with current values has the steeper slope. Since the ultimate target is to reduce the network error, GD makes small steps in the opposite direction -**G**. This iterative process is executed a number of times, so the error E would move down towards the global minima. This way, the ultimate target is to reach a point where **G = 0**, where no further optimization is possible:

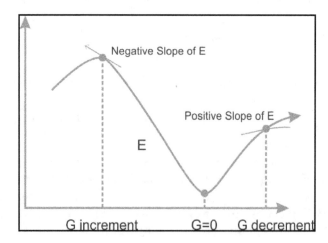

Searching for the minimum for the error function E; we move in the direction in which the gradient G of E is minimal

The downside is that it takes too long to converge, which makes it impossible to meet the demand of handling large-scale training data. Therefore, a faster GD called **Stochastic Gradient Descent** (**SDG**) is proposed, which is also a widely used optimizer in DNN training. In SGD, we use only one training sample per iteration from the training set to update the network parameters.

 I'm not saying SGD is the only available optimization algorithm, but there are so many advanced optimizers available nowadays, for example, Adam, RMSProp, ADAGrad, Momentum, and so on. More or less, most of them are either direct or indirect optimized versions of SGD.

By the way, the term **stochastic** comes from the fact that the gradient based on a single training sample per iteration is a stochastic approximation of the true cost gradient.

Activation functions

To allow a neural network to learn complex decision boundaries, we apply a non-linear activation function to some of its layers. Commonly used functions include Tanh, ReLU, softmax, and variants of these. More technically, each neuron receives as input signal the weighted sum of the synaptic weights and the activation values of the neurons connected. One of the most widely used functions for this purpose is the so-called **sigmoid function**. It is a special case of the logistic function, which is defined by the following formula:

$$Out_i = \frac{1}{(1 + e^{-x})}$$

The domain of this function includes all real numbers, and the co-domain is *(0, 1)*. This means that any value obtained as an output from a neuron (as per the calculation of its activation state), will always be between zero and one. The sigmoid function, as represented in the following diagram, provides an interpretation of the saturation rate of a neuron, from not being active (= *0*) to complete saturation, which occurs at a predetermined maximum value (= *1*).

On the other hand, a hyperbolic tangent, or **tanh**, is another form of the activation function. Tanh squashes a real-valued number to the range *[-1, 1]*. In particular, mathematically, tanh activation function can be expressed as follows:

$$tanh(x) = 2\sigma(2x) - 1$$

The preceding equation can be represented in the following figure:

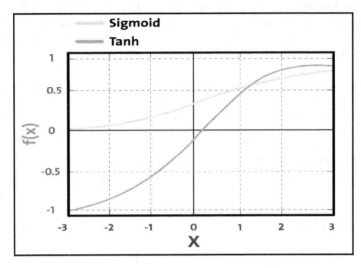

Sigmoid versus tanh activation function

In general, in the last level of an **feedforward neural network (FFNN)**, the softmax function is applied as the decision boundary. This is a common case, especially when solving a classification problem. In probability theory, the output of the softmax function is squashed as the probability distribution over K different possible outcomes. Nevertheless, the softmax function is used in various multiclass classification methods, such that the network's output is distributed across classes (that is, probability distribution over the classes) having a dynamic range between *-1* and *1* or *0* and *1*.

For a regression problem, we do not need to use any activation function since the network generates continuous values—probabilities. However, I've seen people using the IDENTITY activation function for regression problems nowadays. We'll see this in later chapters.

To conclude, choosing proper activation functions and network weights initialization are two problems that make a network perform at its best and help to obtain good training. We'll discuss more in upcoming chapters; we will see where to use which activation function.

Neural network architectures

There are various types of architectures in neural networks. We can categorize DL architectures into four groups: **Deep Neural Networks (DNNs)**, **Convolutional Neural Networks (CNNs)**, **Recurrent Neural Networks (RNNs)**, and **Emergent Architectures (EAs)**.

Nowadays, based on these architectures, researchers come up with so many variants of these for domain-specific use cases and research problems. The following sections of this chapter will give a brief introduction to these architectures. More detailed analysis, with examples of applications, will be the subject of later chapters of this book.

Deep neural networks

DNNs are neural networks having complex and deeper architecture with a large number of neurons in each layer, and there are many connections. The computation in each layer transforms the representations in the subsequent layers into slightly more abstract representations. However, we will use the term DNN to refer specifically to the MLP, the **Stacked Auto-Encoder (SAE)**, and **Deep Belief Networks (DBNs)**.

SAEs and DBNs use AEs and **Restricted Boltzmann Machines (RBMs)** as building blocks of the architectures. The main difference between these and MLPs is that training is executed in two phases: unsupervised pre-training and supervised fine-tuning.

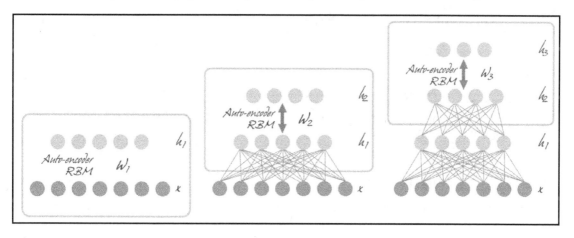

SAE and DBN using AE and RBM respectively

In unsupervised pre-training, shown in the preceding diagram, the layers are stacked sequentially and trained in a layer-wise manner, like an AE or RBM using unlabeled data. Afterwards, in supervised fine-tuning, an output classifier layer is stacked and the complete neural network is optimized by retraining with labeled data.

Multilayer Perceptron

As discussed earlier, a single perceptron is even incapable of approximating an XOR function. To overcome this limitation, multiple perceptrons are stacked together as MLPs, where layers are connected as a directed graph. This way, the signal propagates one way, from input layer to hidden layers to output layer, as shown in the following diagram:

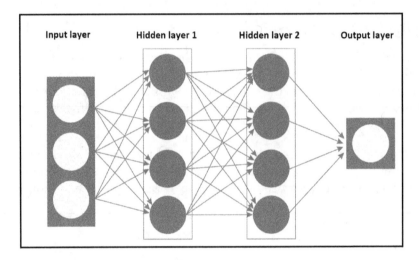

An MLP architecture having an input layer, two hidden layers, and an output layer

Fundamentally, an MLP is one the most simple FFNNs having at least three layers: an input layer, a hidden layer, and an output layer. An MLP was first trained with a backpropogation algorithm in the 1980s.

Deep belief networks

To overcome the overfitting problem in MLPs, the DBN was proposed by Hinton et al. It uses a greedy, layer-by-layer, pre-training algorithm to initialize the network weights through probabilistic generative models.

DBNs are composed of a visible layer and multiple layers—**hidden units**. The top two layers have undirected, symmetric connections in between and form an associative memory, whereas lower layers receive top-down, directed connections from the preceding layer. The building blocks of a DBN are RBMs, as you can see in the following figure, where several RBMs are *stacked* one after another to form DBNs:

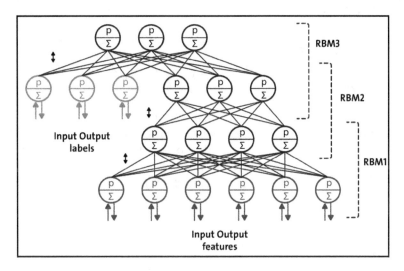

A DBN configured for semi-supervised learning

A single RBM consists of two layers. The first layer is composed of visible neurons, and the second layer consists of hidden neurons. *Figure 16* shows the structure of a simple RBM, where the neurons are arranged according to a symmetrical bipartite graph:

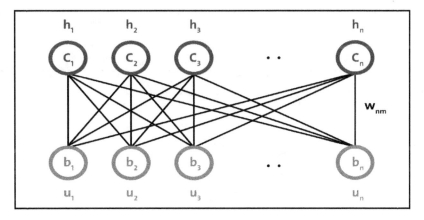

RBM architecture

In DBNs, an RBM is trained first with input data, called unsupervised pre-training, and the hidden layer represents the features learned using a greedy learning approach called supervised fine-tuning. Despite numerous successes, DBNs are being replaced by AEs.

Autoencoders

An AE is a network with three or more layers, where the input layer and the output layer have the same number of neurons, and those intermediate (hidden layers) have a lower number of neurons. The network is trained to reproduce in the output, for each piece of input data, the same pattern of activity as in the input.

Useful applications of AEs are data denoising and dimensionality reduction for data visualization. The following diagram shows how an AE typically works. It reconstructs the received input through two phases: an encoding phase, which corresponds to a dimensional reduction for the original input, and a decoding phase, which is capable of reconstructing the original input from the encoded (compressed) representation:

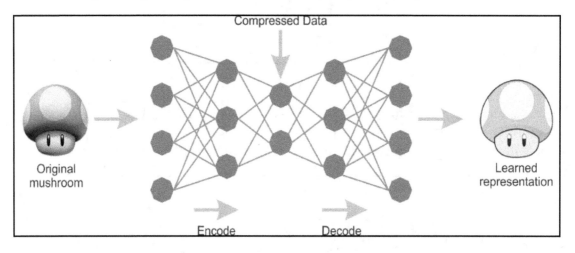

Encoding and decoding phases of an AE

Convolutional neural networks

CNNs have achieved much and wide adoption in computer vision (for example, image recognition). In CNN networks, the connection scheme that defines the convolutional layer (conv) is significantly different compared to an MLP or DBN.

Importantly, a DNN has no prior knowledge of how the pixels are organized; it does not know that nearby pixels are close. A CNN's architecture embeds this prior knowledge. Lower layers typically identify features in small areas of the image, while higher layers combine lower-level features into larger features. This works well with most natural images, giving CNNs a decisive head start over DNNs:

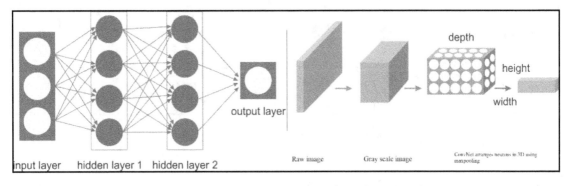

A regular DNN versus a CNN

Take a close look at the preceding diagram; on the left is a regular three-layer neural network, and on the right, a CNN arranges its neurons in three dimensions (width, height, and depth). In a CNN architecture, a few convolutional layers are connected in a cascade style, where each layer is followed by a ReLU layer, then a pooling layer, then a few more convolutional layers (+ReLU), then another pooling layer, and so on.

The output from each conv layer is a set of objects called feature maps that are generated by a single kernel filter. Then the feature maps can be used to define a new input to the next layer. Each neuron in a CNN network produces an output followed by an activation threshold, which is proportional to the input and not bound. This type of layer is called a convolutional layer. The following diagram is a schematic of the architecture of a CNN used for facial recognition:

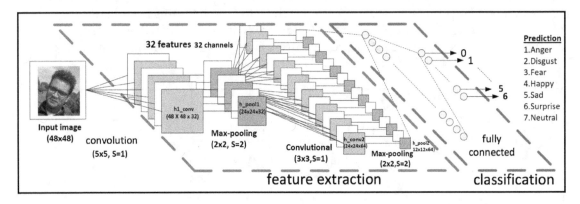

A schematic architecture of a CNN used for facial recognition

Recurrent neural networks

A **recurrent neural network (RNN)** is a class of **artificial neural network** (**ANN**) where connections between units form a directed cycle. RNN architecture was originally conceived by Hochreiter and Schmidhuber in 1997. RNN architectures have standard MLPs plus added loops (as shown in the following diagram), so they can exploit the powerful nonlinear mapping capabilities of the MLP; and they have some form of memory:

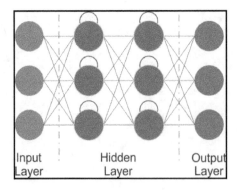

RNN architecture

The preceding image shows a a very basic RNN having an input layer, 2 recurrent layers and an output layer. However, this basic RNN suffers from gradient vanishing and exploding problem and cannot model the long-term depedencies. Therefore, more advanced architectures are designed to utilize sequential information of input data with cyclic connections among building blocks such as perceptrons. These architectures include **Long-Short-Term Memory (LSTM)**, **Gated Recurrent Units (GRUs)**, **Bidirectional-LSTM** and other variants.

Consequently, LSTM and GR can overcome the drawbacks of regular RNNs: gradient vanishing/exploding problem and the long-short term dependency. We will look at these architectures in chapter 2.

Emergent architectures

Many other emergent DL architectures have been suggested, such as **Deep SpatioTemporal Neural Networks (DST-NNs)**, **Multi-Dimensional Recurrent Neural Networks (MD-RNNs)**, and **Convolutional AutoEncoders (CAEs)**.

Nevertheless, there are a few more emerging networks, such as **CapsNets** (which is an improved version of a CNN, designed to remove the drawbacks of regular CNNs), RNN for image recognition, and **Generative Adversarial Networks (GANs)** for simple image generation. Apart from these, factorization machines for personalization and deep reinforcement learning are also being used widely.

Residual neural networks

Since there are sometimes millions of billions of hyperparameters and other practical aspects, it's really difficult to train deeper neural networks. To overcome this limitation, Kaiming He et al. (see `https://arxiv.org/abs/1512.03385v1`) proposed a residual learning framework to ease the training of networks that are substantially deeper than those used previously.

They also explicitly reformulated the layers as learning residual functions with reference to the layer inputs, instead of learning unreferenced functions. This way, these residual networks are easier to optimize and can gain accuracy from considerably increased depth.

The downside is that building a network by simply stacking residual blocks inevitably limits its optimization ability. To overcome this limitation, Ke Zhang et al. also proposed using a Multilevel Residual Network (`https://arxiv.org/abs/1608.02908`).

Generative adversarial networks

GANs are deep neural net architectures that consist of two networks pitted against each other (hence the name "adversarial"). Ian Goodfellow et al. introduced GANs in a paper (see more at `https://arxiv.org/abs/1406.2661v1`). In GANs, the two main components are the **generator and discriminator**.

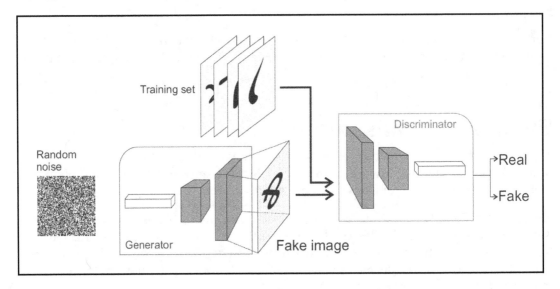

Working principle of Generative Adversarial Networks (GANs)

The Generator will try to generate data samples out of a specific probability distribution, which is very similar to the actual object. The discriminator will judge whether its input is coming from the original training set or from the generator part.

Capsule networks

CNNs perform well at classifying images. However, if the images have rotation, tilt, or any other different orientation, then CNNs show relatively very poor performance. Even the pooling operation in CNNs cannot much help against the positional invariance.

This issue in CNNs has led us to the recent advancement of CapsNet through the paper titled *Dynamic Routing Between Capsules* (see more at `https://arxiv.org/abs/1710.09829`) by Geoffrey Hinton et al.

Unlike a regular DNN, where we keep on adding layers, in CapsNets, the idea is to add more layers inside a single layer. This way, a CapsNet is a nested set of neural layers. We'll discuss more in `Chapter 11`, *Discussion, Current Trends, and Outlook*.

DL frameworks and cloud platforms

In this section, we'll present some of the most popular deep learning frameworks. Then we will discuss some cloud based platforms where you can deploy/run your DL applications. In short, almost all of the libraries provide the possibility of using a graphics processor to speed up the learning process, are released under an open license, and are the result of university research groups.

Deep learning frameworks

TensorFlow is mathematical software, and an open source software library for machine intelligence. The Google Brain team developed it in 2011 and open-sourced it in 2015. The main features offered by the latest release of TensorFlow (v1.8 during the writing of this book) are faster computing, flexibility, portability, easy debugging, a unified API, transparent use of GPU computing, easy use, and extensibility. Once you have constructed your neural network model, after the necessary feature engineering, you can simply perform the training interactively using plotting or TensorBoard.

Keras is a deep learning library that sits atop TensorFlow and Theano, providing an intuitive API inspired by Torch. It is perhaps the best Python API in existence. DeepLearning4J relies on Keras as its Python API and imports models from Keras and through Keras from Theano and TensorFlow.

Theano is also a deep learning framework written in Python. It allows using GPU, which is 24x faster than a single CPU. Defining, optimizing, and evaluating complex mathematical expressions is very straightforward in Theano.

Neon is a Python-based deep learning framework developed by Nirvana. Neon has a syntax similar to Theano's high-level framework (for example, Keras). Currently, Neon is considered the fastest tool for GPU-based implementation, especially for CNNs. But its CPU-based implementation is relatively worse than most other libraries.

PyTorch is a vast ecosystem for ML that offers a large number of algorithms and functions, including for DL and for processing various types of multimedia data, with a particular focus on parallel computing. Torch is a highly portable framework supported on various platforms, including Windows, macOS, Linux, and Android.

Caffe, developed primarily by **Berkeley Vision and Learning Center** (**BVLC**), is a framework designed to stand out because of its expression, speed, and modularity.

MXNet (`http://mxnet.io/`) is a deep learning framework that supports many languages, such as R, Python, C++, and Julia. This is helpful because if you know any of these languages, you will not need to step out of your comfort zone at all to train your deep learning models. Its backend is written in C++ and CUDA and it is able to manage its own memory in a way similar to Theano.

The **Microsoft Cognitive Toolkit** (**CNTK**) is a unified deep learning toolkit from Microsoft Research that makes it easy to train and combine popular model types across multiple GPUs and servers. CNTK implements highly efficient CNN and RNN training for speech, image, and text data. It supports cuDNN v5.1 for GPU acceleration.

DeepLearning4J is one of the first commercial-grade, open source, distributed deep learning libraries written for Java and Scala. This also provides integrated support for Hadoop and Spark. DeepLearning4 is designed to be used in business environments on distributed GPUs and CPUs.

DeepLearning4J aims to be cutting-edge and plug-and-play, with more convention than configuration, which allows for fast prototyping for non-researchers. The following libraries can be integrated with DeepLearning4 and will make your JVM experience easier whether you are developing your ML application in Java or Scala.

ND4J is just like NumPy for JVM. It comes with some basic operations of linear algebra such as matrix creation, addition, and multiplication. ND4S, on the other hand, is a scientific computing library for linear algebra and matrix manipulation. It supports n-dimensional arrays for JVM-based languages.

To conclude, the following figure shows the last 1 year's Google trends concerning the popularity of different DL frameworks:

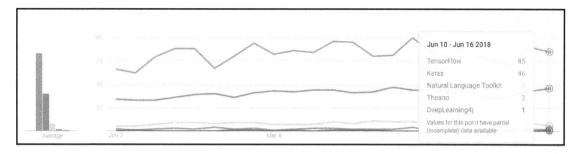

The trends of different DL frameworks. TensorFlow and Keras are most dominating. Theano is losing its popularity. On the other hand, DeepLearning4J is emerging for JVM.

Cloud-based platforms for DL

Apart from the preceding libraries, there have been some recent initiatives for deep learning on the cloud. The idea is to bring deep learning capabilities to big data with millions of billions of data points and high-dimensional data. For example, **Amazon Web Services** (**AWS**), Microsoft Azure, Google Cloud Platform, and **NVIDIA GPU Cloud** (**NGC**) all offer machine and deep learning services that are native to their public clouds.

In October 2017, AWS released deep learning **Amazon Machine Images** (**AMIs**) for Amazon **Elastic Compute Cloud** (**EC2**) P3 instances. These AMIs come pre-installed with deep learning frameworks, such as TensorFlow, Gluon, and Apache MXNet, that are optimized for the NVIDIA Volta V100 GPUs within Amazon EC2 P3 instances.

The Microsoft Cognitive Toolkit is Azure's open source, deep learning service. Similar to AWS's offering, it focuses on tools that can help developers build and deploy deep learning applications.

On the other hand, NGC empowers AI scientists and researchers with GPU-accelerated containers (see `https://www.nvidia.com/en-us/data-center/gpu-cloud-computing/`). NGC features containerized deep learning frameworks such as TensorFlow, PyTorch, MXNet, and more that are tuned, tested, and certified by NVIDIA to run on the latest NVIDIA GPUs.

Now that we have a minimum of knowledge about available DL libraries, frameworks, and cloud-based platforms for running and deploying our DL applications, we can dive into coding. First, we will start by solving the famous Titanic survival prediction problem. However, we won't use the previously listed frameworks; we will be using the Apache Spark ML library. Since we will be using Spark along with other DL libraries, knowing a little bit of Spark would help us grasp things in the upcoming chapters.

Deep learning from a disaster – Titanic survival prediction

In this section, we are going to solve the famous Titanic survival prediction problem available on Kaggle (see `https://www.kaggle.com/c/titanic/data`). The task is to complete the analysis of what sorts of people are likely to survive using an ML algorithm.

Problem description

Before diving into the coding, let's see a short description of the problem. This paragraph is directly quoted from the Kaggle Titanic survival prediction page:

> *"The sinking of the RMS Titanic is one of the most infamous shipwrecks in history. On April 15, 1912, during her maiden voyage, the Titanic sank after colliding with an iceberg, killing 1502 out of 2224 passengers and crew. This sensational tragedy shocked the international community and led to better safety regulations for ships. One of the reasons that the shipwreck led to such loss of life was that there were not enough lifeboats for the passengers and crew. Although there was some element of luck involved in surviving the sinking, some groups of people were more likely to survive than others, such as women, children, and the upper class. In this challenge, we ask you to complete the analysis of what sorts of people were likely to survive. In particular, we ask you to apply the tools of machine learning to predict which passengers survived the tragedy."*

Now, before going even deeper, we need to know about the data of the passengers traveling on the Titanic during the disaster so that we can develop a predictive model that can be used for survival analysis. The dataset can be downloaded from `https://github.com/rezacsedu/TitanicSurvivalPredictionDataset`. There are two `.csv` files:

- **The training set** (`train.csv`): Can be used to build your ML models. This file also includes labels as the *ground truth* for each passenger for the training set.
- **The test set** (`test.csv`): Can be used to see how well your model performs on unseen data. However, for the test set, we do not provide the ground truth for each passenger.

In short, for each passenger in the test set, we have to use the trained model to predict whether they'll survive the sinking of the Titanic. *Table 1* shows the metadata of the training set:

Variable	Definition
survival	Two labels: • *0 = No* • *1 = Yes*
pclass	This is a proxy for the **Socioeconomic Status (SES)** of a passenger and is categorized as upper, middle, and lower. In particular, *1 = 1ˢᵗ, 2 = 2ⁿᵈ, 3 = 3ʳᵈ*.
sex	Male or female.
Age	Age in years.
sibsp	This signifies family relations as follows: • *Sibling = brother, sister, stepbrother, stepsister* • *Spouse = husband, wife (mistresses and fiancés were ignored)*
parch	In the dataset, family relations are defined as follows: • *Parent = mother, father* • *Child = daughter, son, stepdaughter, stepson* Some children traveled only with a nanny, therefore *parch=0* for them.
ticket	Ticket number.
fare	Passenger ticket fare.
cabin	Cabin number.
embarked	Three ports: • *C = Cherbourg* • *Q = Queenstown* • *S = Southampton*

Now the question would be: using this labeled data, can we draw some straightforward conclusions? Say that being a woman, being in first class, and being a child were all factors that could boost a passenger's chances of survival during this disaster.

To solve this problem, we can start from the basic MLP, which is one of the oldest deep learning algorithms. For this, we use the Spark-based `MultilayerPerceptronClassifier`. At this point, you might be wondering why I am talking about Spark since it is not a DL library. However, Spark has an MLP implementation, which would be enough to serve our objective.

Then from the next chapter, we'll gradually start using more robust DNN by using DeepLearning4J, a JVM-based framework for developing deep learning applications. So let's see how to configure our Spark environment.

Configuring the programming environment

I am assuming that Java is already installed on your machine and the JAVA_HOME is set too. Also, I'm assuming that your IDE has the Maven plugin installed. If so, then just create a Maven project and add the project properties as follows:

```
<properties>
        <project.build.sourceEncoding>UTF-8</project.build.sourceEncoding>
        <java.version>1.8</java.version>
        <jdk.version>1.8</jdk.version>
        <spark.version>2.3.0</spark.version>
</properties>
```

In the preceding tag, I specified Spark (that is, 2.3.0), but you can adjust it. Then add the following dependencies in the pom.xml file:

```
<dependencies>
        <dependency>
                <groupId>org.apache.spark</groupId>
                <artifactId>spark-core_2.11</artifactId>
                <version>${spark.version}</version>
        </dependency>
        <dependency>
                <groupId>org.apache.spark</groupId>
                <artifactId>spark-sql_2.11</artifactId>
                <version>${spark.version}</version>
        </dependency>
        <dependency>
                <groupId>org.apache.spark</groupId>
                <artifactId>spark-mllib_2.11</artifactId>
                <version>${spark.version}</version>
        </dependency>
        <dependency>
                <groupId>org.apache.spark</groupId>
                <artifactId>spark-graphx_2.11</artifactId>
                <version>${spark.version}</version>
        </dependency>
        <dependency>
                <groupId>org.apache.spark</groupId>
                <artifactId>spark-yarn_2.11</artifactId>
                <version>${spark.version}</version>
        </dependency>
        <dependency>
                <groupId>org.apache.spark</groupId>
                <artifactId>spark-network-shuffle_2.11</artifactId>
                <version>${spark.version}</version>
        </dependency>
```

```xml
<dependency>
    <groupId>org.apache.spark</groupId>
    <artifactId>spark-streaming-flume_2.11</artifactId>
    <version>${spark.version}</version>
</dependency>
<dependency>
    <groupId>com.databricks</groupId>
    <artifactId>spark-csv_2.11</artifactId>
    <version>1.3.0</version>
</dependency>
</dependencies>
```

Then if everything goes smoothly, all the JAR files will be downloaded in the project home as Maven dependencies. Alright! Then we can start writing the code.

Feature engineering and input dataset preparation

In this sub-section, we will see some basic feature engineering and dataset preparation that can be fed into the MLP classifier. So let's start by creating `SparkSession`, which is the gateway to access Spark:

```java
SparkSession spark = SparkSession
                .builder()
                .master("local[*]")
                .config("spark.sql.warehouse.dir", "/tmp/spark")
                .appName("SurvivalPredictionMLP")
                .getOrCreate();
```

Then let's read the training set and see a glimpse of it:

```java
Dataset<Row> df = spark.sqlContext()
                .read()
                .format("com.databricks.spark.csv")
                .option("header", "true")
                .option("inferSchema", "true")
                .load("data/train.csv");
df.show();
```

A snapshot of the dataset can be seen as follows:

```
+-----------+--------+------+--------------------+------+----+-----+-----+--------------+-------+-----+--------+
|PassengerId|Survived|Pclass|                Name|   Sex| Age|SibSp|Parch|        Ticket|   Fare|Cabin|Embarked|
+-----------+--------+------+--------------------+------+----+-----+-----+--------------+-------+-----+--------+
|          1|       0|     3|Braund, Mr. Owen ...|  male|22.0|    1|    0|     A/5 21171|   7.25| null|       S|
|          2|       1|     1|Cumings, Mrs. Joh...|female|38.0|    1|    0|      PC 17599|71.2833|  C85|       C|
|          3|       1|     3|Heikkinen, Miss. ...|female|26.0|    0|    0|STON/O2. 3101282|  7.925| null|       S|
|          4|       1|     1|Futrelle, Mrs. Ja...|female|35.0|    1|    0|        113803|   53.1| C123|       S|
|          5|       0|     3|Allen, Mr. Willia...|  male|35.0|    0|    0|        373450|   8.05| null|       S|
|          6|       0|     3|    Moran, Mr. James|  male|null|    0|    0|        330877| 8.4583| null|       Q|
|          7|       0|     1|McCarthy, Mr. Tim...|  male|54.0|    0|    0|         17463|51.8625|  E46|       S|
|          8|       0|     3|Palsson, Master. ...|  male| 2.0|    3|    1|        349909| 21.075| null|       S|
|          9|       1|     3|Johnson, Mrs. Osc...|female|27.0|    0|    2|        347742|11.1333| null|       S|
|         10|       1|     2|Nasser, Mrs. Nich...|female|14.0|    1|    0|        237736|30.0708| null|       C|
|         11|       1|     3|Sandstrom, Miss. ...|female| 4.0|    1|    1|       PP 9549|   16.7|   G6|       S|
|         12|       1|     1|Bonnell, Miss. El...|female|58.0|    0|    0|        113783|  26.55| C103|       S|
|         13|       0|     3|Saundercock, Mr. ...|  male|20.0|    0|    0|     A/5. 2151|   8.05| null|       S|
|         14|       0|     3|Andersson, Mr. An...|  male|39.0|    1|    5|        347082| 31.275| null|       S|
|         15|       0|     3|Vestrom, Miss. Hu...|female|14.0|    0|    0|        350406| 7.8542| null|       S|
|         16|       1|     2|Hewlett, Mrs. (Ma...|female|55.0|    0|    0|        248706|   16.0| null|       S|
|         17|       0|     3|Rice, Master. Eugene|  male| 2.0|    4|    1|        382652| 29.125| null|       Q|
|         18|       1|     2|Williams, Mr. Cha...|  male|null|    0|    0|        244373|   13.0| null|       S|
|         19|       0|     3|Vander Planke, Mr...|female|31.0|    1|    0|        345763|   18.0| null|       S|
|         20|       1|     3|Masselmani, Mrs. ...|female|null|    0|    0|          2649|  7.225| null|       C|
+-----------+--------+------+--------------------+------+----+-----+-----+--------------+-------+-----+--------+
only showing top 20 rows
```

A snapshot of the Titanic survival dataset

Now we can see that the training set has both categorical as well as numerical features. In addition, some features are not important, such as `PassengerID`, `Ticket`, and so on. The same also applies to the `Name` feature unless we manually create some features based on the title. However, let's keep it simple. Nevertheless, some columns contain null values. Therefore, lots of consideration and cleaning are required.

I ignore the `PassengerId`, `Name`, and `Ticket` columns. Apart from these, the `Sex` column is categorical, so I've encoded the passengers based on `male` and `female`. Then the `Embarked` column is encoded too. We can encode `S` as 0, `C` as 1, and `Q` as 2.

For this also, we can write user-defined-functions (also known as UDFs) called `normSex` and `normEmbarked` for `Sex` and `Embarked`, respectively. Let's see their signatures:

```
private static UDF1<String,Option<Integer>> normEmbarked=(String d) -> {
    if (null == d)
        return Option.apply(null);
    else {
        if (d.equals("S"))
            return Some.apply(0);
        else if (d.equals("C"))
            return Some.apply(1);
        else
            return Some.apply(2);
    }
};
```

Therefore, this UDF takes a `String` type and encodes as an integer. Now the `normSex` UDF also works similarly:

```
private static UDF1<String, Option<Integer>> normSex = (String d) -> {
    if (null == d)
        return Option.apply(null);
    else {
        if (d.equals("male"))
            return Some.apply(0);
        else
            return Some.apply(1);
    }
};
```

So we can now select only useful columns but for the `Sex` and `Embarked` columns with the aforementioned UDFs:

```
Dataset<Row> projection = df.select(
            col("Survived"),
            col("Fare"),
            callUDF("normSex", col("Sex")).alias("Sex"),
            col("Age"),
            col("Pclass"),
            col("Parch"),
            col("SibSp"),
             callUDF("normEmbarked",
            col("Embarked")).alias("Embarked"));
projectin.show();
```

```
+--------+-------+---+----+------+-----+-----+--------+
|Survived|   Fare|Sex| Age|Pclass|Parch|SibSp|Embarked|
+--------+-------+---+----+------+-----+-----+--------+
|       0|   7.25|  0|22.0|     3|    0|    1|       0|
|       1|71.2833|  1|38.0|     1|    0|    1|       1|
|       1|  7.925|  1|26.0|     3|    0|    0|       0|
|       1|   53.1|  1|35.0|     1|    0|    1|       0|
|       0|   8.05|  0|35.0|     3|    0|    0|       0|
|       0| 8.4583|  0|null|     3|    0|    0|       2|
|       0|51.8625|  0|54.0|     1|    0|    0|       0|
|       0| 21.075|  0| 2.0|     3|    1|    3|       0|
|       1|11.1333|  1|27.0|     3|    2|    0|       0|
|       1|30.0708|  1|14.0|     2|    0|    1|       1|
|       1|   16.7|  1| 4.0|     3|    1|    1|       0|
|       1|  26.55|  1|58.0|     1|    0|    0|       0|
|       0|   8.05|  0|20.0|     3|    0|    0|       0|
|       0| 31.275|  0|39.0|     3|    5|    1|       0|
|       0| 7.8542|  1|14.0|     3|    0|    0|       0|
|       1|   16.0|  1|55.0|     2|    0|    0|       0|
|       0| 29.125|  0| 2.0|     3|    1|    4|       2|
|       1|   13.0|  0|null|     2|    0|    0|       0|
|       0|   18.0|  1|31.0|     3|    0|    1|       0|
|       1|  7.225|  1|null|     3|    0|    0|       1|
+--------+-------+---+----+------+-----+-----+--------+
only showing top 20 rows
```

Now we have been able to convert a categorical column into a numeric; however, as we can see, there are still null values. Therefore, what can we do? We can either drop the `null` values altogether or apply some `null` imputing techniques with the mean value of those particular columns. I believe the second approach is better.

Now, again for this null imputation, we can write UDFs too. However, for that we need to know some statistics about those numerical columns. Unfortunately, we cannot perform the summary statistics on DataFrame. Therefore, we have to convert the DataFrame into `JavaRDD<Vector>`. Well, we also ignore the `null` entries for calculating this:

```
JavaRDD<Vector> statsDf =projection.rdd().toJavaRDD().map(row ->
Vectors.dense( row.<Double>getAs("Fare"),
            row.isNullAt(3) ? 0d : row.Double>getAs("Age")
            ));
```

Now let's compute the multivariate statistical `summary`. The `summary` statistical will be further used to calculate the `meanAge` and `meanFare` for the corresponding missing entries for these two features:

```
MultivariateStatisticalSummary summary =
Statistics.colStats(statsRDD.rdd());
double meanFare = summary.mean().apply(0);
double meanAge = summary.mean().apply(1);
```

Now let's create two more UDFs for the null imputation on the `Age` and `Fare` columns:

```
UDF1<String, Option<Double>> normFare = (String d) -> {
        if (null == d) {
            return Some.apply(meanFare);
        }
        else
            return Some.apply(Double.parseDouble(d));
    };
```

Therefore, we have defined a UDF, which fills in the `meanFare` values if the data has no entry. Now let's create another UDF for the `Age` column:

```
UDF1<String, Option<Double>> normAge = (String d) -> {
        if (null == d)
            return Some.apply(meanAge);
        else
            return Some.apply(Double.parseDouble(d));
    };
```

Now we need to register the UDFs as follows:

```
spark.sqlContext().udf().register("normFare", normFare,
DataTypes.DoubleType);
spark.sqlContext().udf().register("normAge", normAge,
DataTypes.DoubleType);
```

Therefore, let's apply the preceding UDFs for `null` imputation:

```
Dataset<Row> finalDF = projection.select(
                col("Survived"),
                callUDF("normFare",
                col("Fare").cast("string")).alias("Fare"),
                col("Sex"),
                callUDF("normAge",
                col("Age").cast("string")).alias("Age"),
                col("Pclass"),
                col("Parch"),
                col("SibSp"),
                col("Embarked"));
finalDF.show();
```

```
+--------+-------+---+------------------+------+-----+-----+--------+
|Survived|   Fare|Sex|               Age|Pclass|Parch|SibSp|Embarked|
+--------+-------+---+------------------+------+-----+-----+--------+
|       0|   7.25|  0|              22.0|     3|    0|    1|       0|
|       1|71.2833|  1|              38.0|     1|    0|    1|       1|
|       1|  7.925|  1|              26.0|     3|    0|    0|       0|
|       1|   53.1|  1|              35.0|     1|    0|    1|       0|
|       0|   8.05|  0|              35.0|     3|    0|    0|       0|
|       0| 8.4583|  0|23.799292929292942|     3|    0|    0|       2|
|       0|51.8625|  0|              54.0|     1|    0|    0|       0|
|       0| 21.075|  0|               2.0|     3|    1|    3|       0|
|       1|11.1333|  1|              27.0|     3|    2|    0|       0|
|       1|30.0708|  1|              14.0|     2|    0|    1|       1|
|       1|   16.7|  1|               4.0|     3|    1|    1|       0|
|       1|  26.55|  1|              58.0|     1|    0|    0|       0|
|       0|   8.05|  0|              20.0|     3|    0|    0|       0|
|       0| 31.275|  0|              39.0|     3|    5|    1|       0|
|       0| 7.8542|  1|              14.0|     3|    0|    0|       0|
|       1|   16.0|  1|              55.0|     2|    0|    0|       0|
|       0| 29.125|  0|               2.0|     3|    1|    4|       2|
|       1|   13.0|  0|23.799292929292942|     2|    0|    0|       0|
|       0|   18.0|  1|              31.0|     3|    0|    1|       0|
|       1|  7.225|  1|23.799292929292942|     3|    0|    0|       1|
+--------+-------+---+------------------+------+-----+-----+--------+
only showing top 20 rows
```

Great! We now can see that the `null` values are replaced with the mean value for the `Age` and `Fare` columns. However, still the numeric values are not scaled. Therefore, it would be a better idea to scale them. However, for that, we need to compute the mean and variance and then store them as a model to be used for later scaling:

```
Vector stddev = Vectors.dense(Math.sqrt(summary.variance().apply(0)),
Math.sqrt(summary.variance().apply(1)));

Vector mean = Vectors.dense(summary.mean().apply(0),
summary.mean().apply(1));
StandardScalerModel scaler = new StandardScalerModel(stddev, mean);
```

Then we need an encoder for the numeric values (that is, `Integer`; either `BINARY` or `Double`):

```
Encoder<Integer> integerEncoder = Encoders.INT();
Encoder<Double> doubleEncoder = Encoders.DOUBLE();
Encoders.BINARY();

Encoder<Vector> vectorEncoder = Encoders.kryo(Vector.class);
Encoders.tuple(integerEncoder, vectorEncoder);
Encoders.tuple(doubleEncoder, vectorEncoder);
```

Then we can create a `VectorPair` consisting of the label (that is, `Survived`) and the features. Here the encoding is, basically, creating a scaled feature vector:

```
JavaRDD<VectorPair> scaledRDD = trainingDF.toJavaRDD().map(row -> {
            VectorPair vectorPair = new VectorPair();
            vectorPair.setLable(new
            Double(row.<Integer> getAs("Survived")));

            vectorPair.setFeatures(Util.getScaledVector(
                    row.<Double>getAs("Fare"),
                    row.<Double>getAs("Age"),
                    row.<Integer>getAs("Pclass"),
                    row.<Integer>getAs("Sex"),
                    row.isNullAt(7) ? 0d :
                    row.<Integer>getAs("Embarked"),
                    scaler));
            return vectorPair;
    });
```

In the preceding code block, the `getScaledVector()` method does perform the scaling operation. The signature of this method can be seen as follows:

```
public static org.apache.spark.mllib.linalg.Vector getScaledVector(double
fare,
        double age, double pclass,  double sex, double embarked,
StandardScalerModel scaler) {
        org.apache.spark.mllib.linalg.Vector scaledContinous =
scaler.transform(Vectors.dense(fare, age));
        Tuple3<Double, Double, Double> pclassFlat = flattenPclass(pclass);
        Tuple3<Double, Double, Double> embarkedFlat =
flattenEmbarked(embarked);
        Tuple2<Double, Double> sexFlat = flattenSex(sex);

        return Vectors.dense(
                scaledContinous.apply(0),
                scaledContinous.apply(1),
                sexFlat._1(),
                sexFlat._2(),
                pclassFlat._1(),
                pclassFlat._2(),
                pclassFlat._3(),
                embarkedFlat._1(),
                embarkedFlat._2(),
                embarkedFlat._3());
    }
```

Since we planned to use a Spark ML-based classifier (that is, an MLP implementation), we need to convert this RDD of the vector to an ML vector:

```
Dataset<Row> scaledDF = spark.createDataFrame(scaledRDD, VectorPair.class);
```

Finally, let's see how the resulting DataFrame looks:

```
scaledDF.show();
```

```
+-------------------+-----+
|          features|lable|
+-------------------+-----+
|[-0.5021631365156...|  0.0|
|[0.78640361783453...|  1.0|
|[-0.4885798515812...|  1.0|
|[0.42049406976541...|  1.0|
|[-0.4860644284452...|  0.0|
|[-0.4778480503138...|  0.0|
|[0.39559138071911...|  0.0|
|[-0.2239573376751...|  0.0|
|[-0.4240179952036...|  1.0|
|[-0.0429313901012...|  1.0|
|[-0.3119971474347...|  1.0|
|[-0.1137818043187...|  1.0|
|[-0.4860644284452...|  0.0|
|[-0.0186988097783...|  0.0|
|[-0.4900045872454...|  0.0|
|[-0.3260835169963...|  1.0|
|[-0.0619640877174...|  0.0|
|[-0.3864536722600...|  1.0|
|[-0.2858367468204...|  0.0|
|[-0.5026662211428...|  1.0|
+-------------------+-----+
only showing top 20 rows
```

Up to this point, we have been able to prepare our features. Still, this is an MLlib-based vector, so we need to further convert this into an ML vector:

```
Dataset<Row> scaledData2 = MLUtils.convertVectorColumnsToML(scaledDF);
```

Fantastic! Now were' almost done preparing a training set that can be consumed by the MLP classifier. Since we also need to evaluate the model's performance, we can randomly split the training data for the training and test sets. Let's allocate 80% for training and 20% for testing. These will be used to train the model and evaluate the model, respectively:

```
Dataset<Row> data = scaledData2.toDF("features", "label");
Dataset<Row>[] datasets = data.randomSplit(new double[]{0.80, 0.20},
12345L);

Dataset<Row> trainingData = datasets[0];
Dataset<Row> validationData = datasets[1];
```

Alright. Now that we have the training set, we can perform training on an MLP model.

Training MLP classifier

In Spark, an MLP is a classifier that consists of multiple layers. Each layer is fully connected to the next layer in the network. Nodes in the input layer represent the input data, whereas other nodes map inputs to outputs by a linear combination of the inputs with the node's weights and biases and by applying an activation function.

 Interested readers can take a look at `https://spark.apache.org/docs/latest/ml-classification-regression.html#multilayer-perceptron-classifier`.

So let's create the layers for the MLP classifier. For this example, let's make a shallow network considering the fact that our dataset is not that highly dimensional.

Let's assume that only 18 neurons in the first hidden layer and 8 neurons in the second hidden layer would be sufficient. Note that the input layer has 10 inputs, so we set 10 neurons and 2 neurons in the output layers since our MLP will predict only 2 classes. One thing is very important—the number of inputs has to be equal to the size of the feature vectors and the number of outputs has to be equal to the total number of labels:

```
int[] layers = new int[] {10, 8, 16, 2};
```

Then we instantiate the model with the trainer and set its parameters:

```
MultilayerPerceptronClassifier mlp = new MultilayerPerceptronClassifier()
                            .setLayers(layers)
                            .setBlockSize(128)
                            .setSeed(1234L)
                            .setTol(1E-8)
                            .setMaxIter(1000);
```

So, as you can understand, the preceding `MultilayerPerceptronClassifier()` is the classifier trainer based on the MLP. Each layer has a sigmoid activation function except the output layer, which has the softmax activation. Note that Spark-based MLP implementation supports only minibatch GD and LBFGS optimizers.

In short, we cannot use other activation functions such as ReLU or tanh in the hidden layers. Apart from this, other advanced optimizers are also not supported, nor are batch normalization and so on. This is a serious constraint of this implementation. In the next chapter, we will try to overcome this with DL4J.

We have also set the convergence tolerance of iterations as a very small value so that it will lead to higher accuracy with the cost of more iterations. We set the block size for stacking input data in matrices to speed up the computation.

 If the size of the training set is large, then the data is stacked within partitions. If the block size is more than the remaining data in a partition, then it is adjusted to the size of this data. The recommended size is between 10 and 1,000, but the default block size is 128.

Finally, we plan to iterate the training 1,000 times. So let's start training the model using the training set:

```
MultilayerPerceptronClassificationModel model = mlp.fit(trainingData);
```

Evaluating the MLP classifier

When the training is completed, we compute the prediction on the test set to evaluate the robustness of the model:

```
Dataset<Row> predictions = model.transform(validationData);
```

Now, how about seeing some sample predictions? Let's observe both the true labels and the predicted labels:

```
predictions.show();
```

```
+--------------------+-----+--------------------+--------------------+----------+
|            features|label|       rawPrediction|         probability|prediction|
+--------------------+-----+--------------------+--------------------+----------+
|[-0.6480576784030...|  0.0|[1.43363517591707...|[0.96893349593122...|       0.0|
|[-0.6480576784030...|  0.0|[-8.1082996435819...|[4.02626228259359...|       1.0|
|[-0.6480576784030...|  0.0|[-8.1082996435819...|[4.02626228259359...|       1.0|
|[-0.5673125957377...|  0.0|[-0.1640322959336...|[0.39260137197488...|       1.0|
|[-0.5474407529634...|  0.0|[-2.0356964860504...|[0.03642107039370...|       1.0|
|[-0.5225380639171...|  0.0|[9.52109001355164...|[0.99999999757694...|       0.0|
|[-0.5061878135331...|  0.0|[0.78136459169634...|[0.85958947041939...|       0.0|
|[-0.5046785596515...|  0.0|[0.78485553806333...|[0.86092086461934...|       0.0|
|[-0.5043424991206...|  1.0|[0.81165826965175...|[0.86973786781644...|       0.0|
|[-0.5026662211428...|  0.0|[0.99991945120328...|[0.90539585458035...|       0.0|
|[-0.5025817029254...|  0.0|[2.02941913478983...|[0.97832651549972...|       0.0|
|[-0.5025817029254...|  0.0|[0.72874407797616...|[0.83968520050639...|       0.0|
|[-0.5021631365156...|  1.0|[-0.7715748122114...|[0.53732167552789...|       0.0|
|[-0.5021631365156...|  0.0|[0.94526514986850...|[0.89986599681597...|       0.0|
|[-0.5021631365156...|  0.0|[0.83225452435252...|[0.87478522475214...|       0.0|
|[-0.5021631365156...|  0.0|[0.76414347561137...|[0.85732315266212...|       0.0|
|[-0.5021631365156...|  0.0|[0.67965344587190...|[0.83225668146381...|       0.0|
|[-0.4961261209892...|  1.0|[-0.7703785744727...|[0.53787966880031...|       0.0|
|[-0.4941137824804...|  0.0|[1.13917954766187...|[0.93314414983304...|       0.0|
|[-0.4924375045026...|  1.0|[-1.4101139215228...|[0.25222774913860...|       1.0|
+--------------------+-----+--------------------+--------------------+----------+
only showing top 20 rows
```

We can see that some predictions are correct but some of them are wrong too. Nevertheless, in this way, it is difficult to guess the performance. Therefore, we can compute performance metrics such as precision, recall, and f1 measure:

```
MulticlassClassificationEvaluator evaluator = new
MulticlassClassificationEvaluator()
                                          .setLabelCol("label")
.setPredictionCol("prediction");

MulticlassClassificationEvaluator evaluator1 =
evaluator.setMetricName("accuracy");
MulticlassClassificationEvaluator evaluator2 =
evaluator.setMetricName("weightedPrecision");
MulticlassClassificationEvaluator evaluator3 =
evaluator.setMetricName("weightedRecall");
MulticlassClassificationEvaluator evaluator4 =
evaluator.setMetricName("f1");
```

Now let's compute the classification's accuracy, precision, recall, f1 measure, and error on test data:

```
double accuracy = evaluator1.evaluate(predictions);
double precision = evaluator2.evaluate(predictions);
double recall = evaluator3.evaluate(predictions);
double f1 = evaluator4.evaluate(predictions);

// Print the performance metrics
System.out.println("Accuracy = " + accuracy);
System.out.println("Precision = " + precision);
System.out.println("Recall = " + recall);
System.out.println("F1 = " + f1);

System.out.println("Test Error = " + (1 - accuracy));

>>>
Accuracy = 0.7796476846282568
Precision = 0.7796476846282568
Recall = 0.7796476846282568
F1 = 0.7796476846282568
Test Error = 0.22035231537174316
```

Well done! We have been able to achieve a fair accuracy rate, that is, 78%. Still we can improve the with additional feature engineering. More tips will be given in the next section! Now, before concluding this chapter, let's try to utilize the trained model to get the prediction on the test set. First, we read the test set and create the DataFrame:

```
Dataset<Row> testDF = Util.getTestDF();
```

Nevertheless, even if you see the test set, it has some null values. So let's do null imputation on the Age and Fare columns. If you don't prefer using UDF, you can create a MAP where you include your imputing plan:

```
Map<String, Object> m = new HashMap<String, Object>();
m.put("Age", meanAge);
m.put("Fare", meanFare);
Dataset<Row> testDF2 = testDF.na().fill(m);
```

Then again, we create an RDD of vectorPair consisting of features and labels (target column):

```
JavaRDD<VectorPair> testRDD = testDF2.javaRDD().map(row -> {
        VectorPair vectorPair = new VectorPair();
        vectorPair.setLable(row.<Integer>getAs("PassengerId"));
        vectorPair.setFeatures(Util.getScaledVector(
                row.<Double>getAs("Fare"),
                row.<Double>getAs("Age"),
                row.<Integer>getAs("Pclass"),
                row.<Integer>getAs("Sex"),
                row.<Integer>getAs("Embarked"),
                scaler));
        return vectorPair;
    });
```

Then we create a Spark DataFrame:

```
Dataset<Row> scaledTestDF = spark.createDataFrame(testRDD,
VectorPair.class);
```

Finally, let's convert the MLib vectors to ML based vectors:

```
Dataset<Row> finalTestDF =
MLUtils.convertVectorColumnsToML(scaledTestDF).toDF("features",
"PassengerId");
```

Now, let's perform the model inferencing, that is, create a prediction for the `PassengerId` column and show the sample `prediction`:

```
Dataset<Row> resultDF = model.transform(finalTestDF).select("PassengerId",
"prediction");
resultDF.show();
```

```
+-----------+----------+
|PassengerId|prediction|
+-----------+----------+
|      892.0|       0.0|
|      893.0|       0.0|
|      894.0|       0.0|
|      895.0|       1.0|
|      896.0|       0.0|
|      897.0|       0.0|
|      898.0|       1.0|
|      899.0|       0.0|
|      900.0|       1.0|
|      901.0|       0.0|
|      902.0|       0.0|
|      903.0|       0.0|
|      904.0|       1.0|
|      905.0|       0.0|
|      906.0|       1.0|
|      907.0|       1.0|
|      908.0|       0.0|
|      909.0|       1.0|
|      910.0|       1.0|
|      911.0|       0.0|
+-----------+----------+
only showing top 20 rows
```

Finally, let's write the result in a CSV file:

```
resultDF.write().format("com.databricks.spark.csv").option("header",
true).save("result/result.csv");
```

Frequently asked questions (FAQs)

Now that we have solved the Titanic survival prediction problem with an acceptable level of accuracy, there are other practical aspects of this problem and of overall deep learning phenomena that need to be considered too. In this section, we will see some frequently asked questions that might be already in your mind. Answers to these questions can be found in *Appendix A*.

1. Draw an ANN using the original artificial neurons that compute the XOR operation: $A \oplus B$. Describe this problem formally as a classification problem. Why can't simple neurons solve this problem? How does an MLP solve this problem by stacking multiple perceptrons?
2. We have briefly seen the history of ANNs. What are the most significant milestones in the era of deep learning? Can we explain the timeline in a single figure?
3. Can I use another deep learning framework for solving this Titanic survival prediction problem more flexibly?
4. Can I use `Name` as a feature to be used in the MLP in the code?
5. I understand the number of neurons in the input and output layers. But how many neurons should I set for the hidden layers?
6. Can't we improve the predictive accuracy by the cross-validation and grid search technique?

Summary

In this chapter, we introduced some fundamental themes of DL. We started our journey with a basic but comprehensive introduction to ML. Then we gradually moved on to DL and different neural architectures. Then we got a brief overview of the most important DL frameworks. Finally, we saw some frequently asked questions related to deep learning and the Titanic survival prediction problem.

In the next chapter, we'll begin our journey into DL by solving the Titanic survival prediction problem using MLP. Then'll we start developing an end-to-end project for cancer type classification using a recurrent LSTM network. A very-high-dimensional gene expression dataset will be used for training and evaluating the model.

Answers to FAQs

Answer to question 1: There are many ways to solve this problem:

1. $A \oplus B = (A \vee \neg B) \vee (\neg A \wedge B)$
2. $A \oplus B = (A \vee B) \wedge \neg(A \vee B)$
3. $A \oplus B = (A \vee B) \wedge (\neg A \vee \wedge B)$, and so on

If we go with the first approach, the resulting ANNs would look like this:

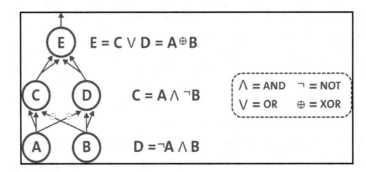

Now from computer science literature, we know that only two input combinations and one output are associated with the XOR operation. With inputs (0, 0) or (1, 1) the network outputs 0; and with inputs (0, 1) or (1, 0), it outputs 1. So we can formally represent the preceding truth table as follows:

X0	X1	Y
0	0	0
0	1	1
1	0	1
1	1	0

Here, each pattern is classified into one of two classes that can be separated by a single line L. They are known as linearly separable patterns, as represented here:

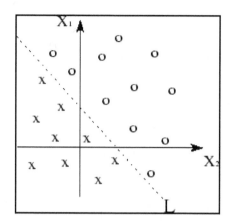

Answer to question 2: The most significant progress in ANN and DL can be described in the following timeline. We have already seen how artificial neurons and perceptrons provided the base in 1943s and 1958s respectively. Then, XOR was formulated as a linearly non-separable problem in 1969 by Minsky et al. But later in 1974, Werbos et al. demonstrated the backpropagation algorithm for training the perceptron in 1974.

However, the most significant advancement happened in the 1980s, when John Hopfield et al. proposed the Hopfield Network in 1982. Then, Hinton, one of the godfathers of neural networks and deep learning, and his team proposed the Boltzmann machine in 1985. However, probably one of the most significant advances happened in 1986, when Hinton et al. successfully trained the MLP, and Jordan et. al. proposed RNNs. In the same year, Smolensky et al. also proposed an improved version of the RBM.

In the 1990s, the most significant year was 1997. Lecun et al. proposed LeNet in 1990, and Jordan et al. proposed RNN in 1997. In the same year, Schuster et al. proposed an improved version of LSTM and an improved version of the original RNN, called **bidirectional RNN**.

Despite significant advances in computing, from 1997 to 2005, we hadn't experienced much advancement, until Hinton struck again in 2006. He and his team proposed a DBN by stacking multiple RBMs. Then in 2012, again Hinton invented dropout, which significantly improved regularization and overfitting in a DNN.

After that, Ian Goodfellow et al. introduced GANs, a significant milestone in image recognition. In 2017, Hinton proposed CapsNets to overcome the limitations of regular CNNs—so far one of the most significant milestones.

Answer to question 3: Yes, you can use other deep learning frameworks described in the *Deep learning frameworks* section. However, since this book is about using Java for deep learning, I would suggest going for DeepLearning4J. We will see how flexibly we can create networks by stacking input, hidden, and output layers using DeepLearning4J in the next chapter.

Answer to question 4: Yes, you can, since the passenger's name containing a different title (for example, Mr., Mrs., Miss, Master, and so on) could be significant too. For example, we can imagine that being a woman (that is, Mrs.) and being a junior (for example, Master.) could give a higher chance of survival.

Even, after watching the famous movie Titanic (1997), we can imagine that being in a relationship, a girl might have a good chance of survival since his boyfriend would try to save her! Anyway, this is just for imagination, so do not take it seriously. Now, we can write a user-defined function to encode this using Apache Spark. Let's take a look at the following UDF in Java:

```java
private static final UDF1<String, Option<String>> getTitle = (String name)
    -> {
    if(name.contains("Mr.")) { // If it has Mr.
        return Some.apply("Mr.");
    } else if(name.contains("Mrs.")) { // Or if has Mrs.
        return Some.apply("Mrs.");
    } else if(name.contains("Miss.")) { // Or if has Miss.
        return Some.apply("Miss.");
    } else if(name.contains("Master.")) { // Or if has Master.
        return Some.apply("Master.");
    } else{ // Not any.
        return Some.apply("Untitled");
    }
};
```

Next, we can register the UDF. Then I had to register the preceding UDF as follows:

```java
spark.sqlContext().udf().register("getTitle", getTitle,
DataTypes.StringType);

Dataset<Row> categoricalDF = df.select(callUDF("getTitle",
col("Name")).alias("Name"), col("Sex"),
                                    col("Ticket"), col("Cabin"),
col("Embarked"));
categoricalDF.show();
```

The resulting column would look like this:

```
+-----+------+--------------------+-----+--------+
| Name|   Sex|              Ticket|Cabin|Embarked|
+-----+------+--------------------+-----+--------+
|  Mr.|  male|          A/5 21171| null|       S|
| Mrs.|female|          PC 17599|  C85|       C|
|Miss.|female|STON/02. 3101282| null|       S|
| Mrs.|female|            113803| C123|       S|
|  Mr.|  male|            373450| null|       S|
+-----+------+--------------------+-----+--------+
only showing top 5 rows
```

Answer to question 5: For many problems, you can start with just one or two hidden layers. This setting will work just fine using two hidden layers with the same total number of neurons (continue reading to get an idea about a number of neurons) in roughly the same amount of training time. Now let's see some naïve estimation about setting the number of hidden layers:

- **0:** Only capable of representing linear separable functions
- **1:** Can approximate any function that contains a continuous mapping from one finite space to another
- **2:** Can represent an arbitrary decision boundary to arbitrary accuracy

However, for a more complex problem, you can gradually ramp up the number of hidden layers, until you start overfitting the training set. Nevertheless, you can try increasing the number of neurons gradually until the network starts overfitting. This means the upper bound on the number of hidden neurons that will not result in overfitting is:

$$N_h = \frac{N_s}{(\alpha * (N_i + N_o))}$$

In the preceding equation:

- N_i = number of input neurons
- N_o = number of output neurons
- N_s = number of samples in training dataset
- α = an arbitrary scaling factor, usually *2-10*

Note that the preceding equation does not come from any research but from my personal working experience.

Answer to question 6: Of course, we can. We can cross-validate the training and create a grid search technique for finding the best hyperparameters. Let's give it a try.

First, we have the layers defined. Unfortunately, we cannot cross-validate layers. Probably, it's either a bug or made intentionally by the Spark guys. So we stick to a single layering:

```
int[] layers = new int[] {10, 16, 16, 2};
```

Then we create the trainer and set only the layer and seed parameters:

```
MultilayerPerceptronClassifier mlp = new MultilayerPerceptronClassifier()
                    .setLayers(layers)
                    .setSeed(1234L);
```

We search through the MLP's different hyperparameters for the best model:

```
ParamMap[] paramGrid = new ParamGridBuilder()
                    .addGrid(mlp.blockSize(), new int[] {32, 64, 128})
                    .addGrid(mlp.maxIter(), new int[] {10, 50})
                    .addGrid(mlp.tol(), new double[] {1E-2, 1E-4, 1E-6})
                    .build();
MulticlassClassificationEvaluator evaluator = new
MulticlassClassificationEvaluator()
            .setLabelCol("label")
            .setPredictionCol("prediction");
```

We then set up the cross-validator and perform 10-fold cross-validation:

```
int numFolds = 10;
CrossValidator crossval = new CrossValidator()
            .setEstimator(mlp)
            .setEvaluator(evaluator)
            .setEstimatorParamMaps(paramGrid)
            .setNumFolds(numFolds);
```

Then we perform training using the cross-validated model:

```
CrossValidatorModel cvModel = crossval.fit(trainingData);
```

Finally, we evaluate the cross-validated model on the test set, as follows:

```
Dataset<Row> predictions = cvModel.transform(validationData);
```

Now we can compute and show the performance metrics, similar to our previous example:

```
double accuracy = evaluator1.evaluate(predictions);
double precision = evaluator2.evaluate(predictions);
double recall = evaluator3.evaluate(predictions);
double f1 = evaluator4.evaluate(predictions);

// Print the performance metrics
System.out.println("Accuracy = " + accuracy);
System.out.println("Precision = " + precision);
System.out.println("Recall = " + recall);
System.out.println("F1 = " + f1);
System.out.println("Test Error = " + (1 - accuracy));
```

```
>>>
Accuracy = 0.7810132575757576
Precision = 0.7810132575757576
Recall = 0.7810132575757576
F1 = 0.7810132575757576
Test Error = 0.21898674242424243
```

Cancer Types Prediction Using Recurrent Type Networks

2

Large-scale cancer genomics data often comes in multiplatform and heterogeneous forms. These datasets impose great challenges in terms of the bioinformatics approach and computational algorithms. Numerous researchers have proposed to utilize this data to overcome several challenges, using classical machine learning algorithms as either the primary subject or a supporting element for cancer diagnosis and prognosis.

In this chapter, we will use some deep learning architectures for cancer type classification from a very-high-dimensional dataset curated from The Cancer Genome Atlas (TCGA). First, we will describe the dataset and perform some preprocessing such that the dataset can be fed to our networks. We will then see how to prepare our programming environment, before moving on to coding with an open source, deep learning library called **Deeplearning4j (DL4J)**. First, we will revisit the Titanic survival prediction problem again using a **Multilayer Perceptron (MLP)** implementation from DL4J.

Then we will use an improved architecture of **Recurrent Neural Networks (RNN)** called **Long Short-Term Memory (LSTM)** for cancer type prediction. Finally, we will see some frequent questions related to this project and DL4J hyperparameters/nets tuning.

In a nutshell, we will be learning the following topics in the chapter:

- Deep learning in cancer genomics
- Cancer genomics dataset description
- Getting started with Deeplearning4j
- Developing a cancer type predictive model using LSTM-RNN
- Frequently asked questions

Deep learning in cancer genomics

Biomedical informatics includes all techniques regarding the development of data analytics, mathematical modeling, and computational simulation for the study of biological systems. In recent years, we've witnessed huge leaps in biological computing that has resulted in large, information-rich resources being at our disposal. These cover domains such as anatomy, modeling (3D printers), genomics, and pharmacology, among others.

One of the most famous success stories of biomedical informatics is from the domain of genomics. The **Human Genome Project** (**HGP**) was an international research project with the objective of determining the full sequence of human DNA. This project has been one of the most important landmarks in computational biology and has been used as a base for other projects, including the Human Brain Project, which is determined to sequence the human brain. The data that was used in this thesis is also the indirect result of the HGP.

The era of big data starts from the last decade or so, which was marked by an overflow of digital information in comparison to its analog counterpart. Just in the year 2016, 16.1 zettabytes of digital data were generated, and it is predicted to reach 163 ZB/year by 2025. As good a piece of news as this is, there are some problems lingering, especially of data storage and analysis. For the latter, simple machine learning methods that were used in normal-size data analysis won't be effective anymore and should be substituted by deep neural network learning methods. Deep learning is generally known to deal very well with these types of large and complex datasets.

Along with other crucial areas, the biomedical area has also been exposed to these big data phenomena. One of the main largest data sources is omics data such as genomics, metabolomics, and proteomics. Innovations in biomedical techniques and equipment, such as DNA sequencing and mass spectrometry, have led to a massive accumulation of -omics data.

Typically -omics data is full of veracity, variability and high dimensionality. These datasets are sourced from multiple, and even sometimes incompatible, data platforms. These properties make these types of data suitable for applying DL approaches. Deep learning analysis of -omics data is one of the main tasks in the biomedical sector as it has a chance to be the leader in personalized medicine. By acquiring information about a person's omics data, diseases can be dealt with better and treatment can be focused on preventive measures.

Cancer is generally known to be one of the deadliest diseases in the world, which is mostly due to its complexity of diagnosis and treatment. It is a genetic disease that involves multiple gene mutations. As the importance of genetic knowledge in cancer treatment is increasingly addressed, several projects to document the genetic data of cancer patients has emerged recently. One of the most well known is **The Cancer Genome Atlas (TCGA)** project, which is available on the TCGA research network: `http://cancergenome.nih.gov/`
.

As mentioned before, there have been a number of deep learning implementations in the biomedical sector, including cancer research. For cancer research, most researchers usually use -omics or medical imaging data as inputs. Several research works have focused on cancer analysis. Some of them use either a histopathology image or a PET image as a source. Most of that research focuses on classification based on that image data with **convolutional neural networks (CNNs)**.

However, many of them use -omics data as their source. Fakoor et al. classified the various types of cancer using patients' gene expression data. Due to the different dimensionality of each data from each cancer type, they used **principal component analysis (PCA)** first to reduce the dimensionality of microarray gene expression data.

 PCA is a statistical technique used to emphasize variation and extract the most significant patterns from a dataset; principal components are the simplest of the true eigenvector-based multivariate analyses. PCA is frequently used for making data exploration easy to visualize. Consequently, PCA is one of the most used algorithms in exploratory data analysis and for making predictive models.

Then they applied sparse and stacked autoencoders to classify various cancers, including acute myeloid leukemia, breast cancer, and ovarian cancer.

 For detailed information, refer to the following publication, entitled *Using deep learning to enhance cancer diagnosis and classification* by R. Fakoor et al. in proceedings of the International Conference on Machine Learning, 2013.

Ibrahim et al. , on the other hand, used miRNA expression data from six types of cancer genes/miRNA feature selection. They proposed a novel multilevel feature selection approach named **MLFS** (short for **Multilevel gene/miRNA feature selection**), which was based on **Deep Belief Networks (DBN)** and unsupervised active learning.

You can read more in the publication titled *Multilevel gene/miRNA feature selection using deep belief nets and active learning* (R. Ibrahim, et al.) in Proceedings 36th annual International Conference Eng. Med. Biol. Soc. (EMBC), pp. 3957-3960, IEEE, 2014.

Finally, Liang et al. clustered ovarian and breast cancer patients using multiplatform genomics and clinical data. The ovarian cancer dataset contained gene expression, DNA methylation, and miRNA expression data across 385 patients, which were downloaded from **The Cancer Genome Atlas (TCGA)**.

 You can read more more in the following publication entitled *Integrative data analysis of multi-platform cancer data with a multimodal deep learning approach* (by M. Liang et al.) in Molecular Pharmaceutics, vol. 12, pp. 928{937, IEEE/ACM Transaction Computational Biology and Bioinformatics, 2015.

The breast cancer dataset included GE data and corresponding clinical information, such as survival time and time to recurrence data, which was collected by the Netherlands Cancer Institute. To deal with this multiplatform data, they used **multimodal Deep Belief Networks (mDBN)**.

First, they implemented a DBN for each of those data to get their latent features. Then, another DBN used to perform the clustering is implemented using those latent features as the input. Apart from these researchers, much research work is going on to give cancer genomics, identification, and treatment a significant boost.

Cancer genomics dataset description

Genomics data covers all data related to DNA on living things. Although in this thesis we will also use other types of data like transcriptomic data (RNA and miRNA), for convenience purposes, all data will be termed as genomics data. Research on human genetics found a huge breakthrough in recent years due to the success of the HGP (1984-2000) on sequencing the full sequence of human DNA.

One of the areas that have been helped a lot due to this is the research of all diseases related to genetics, including cancer. Due to various biomedical analyses done on DNA, there exist various types of -omics or genomics data. Here are some types of -omics data that were crucial to cancer analysis:

- **Raw sequencing data:** This corresponds to the DNA coding of whole chromosomes. In general, every human has 24 types of chromosomes in each cell of their body, and each chromosome consists of 4.6-247 million base pairs. Each base pair can be coded in four different types, which are **adenine (A)**, **cytosine (C)**, **guanine (G)**, and **thymine (T)**. Therefore, raw sequencing data consists of billions of base pair data, with each coded in one of these four different types.

- **Single-Nucleotide Polymorphism (SNP) data:** Each human has a different raw sequence, which causes genetic mutation. Genetic mutation can cause an actual disease, or just a difference in physical appearance (such as hair color), or nothing at all. When this mutation happens only on a single base pair instead of a sequence of base pairs, it is called **Single-Nucleotide Polymorphism (SNP)**.

- **Copy Number Variation (CNV) data:** This corresponds to a genetic mutation that happens in a sequence of base pairs. Several types of mutation can happen, including deletion of a sequence of base pairs, multiplication of a sequence of base pairs, and relocation of a sequence of base pairs into other parts of the chromosome.

- **DNA methylation data**: Which corresponds to the amount of methylation (methyl group connected to base pair) that happens to areas in the chromosome. A large amount of methylation in promoter regions of a gene can cause gene repression. DNA methylation is the reason each of our organs acts differently even though all of them have the same DNA sequence. In cancer, this DNA methylation is disrupted.

- **Gene expression data**: This corresponds to the number of proteins that were expressed from a gene at a given time. Cancer happens either because of high expression of an oncogene (that is, a gene that causes a tumor), low expression of a tumor suppressor gene (a gene that prevents a tumor), or both. Therefore, the analysis of gene expression data can help discover protein biomarkers in cancer. We will use this in this project.

- **miRNA expression data**: Corresponds to the amount of microRNA that was expressed at a given time. miRNA plays a role in protein silencing at the mRNA stage. Therefore, an analysis of gene expression data can help discover miRNA biomarkers in cancer.

There are several databases of genomics datasets, where the aforementioned data can be found. Some of them focus on the genomics data of cancer patients. These databases include:

- **The Cancer Genome Atlas (TCGA)**: https://cancergenome.nih.gov/
- **International Cancer Genome Consortium (ICGC)**: https://icgc.org/
- **Catalog of Somatic Mutations in Cancer (COSMIC)**: https://cancer.sanger.ac.uk/cosmic

This genomics data is usually accompanied by clinical data of the patient. This clinical data can comprise general clinical information (for example, age or gender) and their cancer status (for example, cancer location or cancer stage). All of this genomics data itself has a characteristic of high dimensions. For example, the gene expression data for each patient is structured based on the gene ID, which reaches around 60,000 types.

Moreover, some of the data itself comes from more than one format. For example, 70% of the DNA methylation data is collected from breast cancer patients and the remaining 30% are curated from different platforms. Therefore, there are two different structures on in this dataset. Therefore, to analyze genomics data by dealing with the heterogeneity, researchers have often used powerful machine learning techniques or even deep neural networks.

Now let's see what a real-life dataset looks like that can be used for our purpose. We will be using the gene expression cancer RNA-Seq dataset downloaded from the UCI machine learning repository (see https://archive.ics.uci.edu/ml/datasets/gene+expression+cancer+RNA-Seq# for more information).

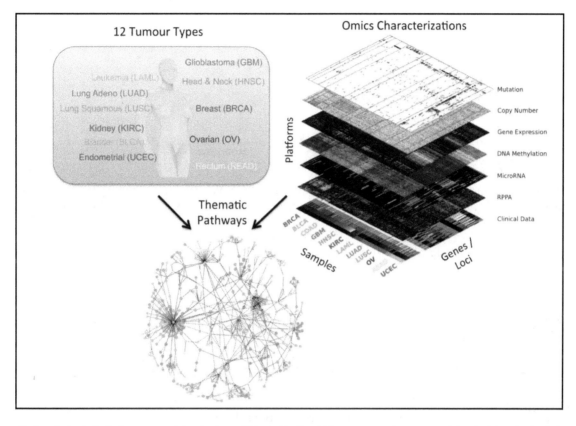

The data collection pipeline for the pan-cancer analysis project (source: "Weinstein, John N., et al. 'The cancer genome atlas pan-cancer analysis project.' Nature Genetics 45.10 (2013): 1113-1120")

This dataset is a random subset of another dataset reported in the following paper: Weinstein, John N., et al. *The cancer genome atlas pan-cancer analysis project. Nature Genetics 45.10 (2013): 1113-1120*. The preceding diagram shows the data collection pipeline for the pan-cancer analysis project.

The name of the project is The Pan-Cancer analysis project. It assembled data from thousands of patients with primary tumors occurring in different sites of the body. It covered 12 tumor types (see the upper-left panel in the preceding figure) including:

- **Glioblastoma Multiform** (GBM)
- **Lymphoblastic acute myeloid leukemia** (AML)
- **Head and Neck Squamous Carcinoma** (HNSC)
- **Lung Adenocarcinoma** (LUAD)

- **lung Squamous Carcinoma (LUSC)**
- **Breast Carcinoma (BRCA)**
- **kidney Renal Clear Cell Carcinoma (KIRC)**
- **ovarian Carcinoma (OV)**
- **Bladder Carcinoma (BLCA)**
- **Colon Adenocarcinoma (COAD)**
- **Uterine Cervical and Endometrial Carcinoma (UCEC)**
- **Rectal Adenocarcinoma (READ)**

This collection of data is part of the RNA-Seq (HiSeq) PANCAN dataset. It is a random extraction of gene expressions of patients having different types of tumors: BRCA, KIRC, COAD, LUAD, and PRAD.

This dataset is a random collection of cancer patients from 801 patients, each having 20,531 attributes. Samples (instances) are stored row-wise. Variables (attributes) of each sample are RNA-Seq gene expression levels measured by the illumina HiSeq platform. A dummy name (gene_XX) is given to each attribute. The attributes are ordered consistently with the original submission. For example, gene_1 on sample_0 is significantly and differentially expressed with a a value of 2.01720929003.

When you download the dataset, you will see there are two CSV files:

- data.csv: Contains the gene expression data of each sample
- labels.csv: The labels associated with each sample

Let's take a look at the processed dataset. Note we will see only a few selected features considering the high dimensionality in the following screenshot, where the first column represents sample IDs (that is, anonymous patient IDs). The rest of the columns represent how a certain gene expression occurs in the tumor samples of the patients:

```
|       id|gene_0|         gene_1|         gene_2|         gene_3|         gene_4|
+---------+------+---------------+---------------+---------------+---------------+
| sample_0|   0.0| 2.01720929003|3.26552691165|5.47848651208|10.4319989607|
| sample_1|   0.0|0.592732094867|1.58842082049|7.58615673813|9.62301085621|
| sample_2|   0.0|  3.5117589779|4.32719871937|6.88178695937|9.87072997113|
| sample_3|   0.0| 3.66361787431|4.50764877794|6.65906827484|10.1961840717|
| sample_4|   0.0| 2.65574107476|2.82154695883|6.53945352515|9.73826456185|
| sample_5|   0.0| 3.46785331372|3.58191760772|6.62024328973|9.70682924127|
| sample_6|   0.0|   1.224966365|1.69117679681|6.57200741498|9.64051067136|
| sample_7|   0.0| 2.85485342652|1.75047787844|7.22672044861|9.75869126501|
| sample_8|   0.0| 3.99212487426|2.77273024777|6.54669231412|10.4882518866|
| sample_9|   0.0| 3.64249364243|4.42355800269|6.84951144203|9.46446610892|
|sample_10|   0.0| 3.49207108711|  3.553372792|7.15170663424|10.2534456958|
|sample_11|   0.0| 2.94118144936|2.66327629754|6.56168966691|9.37629255419|
|sample_12|   0.0|  3.9703475182|2.36429227014| 7.1454431001|9.24060531982|
|sample_13|   0.0| 1.5510483733|3.52984592804|  6.3268249381|10.6338489327|
|sample_14|   0.0| 1.9648421858|2.18301003676|6.59683230199|10.2481410545|
|sample_15|   0.0| 2.90137860229|3.68536833781|6.66966460873|9.99909803371|
|sample_16|   0.0|  3.4609128992|3.61847360308|5.66104837265|9.73121719013|
|sample_17|   0.0| 3.00451936963|3.00717755732|6.52420475302|9.06266141243|
|sample_18|   0.0| 1.54146527849|2.54153961931|6.84325527996|9.44446829832|
|sample_19|   0.0| 4.16758272913|3.84138948407|6.97612301373|9.98225207842|
+---------+------+---------------+---------------+---------------+---------------+
only showing top 20 rows
```

Sample gene expression dataset

Now look at the labels in *Figure 3*. Here, `id` contains the sample ids and `Class` represents the cancer labels:

```
+---------+-----+
|       id|Class|
+---------+-----+
|sample_0| PRAD|
|sample_1| LUAD|
|sample_2| PRAD|
|sample_3| PRAD|
|sample_4| BRCA|
|sample_5| PRAD|
|sample_6| KIRC|
|sample_7| PRAD|
|sample_8| BRCA|
|sample_9| PRAD|
+---------+-----+
only showing top 10 rows
```

Samples are classified into different cancer types

Now you can imagine why I have chosen this dataset. Well, although we will not have so many samples, the dataset is still very high dimensional. In addition, this type of high-dimensional dataset is very suitable for applying a deep learning algorithm.

Alright. Therefore, if the features and labels are given, can we classify these samples based on features and the ground truth. Why not? We will try to solve the problem with the DL4J library. First, we have to configure our programming environment so that we can start writing our codes.

Preparing programming environment

In this section, we will discuss how to configure DL4J, ND4s, Spark, and ND4J before getting started with the coding. The following are prerequisites when working with DL4J:

- Java 1.8+ (64-bit only)
- Apache Maven for automated build and dependency manager
- IntelliJ IDEA or Eclipse IDE
- Git for version control and CI/CD

The following libraries can be integrated with DJ4J to enhance your JVM experience while developing your ML applications:

- **DL4J**: The core neural network framework, which comes up with many DL architectures and underlying functionalities.
- **ND4J**: Can be considered as the NumPy of the JVM. It comes with some basic operations of linear algebra. Examples are matrix creation, addition, and multiplication.
- **DataVec**: This library enables ETL operation while performing feature engineering.
- **JavaCPP**: This library acts as the bridge between Java and Native C++.
- **Arbiter**: This library provides basic evaluation functionalities for the DL algorithms.
- **RL4J**: Deep reinforcement learning for the JVM.
- **ND4S**: This is a scientific computing library, and it also supports n-dimensional arrays for JVM-based languages.

If you are using Maven on your preferred IDE, let's define the project properties to mention the versions in the `pom.xml` file:

```
<properties>
        <project.build.sourceEncoding>UTF-8</project.build.sourceEncoding>
        <java.version>1.8</java.version>
        <nd4j.version>1.0.0-alpha</nd4j.version>
        <dl4j.version>1.0.0-alpha</dl4j.version>
        <datavec.version>1.0.0-alpha</datavec.version>
        <arbiter.version>1.0.0-alpha</arbiter.version>
        <logback.version>1.2.3</logback.version>
        <dl4j.spark.version>1.0.0-alpha_spark_2</dl4j.spark.version>
</properties>
```

Then use the following dependencies required for DL4J, ND4S, ND4J, and so on:

```
<dependencies>
    <dependency>
        <groupId>org.nd4j</groupId>
        <artifactId>nd4j-native</artifactId>
        <version>${nd4j.version}</version>
    </dependency>
    <dependency>
        <groupId>org.deeplearning4j</groupId>
        <artifactId>dl4j-spark_2.11</artifactId>
        <version>1.0.0-alpha_spark_2</version>
    </dependency>
    <dependency>
        <groupId>org.nd4j</groupId>
        <artifactId>nd4j-native</artifactId>
        <version>1.0.0-alpha</version>
        <type>pom</type>
    </dependency>
    <dependency>
        <groupId>org.deeplearning4j</groupId>
        <artifactId>deeplearning4j-core</artifactId>
        <version>${dl4j.version}</version>
    </dependency>
    <dependency>
        <groupId>org.deeplearning4j</groupId>
        <artifactId>deeplearning4j-nlp</artifactId>
        <version>${dl4j.version}</version>
    </dependency>
    <dependency>
        <groupId>org.deeplearning4j</groupId>
        <artifactId>deeplearning4j-zoo</artifactId>
        <version>${dl4j.version}</version>
```

```
        </dependency>
        <dependency>
            <groupId>org.deeplearning4j</groupId>
            <artifactId>arbiter-deeplearning4j</artifactId>
            <version>${arbiter.version}</version>
        </dependency>
        <dependency>
            <groupId>org.deeplearning4j</groupId>
            <artifactId>arbiter-ui_2.11</artifactId>
            <version>${arbiter.version}</version>
        </dependency>
        <dependency>
            <artifactId>datavec-data-codec</artifactId>
            <groupId>org.datavec</groupId>
            <version>${datavec.version}</version>
        </dependency>
        <dependency>
            <groupId>org.apache.httpcomponents</groupId>
            <artifactId>httpclient</artifactId>
            <version>4.3.5</version>
        </dependency>
        <dependency>
            <groupId>ch.qos.logback</groupId>
            <artifactId>logback-classic</artifactId>
            <version>${logback.version}</version>
        </dependency>
</dependencies>
```

By the way, DL4J comes with Spark 2.1.0. Additionally, if a native system BLAS is not configured on your machine, ND4J's performance will be reduced. You will experience the following warning once you execute simple code written in Scala:

```
******************************************************************
WARNING: COULD NOT LOAD NATIVE SYSTEM BLAS
ND4J performance WILL be reduced
******************************************************************
```

However, installing and configuring BLAS such as `OpenBLAS` or `IntelMKL` is not that difficult; you can invest some time and do it. Refer to the following URL for further details: `http://nd4j.org/getstarted.html#open`.

Well done! Our programming environment is ready for simple deep learning application development. Now it's time to get your hands dirty with some sample code.

Titanic survival revisited with DL4J

In the preceding chapter, we solved the Titanic survival prediction problem using Spark-based MLP. We also saw that by using Spark-based MLP, the user has very little transparency of using the layering structure. Moreover, it was not explicit to define hyperparameters and so on.

Therefore, what I have done is used the training dataset and then performed some preprocessing and feature engineering. Then I randomly split the pre-processed dataset into training and testing (to be precise, 70% for training and 30% for testing). First, we create the Spark session as follows:

```
SparkSession spark = SparkSession.builder()
                .master("local[*]")
                .config("spark.sql.warehouse.dir", "temp/")// change
accordingly
                .appName("TitanicSurvivalPrediction")
                .getOrCreate();
```

In this chapter, we have seen that there are two CSV files. However, `test.csv` one does not provide any ground truth. Therefore, I decided to use only the `training.csv` one, so that we can compare the model's performance. So let's read the training dataset using the spark `read()` API:

```
Dataset<Row> df = spark.sqlContext()
                .read()
                .format("com.databricks.spark.csv")
                .option("header", "true") // Use first line of all files as
header
                .option("inferSchema", "true") // Automatically infer data
types
                .load("data/train.csv");
```

We have seen in `Chapter 1`, *Getting Started with Deep Learning* that the `Age` and `Fare` columns have many null values. So, instead of writing UDF for each column, here I just replace the missing values of the age and fare columns by their mean:

```
Map<String, Object> m = new HashMap<String, Object>();
m.put("Age", 30);
m.put("Fare", 32.2);
Dataset<Row> trainingDF1 = df2.na().fill(m);
```

To get more detailed insights into handling missing/null values and machine learning, interested readers can take a look at Boyan Angelov's blog at `https://towardsdatascience.com/working-with-missing-data-in-machine-learning-9c0a430df4ce`.

For simplicity, we can drop a few more columns too, such as `"PassengerId"`, `"Name"`, `"Ticket"`, and `"Cabin"`:

```
Dataset<Row> trainingDF2 = trainingDF1.drop("PassengerId", "Name",
"Ticket", "Cabin");
```

Now, here comes the tricky part. Similar to Spark ML-based estimators, DL4J-based networks also need training data in numeric form. Therefore, we now have to convert the categorical features into numerics. For that, we can use a `StringIndexer()` transformer. What we will do is we will create two that is, `StringIndexer` for the `"Sex"` and `"Embarked"` columns:

```
StringIndexer sexIndexer = new StringIndexer()
                            .setInputCol("Sex")
                            .setOutputCol("sexIndex")
                            .setHandleInvalid("skip");//// we skip
column having nulls
StringIndexer embarkedIndexer = new StringIndexer()
                            .setInputCol("Embarked")
                            .setOutputCol("embarkedIndex")
                            .setHandleInvalid("skip");//// we skip
column having nulls
```

Then we will chain them into a single pipeline. Next, we will perform the transformation operation:

```
Pipeline pipeline = new Pipeline().setStages(new PipelineStage[]
{sexIndexer, embarkedIndexer});
```

Then we will fit the pipeline, transform, and drop both the `"Sex"` and `"Embarked"` columns to get the transformed dataset:

```
Dataset<Row> trainingDF3 =
pipeline.fit(trainingDF2).transform(trainingDF2).drop("Sex", "Embarked");
```

Then our final pre-processed dataset will have only the numerical features. Note that DL4J considers the last column as the label column. That means DL4J will consider `"Pclass"`, `"Age"`, `"SibSp"`, `"Parch"`, `"Fare"`, `"sexIndex"`, and `"embarkedIndex"` as features. Therefore, I placed the `"Survived"` column as the last column:

```
Dataset<Row> finalDF = trainingDF3.select("Pclass", "Age", "SibSp","Parch",
"Fare",
                                          "sexIndex","embarkedIndex",
"Survived");
finalDF.show();
```

Then we randomly split the dataset into training and testing as 70% and 30%, respectively. That is, we used 70% for training and the rest to evaluate the model:

```
Dataset<Row>[] splits = finalDF.randomSplit(new double[] {0.7, 0.3});
Dataset<Row> trainingData = splits[0];
Dataset<Row> testData = splits[1];
```

Finally, we have both the DataFrames as separate CSV files to be used by DL4J:

```
trainingData
        .coalesce(1)// coalesce(1) writes DF in a single CSV
        .write()
        .format("com.databricks.spark.csv")
        .option("header", "false") // don't write the header
        .option("delimiter", ",") // comma separated
        .save("data/Titanic_Train.csv"); // save location

testData
        .coalesce(1)// coalesce(1) writes DF in a single CSV
        .write()
        .format("com.databricks.spark.csv")
        .option("header", "false") // don't write the header
        .option("delimiter", ",") // comma separated
        .save("data/Titanic_Test.csv"); // save location
```

Additionally, DL4J does not support the header info in the training set, so I intentionally skipped writing the header.

Multilayer perceptron network construction

As I informed you in the preceding chapter, DL4J-based neural networks are made of multiple layers. Everything starts with a `MultiLayerConfiguration`, which organizes those layers and their hyperparameters.

 Hyperparameters are a set of variables that determine how a neural network would learn. There are many parameters, for example, how many times and how often to update the weights of the model (called an **epoch**), how to initialize network weights, which activation function to be used, which updater and optimization algorithms to be used, the learning rate (that is, how fast the model should learn), how many hidden layers are there, how many neurons are there in each layer, and so on.

We now create the network. First, let us create the layers. Similar to the MLP we created in `Chapter 1`, *Getting Started with Deep Learning*, our MLP will have four layers:

- **Layer 0**: Input layer
- **Lauer 1**: Hidden layer 1
- **Layer 2**: Hidden layer 2
- **Layer 3**: Output layer

More technically, the first layer is the input layer, and then two layers are placed as hidden layers. For the first three layers, we initialized the weights using Xavier and the activation function is ReLU. Finally, the output layer is placed. This setting is shown in the following figure:

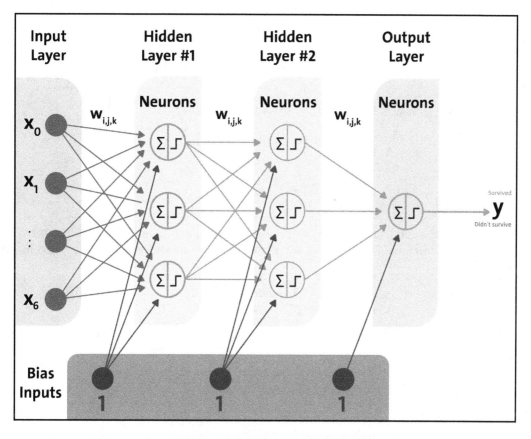

Multilayer perceptron for Titanic survival prediction input layer

We have specified the neurons (that is, nodes), which are an equal number of inputs, and an arbitrary number of neurons as output. We set a smaller value considering very few inputs and features:

```
DenseLayer input_layer = new DenseLayer.Builder()
                .weightInit(WeightInit.XAVIER)
                .activation(Activation.RELU)
                .nIn(numInputs)
                .nOut(16)
                .build();
```

Hidden layer 1

The number of input neurons is equal to the output of the input layer. Then the number of outputs is an arbitrary value. We set a smaller value considering very few inputs and features:

```
DenseLayer hidden_layer_1 = new DenseLayer.Builder()
                .weightInit(WeightInit.XAVIER)
                .activation(Activation.RELU)
                .nIn(16).nOut(32)
                .build();
```

Hidden layer 2

The number of input neurons is equal to the output of hidden layer 1. Then the number of outputs is an arbitrary value. Again we set a smaller value considering very few inputs and features:

```
DenseLayer hidden_layer_2 = new DenseLayer.Builder()
                .weightInit(WeightInit.XAVIER)
                .activation(Activation.RELU)
                .nIn(32).nOut(16)
                .build();
```

Output layer

The number of input neurons is equal to the output of the hidden layer 1. Then the number of outputs is equal to the number of predicted labels. We set a smaller value yet again, considering a very few inputs and features.

Here we used the Softmax activation function, which gives us a probability distribution over classes (the outputs sum to 1.0), and the losses function as cross-entropy for binary classification (XNET) since we want to convert the output (probability) to a discrete class, that is, zero or one:

```
OutputLayer output_layer = new OutputLayer.Builder(LossFunction.XENT) //
XENT for Binary Classification
                .weightInit(WeightInit.XAVIER)
                .activation(Activation.SOFTMAX)
                .nIn(16).nOut(numOutputs)
                .build();
```

XNET is used for binary classification with logistic regression. Check out more about this in `LossFunctions.java` class in DL4J.

Now we create a `MultiLayerConfiguration` by specifying `NeuralNetConfiguration` before conducting the training. With DL4J, we can add a layer by calling `layer` on the `NeuralNetConfiguration.Builder()`, specifying its place in the order of layers (the zero-indexed layer in the following code is the input layer):

```
MultiLayerConfiguration MLPconf = new
NeuralNetConfiguration.Builder().seed(seed)
.optimizationAlgo(OptimizationAlgorithm.STOCHASTIC_GRADIENT_DESCENT)
                .weightInit(WeightInit.XAVIER)
                .updater(new Adam(0.0001))
                .list()
                    .layer(0, input_layer)
                    .layer(1, hidden_layer_1)
                    .layer(2, hidden_layer_2)
                    .layer(3, output_layer)
                .pretrain(false).backprop(true).build();// no pre-traning
    required
```

Apart from these, we also specify how to set the network's weights. For example, as discussed, we use Xavier as the weight initialization and **Stochastic Gradient Descent** (**SGD**) optimization algorithm with Adam as the updater. Finally, we also specify that we do not need to do any pre-training (which is typically needed in DBN or stacked autoencoders). Nevertheless, since MLP is a feedforward network, we set backpropagation as true.

Network training

First, we create a `MultiLayerNetwork` using the preceding `MultiLayerConfiguration`. Then we initialize the network and start the training on the training set:

```
MultiLayerNetwork model = new MultiLayerNetwork(MLPconf);
model.init();
log.info("Train model....");
for( int i=0; i<numEpochs; i++ ){
    model.fit(trainingDataIt);
        }
```

In the preceding code block, we start training the model by invoking the `model.fit()` on the training set (`trainingDataIt` in our case). Now we will discuss how we prepared the training and test set. Well, for reading the training set or test set that are in an inappropriate format (features are numeric and labels are integers), I have created a method called `readCSVDataset()`:

```
private static DataSetIterator readCSVDataset(String csvFileClasspath, int batchSize,
                int labelIndex, int numClasses) throws IOException,
InterruptedException {
        RecordReader rr = new CSVRecordReader();
        File input = new File(csvFileClasspath);
        rr.initialize(new FileSplit(input));
        DataSetIterator iterator = new RecordReaderDataSetIterator(rr,
batchSize, labelIndex, numClasses);
        return iterator;
    }
```

If you see the previous code block, you can realize that it is basically a wrapper that reads the data in CSV format, and then the `RecordReaderDataSetIterator()` method converts the record reader as a dataset iterator.

Technically, `RecordReaderDataSetIterator()` is the main constructor for classification. It takes the following parameters:

- `RecordReader`: This is the `RecordReader` that provides the source of the data
- `batchSize`: Batch size (that is, number of examples) for the output `DataSet` objects
- `labelIndex`: The index of the label writable (usually an `IntWritable`) as obtained by `recordReader.next()`
- `numPossibleLabels`: The number of classes (possible labels) for classification

This will then convert the input class index (at position `labelIndex`, with integer values 0 to `numPossibleLabels-1`, inclusive) to the appropriate one-hot output/labels representation. So let's see how to proceed. First, we show the path of training and test sets:

```
String trainPath = "data/Titanic_Train.csv";
String testPath = "data/Titanic_Test.csv";

int labelIndex = 7; // First 7 features are followed by the labels in
integer
int numClasses = 2; // number of classes to be predicted -i.e survived or
not-survived
int numEpochs = 1000; // Number of training eopich
int seed = 123; // Randome seed for reproducibilty
```

```
int numInputs = labelIndex; // Number of inputs in input layer
int numOutputs = numClasses; // Number of classes to be predicted by the
network
int batchSizeTraining = 128;
```

Now let's prepare the data we want to use for training:

```
DataSetIterator trainingDataIt = readCSVDataset(trainPath,
batchSizeTraining, labelIndex, numClasses);
```

Next, let's prepare the data we want to classify:

```
int batchSizeTest = 128;
DataSetIterator testDataIt = readCSVDataset(testPath, batchSizeTest,
labelIndex, numClasses);
```

Fantastic! We have managed to prepare the training and test `DataSetIterator`.
Remember, we will be following nearly the same approach to prepare the training and test
sets for other problems too.

Evaluating the model

Once the training has been completed, the next task would be evaluating the model. We
will evaluate the model's performance on the test set. For the evaluation, we will be using
`Evaluation()`; it creates an evaluation object with two possible classes (survived or not
survived). More technically, the Evaluation class computes the evaluation metrics such as
precision, recall, F1, accuracy, and Matthews' correlation coefficient. The last one is used to
evaluate a binary classifier. Now let's take a brief overview on these metrics:

Accuracy is the ratio of correctly predicted samples to total samples:

$$Acc = \frac{TP + TN}{TP + FP + FN + TN}$$

Precision is the ratio of correctly predicted positive samples to the total predicted positive
samples:

$$Precision = \frac{TP}{TP + FP}$$

Recall is the ratio of correctly predicted positive samples to all samples in the actual class—yes:

$$Recall = \frac{TP}{TP + FN}$$

F1 score is the weighted average (harmonic mean) of Precision and Recall::

$$F_1 score = \frac{2 * (Precision * Recall)}{Precision + Recall}$$

Matthews Correlation Coefficient (**MCC**) is a measure of the quality of binary (two-class) classifications. MCC can be calculated directly from the confusion matrix as follows (given that TP, FP, TN, and FN are already available):

$$MCC = \frac{TP * TN - FP * FN}{\sqrt{(TP + FP)(TP + FN)(TN + FP)(TN + FN)}}$$

Unlike the Apache Spark-based classification evaluator, when solving a binary classification problem using the DL4J-based evaluator, special care should be taken for binary classification metrics such as F1, precision, recall, and so on.

Well, we will see these later on. First, let's iterate the evaluation over every test sample and get the network's prediction from the trained model. Finally, the `eval()` method checks the prediction against the true classes:

```
log.info("Evaluate model....");
Evaluation eval = new Evaluation(2) // for class 1

while(testDataIt.hasNext()){
DataSet next = testDataIt.next();
INDArray output = model.output(next.getFeatureMatrix());
eval.eval(next.getLabels(), output);
}
log.info(eval.stats());
log.info("****************Example finished********************");
```

```
>>>
==========================Scores============================
# of classes: 2
Accuracy: 0.6496
Precision: 0.6155
Recall: 0.5803
F1 Score: 0.3946
Precision, recall & F1: reported for positive class (class 1 - "1") only
============================================================
```

Oops! Unfortunately, we have not managed to achieve very high classification accuracy for class 1 (that is, 65%). Now, we compute another metric called MCC for this binary classification problem.

```
// Compute Matthews correlation coefficient
EvaluationAveraging averaging = EvaluationAveraging.Macro;
double MCC = eval.matthewsCorrelation(averaging);
System.out.println("Matthews correlation coefficient: "+ MCC);
```

```
>>>
Matthews's correlation coefficient: 0.22308172619187497
```

Now let's try to interpret this result based on the Matthews paper (see more at www.sciencedirect.com/science/article/pii/0005279575901099), which describes the following properties: A correlation of $C = 1$ indicates perfect agreement, $C = 0$ is expected for a prediction no better than random, and $C = -1$ indicates total disagreement between prediction and observation.

Following this, our result shows a weak positive relationship. Alright! Although we have not achieved good accuracy, you guys can still try by tuning hyperparameters or even by changing other networks such as LSTM, which we are going to discuss in the next section. But we'll do so for solving our cancer prediction problem, which is the main goal of this chapter. So stay with me!

Cancer type prediction using an LSTM network

In the previous section, we have seen what our data (that is, features and labels) looks like. Now in this section, we try to classify those samples according to their labels. However, as we have seen, DL4J needs the data in a well-defined format so that it can be used to train the model. So let us perform the necessary preprocessing and feature engineering.

Dataset preparation for training

Since we do not have any unlabeled data, I would like to select some samples randomly for test. Well, one more thing is that features and labels come in two separate files. Therefore, we can perform the necessary preprocessing and then join them together so that our pre-processed data will have features and labels together.

Then the rest will be used for training. Finally, we'll save the training and testing set in a separate CSV file to be used later on. First, let's load the samples and see the statistics. By the way, we use the `read()` method of Spark but specify the necessary options and format too:

```
Dataset<Row> data = spark.read()
                .option("maxColumns", 25000)
                .format("com.databricks.spark.csv")
                .option("header", "true") // Use first line of all files as
header
                .option("inferSchema", "true") // Automatically infer data
types
                .load("TCGA-PANCAN-HiSeq-801x20531/data.csv");// set your
path accordingly
```

Then we see some related statistics such as number of features and number of samples:

```
int numFeatures = data.columns().length;
long numSamples = data.count();
System.out.println("Number of features: " + numFeatures);
System.out.println("Number of samples: " + numSamples);

>>>
  Number of features: 20532
  Number of samples: 801
```

Therefore, there are 801 samples from 801 distinct patients and the dataset is too high in dimensions, having 20532 features. In addition, in *Figure 2*, we have seen that the id column represents only the patient's anonymous ID, so we can simply drop it:

```
Dataset<Row> numericDF = data.drop("id"); // now 20531 features left
```

Then we load the labels using the read() method of Spark and also specify the necessary options and format:

```
Dataset<Row> labels = spark.read()
                .format("com.databricks.spark.csv")
                .option("header", "true") // Use first line of all files as
header
                .option("inferSchema", "true") // Automatically infer data
types
                .load("TCGA-PANCAN-HiSeq-801x20531/labels.csv");
labels.show(10);
```

```
+--------+-----+
|      id|Class|
+--------+-----+
|sample_0| PRAD|
|sample_1| LUAD|
|sample_2| PRAD|
|sample_3| PRAD|
|sample_4| BRCA|
|sample_5| PRAD|
|sample_6| KIRC|
|sample_7| PRAD|
|sample_8| BRCA|
|sample_9| PRAD|
+--------+-----+
only showing top 10 rows
```

We have already seen how the labels dataframe looks. We will skip the id. However, the Class column is categorical. Now, as I said, DL4J does not support categorical labels to be predicted. Therefore, we have to convert it to numeric (integer, to be more specific); for that I would use StringIndexer() from Spark.

First, create a `StringIndexer()`; we apply the index operation to the `Class` column and rename it as `label`. Additionally, we skip null entries:

```
StringIndexer indexer = new StringIndexer()
                    .setInputCol("Class")
                    .setOutputCol("label")
                    .setHandleInvalid("skip");// skip null/invalid
values
```

Then we perform the indexing operation by calling the `fit()` and `transform()` operations as follows:

```
Dataset<Row> indexedDF = indexer.fit(labels)
                    .transform(labels)
                    .select(col("label")
                    .cast(DataTypes.IntegerType));// casting data
types to integer
```

Now let's take a look at the indexed DataFrame:

```
indexedDF.show();
```

```
+-----+
|label|
+-----+
|    3|
|    2|
|    3|
|    3|
|    0|
|    3|
|    1|
|    3|
|    0|
|    3|
+-----+
only showing top 10 rows
```

Fantastic! Now all of our columns (including features and labels) are numeric. Thus, we can join both features and labels into a single DataFrame. For that, we can use the `join()` method from Spark as follows:

```
Dataset<Row> combinedDF = numericDF.join(indexedDF);
```

Now we can generate both the training and test sets by randomly splitting the combindedDF, as follows:

```
Dataset<Row>[] splits = combinedDF.randomSplit(newdouble[] {0.7,
0.3});//70% for training, 30% for testing
Dataset<Row> trainingData = splits[0];
Dataset<Row> testData = splits[1];
```

Now let's see the count of samples in each set:

```
System.out.println(trainingData.count());// number of samples in training
set
System.out.println(testData.count());// number of samples in test set

>>>
 561
 240
```

Thus, our training set has `561` samples and the test set has `240` samples. Finally, save these two sets as separate CSV files to be used later on:

```
trainingData.coalesce(1).write()
                .format("com.databricks.spark.csv")
                .option("header", "false")
                .option("delimiter", ",")
                .save("data/TCGA_train.csv");
testData.coalesce(1).write()
                .format("com.databricks.spark.csv")
                .option("header", "false")
                .option("delimiter", ",")
                .save("data/TCGA_test.csv");
```

Now that we have the training and test sets, we can now train the network with the training set and evaluate the model with the test set. Considering the high dimensionality, I would rather try a better network such as LSTM, which is an improved variant of RNN. At this point, some contextual information about LSTM would be helpful to grasp the idea.

Recurrent and LSTM networks

As discussed in `Chapter 1`, *Getting Started with Deep Learning*, RNNs make use of information from the past; they can make predictions in data with high temporal dependencies. A more explicit architecture can be found in following diagram where the temporally shared weights **w2** (for the hidden layer) must be learned in addition to **w1** (for the input layer) and **w3** (for the output layer). From a computational point of view, an RNN takes many input vectors to process and generate output vectors. Imagine that each rectangle in the following diagram has a vectorial depth and other special hidden quirks:

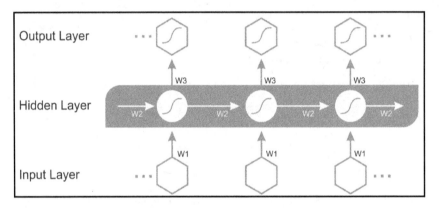

An RNN architecture where all weights in all layers have to be learned with time

However, we often need to look at only recent information to perform the present task, rather than stored information or information that arrived a long time ago. This happens frequently in NLP for language modeling. Let's see a common example:

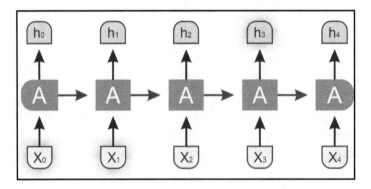

If the gap between the relevant information is small, RNNs can learn to use past information

Suppose we want to develop a DL-based NLP model to predict the next word based on the previous words. As a human being, if we try to predict the last word in *Berlin is the capital of...*, without further context, the next word is most likely *Germany*. In such cases, the gap between the relevant information and the position is small. Thus, RNNs can learn to use past information easily.

However, consider another example that is a bit longer: *Reza grew up in Bangladesh. He studied in Korea. He speaks fluent...* Now to predict the last word, we would need a little bit more context. In this sentence, the most recent information advises the network that the next word would probably be the name of a language. However, if we narrow down to language level, the context of Bangladesh (from the previous words) would be needed.

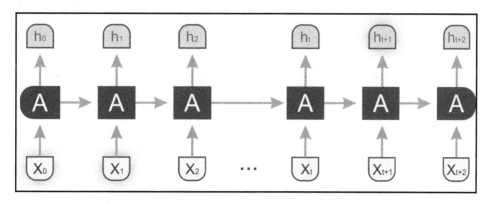

If the gap between the relevant information and the place that is needed is bigger, RNNs can't learn to use past information

Here, the gap is larger than in the previous example, so an RNN is unable to learn to map the information. Nevertheless, gradients for deeper layers are calculated by multiplication (that is, the product) of many gradients coming from activation functions in the multilayer network. If those gradients are very small or close to zero, gradients will easily vanish. On the other hand, when they are bigger than 1, it will possibly explode. So, it becomes very hard to calculate and update. Let's explain them in more detail.

These two issues of RNN are jointly called a **vanishing-exploding gradient** problem, which directly affects performance. In fact, the backpropagation time rolls out the RNN, creating *a very deep* feedforward neural network. The impossibility of getting a long-term context from the RNN is precisely due to this phenomenon; if the gradient vanishes or explodes within a few layers, the network will not be able to learn high-temporal-distance relationships between the data.

Therefore, the inability of handling long-term dependency, gradient exploding and vanishing problems is a serious drawback of RNNs. Here comes LSTM as the savior.

As the name signifies, short-term patterns are not forgotten in the long term. An LSTM network is composed of cells (LSTM blocks) linked to each other. Each LSTM block contains three types of gates: an input gate, an output gate, and a forget gate. They implement the functions of writing, reading, and reset on the cell memory, respectively. These gates are not binary but analog (generally managed by a sigmoidal activation function mapped in the range *[0, 1]*, where zero indicates total inhibition and one shows total activation).

We can consider an LSTM cell very much like a basic cell, but still the training will converge more quickly and it will detect long-term dependencies in the data. Now the question would be: how does an LSTM cell work? The architecture of a basic LSTM cell is shown in the following diagram:

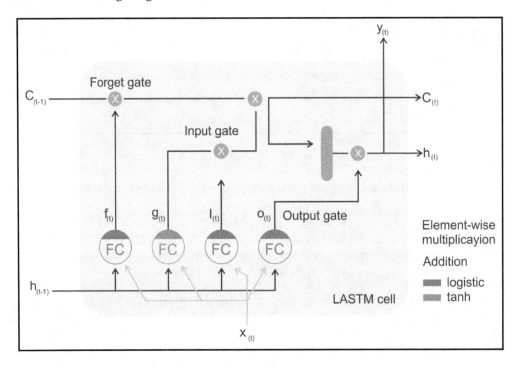

Block diagram of an LSTM cell

Now, let's see the mathematical notation behind this architecture. If we don't look at what's inside the LSTM box, the LSTM cell itself looks exactly like a regular memory cell, except that its state is split into two vectors, $h(t)$ and $c(t)$:

- c is a cell
- $h(t)$ is the short-term state
- $c(t)$ is the long-term state

Now, let's open the box! The key idea is that the network can learn the following:

- What to store in the long-term state
- What to throw away
- What to read

In more simplified words, in an STM, all hidden units of the original RNN are replaced by memory blocks, where each memory block contains a memory cell to store input history information and three gates to define how to update the information. These gates are an input gate, a forget gate, and an output gate.

The presence of these gates allows LSTM cells to remember information for an indefinite period. In fact, if the input gate is below the activation threshold, the cell will retain the previous state, and if the current state is enabled, it will be combined with the input value. As the name suggests, the forget gate resets the current state of the cell (when its value is cleared to zero), and the output gate decides whether the value of the cell must be carried out or not.

Although the long-term state is copied and passed through the tanh function, internally in an LSTM cell, incorporation between two activation functions is needed. For example, in the following diagram, tanh decides which values to add to the state, with the help of the sigmoid gate:

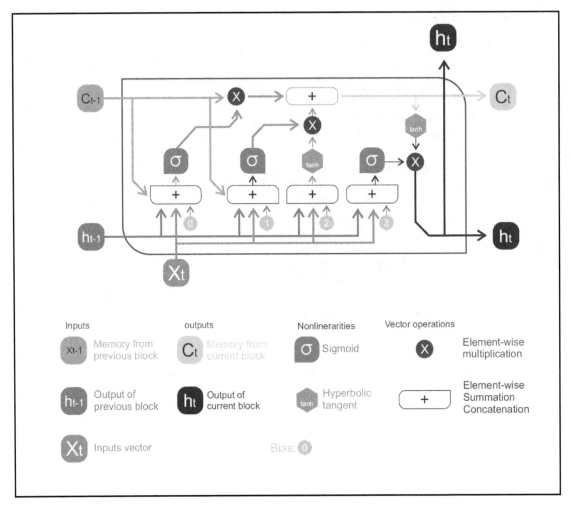

The internal organization of the LSTM cell structure

Now, since this book is not meant to teach theory, I would like to stop the discussion here, but interested readers can find more details on the DL4J website at `https://deeplearning4j.org/lstm.html`.

Dataset preparation

In the previous section, we prepared the training and test sets. However, we need to put some extra efforts into making them consumable by DL4J. To be more specific, DL4J expects the training data as numeric and the last column to be the label column, and the remaining are features.

We will now try to prepare our training and test sets like that. First, we show the files where we saved the training and test sets:

```
String trainPath = "data/TCGA_train.csv"; // training set
String testPath = "data/TCGA_test.csv"; // test set
```

Then, we define the required parameters, such as the number of features, number of classes, and batch size. Here, I use `128` as the `batchSize` but adjust it accordingly:

```
int labelIndex = 20531;// number of features
int numClasses = 5; // number of classes to be predicted
int batchSize = 128; // batch size (feel free to adjust)
```

This dataset is used for training:

```
DataSetIterator trainingDataIt = readCSVDataset(trainPath, batchSize,
labelIndex, numClasses);
```

This is the data we want to classify:

```
DataSetIterator testDataIt = readCSVDataset(testPath, batchSize,
labelIndex, numClasses);
```

If you see the preceding two lines, you can realize that `readCSVDataset()` is basically a wrapper that reads the data in CSV format, and then the `RecordReaderDataSetIterator()` method converts the record reader as a dataset iterator. For more details, refer to the *Titanic survival revisited with DL4J* section.

LSTM network construction

As discussed in the Titanic survival prediction section, again everything starts with `MultiLayerConfiguration`, which organizes those layers and their hyperparameters. Our LSTM network consists of five layers. The input layer is followed by three LSTM layers. Then the last layer is an RNN layer, which is also the output layer.

More technically, the first layer is the input layer, and then three layers are placed as LSTM layers. For the LSTM layers, we initialized the weights using Xavier. We use SGD as the optimization algorithm with Adam updater and the activation function is tanh.

Finally, the RNN output layer has a softmax activation function, which gives us a probability distribution over classes (that is, outputs sum to *1.0*), and MCXENT, which is the Multiclass cross-entropy loss function. This setting is shown in the following figure:

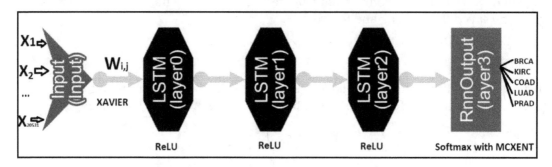

Multilayer perceptron for Titanic survival prediction. It takes 20,531 features and fixed bias (that is, 1) and generates multi-class outputs.

For creating LSTM layers, DL4J provides both LSTM and GravesLSTM classes. The latter is an LSTM recurrent net, based on *Supervised Sequence Labelling with Recurrent Neural Networks* (see more at http://www.cs.toronto.edu/~graves/phd.pdf).

GravesLSTM is not compatible with CUDA. Thus, using LSTM is recommended while performing the training on GPU. Otherwise, GravesLSTM is faster than LSTM.

Now before, we start creating the network, let's define required hyperparameters such as the number of input/hidden/output nodes (neurons):

```
// Network hyperparameters
int numInputs = labelIndex; // number of input features
int numOutputs = numClasses; // number of classes to be predicted
int numHiddenNodes = 5000; // too many features, so 5000 sounds good
```

We now create a network configuration and conduct network training. With DL4J, you add a layer by calling `layer` on the `NeuralNetConfiguration.Builder()`, specifying its place in the order of layers (the zero-indexed layer in the following code is the input layer):

```
// Create network configuration and conduct network training
MultiLayerConfiguration LSTMconf = new NeuralNetConfiguration.Builder()
            .seed(seed)     //Random number generator seed for improved
repeatability. Optional.
.optimizationAlgo(OptimizationAlgorithm.STOCHASTIC_GRADIENT_DESCENT)
            .weightInit(WeightInit.XAVIER)
            .updater(new Adam(0.001))
            .list()
            .layer(0, new LSTM.Builder()
                        .nIn(numInputs)
                        .nOut(numHiddenNodes)
                        .activation(Activation.RELU)
                        .build())
            .layer(1, new LSTM.Builder()
                        .nIn(numHiddenNodes)
                        .nOut(numHiddenNodes)
                        .activation(Activation.RELU)
                        .build())
            .layer(2, new LSTM.Builder()
                        .nIn(numHiddenNodes)
                        .nOut(numHiddenNodes)
                        .activation(Activation.RELU)
                        .build())
            .layer(3, new RnnOutputLayer.Builder()
                        .activation(Activation.SOFTMAX)
                        .lossFunction(LossFunction.MCXENT)
                        .nIn(numHiddenNodes)
                        .nOut(numOutputs)
                        .build())
            .pretrain(false).backprop(true).build();
```

Finally, we also specify that we do not need to do any pre-training (which is typically needed in DBN or stacked autoencoders).

Network training

First, we create a `MultiLayerNetwork` using the preceding `MultiLayerConfiguration`. Then we initialize the network and start the training on the training set:

```
MultiLayerNetwork model = new MultiLayerNetwork(LSTMconf);
model.init();

log.info("Train model....");
for(int i=0; i<numEpochs; i++ ){
    model.fit(trainingDataIt);
 }
```

Typically, this type of network has so many hyperparameters. Let's print the number of parameters in the network (and for each layer):

```
Layer[] layers = model.getLayers();
int totalNumParams = 0;
for( int i=0; i<layers.length; i++ ){
        int nParams = layers[i].numParams();
        System.out.println("Number of parameters in layer " + i + ": " +
nParams);
        totalNumParams += nParams;
}
System.out.println("Total number of network parameters: " +
totalNumParams);

>>>
 Number of parameters in layer 0: 510655000
 Number of parameters in layer 1: 200035000
 Number of parameters in layer 2: 200035000
 Number of parameters in layer 3: 25005
 Total number of network parameters: 910750005
```

As I said, our network has 910 million parameters, which is huge. This also poses a great challenge while tuning hyperparameters. However, we will see some tricks in the FAQs section.

Evaluating the model

Once the training has been completed, the next task would be evaluating the model. We will evaluate the model's performance on the test set. For the evaluation, we will be using `Evaluation()`. This method creates an evaluation object with five possible classes. First, let's iterate the evaluation over every test sample and get the network's prediction from the trained model. Finally, the `eval()` method checks the prediction against the true class:

```
log.info("Evaluate model....");
Evaluation eval = new Evaluation(5) // for 5 classes
while(testDataIt.hasNext()){
        DataSet next = testDataIt.next();
        INDArray output = model.output(next.getFeatureMatrix());
        eval.eval(next.getLabels(), output);
}
log.info(eval.stats());
log.info("***************Example finished*******************");
```

```
>>>
========================Scores=========================================
# of classes:  5
Accuracy:      0.9950
Precision:     0.9944
Recall:        0.9889
F1 Score:      0.9915
Precision, recall & F1: macro-averaged (equally weighted avg. of 5 classes)
=======================================================================
***************Example finished*******************
```

Wow! Unbelievable! Our LSTM network has accurately classified the samples so accurately. Finally, let's see how the classifier predicts across each class:

```
Predictions labeled as 0 classified by model as 0: 82 times
Predictions labeled as 1 classified by model as 1: 17 times
Predictions labeled as 1 classified by model as 2: 1 times
Predictions labeled as 2 classified by model as 2: 35 times
Predictions labeled as 3 classified by model as 3: 31 times
Predictions labeled as 4 classified by model as 4: 35 times
```

The predictive accuracy for cancer type prediction using LSTM is suspiciously higher. Did our network underfit? Is there any way to observe how the training went? In other words, the question would be why our LSTM neural net shows 100% accuracy. We will try to answer these questions in the next section. So stay with me!

Frequently asked questions (FAQs)

Now that we have solved the Titanic survival prediction problem with an acceptable level of accuracy, there are other practical aspects of this problem and overall deep learning phenomena that need to be considered too. In this section, we will see some frequently asked questions that might be already in your mind. Answers to these questions can be found in *Appendix A*.

1. Can't we use MLP to solve the cancer type prediction by handling this too high-dimensional data?
2. Which activation and loss function can be used with RNN type nets?
3. What is the best way of recurrent net weight initialization?
4. Which updater and optimization algorithm should be used?
5. In the Titanic survival prediction problem, we did not experience good accuracy. What could be possible reasons and how can we improve the accuracy?
6. The predictive accuracy for cancer type prediction using LSTM is suspiciously higher. Did our network underfit? Is there any way to observe how the training went?
7. Which type RNN variants should I use, that is, LSTM or GravesLSTM?
8. Why is my neural net throwing nan score values?
9. How to configure/change the DL4J UI port?

Summary

In this chapter, we saw how to classify cancer patients on the basis of tumor types from a very-high-dimensional gene expression dataset curated from TCGA. Our LSTM architecture managed to achieve 100% accuracy, which is outstanding. Nevertheless, we discussed many aspects of DL4J, which will be helpful in upcoming chapters. Finally, we saw answers to some frequent questions related to this project, LSTM network, and DL4J hyperparameters/nets tuning.

In the next chapter, we will see how to develop an end-to-end project for handling a multilabel (each entity can belong to multiple classes) image classification problem using CNN based on Scala and the DL4J framework on real Yelp image datasets. We will also discuss some theoretical aspects of CNNs before getting started. Nevertheless, we will discuss how to tune hyperparameters for better classification results.

Answers to questions

Answer to question 1: The answer is yes, but not very comfortably. That means a very deep feedforward network such as deep MLP or DBN can classify them with too many iterations.

However, also to speak frankly, MLP is the weakest deep architecture and is not ideal for very high dimensions like this. Moreover, DL4J has deprecated DBN since the DL4J 1.0.0-alpha release. Finally, I would still like to show an MLP network config just in case you want to try it:

```
// Create network configuration and conduct network training
MultiLayerConfiguration MLPconf = new
NeuralNetConfiguration.Builder().seed(seed)
.optimizationAlgo(OptimizationAlgorithm.STOCHASTIC_GRADIENT_DESCENT)
                    .updater(new
Adam(0.001)).weightInit(WeightInit.XAVIER).list()
                    .layer(0,new DenseLayer.Builder().nIn(numInputs).nOut(32)
                            .weightInit(WeightInit.XAVIER)
                            .activation(Activation.RELU).build())
                    .layer(1,new
DenseLayer.Builder().nIn(32).nOut(64).weightInit(WeightInit.XAVIER)
                            .activation(Activation.RELU).build())
                    .layer(2,new
DenseLayer.Builder().nIn(64).nOut(128).weightInit(WeightInit.XAVIER)
                            .activation(Activation.RELU).build())
                    .layer(3, new
OutputLayer.Builder(LossFunction.XENT).weightInit(WeightInit.XAVIER)
        .activation(Activation.SOFTMAX).weightInit(WeightInit.XAVIER).nIn(128)
                            .nOut(numOutputs).build())
                    .pretrain(false).backprop(true).build();
```

Then, just change the line from `MultiLayerNetwork model = new MultiLayerNetwork(LSTMconf);` to **MultiLayerNetwork** model = **new MultiLayerNetwork**(MLPconf);. Readers can see the full source in the `CancerPreddictionMLP.java` file.

Answer to question 2: There are two aspects to be aware of with regard to the choice of activation function.

Activation function for hidden layers: Usually, ReLU or leakyrelu activations are good choices. Some other activation functions (tanh, sigmoid, and so on) are more prone to vanishing gradient problems. However, for LSTM layers, the tanh activation function is still commonly used.

A note here: The reason some people do not want to use Rectified Linear Unit (ReLU) is that it seems not to perform very well relative to smoother nonlinearity, such as sigmoid in the case of RNNs (see more at `https://arxiv.org/pdf/1312.4569.pdf`). Even tanh works much better with LSTM. Therefore, I used tanh as the activation function in the LSTM layers.

The activation function for the output layer: For classification problems, using the Softmax activation function combined with the negative log-likelihood / MCXENT is recommended. However, for a regression problem, the "IDENTITY" activation function is a good choice, with MSE as the loss function. In short, the choice is really application-specific.

Answer to question 3: Well, we need to make sure that the network weights are neither too big nor too small. I will not recommend using random or zero; rather, Xavier weight initialization is usually a good choice for this.

Answer to question 4: Unless SGD converges well, momentum/rmsprop/adagrad optimizers are a good choice. However, I've often used Adam as the updater and observed good performance too.

Answer to question 5: Well, there is no concrete answer to this question. In fact, there could be several reasons. For example, probably we have not chosen the appropriate hyperparameters. Secondly, we may not have enough data. Thirdly, we could be using another network such as LSTM. Fourthly, we did not normalize our data.

Well, for the third one, you can of course try using an LSTM network similarly; I did it for cancer type prediction. For the fourth one, of course normalized data always gives better classification accuracy. Now the question would be: what is the distribution of your data? Are you scaling it properly? Well, continuous values have to be in the range of -1 to 1, 0 to 1, or distributed normally with mean 0 and standard deviation 1.

Finally, I would like to give you a concrete example of data normalization in the Titanic example. For that, we can use DL4J's `NormalizerMinMaxScaler()`. Once we created the training dataset iterator, we can instantiate a `NormalizerMinMaxScaler()` object and then normalize the data by invoking the `fit()` method. Finally, we perform the transformation using the `setPreProcessor()` method, as follows:

```
NormalizerMinMaxScaler preProcessor = new NormalizerMinMaxScaler();
preProcessor.fit(trainingDataIt);
trainingDataIt.setPreProcessor(preProcessor);
```

Now, for the test dataset iterator, we apply the same normalization for better results but without invoking the `fit()` method:

```
testDataIt.setPreProcessor(preProcessor);
```

More elaborately, `NormalizerMinMaxScaler ()` acts as the pre-processor for datasets that normalizes feature values (and optionally label values) to lie between a minimum and maximum value (by default, between 0 and 1). Readers can see the full source in the `CancerPreddictionMLP.java` file. After this normalization, I experienced slightly better result for class 1, as follows (you could try the same for class 0 too):

```
==========================Scores========================================
# of classes: 2
Accuracy: 0.6654
Precision: 0.7848
Recall: 0.5548
F1 Score: 0.2056
Precision, recall & F1: reported for positive class (class 1 - "1") only
========================================================================
```

Answer to question 6: In the real world, it's a rare case that a neural net would achieve 100% accuracy. However, if the data is linearly separable, then yes, it's possible! Take a look at the following scatter plots, which show that the black line clearly separates the red points and the dark blue points:

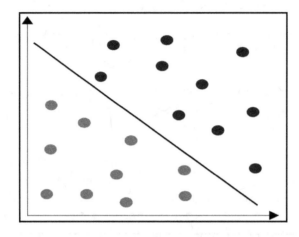

Very clearly and linearly separable data points

More technically, since a neuron's output (before it passes through an activation function) is a linear combination of its inputs, a network consisting of a single neuron can learn this pattern. That means if our neural net got the line right, it is possible to achieve 100% accuracy.

Now, to answer the second part: probably no. To prove this, we can observe the training loss, score, and so on on the DL4J UI, which is the interface used to visualize the current network status and progress of training in real time on your browser.

The UI is typically used to help with tuning neural networks, that is, the selection of hyperparameters to obtain good performance for a network. These are already in the `CancerPreddictionLSTM.java` file, so do not worry but just keep going.

Step 1: Adding the dependency for DL4J to your project

In the following dependency tag, `_2.11 suffix` is used to specify which Scala version should be used for the Scala play framework. You should setting accordingly:

```
<dependency>
    <groupId>org.deeplearning4j</groupId>
    <artifactId>deeplearning4j-ui_2.11</artifactId>
    <version>${dl4j.version}</version>
</dependency>
```

Step 2: Enabling UI in your project

This is relatively straightforward. First, you have to initialize the user interface backend as follows:

```
UIServer uiServer = UIServer.getInstance();
```

You then configure where the network information is to be stored. Then the StatsListener can be added to collect this information:

```
StatsStorage statsStorage = new InMemoryStatsStorage();
```

Finally, we attach the StatsStorage instance to the UI:

```
uiServer.attach(statsStorage);
int listenerFrequency = 1;
model.setListeners(new StatsListener(statsStorage, listenerFrequency));
```

Step 3: Start collecting information by invoking the fit() method
Information will then be collected and routed to the UI when you call the `fit` method on your network.

Step 4: Accessing the UI
Once it is configured, the UI can be accessed at `http://localhost:9000/train`. Now to answer "Did our network under fit? Is there any way to observe how the training went?" We can observe the **Model Score versus Iteration Chart** on the overview page. As suggested in the model tuning section at `https://deeplearning4j.org/visualization`, we have the following observation:

- The overall score versus iteration should go down over time
- The score does not increase consistently but decreases drastically when the iteration moves on

The issue might be that there is no noise in the line chart, which is ideally expected (that is, the line will go up and down within a small range).

Now to deal with this, again we can normalize the data and perform the training again to see how the performance differs. Well, I would like to leave this up to you, folks. One more clue would be following the same data normalization that we discussed in question 5.

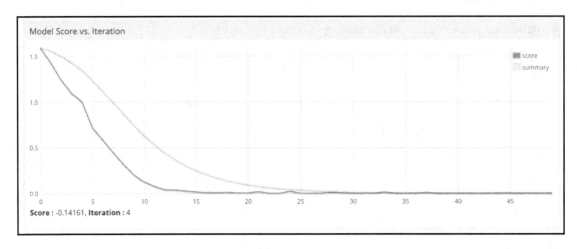

LSTM model score over iterations

Now, another observation would be worth mentioning too. For example, the gradients did not vanish until the end, which becomes clearer from this figure:

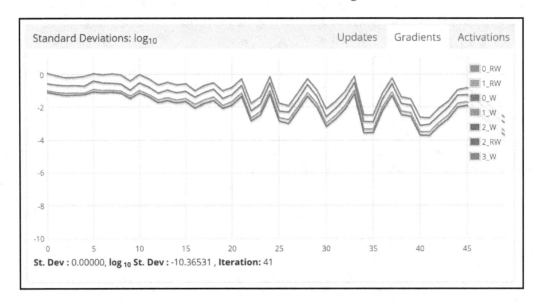

The LSTM network's gradients across different iterations

Finally, the activation functions performed their role consistently, which becomes clearer from the following figure:

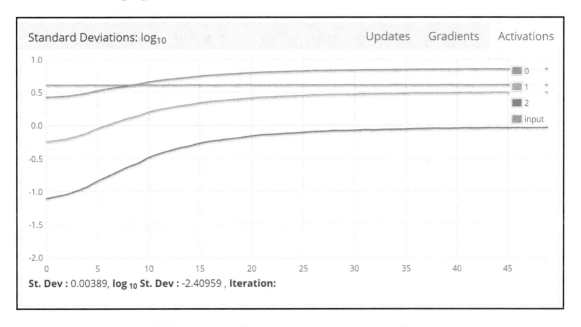

The LSTM network's activation functions performed their role consistently across different layers

The thing is that there are many more factors to be considered too. However, in reality, tuning a neural network is often more an art than a science, and we have not considered many aspects as I said. Yet, do not worry; we will see them in upcoming projects. So hang on and let's move on to the next question.

Answer to question 7: LSTM allows both GPU/CUDA support, but GravesLSTM supports only CUDA, hence no support for CuDNN yet. Nonetheless, if you want faster training and convergence, using LSTM type is recommended.

Answer to question 8: While training a neural network, the backpropagation involves multiplications across very small gradients. This happens due to limited precision when representing real numbers; values very close to zero cannot be represented.

It introduces an arithmetic underflow issue, which often happens in a deeper network such as DBN, MLP, or CNN. Moreover, if your network throws NaN, then you'll need to retune your network to avoid very small gradients.

Answer to question 9: You can set the port by using the org.deeplearning4j.ui.port system property. To be more specific, to use port 9001 for example, pass the following to the JVM on launch:

```
-Dorg.deeplearning4j.ui.port=9001
```

3
Multi-Label Image Classification Using Convolutional Neural Networks

In the previous chapter, we developed a project that accurately classifies cancer patients based on cancer types using an LSTM network. This is a challenging problem in biomedical informatics. Unfortunately, when it comes to classifying multimedia objects such as images, audio, or videos, linear ML models and other regular **deep neural network** (**DNN**) models, such as **Multilayer Perceptron** (**MLP**) or **Deep Belief Networks** (**DBN**), often fail to learn or model non-linear features from images.

On the other hand, **convolutional neural networks** (**CNNs**) can be utilized to overcome these limitations. In CNNs, the connectivity pattern between neurons is inspired by the human visual cortex, which more accurately resembles human vision, so it is perfect for image processing-related tasks. Consequently, CNNs have shown outstanding successes in numerous domains: computer vision, NLP, multimedia analytics, image searches, and so on.

Considering this motivation, in this chapter, we will see how to develop an end-to-end project for handling multi-label (that is, each entity can belong to multiple classes) image classification problems using CNNs based on the Scala and **Deeplearning4j** (**DL4J**) frameworks on real Yelp image datasets. We will also discuss some theoretical aspects of CNNs before getting started. Nevertheless, we will discuss how to tune hyperparameters for better classification results. Concisely, we will learn the following topics throughout our end-to-end project:

- Drawbacks of regular DNNs
- CNN architectures: convolution operations and pooling layers

- Large-scale image classification using CNNs
- Frequently asked questions (FAQs)

Image classification and drawbacks of DNNs

In this project, we will show a step-by-step example of developing real-life ML projects for image classification using Scala and CNN. One such image data source is Yelp, where there are many photos and many users uploading photos. These photos provide rich local business information across categories. Thus, using these photos, developing an ML application by understanding the context of these photos is not an easy task. We will see how to use the DL4j platform to do so using Java. However, some theoretical background is a prior mandate before we start formally.

Before we start developing the end-to-end project for image classification using CNN, let's take a look at the drawbacks of regular DNNs. Although regular DNNs work fine for small images (for example, MNIST and CIFAR-10), it breaks down for large-scale and high-quality images because of the huge number of hyperparameters it requires. For example, a 200 × 200 image has 40,000 pixels, and if the first layer has just 2,000 neurons, this means there will have 80 million different connections just in the first layer. Thus, if your network is very deep, there might be even billions of parameters.

CNNs solve this problem using partially connected layers. Because consecutive layers are only partially connected and because it heavily reuses its weights, a CNN has far fewer parameters than a fully connected DNN, which makes it much faster to train, reduces the risk of overfitting, and requires much less training data.

Moreover, when a CNN has learned a kernel that can detect a particular feature, it can detect that feature anywhere on the image. In contrast, when a DNN learns a feature in one location, it can detect it only in that particular location. Since images typically have very repetitive features, CNNs are able to generalize much better than DNNs for image processing tasks such as classification, using fewer training examples.

Importantly, DNN has no prior knowledge of how pixels are organized: it does not know that nearby pixels are close. A CNN's architecture embeds this prior knowledge. Lower layers typically identify features in small areas of the images, while higher layers combine the lower-level features into larger features. This works well with most natural images, giving CNNs a decisive head start compared to DNNs:

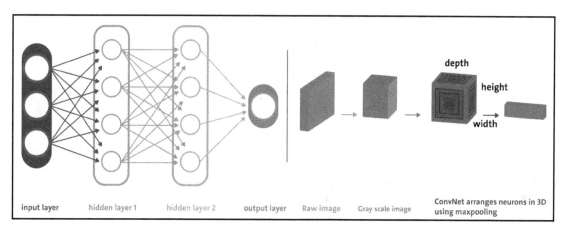

Regular DNN versus CNN where each layer has neurons arranged in 3D

For example, in the preceding diagram, on the left, you can see a regular three-layer neural network. On the right, a ConvNet arranges its neurons into three dimensions (width, height, and depth), as visualized in one of the layers. Every layer of a CNN transforms the 3D structure into a 3D output structure of neuron activations. The red input layer holds the image, so its width and height would be the dimensions of the image, and the depth would be three (red, green, and blue channels).

Therefore, all the multilayer neural networks we looked at had layers composed of a long line of neurons, and we had to flatten input images to 1D before feeding them to the network. However, feeding 2D images directly to CNNs is possible since each layer in CNN is represented in 2D, which makes it easier to match neurons with their corresponding inputs. We will see examples of this in the upcoming sections.

Another important fact is that all the neurons in a feature map share the same parameters, so it dramatically reduces the number of parameters in the model. Also, more importantly, once a CNN has learned to recognize a pattern in one location, it can do the same for other locations as well.

CNN architecture

In CNN networks, the way connectivity is defined among layers is significantly different compared to MLP or DBN. The **convolutional (conv)** layer is the main type of layer in a CNN, where each neuron is connected to a certain region of the input image, which is called a **receptive field**.

To be more specific, in a CNN architecture, a few conv layers are connected in a cascade style: each layer is followed by a **rectified linear unit (ReLU)** layer, then a pooling layer, then a few more conv layers (+ReLU), then another pooling layer, and so on. The output from each conv layer is a set of objects called feature maps, which are generated by a single kernel filter. Then, the feature maps are fed to the next layer as a new input. In the fully connected layer, each neuron produces an output followed by an activation layer (that is, the Softmax layer):

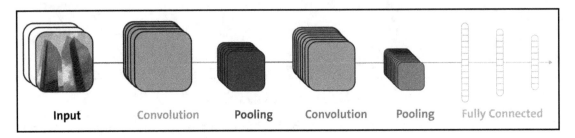

A conceptual architecture of CNN

As you can see in the preceding diagram, the pooling layers are usually placed after the convolutional layers (that is, between two such layers). A pooling layer into sub-regions then divides the convolutional region. Then, a single representative value is selected using either a max-pooling or an average pooling technique to reduce the computational time of subsequent layers. This way, a CNN can be thought of as a feature extractor. To understand this more clearly, refer to the following diagram:

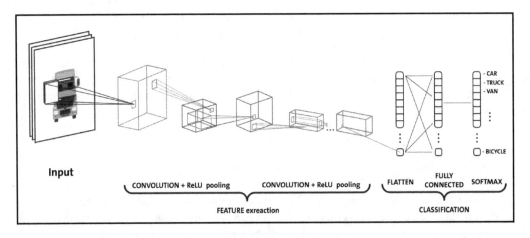

A CNN is an end-to-end network that acts as both a feature extractor and a classifier. This way, it can accurately identify (under the given condition that it gets sufficient training data) the label of a given input image. For example, it can classify that the input image is really a tiger.

The robustness of the feature with respect to its spatial position is increased too. To be more specific, when feature maps are used as image properties and pass through the grayscale image, it gets smaller and smaller as it progresses through the network, but it also typically gets deeper and deeper since more feature maps will be added. The convolution operation brings a solution to this problem as it reduces the number of free parameters, allowing the network to be deeper with fewer parameters.

Convolutional operations

A convolution is a mathematical operation that slides one function over another and measures the integrity of their pointwise multiplication. Convolutional layers are probably the most important building blocks in a CNN. For the first conv layer, neurons are not connected to every single pixel in the input image, but only to pixels in their receptive fields (refer to the preceding diagram), whereas each neuron in the second conv layer is only connected to neurons located within a small rectangle in the first layer:

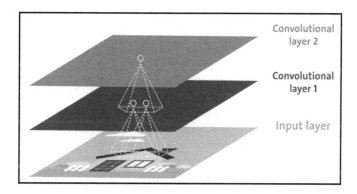

Each convolutional neuron only processes data for its receptive field

In `Chapter 2`, *Cancer Types Prediction Using Recurrent Type Networks,* we have seen that all multilayer neural networks (for example, MLP) have layers composed of so many neurons, and we had to flatten input images to 1D before feeding them to the network. Instead, in a CNN, each layer is represented in 2D, which makes it easier to match neurons with their associated inputs.

The receptive field is used to exploit spatial locality by enforcing a local connectivity pattern between neurons of adjacent layers.

This architecture allows the network to concentrate on low-level features in the first hidden layer, and then assemble them into higher-level features in the next hidden layer, and so on. This hierarchical structure is common in real-world images, which is one of the reasons why CNNs work so well for image recognition.

Pooling and padding operations

Once you understand how convolutional layers work, pooling layers are quite easy to grasp. A pooling layer typically works on every input channel independently, so the output depth is the same as the input depth. Alternatively, you may pool over the depth dimension, as we will see next, in which case the image's spatial dimensions (for example, height and width) remain unchanged, but the number of channels is reduced. Let's see a formal definition of pooling layers from TensorFlow API documentation (see more at `https://github.com/petewarden/tensorflow_makefile/blob/master/tensorflow/python/ops/nn.py`):

> *"The pooling ops sweep a rectangular window over the input tensor, computing a reduction operation for each window (average, max, or max with argmax). Each pooling op uses rectangular windows of size called ksize separated by offset strides. For example, if strides are all ones, every window is used, if strides are all twos, every other window is used in each dimension, and so on."*

Similar to a conv layer, each neuron in a pooling layer is connected to the outputs of a limited number of neurons in the previous layer that are located within a small rectangular receptive field. However, the size, the stride, and the padding type have to be defined. So, in summary, the output from a pooling layer can be computed as follows:

```
output[i] = reduce(value[strides * i:strides * i + ksize])
```

where indices are also taken into consideration along with the padding values. In other words, the goal of using pooling is to subsample the input image in order to reduce the computational load, the memory usage, and the number of parameters. This helps to avoid overfitting in the training stage.

A pooling neuron has no weights. Therefore, it only aggregate the inputs using an aggregation function such as the max or mean.

The spatial semantics of the convolution ops depend on the padding scheme chosen. Padding is an operation to increase the size of the input data:

- **For 1D input**: Just an array is appended with a constant, say, c
- **For a 2D input**: A matrix that is surrounded with c
- **For a milt-dimensional (that is, nD) input**: The nD hypercube is surrounded with c

Now, the question is, what's this constant c? Well, in most of the cases (but not always), c is zero called **zero padding**. This concept can be further broken down into two types of padding called VALID and SAME, which are outlined as follows:

- **VALID padding**: Only drops the right-most columns (or bottom-most rows).
- **SAME padding**: In this scheme, padding is applied evenly or both left and right. However, if the number of columns to be added is odd, then an extra column is added to the right.

We've explained the previous definition graphically in the following diagram. If we want a layer to have the same height and width as the previous layer, it is common to add zeros around the inputs. This is called SAME or zero padding.

 The term SAME means that the output feature map has the same spatial dimensions as the input feature map.

On the other hand, zero padding is introduced to make the shapes match as needed, equally on every side of the input map. On the other hand, `VALID` means no padding and only drops the right-most columns (or bottom-most rows):

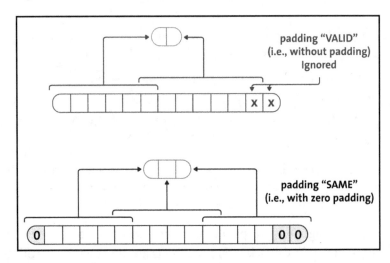

SAME versus VALID padding with CNN

In the following diagram, we use a 2 × 2 pooling kernel, a stride of 2 with no padding. Only the max input value in each kernel makes it to the next layer since the other inputs are dropped (we will see this later on):

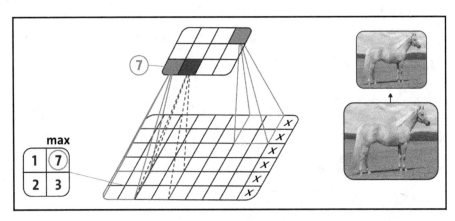

An example using max pooling, that is, subsampling

Fully connected layer (dense layer)

At the top of the stack, a regular fully connected layer (feedforward neural network or dense layer) is added, which acts similar to an MLP that might be composed of a few fully connected layers (+ReLUs), and the final layer outputs the prediction: typically, a Softmax layer is used that outputs estimated class probabilities for a multiclass classification.

Well, up to this point, we have minimum theoretical knowledge about CNNs and their architectures for image classification. Now, it is time to do a hands-on project, which is about classifying large-scale Yelp images. At Yelp, there are many photos and many users uploading photos. These photos provide rich local business information across categories. Teaching a computer to understand the context of these photos is not an easy task.

Yelp engineers work on deep learning-based image classification projects in-house (see more at `https://engineeringblog.yelp.com/2015/10/how-we-use-deep-learning-to-classify-business-photos-at-yelp.html`).

Multi-label image classification using CNNs

In this section, we will show you a systematic example of developing real-life ML projects for image classification. However, we need to know the problem description first so as to know what sort of image classification needs to be done. Moreover, knowledge about the dataset is a mandate before getting started.

Problem description

Nowadays, food selfies and photo-centric social storytelling are becoming social trends. Consequently, an enormous amount of selfies that include foods and a picture of the restaurant are being uploaded on social media and websites. In many instances, food lovers also provide the written reviews that can significantly boost the popularity of a business (for example, a restaurant).

For example, millions of unique visitors have visited the Yelp website and have written more than 135 million reviews. Besides, many photos and users are uploading photos. Nevertheless, business owners can post photos and message their customers. This way, Yelp makes money by **selling ads** to those local businesses.

An interesting fact is that these photos provide rich local business information across categories. Thus, developing deep learning applications to understand the context of these photos would be a useful task. Take a look at the following screenshot to get an insight:

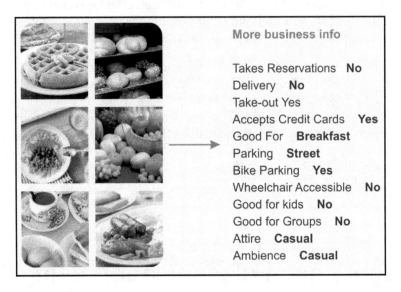

Mining some insights about a business from a Yelp dataset

Thus, if we're given photos that belong to a business, we need to build a model so that it can tag restaurants with multiple labels of the user-submitted photos automatically in order to predict business attributes. Eventually, the goal of this project is to turn Yelp pictures into words.

Description of the dataset

The Yelp dataset for this fun project was downloaded from `https://www.kaggle.com/c/yelp-restaurant-photo-classification`. We got permission from the Yelp guys under the condition that the images won't be redistributed. However, you need to get usage permission from `https://www.yelp.com/dataset`.

Submitting a review is tricky. When Yelp users want to submit a review, they have to select the labels of the restaurants manually from nine different labels that are annotated by the Yelp community, which are associated with the dataset. These are as follows:

- 0: `good_for_lunch`
- 1: `good_for_dinner`
- 2: `takes_reservations`
- 3: `outdoor_seating`
- 4: `restaurant_is_expensive`
- 5: `has_alcohol`
- 6: `has_table_service`
- 7: `ambience_is_classy`
- 8: `good_for_kids`

Thus, this is a multiple label multiclass classification problem, where each business can have one or more of the nine characteristics listed previously. Therefore, we have to predict these labels as accurately as possible. There are six files in the dataset, as follows:

- `train_photos.tgz`: Photos to be used as the training set (234,842 images)
- `test_photos.tgz`: Photos to be used as the test set (237,152 images)
- `train_photo_to_biz_ids.csv`: Provides the mapping between the photo ID and the business ID (234,842 rows)
- `test_photo_to_biz_ids.csv`: Provides the mapping between the photo ID and business the ID (1,190,225 rows)
- `train.csv`: This is the main training dataset, which includes business IDs and their corresponding labels (2,000 rows)
- `sample_submission.csv`: A sample submission—reference the correct format for your predictions including `business_id` and the corresponding predicted labels

Removing invalid images

I do not know why, but each image folder (train and test) also contains some temporary images with the `_*.jpg` name pattern, but not actual images. Therefore, I removed them using a UNIX command as follows:

```
$ find . -type f -name "._*.jpg" -exec rm -f {} ;
```

Then, I unzipped and copied each `.csv` file into a folder called `label`. Additionally, I moved the training and test images into the `train` and `test` folders (that is, inside the `images` folder), respectively. In short, after extraction and copying, the following folder structure is used in our projects. Therefore, the resulting structure will be as follows:

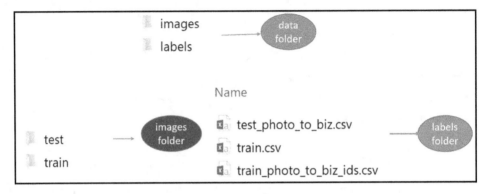

Folder structure in the Large Movie Review Dataset

Workflow of the overall project

Since we already know that this is a multi-label multiclass image classification problem, we have to deal with the multiple-instance issue. Since DL4J does not provide an example of how to solve a multi-label multiclass image classification problem, I found Andrew Brooks's blog article (see `http://brooksandrew.github.io/simpleblog/articles/convolutional-neural-network-training-with-dl4j/`) motivation for this project.

I simply applied the labels of the restaurant to all of the images associated with it and treated each image as a separate record. To be more technical, I handled each class as a separate binary classification problem. Nevertheless, at the beginning of this project, we will see how to read images from `.jpg` format into a matrix representation in Java. Then, we will further process and prepare those images so that they are feedable by the CNNs. Also, since images do not come with uniform shapes and sizes, we need to apply several rounds of image preprocessing ops, such as squaring and resizing every image to the uniform dimensions, before we apply a grayscale filter to the image:

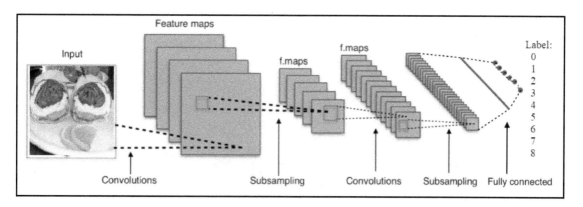

Feature maps

A conceptualized view of a CNN for image classification

Then, we train nine CNNs on training data for each class. Once the training is complete, we save the trained model, CNN configurations, and parameters so that they can be restored later on. Then, we apply a simple aggregate function to assign classes to each restaurant, where each one has multiple images associated with it, each with its own vector of probabilities for each of the nine classes. Then, we score test data and finally, we evaluate the model using test images.

Now, let's see the structure of each CNN. Well, each network will have two convolutional layers, two subsampling layers, one dense layer, and the output layer as the dense layer. The first layer is a conv layer, followed by a subsampling layer, which is again followed by another conv layer, then a subsampling layer, then a dense layer, which is followed by an output layer. We will see each layer's structure later on. In short, the Java class (`YelpImageClassifier.java`) has the following workflow:

1. We read all the business labels from the `train.csv` file
2. We then read and create a map from the image ID to the business ID as **imageID | busID**
3. Then, we generate a list of images from the `photoDir` directory to load and process, which helps us to retrieve image IDs of a certain number of images
4. We then read and process images into a **photoID | vector map**
5. We chain the output of step 3 and step 4 to align the business feature, image IDs, and label IDs to extract image features
6. Then, we construct nine CNNs for nine possible labels in a multi-label setting

7. We then train all the CNNs and specify the model savings locations
8. *Steps 2 to 6* are repeated several times to extract the features from the test set as well
9. Finally, we evaluate the model and save the prediction in a CSV file

Now, let's see what the preceding steps would look like in a high-level diagram, as follows:

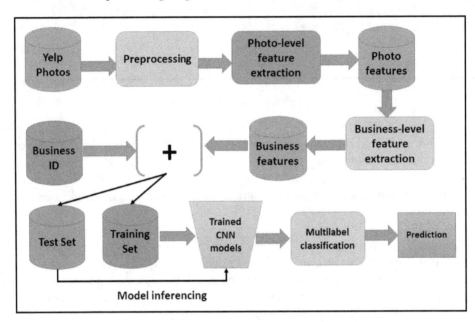

DL4j image processing pipeline for image classification

Too much of a mouthful? Don't worry; we will now see each step in detail. If you look at the previous steps carefully, you will see that steps 1 to 5 are image processing and feature constructions. Then, step 6 is training nine CNNs and then, in step 7, we save the trained CNNs so that we can restore them during result submission.

Image preprocessing

When I tried to develop this application, I found that the photos are different shapes and sizes: some images are tall, some of them are wide, some of them are outside, some images are inside, and most of them are food. Also, images come in different shapes (most were roughly square, though), of pixel and many of them are exactly 500 x 375 in dimension:

Resized figure (left, the original and tall one, right, the squared one)

We have already seen that CNN cannot work with images with heterogeneous shapes and sizes. There are many robust and efficient image processing techniques to extract only the **region of interest (ROI)**, but honestly, I am not an image-processing expert, so I decided to keep this resizing step simple. In simple terms, I made all the images square but still, I tried to preserve their quality. The thing is that ROIs are cantered in most cases. So, capturing only the middle-most square of each image is not a trivial task. Nevertheless, we also need to convert each image into a grayscale image. Let's make irregularly shaped images square. Look at the preceding image, where the one on the left is the original one and the one on the right is the squared one.

We have generated a square image, but how did we achieve this? Well, I first checked whether the height and the width were the same, and then I resized the image. In the other two cases, I cropped the central region. The following method does the trick (but feel free to execute the `SquaringImage.java` script to see the output):

```
private static BufferedImage makeSquare(BufferedImage img) {
        int w = img.getWidth();
        int h = img.getHeight();
        int dim = Math.min(w, h);

        if (w == h) {
            return img;
```

```
        } else if (w > h) {
            return Scalr.crop(img, (w - h) / 2, 0, dim, dim);
        } else {
            return Scalr.crop(img, 0, (h - w) / 2, dim, dim);
        }
    }
```

Well done! Now that all of our training images are squared, the next step is to use the import-preprocessing task to resize them all. I decided to make all the images 128 x 128 in size. Let's see what the previous image (the original one) looks like after resizing:

Image resizing (256 x 256, 128 x 128, 64 x 64 and 32 x 32, respectively)

The following method does this trick (but feel free to execute the imageUtils.java script to see a demo):

```
// resize pixels
    public static BufferedImage resizeImg(BufferedImage img, int width, int
height) {
        return Scalr.resize(img, Scalr.Method.BALANCED, width, height);
    }
```

By the way, for the image resizing and squaring, I used some built-in package for image reading and some third-party packages for processing:

```
import javax.imageio.ImageIO;
import org.imgscalr.Scalr;
```

To use the previous packages, add the following dependencies in a Maven-friendly `pom.xml` file (for the complete list of dependencies, refer to the `pom.xml` file provided for this chapter):

```
<dependency>
        <groupId>org.imgscalr</groupId>
        <artifactId>imgscalr-lib</artifactId>
        <version>4.2</version>
</dependency>
<dependency>
        <groupId>org.datavec</groupId>
        <artifactId>datavec-data-image</artifactId>
        <version>${dl4j.version}</version>
</dependency>
```

Processing color images is more exciting and effective, and DL4J-based CNNs can handle color images, too. However, it's better to simplify the computation with the grayscale images. Nevertheless, this way, we can make the overall representation simpler and space efficient.

Let's give an example for our previous step; we resized each 256 x 256 pixel image—which is represented by 16,384 features rather than 16,384 x 3 for a color image having three RGB channels (execute `GrayscaleConverter.java` to see a demo). Let's see what the converted image would look like:

On the left—the original image, on the right—the grayscale one with RGB averaging

The previous conversion is done using two methods called `pixels2Gray()` and
`makeGray()`. The former converts RGB pixels into corresponding grayscale ones. Let's see
the signature for this:

```
private static int pixels2Gray(int R, int G, int B) {
      return (R + G + B) / 3;
   }
private static BufferedImage makeGray(BufferedImage testImage) {
      int w = testImage.getWidth();
      int h = testImage.getHeight();
      for (int w1 = 0; w1 < w; w1++) {
         for (int h1 = 0; h1 < h; h1++) {
            int col = testImage.getRGB(w1, h1);
            int R = (col & 0xff0000) / 65536;
            int G = (col & 0xff00) / 256;
            int B = (col & 0xff);
            int graycol = pixels2Gray(R, G, B);
            testImage.setRGB(w1, h1, new Color(graycol, graycol,
graycol).getRGB());
         }
      }
      return testImage;
   }
```

So, what happens under the hood? We chain all the previous three steps: make all the
images square, then convert all of them to 256 x 256, and finally convert the resized image
into a grayscale one (I assume that x is the image to be converted):

```
convertedImage = ImageIO.read(new File(x))
         .makeSquare()
         .resizeImg(resizeImgDim, resizeImgDim) // (128, 128)
         .image2gray();
```

Therefore, in summary, now all of the images are in grey, but only after squaring and resizing. The following image gives some sense of the conversion step:

Resized figure (left, the original and tall one, right, the squared one)

The previous chaining also comes with some additional effort. Now, putting all these three coding steps together, we can finally prepare all of our images:

```java
//imageUtils.java
public class imageUtils {
    // image 2 vector processing
    private static Integer pixels2gray(Integer red, Integer green, Integer blue){
        return (red + green + blue) / 3;
    }
    private static List<Integer> pixels2color(Integer red, Integer green, Integer blue) {
        return Arrays.asList(red, green, blue);
    }

private static <T> List<T> image2vec(BufferedImage img,
Function<Triple<Integer, Integer, Integer>, T> f) {
        int w = img.getWidth();
        int h = img.getHeight();

        ArrayList<T> result = new ArrayList<>();
        for (int w1 = 0; w1 < w; w1++ ) {
            for (int h1 = 0; h1 < h; h1++) {
                int col = img.getRGB(w1, h1);
                int red =   (col & 0xff0000) / 65536;
                int green = (col & 0xff00) / 256;
                int blue = (col & 0xff);
                result.add(f.apply(new Triple<>(red, green, blue)));
```

```
                }
            }
            return result;
        }

    public static List<Integer> image2gray(BufferedImage img) {
        return image2vec(img, t -> pixels2gray(t.getFirst(), t.getSecond(),
t.getThird()));
    }

    public static List<Integer> image2color(BufferedImage img) {
        return image2vec(img, t -> pixels2color(t.getFirst(),
t.getSecond(), t.getThird()))
                .stream()
                .flatMap(l -> l.stream())
                .collect(Collectors.toList());
    }

    // make image square
    public static BufferedImage makeSquare(BufferedImage img) {
        int w = img.getWidth();
        int h = img.getHeight();
        int dim = Math.min(w, h);

        if (w == h) {
            return img;
        } else if (w > h) {
            return Scalr.crop(img, (w-h)/2, 0, dim, dim);
        } else {
            return Scalr.crop(img, 0, (h-w)/2, dim, dim);
        }
    }

    // resize pixels
public static BufferedImage resizeImg(BufferedImage img, int width, int
height) {
        return Scalr.resize(img, Scalr.Method.BALANCED, width, height);
    }
}
```

Extracting image metadata

Up to this point, we have loaded and pre-processed raw images. However, we have no idea about the image metadata that is added, which is needed so that our CNNs can learn. Thus, it's time to load those CSV files containing metadata about each image.

I wrote a method called readMetadata() to read such metadata in CSV format so that it can be used by two other methods called readBusinessLabels and readBusinessToImageLabels. These three methods are defined in the CSVImageMetadataReader.java script. Here's the signature of the readMetadata() method:

```java
public static List<List<String>> readMetadata(String csv, List<Integer>
rows) throws IOException {
        boolean defaultRows = rows.size() == 1 && rows.get(0) == -1;
        LinkedList<Integer> rowsCopy = null;
        if (!defaultRows) {
            rowsCopy = new LinkedList<>(rows);
        }
        try(BufferedReader bufferedReader = new BufferedReader(new
InputStreamReader(new FileInputStream(new File(csv))))) {
            ArrayList<List<String>> arrayList = new ArrayList<>();
            String line = bufferedReader.readLine();
            int i = 0;
            while (line != null) {
                if (defaultRows || rowsCopy.getFirst() == i) {
                    if (!defaultRows) {
                        rowsCopy.removeFirst();
                    }
                    arrayList.add(Arrays.asList(line.split(",")));
                }
                line = bufferedReader.readLine();
                i++;
            }
            return arrayList;
        }
    }
```

The `readBusinessLabels()` method maps from the business ID to labels of the form **businessID | Set(labels)**:

```
public static Map<String, Set<Integer>> readBusinessLabels(String csv)
throws IOException {
        return readBusinessLabels(csv, DEFAULT_ROWS);
    }

public static Map<String, Set<Integer>> readBusinessLabels(String csv,
List<Integer> rows) throws IOException {
        return readMetadata(csv, rows).stream()
                .skip(1)
                .map(l -> parseBusinessLabelsKv(l))
                .collect(Collectors.toMap(e -> e.getKey(), e ->
e.getValue()));
    }
```

The `readBusinessToImageLabels()` method maps from the image ID to the business ID of the form **imageID | businessID**:

```
public static Map<Integer, String> readBusinessToImageLabels(String csv)
throws IOException {
        return readBusinessToImageLabels(csv, DEFAULT_ROWS);
    }

public static Map<Integer, String> readBusinessToImageLabels(String csv,
List<Integer> rows) throws IOException {
        return readMetadata(csv, rows).stream()
                .skip(1)
                .map(l -> parseBusinessToImageLabelsKv(l))
                .collect(Collectors.toMap(e -> e.getKey(), e ->
e.getValue(), useLastMerger()));
    }
```

Image feature extraction

So far, we have seen how to preprocess images and extract image metadata by linking them with the original images. Now, we need to extract features from those preprocessed images so that they can be fed into CNNs.

We need the map operations for feature extractions for business, data, and labels. These three operations will ensure that we don't lose any image provenance (see the `imageFeatureExtractor.java` script):

- Business mapping with the form **imageID | businessID**
- Data map of the form **imageID | image data**
- Label map of the form **businessID | labels**

First, we must define a regular expression pattern to extract a jpg name from the `CSVImageMetadataReaderclass`, which is used to match against training labels:

```
public static Pattern patt_get_jpg_name = Pattern.compile("[0-9]");
```

Then, we extract all of the image IDs associated with their respective business IDs:

```
public static List<Integer> getImgIdsFromBusinessId(Map<Integer, String>
bizMap, List<String> businessIds) {
        return bizMap.entrySet().stream().filter(x ->
                businessIds.contains(x.getValue())).map(Map.Entry::getKey)
        .collect(Collectors.toList());
}
```

Now, we need to load and process all the images that are already preprocessed to extract the image IDs by mapping them with the IDs extracted from the business IDs in the earlier examples:

```
public static List<String> getImageIds(String photoDir, Map<Integer,
String> businessMap,
                                        List<String> businessIds) {
        File d = new File(photoDir);
        List<String> imgsPath = Arrays.stream(d.listFiles()).map(f ->
                        f.toString()).collect(Collectors.toList());
        boolean defaultBusinessMap = businessMap.size() == 1 &&
businessMap.get(-1).equals("-1");
        boolean defaultBusinessIds = businessIds.size() == 1 &&
businessIds.get(0).equals("-1");
        if (defaultBusinessMap || defaultBusinessIds) {
            return imgsPath;
        } else {
            Map<Integer, String> imgsMap = imgsPath.stream()
                    .map(x -> new AbstractMap.SimpleEntry<Integer,
String>(extractInteger(x), x))
                    .collect(Collectors.toMap(e -> e.getKey(), e ->
e.getValue()));
            List<Integer> imgsPathSub =
imageFeatureExtractor.getImgIdsFromBusinessId(
```

```
                                              businessMap, businessIds);
            return imgsPathSub.stream().filter(x ->
imgsMap.containsKey(x)).map(x -> imgsMap.get(x))
                    .collect(Collectors.toList());
        }
    }
```

In the preceding code block, we get a list of images from the photoDir directory (which is where the raw images reside). The `ids` parameter is an optional parameter to subset the images loaded from the photoDir. So far, we have been able to extract all the image IDs that are somehow associated with at least one business. The next move will be to read and process the images into an imageID → vector map:

```
public static Map<Integer, List<Integer>> processImages(List<String> imgs,
int resizeImgDim, int nPixels) {
        Function<String, AbstractMap.Entry<Integer, List<Integer>>>
handleImg = x -> {
            BufferedImage img = null;
            try {
                img = ImageIO.read(new File(x));
            } catch (IOException e) {
                e.printStackTrace();
            }
            img = makeSquare(img);
            img = resizeImg(img, resizeImgDim, resizeImgDim);
            List<Integer> value = image2gray(img);
            if(nPixels != -1) {
                value = value.subList(0, nPixels);
            }
            return new AbstractMap.SimpleEntry<Integer,
List<Integer>>(extractInteger(x), value);
        };

        return imgs.stream().map(handleImg).filter(e ->
!e.getValue().isEmpty())
                .collect(Collectors.toMap(e -> e.getKey(), e ->
e.getValue()));
    }
```

In the preceding code block, we read and processed the images into a photoID → vector map. The `processImages()` method takes the following parameters:

- `images`: A list of images in the `getImageIds()` method
- `resizeImgDim`: Dimension to rescale square images
- `nPixels`: Number of pixels used to sample the image to drastically reduce runtime while testing features

Well done! We are just one step away from extracting the data that is required to train our CNNs. The final step in feature extraction is to extract the pixel data, which consists of four objects to keep track of each image -- that is, imageID, businessID, labels, and pixel data:

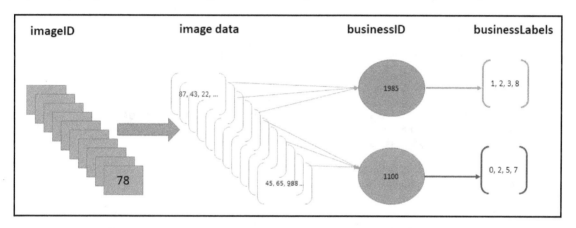

Image data representation

Thus, as shown in the preceding diagram, the primary data structure is constructed with four data types (that is, four tuples) -- `imgID`, `businessID`, `pixel data vector`, and `labels`:

Thus, we should have a class containing all of the parts of these objects. Don't worry; all we need is defined in the `FeatureAndDataAligner.java` script. Once we have the instantiated instance of `FeatureAndDataAligner` using the following line of code in the `YelpImageClassifier.java` script (under the main method), `businessMap`, `dataMap`, and `labMap` are provided:

```
FeatureAndDataAligner alignedData = new FeatureAndDataAligner(dataMap,
businessMap, Optional.of(labMap));
```

Here, the option type for `labMap` is used since we don't have this information when we score on test data -- that is, it is optional for invocation. Now, let's see how I did this. We start from the constructor of the class that is being used, initializing the preceding data structure:

```
private Map<Integer, List<Integer>> dataMap;
private Map<Integer, String> bizMap;
private Optional<Map<String, Set<Integer>>> labMap;
private List<Integer> rowindices;

public FeatureAndDataAligner(Map<Integer, List<Integer>> dataMap,
Map<Integer, String> bizMap, Optional<Map<String, Set<Integer>>> labMap) {
        this(dataMap, bizMap, labMap,
dataMap.keySet().stream().collect(Collectors.toList()));
    }
```

Now, we initialize the values through the constructor of the `FeatureAndDataAligner.java` class as follows:

```
public FeatureAndDataAligner(Map<Integer, List<Integer>> dataMap,
Map<Integer, String> bizMap, Optional<Map<String, Set<Integer>>>
labMap,List<Integer> rowindices) {
        this.dataMap = dataMap;
        this.bizMap = bizMap;
        this.labMap = labMap;
        this.rowindices = rowindices;
    }
```

Now, when aligning the data, if `labMap` is empty -- which is not provided with the training data -- the following can be used too:

```
public FeatureAndDataAligner(Map<Integer, List<Integer>> dataMap,
Map<Integer, String> bizMap) {
        this(dataMap, bizMap, Optional.empty(),
dataMap.keySet().stream().collect(Collectors.toList()));
    }
```

Now, we have to align the image IDs and image data with the business IDs. For this, I have written the `BusinessImgageIds()` method:

```
public List<Triple<Integer, String, List<Integer>>>
alignBusinessImgageIds(Map<Integer, List<Integer>> dataMap, Map<Integer,
String> bizMap) {
        return alignBusinessImgageIds(dataMap, bizMap,
dataMap.keySet().stream().collect(Collectors.toList()));
    }
```

The actual implementation lies in the following overloaded method, which returns optional if an image does not have a business ID:

```java
public List<Triple<Integer, String, List<Integer>>>
alignBusinessImgageIds(Map<Integer, List<Integer>> dataMap, Map<Integer,
String> bizMap, List<Integer> rowindices) {
        ArrayList<Triple<Integer, String, List<Integer>>> result = new
ArrayList<>();
        for (Integer pid : rowindices) {
            Optional<String> imgHasBiz =
Optional.ofNullable(bizMap.get(pid));
            String bid = imgHasBiz.orElse("-1");
            if (dataMap.containsKey(pid) && imgHasBiz.isPresent()) {
                result.add(new ImmutableTriple<>(pid, bid,
dataMap.get(pid)));
            }
        }
        return result;
    }
```

Finally, as shown in the preceding diagram, we now need to align the labels, which is a four-tuple list compromising of `dataMap`, `bizMap`, `labMap`, and `rowindices`:

```java
private List<Quarta<Integer, String, List<Integer>, Set<Integer>>>
alignLabels(Map<Integer, List<Integer>>
                                                     dataMap,
Map<Integer, String>
bizMap, Optional<Map<String,
Set<Integer>>> labMap,
List<Integer> rowindices) {
        ArrayList<Quarta<Integer, String, List<Integer>, Set<Integer>>>
result = new ArrayList<>();
        List<Triple<Integer, String, List<Integer>>> a1 =
alignBusinessImgageIds(dataMap,
bizMap, rowindices);
        for (Triple<Integer, String, List<Integer>> p : a1) {
            String bid = p.getMiddle();
            Set<Integer> labs = Collections.emptySet();
            if (labMap.isPresent() && labMap.get().containsKey(bid)) {
                labs = labMap.get().get(bid);
            }
            result.add(new Quarta<>(p.getLeft(), p.getMiddle(),
p.getRight(), labs));
        }
        return result;
    }
```

In the previous code block, `Quarta` is a case class that help us to maintain our desired data structure, shown as follows:

```
public static class Quarta <A, B, C, D> {
        public final A a;
        public final B b;
        public final C c;
        public final D d;

        public Quarta(A a, B b, C c, D d) {
            this.a = a;
            this.b = b;
            this.c = c;
            this.d = d;
        }
    }
```

Finally, we pre-compute and save the data so that the method does not need to re-compute each time it is called:

```
    private volatile List<Quarta<Integer, String, List<Integer>,
Set<Integer>>> _data = null;
    // pre-computing and saving data as a val so method does not need to re-
compute each time it is called.
    public List<Quarta<Integer, String, List<Integer>, Set<Integer>>> data() {
        if (_data == null) {
            synchronized (this) {
                if (_data == null) {
                    _data = alignLabels(dataMap, bizMap, labMap,
rowindices);
                }
            }
        }
        return _data;
    }
```

Finally, as used in the preceding code block, we now create some getter methods so that in each invocation, we can retrieve the image id, business id, business label, and image for each business easily:

```
    // getter functions
    public List<Integer> getImgIds() {
        return data().stream().map(e -> e.a).collect(Collectors.toList());
    }
    public List<String> getBusinessIds() {
        return data().stream().map(e -> e.b).collect(Collectors.toList());
    }
```

```java
public List<List<Integer>> getImgVectors() {
        return data().stream().map(e -> e.c).collect(Collectors.toList());
    }
public List<Set<Integer>> getBusinessLabels() {
        return data().stream().map(e -> e.d).collect(Collectors.toList());
    }
public Map<String, Integer> getImgCntsPerBusiness() {
        return
getBusinessIds().stream().collect(Collectors.groupingBy(Function.identity()
)).entrySet()
                .stream().map(e -> new
AbstractMap.SimpleEntry<>(e.getKey(), e.getValue().size()))
                .collect(Collectors.toMap(e -> e.getKey(), e ->
e.getValue()));
    }
```

Excellent! Up to this point, we have managed to extract the features to train our CNNs. However, the thing is that the feature in its current form is still not suitable to feed into the CNNs. This is because we only have the feature vectors without labels. Thus, it needs another intermediate conversion.

Preparing the ND4J dataset

As I said previously, we need an intermediate conversion to prepare the training set containing feature vectors and labels: features from images, but labels from the business labels.

For this, we have the makeND4jDataSets class (see makeND4jDataSets.java for details). The class creates an ND4J dataset object from the data structure from the alignLables function in the List[(imgID, bizID, labels, pixelVector)] form. First, we prepare the dataset using the makeDataSet() method as follows:

```java
public static DataSet makeDataSet(FeatureAndDataAligner alignedData, int
bizClass) {
        INDArray alignedXData = makeDataSetTE(alignedData);
        List<Set<Integer>> labels = alignedData.getBusinessLabels();
        float[][] matrix2 = labels.stream().map(x -> (x.contains(bizClass)
? new float[]{1, 0}
                                : new float[]{0, 1})).toArray(float[][]::new);
        INDArray alignedLabs = toNDArray(matrix2);
        return new DataSet(alignedXData, alignedLabs);
    }
```

Then, we further need to convert the preceding data structure into an `INDArray`, which can then be consumed by the CNNs:

```
public static INDArray makeDataSetTE(FeatureAndDataAligner alignedData) {
        List<List<Integer>> imgs = alignedData.getImgVectors();
        double[][] matrix = new double[imgs.size()][];
        for (int i = 0; i < matrix.length; i++) {
            List<Integer> img = imgs.get(i);
            matrix[i] =
img.stream().mapToDouble(Integer::doubleValue).toArray();
        }
        return toNDArray(matrix);
    }
```

In the preceding code block, the `toNDArray()` method is used to convert the double or float matrix into `INDArray` format:

```
// For converting floar matrix to INDArray
private static INDArray toNDArray(float[][] matrix) {
        return Nd4j.create(matrix);
        }
// For converting double matrix to INDArray
private static INDArray toNDArray(double[][] matrix) {
        return Nd4j.create(matrix);
        }
```

Fantastic! We were able to extract all the metadata and features from the images and prepared the training data in an ND4J format that can now be consumed by the DL4J-based model. However, since we will be using CNN as our model, we still need to convert this 2D object into 4D by using the `convolutionalFlat` operation during network construction. Anyway, we will see this in the next section.

Training, evaluating, and saving the trained CNN models

So far, we have seen how to prepare the training set. Now that we have, a more challenging part lies ahead as we have to train our CNNs with 234,545 images, although the testing phase could be less exhaustive with a limited number of images, for example, 500 images. Therefore, it is better to train each CNN involving batchmode using DL4j's `MultipleEpochsIterator`, which is a dataset iterator for doing multiple passes over a dataset.

`MultipleEpochsIterator` is a dataset iterator for doing multiple passes over a dataset. See more at https://deeplearning4j.org/doc/org/deeplearning4j/datasets/iterator/MultipleEpochsIterator.html.

Network construction

The following is a list of important hyperparameters and their details. Here, I will try to construct a five-layered CNN, as follows:

- Layer 0 has a `ConvolutionLayer` having a 6 x 6 kernel, one channel (since they are grayscale images), a stride of 2 x 2, and 20 feature maps where ReLU is the activation function:

```
ConvolutionLayer layer_0 = new ConvolutionLayer.Builder(6,6)
            .nIn(nChannels)
            .stride(2,2) // default stride(2,2)
            .nOut(20) // # of feature maps
            .dropOut(0.7) // dropout to reduce overfitting
            .activation(Activation.RELU) // Activation: rectified
linear units
            .build();
```

- Layer 1 has `SubsamplingLayer` max pooling, and a stride of 2x2. Thus, by using stride, we down sample by a factor of 2. Note that only MAX, AVG, SUM, and PNORM are supported. Here, the kernel size will be the same as the filter size from the last `ConvolutionLayer`. Therefore, we do not need to define the kernel size explicitly:

```
SubsamplingLayer layer_1 = new SubsamplingLayer
            .Builder(SubsamplingLayer.PoolingType.MAX)
            .stride(2, 2)
            .build();
```

- Layer 2 has a `ConvolutionLayer` having a 6 x 6 kernel, one channel (since they are grayscale images), a stride of 2 x 2, and 20 output neurons where RELU is the activation function. We will use Xavier for network weight initialization:

```
ConvolutionLayer layer_2= new ConvolutionLayer.Builder(6, 6)
            .stride(2, 2) // nIn need not specified in later layers
            .nOut(50)
            .activation(Activation.RELU) // Activation: rectified
linear units
            .build();
```

- Layer 3 has `SubsamplingLayer` max pooling and a stride of 2 x 2. Thus, by using stride, we down sample by a factor of 2. Note that only MAX, AVG, SUM, and PNORM are supported. Here, the kernel size will be the same as the filter size from the last `ConvolutionLayer`. Therefore, we do not need to define the kernel size explicitly:

```
SubsamplingLayer layer_3 = new SubsamplingLayer
            .Builder(SubsamplingLayer.PoolingType.MAX)
            .stride(2, 2)
            .build();
```

- Layer 4 has a `DenseLayer`, that is, a fully connected feed forward layer trainable by backpropagation with 50 neurons and ReLU as an activation function. It should be noted that we do not need to specify the number of input neurons as it assumes the input from the previous `ConvolutionLayer`:

```
DenseLayer layer_4 = new DenseLayer.Builder() // Fully connected
layer
                .nOut(500)
                .dropOut(0.7) // dropout to reduce overfitting
                .activation(Activation.RELU) // Activation: rectified
linear units
                .build();
```

- Layer 5 is an `OutputLayer` having two output neurons driven by the softmax activation (that is, probability distribution over the classes). We compute the loss using XENT (that is, cross entropy for binary classification) as the loss function:

```
OutputLayer layer_5 = new
OutputLayer.Builder(LossFunctions.LossFunction.XENT)
                .nOut(outputNum) // number of classes to be predicted
                .activation(Activation.SOFTMAX)
                .build();
```

Apart from these layers, we also need to perform image flattening—that is, converting a 2D object into a 4D consumable using CNN layers by invoking the following method:

```
convolutionalFlat(numRows, numColumns, nChannels))
```

Therefore, in summary, using DL4J, our CNN will be as follows:

```
MultiLayerConfiguration conf = new NeuralNetConfiguration.Builder()
            .seed(seed)a
            .miniBatch(true) // for MultipleEpochsIterator
    .optimizationAlgo(OptimizationAlgorithm.STOCHASTIC_GRADIENT_DESCENT)
            .updater(new Adam(0.001)) // Aama for weight updater
```

```
                     .weightInit(WeightInit.XAVIER) //Xavier weight init
                     .list()
                              .layer(0, layer_0)
                              .layer(1, layer_1)
                              .layer(2, layer_2)
                              .layer(3, layer_3)
                              .layer(4, layer_4)
                              .layer(5, layer_5)
                     .setInputType(InputType.convolutionalFlat(numRows, numColumns,
     nChannels))
                     .backprop(true).pretrain(false)
                     .build();
```

The other important aspects related to the training are described as follows:

- **The number of samples**: If you were training all the images other than GPU, that is, CPU, it would take days. When I tried with 50,000 images, it took one whole day with a machine having a core i7 processor and 32 GB of RAM. Now, you can imagine how long it would take for the whole dataset. In addition, it will require at least 256 GB of RAM even if you do the training in batch mode.
- **Number of epochs**: This is the number of iterations through all the training records. I iterated for 10 epochs due to time constraints.
- **Number of batches**: This is the number of records in each batch, for example, 32, 64, and 128. I used 128.

Now, with the preceding hyperparameters, we can start training our CNNs. The following code does the trick. The thing is that at first, we prepare the training set, then we define the required hyperparameters, and then we normalize the dataset so the ND4j data frame is encoded so that any labels that are considered true are ones and the rest zeros. Then, we shuffle both the rows and labels of the encoded dataset.

Then, we need to create epochs for the dataset iterator using `ListDataSetIterator` and `MultipleEpochsIterator`, respectively. Once the dataset is converted into the batchmodel, we are then ready to train the constructed CNNs:

```
log.info("Train model....");
for( int i=0; i<nepochs; i++ ){
    model.fit(epochitTr);
}
```

Once we finish the training, we can evaluate the model on the test set:

```
log.info("Evaluate model....");
Evaluation eval = new Evaluation(outputNum)
```

```
while (epochitTe.hasNext()) {
        DataSet testDS = epochitTe.next(nbatch);
        INDArray output = model.output(testDS.getFeatureMatrix());
        eval.eval(testDS.getLabels(), output);
}
```

When the evaluation is finished, we can now inspect the result of each CNN (run the
YelpImageClassifier.java script):

```
System.out.println(eval.stats())

>>>
========================Scores========================================
Accuracy: 0.5600
Precision: 0.5584
Recall: 0.5577
F1 Score: 0.5926
Precision, recall & F1: reported for positive class (class 1 - "1") only
======================================================================
```

Oops! Unfortunately, we have not seen good accuracy. However, do not worry, since in the
FAQ section, we will see how to improve upon this. Finally, we can save the layer-wise
network configuration and network weights to be used later on (that is, scoring before
submission):

```
if (!saveNN.isEmpty()) {
        // model config
        FileUtils.write(new File(saveNN + ".json"),
model.getLayerWiseConfigurations().toJson());
        // model parameters
        DataOutputStream dos = new
DataOutputStream(Files.newOutputStream(Paths.get(saveNN + ".bin")));
        Nd4j.write(model.params(), dos);
        }
    log.info("****************Example finished*******************");
}
```

In the previous code, we also saved a JSON file containing all the network configurations
and a binary file for holding all the weights and parameters of all the CNNs. This is done
using two methods, namely saveNN() and loadNN(), which are defined in the
NetwokSaver.java script. First, let's look at the signature of the saveNN() method, as
follows:

```
public void saveNN(MultiLayerNetwork model, String NNconfig, String
NNparams) throws IOException {
        // save neural network config
        FileUtils.write(new File(NNconfig),
```

```
model.getLayerWiseConfigurations().toJson());

        // save neural network parms
        DataOutputStream dos = new
DataOutputStream(Files.newOutputStream(Paths.get(NNparams)));
        Nd4j.write(model.params(), dos);
    }
```

The idea is visionary as well as important since, as I said earlier, you would not train your whole network for the second time to evaluate a new test set. For example, suppose you want to test just a single image. The thing is, we also have another method named loadNN() that reads back the .json and .bin files we created earlier to a MultiLayerNetwork, which can be used to score new test data. This method is as follows:

```
public static MultiLayerNetwork loadNN(String NNconfig, String NNparams)
throws IOException {
        // get neural network config
        MultiLayerConfiguration confFromJson = MultiLayerConfiguration
                .fromJson(FileUtils.readFileToString(new File(NNconfig)));

        // get neural network parameters
        DataInputStream dis = new DataInputStream    (new
FileInputStream(NNparams));
        INDArray newParams = Nd4j.read(dis);

        // creating network object
        MultiLayerNetwork savedNetwork = new
MultiLayerNetwork(confFromJson);
        savedNetwork.init();
        savedNetwork.setParameters(newParams);

        return savedNetwork;
    }
```

Scoring the model

The scoring approach that we are going to use is simple. It assigns business-level labels by averaging the image-level predictions. I did this in a simplistic manner, but you can try using a better approach. What I did is assign a business as label 0 if the average of the probabilities across all of its images belonging to class 0 are greater than a certain threshold, say, 0.5:

```
public static INDArray scoreModel(MultiLayerNetwork model, INDArray ds) {
        return model.output(ds);
    }
```

Then, I collected the model predictions from the `scoreModel()` method and merged them with `alignedData`:

```
/** Take model predictions from scoreModel and merge with alignedData*/
public static List<Pair<String, Double>> aggImgScores2Business(INDArray
scores,
                                            FeatureAndDataAligner alignedData)
{
        assert(scores.size(0) == alignedData.data().size());
        ArrayList<Pair<String, Double>> result = new ArrayList<Pair<String,
Double>>();

        for (String x :
alignedData.getBusinessIds().stream().distinct().collect(Collectors.toList(
))) {
            //R irows =
getRowIndices4Business(alignedData.getBusinessIds(), x);
            List<String> ids = alignedData.getBusinessIds();
            DoubleStream ret = IntStream.range(0, ids.size())
                    .filter(i -> ids.get(i).equals(x))
                    .mapToDouble(e ->
scores.getRow(e).getColumn(1).getDouble(0,0));
            double mean = ret.sum() / ids.size();
            result.add(new ImmutablePair<>(x, mean));
        }
        return result;
    }
```

Finally, we can restore the trained and saved models, restore them back, and generate the submission file for Kaggle. The thing is that we need to aggregate image predictions to business scores for each model.

Submission file generation

For this, I wrote a class called `ResultFileGenerator.java`. According to the Kaggle web page, we will have to write the result in the `business_ids, labels` format. Here, `business_id` is the ID for the corresponding business, and the label is the multi-label prediction. Let's see how easily we can do that.

First, we aggregate image predictions to business scores for each model. Then, we transform the preceding data structure into a list for each `bizID` containing a Tuple (`bizid`, `List[Double]`) where the `Vector[Double]` is the vector of probabilities:

```
public static List<Pair<String, List<Double>>>
SubmitObj(FeatureAndDataAligner alignedData,
                                        String modelPath,
                                        String model0,
                                        String model1,
                                        String model2,
                                        String model3,
                                        String model4,
                                        String model5,
                                        String model6,
                                        String model7,
                                        String model8) throws
IOException {
        List<String> models = Arrays.asList(model0, model1,
                                        model2, model3,
                                        model4, model5,
                                        model6, model7, model8);
        ArrayList<Map<String, Double>> big = new ArrayList<>();
        for (String m : models) {
            INDArray ds = makeND4jDataSets.makeDataSetTE(alignedData);
            MultiLayerNetwork model = NetworkSaver.loadNN(modelPath + m +
".json",
                                        modelPath + m +
".bin");
            INDArray scores = ModelEvaluation.scoreModel(model, ds);
            List<Pair<String, Double>> bizScores = ModelEvaluation.
aggImgScores2Business(scores, alignedData);
            Map<String, Double> map =
bizScores.stream().collect(Collectors.toMap(
                                        e ->
e.getKey(), e -> e.getValue())));
            big.add(map);
            }

        // transforming the data structure above into a List for each bizID
```

```
containing a Tuple (bizid,
        List[Double]) where the Vector[Double] is the the vector of
probabilities:
        List<Pair<String, List<Double>>> result = new ArrayList<>();
        Iterator<String> iter = alignedData.data().stream().map(e ->
e.b).distinct().iterator();
        while (iter.hasNext()) {
            String x = iter.next();
            result.add(new MutablePair(x, big.stream().map(x2 ->
x2.get(x)).collect(Collectors.toList())));
        }
        return result;
    }
```

Therefore, once we have the result aggregated from each model, we then need to generate the submission file:

```
public static void writeSubmissionFile(String outcsv, List<Pair<String,
List<Double>>> phtoObj, double thresh) throws FileNotFoundException {
        try (PrintWriter writer = new PrintWriter(outcsv)) {
            writer.println("business_ids,labels");
            for (int i = 0; i < phtoObj.size(); i++) {
                Pair<String, List<Double>> kv = phtoObj.get(i);
                StringBuffer sb = new StringBuffer();
                Iterator<Double> iter = kv.getValue().stream().filter(x ->
x >= thresh).iterator();
                for (int idx = 0; iter.hasNext(); idx++) {
                    iter.next();
                    if (idx > 0) {
                        sb.append(' ');
                    }
                    sb.append(Integer.toString(idx));
                }
                String line = kv.getKey() + "," + sb.toString();
                writer.println(line);
            }
        }
    }
```

Now that we have managed to do everything up to this point, we can now wrap this up and generate a sample prediction and submission file for Kaggle. For simplicity, I randomly sliced this to only 20,000 images to save time. Interested readers can try building CNNs for all the images, too. However, it might take days. Nevertheless, we will look at some performance tuning tips in the FAQ section.

Wrapping everything up by executing the main() method

Let's wrap the overall discussion by watching the performance of our model programmatically (see the main `YelpImageClassifier.java` class):

```
public class YelpImageClassifier {
    public static void main(String[] args) throws IOException {
        Map<String, Set<Integer>> labMap =
readBusinessLabels("Yelp/labels/train.csv");
        Map<Integer, String> businessMap =
readBusinessToImageLabels("Yelp/labels
/train_photo_to_biz_ids.csv");
        List<String> businessIds = businessMap.entrySet().stream().map(e ->
e.getValue()).distinct().collect(Collectors.toList());
        // 100 images
        List<String> imgs = getImageIds("Yelp/images/train/", businessMap,
businessIds).subList(0, 100);
        System.out.println("Image ID retreival done!");

        Map<Integer, List<Integer>> dataMap = processImages(imgs, 64);
        System.out.println("Image processing done!");

        FeatureAndDataAligner alignedData = new
FeatureAndDataAligner(dataMap,
businessMap, Optional.of(labMap));
        //System.out.println(alignedData.data());
        System.out.println("Feature extraction done!");

        // Training one model for one class at a time
        CNNEpochs.trainModelEpochs(alignedData, 0,
"results/models/model0");
        CNNEpochs.trainModelEpochs(alignedData, 1,
"results/models/model1");
        CNNEpochs.trainModelEpochs(alignedData, 2,
"results/models/model2");
        CNNEpochs.trainModelEpochs(alignedData, 3,
"results/models/model3");
        CNNEpochs.trainModelEpochs(alignedData, 4,
"results/models/model4");
        CNNEpochs.trainModelEpochs(alignedData, 5,
"results/models/model5");
        CNNEpochs.trainModelEpochs(alignedData, 6,
"results/models/model6");
        CNNEpochs.trainModelEpochs(alignedData, 7,
"results/models/model7");
```

```
        CNNEpochs.trainModelEpochs(alignedData, 8,
"results/models/model8");

        // processing test data for scoring
        Map<Integer, String> businessMapTE =
readBusinessToImageLabels("Yelp/labels
/test_photo_to_biz.csv");
        List<String> imgsTE = getImageIds("Yelp/images/test/",
businessMapTE,

                                businessMapTE.values().stream()
                                .distinct().collect(Collectors.toList()))
                                .subList(0, 100);

        Map<Integer, List<Integer>> dataMapTE = processImages(imgsTE, 64);
// make them 64x64
        FeatureAndDataAligner alignedDataTE = new
FeatureAndDataAligner(dataMapTE,
                                        businessMapTE,
Optional.empty());

        // creating csv file to submit to kaggle (scores all models)
        List<Pair<String, List<Double>>> Results = SubmitObj(alignedDataTE,
"results/models/",
                                                "model0",
"model1", "model2",
                                                "model3",
"model4", "model5",
                                                "model6",
"model7", "model8");
writeSubmissionFile("results/kaggleSubmission/kaggleSubmitFile.csv",
Results, 0.50);
        // example of how to score just model
        INDArray dsTE = makeND4jDataSets.makeDataSetTE(alignedDataTE);
        MultiLayerNetwork model =
NetworkSaver.loadNN("results/models/model0.json",
"results/models/model0.bin");
        INDArray predsTE = ModelEvaluation.scoreModel(model, dsTE);
        List<Pair<String, Double>> bizScoreAgg = ModelEvaluation
.aggImgScores2Business(predsTE, alignedDataTE);
        System.out.println(bizScoreAgg);
    }
}
```

It's true that we haven't achieved outstanding classification accuracy. Nevertheless, we can still try this with tuned hyperparameters. The following sections provide some insight.

Frequently asked questions (FAQs)

Although we have been able to solve this multi-label classification problem, the accuracy we experienced was below par. Therefore, in this section, we will see some **frequently asked questions** (**FAQs**) that might already be on your mind. Knowing the answers to these questions might help you to improve the accuracy of the CNNs we trained. Answers to these questions can be found in the Appendix:

1. What are the hyperparameters that I can try tuning while implementing this project?
2. My machine is getting OOP while running this project. What should I do?
3. While training the networks with full images, my GPU is getting OOP. What should I do?
4. I understand that the predictive accuracy using CNN in this project is still very low. Did our network under or overfit? Is there any way to observe how the training went?
5. I am very interested in implementing the same project in Scala. How can I do that?
6. Which optimizer should I use for this type of project where we need to process large-scale images?
7. How many hyperparameters do we have? I also want to see them for each layer.

Summary

In this chapter, we have seen how to develop a real-life application using CNNs on the DL4J framework. We have seen how to solve a multi-label classification problem through nine CNNs and a series of complex feature engineering and image manipulation operations. Albeit, we couldn't achieve higher accuracy, but readers are encouraged to tune hyperparameters in the code and try the same approach with the same dataset.

Also, training the CNNs with all the images is recommended so that networks can get enough data to learn the features from Yelp images. One more suggestion is improving the feature extraction process so that the CNNs can have more quality features.

In the next chapter, we will see how to implement and deploy a hands-on deep learning project that classifies review texts as either positive or negative based on the words they contain. A large-scale movie review dataset that contains 50,000 reviews (training plus testing) will be used.

A combined approach using Word2Vec (that is, a widely used word embedding technique in NLP) and the LSTM network for modeling will be applied: the pre-trained Google news vector model will be used as the neural word embeddings. Then, the training vectors, along with the labels, will be fed into the LSTM network to classify them as negative or positive sentiments. This will evaluate the trained model on the test set.

Answers to questions

Answer to question 1: The following hyperparameters are very important and must be tuned to achieve optimized results:

- Dropout is used to randomly off certain neurons (that is, feature detectors) to prevent overfitting
- Learning rate optimization—Adagrad can be used for feature-specific learning rate optimization
- Regularization—L1 and/or L2 regularization
- Gradient normalization and clipping
- Finally, apply batch normalization to reduce internal covariate shift in training

Now, for dropout, we can add dropout in each convolutional and dense layer and in case of overfitting, the model is specifically adjusted to the training dataset, so it will not be used for generalization. Therefore, although it performs well on the training set, its performance on the test dataset and subsequent tests is poor because it lacks the generalization property.

Anyway, we can apply dropout on a CNN and DenseLayer. Now, for better learning rate optimization, Adagrad can be used for feature-specific learning rate optimization. Then, for better regularization, we can use either L1 and/or L2. Thus, considering this, our network configuration should look as follows:

```
ConvolutionLayer layer_0 = new ConvolutionLayer.Builder(6, 6)
                .nIn(nChannels)
                .stride(2, 2) // default stride(2,2)
                .nOut(20) // # of feature maps
                .dropOut(0.7) // dropout to reduce overfitting
                .activation(Activation.RELU) // Activation: rectified
linear units
                .build();
        SubsamplingLayer layer_1 = new
SubsamplingLayer.Builder(SubsamplingLayer.PoolingType.MAX)
                .stride(2, 2)
                .build();
        ConvolutionLayer layer_2 = new ConvolutionLayer.Builder(6, 6)
```

```
                .stride(2, 2) // nIn need not specified in later layers
                .nOut(50)
                .activation(Activation.RELU) // Activation: rectified
linear units
                .build();
        SubsamplingLayer layer_3 = new
SubsamplingLayer.Builder(SubsamplingLayer.PoolingType.MAX)
                .stride(2, 2)
                .build();
        DenseLayer layer_4 = new DenseLayer.Builder() // Fully connected
layer
                .nOut(500)
                .dropOut(0.7) // dropout to reduce overfitting
                .activation(Activation.RELU) // Activation: rectified
linear units
.gradientNormalization(GradientNormalization.ClipElementWiseAbsoluteValue)
                .gradientNormalizationThreshold(10)
                .build();
        OutputLayer layer_5 = new
OutputLayer.Builder(LossFunctions.LossFunction.XENT)
                .nOut(outputNum) // number of classes to be predicted
.gradientNormalization(GradientNormalization.ClipElementWiseAbsoluteValue)
                .gradientNormalizationThreshold(10)
                .activation(Activation.SOFTMAX)
                .build();
        MultiLayerConfiguration conf = new
NeuralNetConfiguration.Builder().seed(seed).miniBatch(true)
.optimizationAlgo(OptimizationAlgorithm.STOCHASTIC_GRADIENT_DESCENT
                .l2(0.001) // l2 reg on all layers
                .updater(new AdaGrad(0.001))
                .weightInit(WeightInit.XAVIER) // Xavier weight init
                .list()
                        .layer(0, layer_0)
                        .layer(1, layer_1)
                        .layer(2, layer_2)
                        .layer(3, layer_3)
                        .layer(4, layer_4)
                         .layer(5, layer_5)
                .setInputType(InputType.convolutionalFlat(numRows,
numColumns, nChannels))
                .backprop(true).pretrain(false) // Feedforward hence no
pre-train.
                .build();
```

Answer to question 2: Due to the layering architecture's perspective and convolutional layers, training a CNN requires a huge amount of RAM. This is because the reverse pass of backpropagation requires all the intermediate values computed during the forward pass. Fortunately, during the inferencing stage, memory occupied by one layer is released as soon as the computation is completed when the next layer has been computed.

Also, as stated earlier, DL4J is built upon ND4J and ND4J utilizes off-heap memory management. This enables us to control the maximum amount of off-heap memory. We can set the `org.bytedeco.javacpp.maxbytes` system property. For example, for a single JVM run, you can pass `-Dorg.bytedeco.javacpp.maxbytes=1073741824` to limit the off-heap memory to 1 GB.

Answer to question 3: As I mentioned previously, training a CNN with Yelp's 50,000 images took one whole day with a machine with a core i7 processor and 32 GB of RAM. Naturally, performing this on all of the images can take a week. Therefore, in such cases, training on GPU makes much more sense.

Fortunately, we have already seen that DL4J works on distributed GPUs, as well as on native. For this, it has what we call **backbends**, or different types of hardware that it works on. Finally, a funny question would be: What should we do if our GPU runs out of memory? Well, if your GPU runs out of memory while training a CNN, here are five things you could do in order to try to solve the problem (other than purchasing a GPU with more RAM):

- Reduce the mini-batch size
- Reduce dimensionality using a larger stride in one or more layers, but don't go with PCA or SVD
- Remove one or more layers unless it's strictly essential to have a very deep network
- Use 16-bit floats instead of 32-bit (but precision has to be compromised)
- Distribute the CNN across multiple devices (that is, GPUs/CPUs)

For more on distributed training on GPUs using DL4J, refer to `Chapter 8`, *Distributed Deep Learning – Video Classification Using Convolutional LSTM Networks*.

Answer to question 4: It is true that we did not experience good accuracy. However, there are several reasons as to why we have not performed hyperparameter tuning. Secondly, we have not trained our network with all the images, so our network does not have enough data to learn the Yelp images. Finally, we can still see the model versus iteration score and other parameters from the following graph, so we can see that our model was not overfitted:

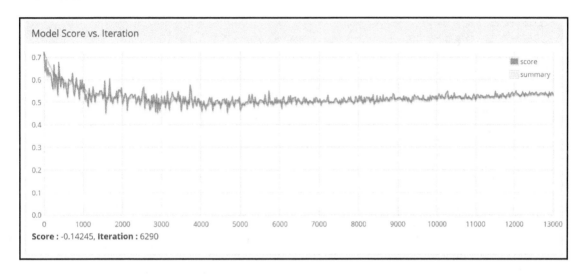

Model versus iteration score and other parameters of the LSTM sentiment analyzer

Answer to question 5: Yes, it is possible since Scala is also a JVM language, so it would not be that difficult to convert this Java project into Scala. Nevertheless, one of my previous books solves this same problem in Scala.

Here is the reference: Md. Rezaul Karim, *Scala Machine Learning Projects*, Packt Publishing Ltd., January 2018. Note that in that book, I used an old version of ND4J and DL4J, but I believe you can upgrade it by following this project.

Answer to question 6: Since, in CNN, one of the objective functions is to minimize the evaluated cost, we must define an optimizer. DL4j supports the following optimizers:

- SGD (learning rate only)
- Nesterovs momentum
- Adagrad
- RMSProp
- Adam
- AdaDelta

For more information, interested readers can refer to the DL4J page on available updaters at `https://deeplearning4j.org/updater`.

Answer to question 7: Just use the following code immediately after network initialization:

```
//Print the number of parameters in the network (and for each layer)
Layer[] layers = model.getLayers();
int totalNumParams = 0;
for( int i=0; i<layers.length; i++ ){
        int nParams = layers[i].numParams();
        System.out.println("Number of parameters in layer " + i + ": " +
nParams);
        totalNumParams += nParams;
    }
System.out.println("Total number of network parameters: " +
totalNumParams);

>>>
  Number of parameters in layer 0: 740
  Number of parameters in layer 1: 0
  Number of parameters in layer 2: 36050
  Number of parameters in layer 3: 0
  Number of parameters in layer 4: 225500
  Number of parameters in layer 5: 1002
  Total number of network parameters: 263292
```

This also tell us that the subsampling layers do not have any hyperparameters. Nevertheless, if you want to create an MLP or DBN, we will require millions of hyperparameters. However, here, we can see that we only need 263,000 hyperparameters.

4
Sentiment Analysis Using Word2Vec and LSTM Network

Sentiment analysis is a systematic way to identify, extract, quantify, and study effective states and subjective information. This is widely used in **natural language processing** (**NLP**), text analytics, and computational linguistics. This chapter demonstrates how to implement and deploy a hands-on deep learning project that classifies review texts as either positive or negative based on the words they contain. A large-scale movie review dataset that contains 50k reviews (training plus testing) will be used.

A combined approach using Word2Vec (that is, a widely used word embedding technique in NLP) and the **Long Short-Term Memory** (**LSTM**) network for modeling will be applied: the pre-trained Google news vector model will be used as the neural word embeddings. Then, the training vectors, along with the labels, will be fed into the LSTM network to classify them as negative or positive sentiments. Finally, it evaluates the trained model on the test set.

Additionally, it shows how to apply text preprocessing techniques such as tokenizer, stop words removal, and **term frequency-inverse document frequency** (**TF-IDF**), and word-embedding operations in **Deeplearning4j** (**DL4J**).

Nevertheless, it also shows how to save the trained DL4J model. Later on, the saved model will be restored from disk to make sentiment prediction on other small-scale review texts from Amazon cell, Yelp, and IMDb. Finally, it has answers to some frequently asked questions related to the projects and possible outlook.

The following topics will be covered throughout this end-to-end project:

- Sentiment analysis in NLP
- Using Word2Vec for neural word embeddings
- Dataset collection and description

- Saving and restoring pre-trained models with DL4J
- Developing a sentiment-analyzing model using Word2Vec and LSTM
- Frequently asked questions (FAQs)

Sentiment analysis is a challenging task

Text analytics in NLP is all about processing and analyzing large-scale structured and unstructured text to discover hidden patterns and themes and derive contextual meaning and relationships. Text analytics has so many potential use cases, such as sentiment analysis, topic modeling, TF-IDF, named entity recognition, and event extraction.

Sentiment analysis includes many example use cases, such as analyzing the political opinions of people on Facebook, Twitter, and other social media. Similarly, analyzing the reviews of restaurants on Yelp is also another great example of Sentiment Analysis. NLP frameworks and libraries such as OpenNLP and Stanford NLP are typically used to implement sentiment analysis.

However, for analyzing sentiments using text, particularly unstructured texts, we must find a robust and efficient way of feature engineering to convert the text into numbers. However, several stages of transformation of data are possible before a model is trained, and then subsequently deployed and finally performing predictive analytics. Moreover, we should expect the refinement of the features and model attributes. We could even explore a completely different algorithm, repeating the entire sequence of tasks as part of a new workflow.

When you look at a line of text, we see sentences, phrases, words, nouns, verbs, punctuation, and so on, which, when put together, have a meaning and purpose. Humans are very good at understanding sentences, words, slang, annotations, and context extremely well. This comes from years of practice and learning how to read/write proper grammar, punctuation, exclamations, and so on.

For example, the two sentences: *DL4J makes predictive analytics easy*, and *Predictive analytics makes DL4J easy*, might result in the same sentence vector having the same length equal to the size of our vocabulary that we pick. The second drawback is that the words "is" and "DL4J" have the same numerical index value of one, but our intuition says that the word "is" isn't important compared to "DL4J". Let's take a look at the second example: when your search string is *hotels in Berlin* in Google, we want results pertaining to *bnb*, *motel*, *lodging*, and *accommodation* in Berlin, too.

When layman terms come to the party, natural language learning becomes more complicated. Take the word bank as an example. This has several connections with a financial institution and land alongside a body of water. Now, if a natural sentence contains the term "bank" in conjunction with words such as finance, money, treasury, and interest rates, we can understand that its intended meaning is the former. However, if the neighboring words are water, shore, river, and lake, and so on, the case is the latter. Now, the question would be: can we exploit this concept to deal with polysemy and synonyms and make our model learn better?

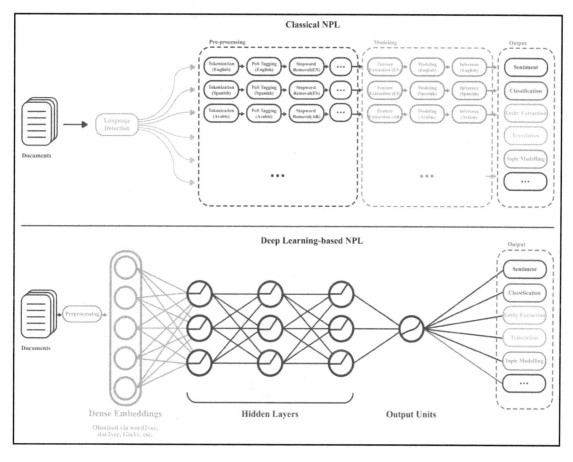

Classical machine learning versus deep learning-based NPL

Nevertheless, natural language sentences also contain vague words, slang, trivial words, and special characters, and all of these make the overall understanding and machine learning troublesome.

We have already seen how to use one-hot encoding or StringIndexer techniques to convert categorical variables (or even words) into numeric form. However, this kind of program often fails to interpret the semantics in a complex sentence, especially for lengthy sentences or even words. Consequently, human words have no natural notion of similarity. Thus, we naturally won't try to replicate this kind of capability, right?

How can we build a simple, scalable, faster way to deal with the regular texts or sentences and derive relations between a word and its contextual words, and then embed them in billions of words that will produce exceedingly good word representations into numeric vector space so that the machine learning models can consume them? Let's look at the Word2Vec model to find the answer to this.

Using Word2Vec for neural word embeddings

Word2Vec is a two-layer neural network that processes texts and turns them into numerical features. This way, the output of the Word2Vec is a vocabulary in which each word is embedded in vector space. The resulting vector can then be fed into a neural network for better understanding of natural languages. The novelist EL Doctorow has expressed this idea quite poetically in his book *Billy Bathgate*:

> *"It's like numbers are language, like all the letters in the language are turned into numbers, and so it's something that everyone understands the same way. You lose the sounds of the letters and whether they click or pop or touch the palate, or go ooh or aah, and anything that can be misread or con you with its music or the pictures it puts in your mind, all of that is gone, along with the accent, and you have a new understanding entirely, a language of numbers, and everything becomes as clear to everyone as the writing on the wall. So as I say there comes a certain time for the reading of the numbers."*

While using BOW and TF-IDF, all words are projected into the same position and their vectors are averaged: we address the word importance without considering the importance of word order in a collection of documents or in a single document.

As the order of words in the history does not influence the projection, both BOW and TF-IDF have no such features that can take care of this issue. Word2Vec encodes each word into a vector by using either context to predict a target word using a **continuous bag-of-words** (**CBOW**) or using a word to predict a target context, which is called **continuous skip-gram**.

- **N-gram versus skip-gram**: Words are read into vectors one at a time and scanned back and forth within a certain range
- **CBOW**: The CBOW technique uses a continuously distributed representation of the context
- **Continuous skip-gram**: Unlike CBOW, this method tries to maximize classification of a word based on another word in the same sentence

I have experienced that an increase in the range improves the quality of the resulting word vectors, but it also increases the computational complexity. Since more distant words are usually less related to the current word than those close to it are, we give less weight to the distant words by sampling less from those words in our training examples. Because of the model building and prediction, times also increase.

A comparative analysis from the architecture's point of view can be seen in the following diagram, where the architecture predicts the current word based on the context, and the skip-gram predicts the surrounding words given the current word:

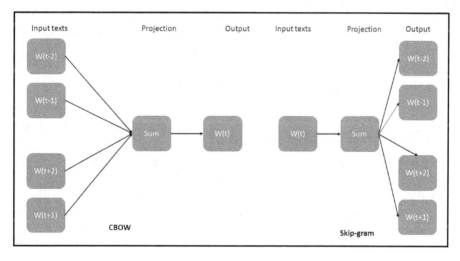

CBOW versus skip-gram (source: Tomas Mikolov et al., Efficient Estimation of Word Representations in Vector Space, https://arxiv.org/pdf/1301.3781.pdf)

Datasets and pre-trained model description

We are going to use the Large Movie Review dataset for training and testing the mode. Additionally, we will be using the Sentiment labeled Sentences dataset for making a single prediction on reviews on products, movies, and restaurants.

Large Movie Review dataset for training and testing

The former one is a dataset for binary sentiment classification containing substantially more data than previous benchmark datasets. The dataset can be downloaded from `http://ai.stanford.edu/~amaas/data/sentiment/`. Alternatively, I have utilized a Java method that comes from DL4J examples that also downloads and extracts this dataset.

I would like to acknowledge the following publications: Andrew L. Maas, Raymond E. Daly, Peter T. Pham, Dan Huang, Andrew Y. Ng, and Christopher Potts. (2011), *Learning Word Vectors for Sentiment Analysis,* The 49th Annual Meeting of the Association for Computational Linguistics (ACL 2011).

This dataset contains 50,000 movie reviews along with their associated binary sentiment polarity labels. The reviews are split evenly into 25,000 for both train and test sets. The overall distribution of labels is balanced (25,000 positive and 25,000 negative). We also include an additional 50 thousand unlabeled documents for unsupervised learning. In the labeled train/test sets, if a reviews has a score <= 4 out of 10, it is treated as a negative review, but having a score >= 7 out of 10 is treated as a positive review. Nevertheless, reviews with more neutral ratings are not included in the datasets.

Folder structure of the dataset

There are two folders, namely `train` and `test` for the training and test sets, respectively. Each folder has two separate subfolders called `pos` and `neg`, which contain reviews with binary labels (pos, neg). Reviews are stored in text files having the name `id_rating.txt`, where `id` is a unique ID and `rating` is the star rating on a 1-10 scale. Take a look at the following diagram to get a clearer view on the directory's structure:

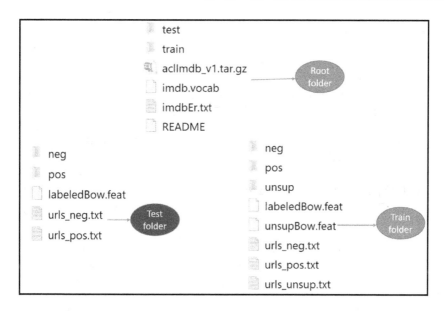

Folder structure in Large Movie Review Dataset

For example, the `test/pos/200_8.txt` file is the text for a positive-labeled test set example with a unique ID of 200 and a star rating of 8/10 from IMDb. The `train/unsup/` directory has zero for all ratings because the ratings are omitted for this portion of the dataset. Let's look at a sample positive review from IMDb:

> "Bromwell High is a cartoon comedy. It ran at the same time as some other programs about school life, such as "Teachers". My 35 years in the teaching profession lead me to believe that Bromwell High's satire is much closer to reality than is "Teachers". The scramble to survive financially, the insightful students who can see right through their pathetic teachers' pomp, the pettiness of the whole situation, all remind me of the schools I knew and their students. When I saw the episode in which a student repeatedly tried to burn down the school, I immediately recalled .... at .... High. A classic line: INSPECTOR: I'm here to sack one of your teachers. STUDENT: Welcome to Bromwell High. I expect that many adults of my age think that Bromwell High is far-fetched. What a pity that it isn't!"

Therefore, from the preceding review text, we can understand that the respective audience gave Bromwell High (a British-Canadian adult animated series about a British high school in South London, which you can see more of at `https://en.wikipedia.org/wiki/Bromwell_High`) a positive review, that is, a positive sentiment.

Description of the sentiment labeled dataset

The sentiment labeled sentences dataset was downloaded from the UCI machine learning repository at `http://archive.ics.uci.edu/ml/datasets/Sentiment+Labelled+Sentences`. This dataset was a research outcome by Kotzias and is used in the following publication: *From Group to Individual Labels using Deep Features*, Kotzias et. al, KDD' 2015.

The dataset contains sentences labeled with a positive or negative sentiment, extracted from reviews of products, movies, and restaurants. The review is a tab-delimited review having review sentences and a score of either 1 (for positive) or 0 (for negative). Let's look at a sample review from Yelp with an associated label:

"I was disgusted because I was pretty sure that was human hair."

In the preceding review text, the score is 0, so it is a negative review and it expresses a negative sentiment on the part of the customer. On the other hand, there are 500 positive and 500 negative sentences.

Those were selected at random for larger datasets of reviews. The author has attempted to select sentences that have a clearly positive or negative connotation; the goal was for no neutral sentences to be selected. The review sentences are collected from three different websites/fields, which are as follows:

- `https://www.imdb.com/`
- `https://www.amazon.com/`
- `https://www.yelp.com/`

Word2Vec pre-trained model

Instead of generating a new Word2Vec model from scratch, Google's pre-trained news word vector model can be used, which provides an efficient implementation of the CBOW and skip-gram architectures for computing vector representations of words. These representations can subsequently be used in many NLP applications and further research.

The model can be downloaded from `https://code.google.com/p/word2vec/` manually. The Word2Vec model takes a text corpus as input and produces the word vectors as output. It first constructs a vocabulary from the training text data and then learns vector representation of words.

There are two ways to achieve a Word2Vec model: by using continuous bag-of-words and continuous skip-gram. Skip-gram is slower, but better for infrequent words, although CBOW is faster.

The resulting word vector file can be used as a feature in many natural language processing and machine learning applications.

Sentiment analysis using Word2Vec and LSTM

First, let's define the problem. Given a movie review (raw text), we have to classify that movie review as either positive or negative based on the words it contains, that is, sentiment. We do this by combining the Word2Vec model and LSTM: each word in a review is vectorized using the Word2Vec model and fed into an LSTM net. As stated earlier, we will train data in the Large Movie Review dataset. Now, here is the workflow of the overall project:

- First, we download the movie/product reviews dataset
- Then we create or reuse an existing Word2Vec model (for example, Google News word vectors)
- Then we load each review text and convert words to vectors and reviews to sequences of vectors
- Then we create and train the LSTM network
- Then we save the trained model
- Then we evaluate the model on the test set
- Then we restore the trained model and evaluate a sample review text from the sentiment labeled dataset

Now, let's take a look at what the `main()` method would look like if we go with the preceding workflow:

```
public static void main(String[] args) throws Exception {
        Nd4j.getMemoryManager().setAutoGcWindow(10000);// see more in the
FAQ section
        wordVectors = WordVectorSerializer.loadStaticModel(new
File(WORD_VECTORS_PATH)); // Word2vec path
        downloadAndExtractData(); // download and extract the dataset
        networkTrainAndSaver(); // create net, train and save the model
        networkEvaluator(); // evaluate the model on test set
```

```
        sampleEvaluator(); // evaluate a simple review from text/file.
    }
```

Let's break the preceding steps down into smaller steps. We'll start with dataset preparation using the Word2Vec model.

Preparing the train and test set using the Word2Vec model

Now, to prepare the dataset for training and testing, first, we have to download three files, which are outlined as follows:

- A Google-trained Word2Vec model
- A large Movie Review dataset
- A sentiment labeled dataset

The pre-trained Word2Vec is downloaded from `https://code.google.com/p/word2vec/` and then we can set the location for the Google News vectors manually:

```
public static final String WORD_VECTORS_PATH = "/Downloads/GoogleNews-
vectors-negative300.bin.gz";
```

Then, we will download and extract the Large Movie Review dataset from the following URL.

```
public static final String DATA_URL =
"http://ai.stanford.edu/~amaas/data/sentiment/aclImdb_v1.tar.gz";
```

Now, let's set the location to save and extract the training/testing data:

```
public static final String DATA_PATH =
FilenameUtils.concat(System.getProperty("java.io.tmpdir"),
"dl4j_w2vSentiment/");
```

Now, we can either manually download or extract the dataset in our preferred location or, alternatively, the following method does it in an automated way. Note that I have slightly modified the original DL4J implementation:

```
public static void downloadAndExtractData() throws Exception {
    //Create directory if required
    File directory = new File(DATA_PATH);

    if(!directory.exists()) directory.mkdir();
    //Download file:
```

```
String archizePath = DATA_PATH + "aclImdb_v1.tar.gz";
File archiveFile = new File(archizePath);
String extractedPath = DATA_PATH + "aclImdb";
File extractedFile = new File(extractedPath);

if( !archiveFile.exists() ){
   System.out.println("Starting data download (80MB)...");
   FileUtils.copyURLToFile(new URL(DATA_URL), archiveFile);
   System.out.println("Data (.tar.gz file) downloaded to " +
archiveFile.getAbsolutePath());

   //Extract tar.gz file to output directory
   DataUtilities.extractTarGz(archizePath, DATA_PATH);
} else {
   //Assume if archive (.tar.gz) exists, then data has already been
extracted
   System.out.println("Data (.tar.gz file) already exists at " +
archiveFile.getAbsolutePath());

   if( !extractedFile.exists()){
   //Extract tar.gz file to output directory
     DataUtilities.extractTarGz(archizePath, DATA_PATH);
   } else {
     System.out.println("Data (extracted) already exists at " +
extractedFile.getAbsolutePath());
   }
 }
}
```

In the preceding method, download the dataset from the URL I mentioned using HTTP protocol. Then, extract the dataset to the location we mentioned. For this, I have used the `TarArchiveEntry`, `TarArchiveInputStream`, and `GzipCompressorInputStream` utilities from Apache Commons. Interested readers can find more details at http://commons.apache.org/.

In short, I have provided a class named `DataUtilities.java` that has two methods, `downloadFile()` and `extractTarGz()`, that are used for downloading and extracting the dataset.

First, the `downloadFile()` method takes the remote URL (that is, the URL of the remote file) and the local path (that is, where to download the file) as parameters and downloads a remote file if it doesn't exist. Now, let's see what the signature looks like:

```
public static boolean downloadFile(String remoteUrl, String localPath)
throws IOException {
  boolean downloaded = false;
```

```
    if (remoteUrl == null || localPath == null)
        return downloaded;

File file = new File(localPath);
if (!file.exists()) {
    file.getParentFile().mkdirs();
    HttpClientBuilder builder = HttpClientBuilder.create();
    CloseableHttpClient client = builder.build();
    try (CloseableHttpResponse response = client.execute(new
HttpGet(remoteUrl))) {
        HttpEntity entity = response.getEntity();
        if (entity != null) {
            try (FileOutputStream outstream = new FileOutputStream(file)) {
                entity.writeTo(outstream);
                outstream.flush();
                outstream.close();
            }
        }
    }
    downloaded = true;
}
if (!file.exists())
throw new IOException("File doesn't exist: " + localPath);
return downloaded;
}
```

Second, the `extractTarGz()` method takes an input path (the `ism` input file path) and the output path (that is, the output directory path) as parameters and extracts the `tar.gz` file to a local folder. Now, let's see what the signature looks like:

```
public static void extractTarGz(String inputPath, String outputPath) throws
IOException {
    if (inputPath == null || outputPath == null)
        return;

    final int bufferSize = 4096;
    if (!outputPath.endsWith("" + File.separatorChar))
        outputPath = outputPath + File.separatorChar;

    try (TarArchiveInputStream tais = new TarArchiveInputStream(
            new GzipCompressorInputStream(new BufferedInputStream(
                                    new FileInputStream(inputPath))))) {
        TarArchiveEntry entry;
        while ((entry = (TarArchiveEntry) tais.getNextEntry()) != null) {
            if (entry.isDirectory()) {
                new File(outputPath + entry.getName()).mkdirs();
            } else {
```

```
        int count;
        byte data[] = newbyte[bufferSize];
        FileOutputStream fos = new FileOutputStream(outputPath +
entry.getName());
        BufferedOutputStream dest = new BufferedOutputStream(fos,
bufferSize);
        while ((count = tais.read(data, 0, bufferSize)) != -1) {
            dest.write(data, 0, count);
        }
        dest.close();
      }
    }
  }
}
```

Now, to utilize the preceding methods, you have to import the following packages:

```
import org.apache.commons.compress.archivers.tar.TarArchiveEntry;
import org.apache.commons.compress.archivers.tar.TarArchiveInputStream;
import
org.apache.commons.compress.compressors.gzip.GzipCompressorInputStream;
```

 By the way, Apache Commons is an Apache project focused on all aspects of reusable Java components. See more at `https://commons.apache.org/`.

Finally, the sentiment labeled dataset can be downloaded from `https://archive.ics.uci.edu/ml/machine-learning-databases/00331/`. Once you have finished these steps, the next task will be to prepare the training and testing set. For this, I have written a class named `SentimentDatasetIterator`, which is a `DataSetIterator` that is specialized for the IMDb review dataset used in our project. However, this can also be applied to any text dataset for text analytics in NLP. This class is a slight extension of the `SentimentExampleIterator.java` class, which is provided by the DL4J example. Thanks to the DL4J folks for making our life easier.

The `SentimentDatasetIterator` class takes either the train or test set from the sentiment labeled dataset and Google pre-trained Word2Vec and generates training data sets. On the other hand, a single class (negative or positive) is used as the label to predict the final time step of each review. Additionally, since we are dealing with reviews of different lengths and only one output at the final time step, we use padding arrays. In short, our training dataset should contain the following items, that is, the 4D object:

- Features from each review text
- Labels in either 1 or 0 (that is, for positive and negative, respectively)
- Feature masks
- Label masks

So, let's get started with the following constructor, which is used for the following purposes:

```java
private final WordVectors wordVectors;
private final int batchSize;
private final int vectorSize;
private final int truncateLength;
private int cursor = 0;
private final File[] positiveFiles;
private final File[] negativeFiles;
private final TokenizerFactory tokenizerFactory;

public SentimentDatasetIterator(String dataDirectory, WordVectors wordVectors,
                                int batchSize, int truncateLength, boolean train) throws IOException {
  this.batchSize = batchSize;
  this.vectorSize =
wordVectors.getWordVector(wordVectors.vocab().wordAtIndex(0)).length;
  File p = new File(FilenameUtils.concat(dataDirectory, "aclImdb/" + (train
? "train" : "test")
                                          + "/pos/") + "/");
  File n = new File(FilenameUtils.concat(dataDirectory, "aclImdb/" + (train
? "train" : "test")
                                          + "/neg/") + "/");
  positiveFiles = p.listFiles();
  negativeFiles = n.listFiles();

  this.wordVectors = wordVectors;
  this.truncateLength = truncateLength;
  tokenizerFactory = new DefaultTokenizerFactory();
  tokenizerFactory.setTokenPreProcessor(new CommonPreprocessor());
}
```

In the preceding signature of the constructor, we used the following purposes:

- To keep track of the positive and negative review files in the directory of the IMDb review data set
- To tokenize the review texts to words with stop words and unknown words removed
- If the longest review exceeds truncateLength, only take the first truncateLength words
- Word2Vec object
- The batch size, which is the size of each minibatch for training

Once initialization is complete, we load each review test as a string. Then, we alternate between positive and negative reviews:

```
List<String> reviews = new ArrayList<>(num);
boolean[] positive = newboolean[num];

for(int i=0; i<num && cursor<totalExamples(); i++ ){
  if(cursor % 2 == 0){
    //Load positive review
    int posReviewNumber = cursor / 2;
    String review =
FileUtils.readFileToString(positiveFiles[posReviewNumber]);
    reviews.add(review);
    positive[i] = true;
  } else {
    //Load negative review
    int negReviewNumber = cursor / 2;
    String review =
FileUtils.readFileToString(negativeFiles[negReviewNumber]);
    reviews.add(review);
    positive[i] = false;
  }
  cursor++;
}
```

Then, we tokenize the reviews and filter out unknown words (that is, words that are not included in the pre-trained Word2Vec model, for example, stop words):

```
List<List<String>> allTokens = new ArrayList<>(reviews.size());
int maxLength = 0;

for(String s : reviews){
  List<String> tokens = tokenizerFactory.create(s).getTokens();
  List<String> tokensFiltered = new ArrayList<>();
```

```
for(String t : tokens ){
    if(wordVectors.hasWord(t)) tokensFiltered.add(t);
}
allTokens.add(tokensFiltered);
maxLength = Math.max(maxLength,tokensFiltered.size());
}
```

Then, if the longest review exceeds the threshold `truncateLength`, we only take the first `truncateLength` words:

```
if(maxLength > truncateLength)
    maxLength = truncateLength;
```

Then, we create data for training. Here, we have `reviews.size()` examples of varying lengths since we have two labels, positive or negative:

```
INDArray features = Nd4j.create(newint[]{reviews.size(), vectorSize,
maxLength}, 'f');
INDArray labels = Nd4j.create(newint[]{reviews.size(), 2, maxLength}, 'f');
```

Now that we are dealing with reviews of different lengths and only one output at the final time step, we use padding arrays, where the mask arrays contain 1 if data is present at that time step for that example, or 0 if the data is just padding:

```
INDArray featuresMask = Nd4j.zeros(reviews.size(), maxLength);
INDArray labelsMask = Nd4j.zeros(reviews.size(), maxLength);
```

It is to be noted that creating the mask arrays for the features and labels are optional and may be null too. Then, we get the truncated sequence length of the ith document, obtain all the word vectors for the current document, and transpose them to fit the second and third feature shape.

Once we have the word vectors ready, we put them into the features array at three indices, which is equal to `NDArrayIndex.interval(0, vectorSize)` having all elements between 0 and the length of the current sequence. Then, we assign 1 to each position where a feature is present, that is, at the interval of 0 and the sequence length.

Now, when it comes to label encoding, we set [0, 1] for a negative review text and [1, 0] for a positive review text. Finally, we specify that an output exists at the final time step for this example:

```
for( int i=0; i<reviews.size(); i++ ){
    List<String> tokens = allTokens.get(i);
    int seqLength = Math.min(tokens.size(), maxLength);
    final INDArray vectors = wordVectors.getWordVectors(tokens.subList(0,
seqLength)).transpose();
```

```
    features.put(new INDArrayIndex[] {
        NDArrayIndex.point(i), NDArrayIndex.all(), NDArrayIndex.interval(0,
seqLength)
        }, vectors);

    featuresMask.get(new INDArrayIndex[] {NDArrayIndex.point(i),
NDArrayIndex.interval(0,
                    seqLength)}).assign(1);
    int idx = (positive[i] ? 0 : 1);
    int lastIdx = Math.min(tokens.size(),maxLength);

    labels.putScalar(newint[]{i,idx,lastIdx-1},1.0);
    labelsMask.putScalar(newint[]{i,lastIdx-1},1.0);
}
```

Note that the main problem hindering dropout in NLP has been that it could not be applied to recurrent connections, as the aggregating dropout masks would effectively zero out embeddings over time—hence, feature masking has been used in the preceding code block.

Now, up to this point, all the required elements are prepared so finally, we return the dataset as an NDArray (that is, 4D) containing the features, labels, featuresMask, and labelsMask:

```
return new DataSet(features,labels,featuresMask,labelsMask);
```

More elaborately, using DataSet, we will create a dataset with the specified input INDArray and labels (output) INDArray, and (optionally) mask arrays for the features and labels.

Finally, our training set will be at hand using the following invocation:

```
SentimentDatasetIterator train = new SentimentDatasetIterator(DATA_PATH,
wordVectors,
                                                batchSize,
truncateReviewsToLength, true);
```

Fantastic! Now we can create our neural networks by specifying the layers and hyperparameters in the next step.

Network construction, training, and saving the model

As discussed in the Titanic survival prediction section, again, everything starts with `MultiLayerConfiguration`, which organizes those layers and their hyperparameters. Our LSTM network consists of five layers. The input layer is followed by three LSTM layers. Then, the last layer is an RNN layer, which is also the output layer.

More technically, the first layer is the input layer, and then three layers are placed as LSTM layers. For the LSTM layers, we initialize the weights using Xavier, we use SGD as the optimization algorithm with the Adam updater, and we use Tanh as the activation function. Finally, the RNN output layer has a softmax activation function that gives us a probability distribution over classes (that is, it outputs the sum to 1.0) and MCXENT, which is the multiclass cross entropy loss function.

For creating LSTM layers, DL4J provides both LSTM and `GravesLSTM` classes. The latter is an LSTM recurrent net, which is based on Graves, but comes up without CUDA support: supervised sequence labelling with RNN (see more at `http://www.cs.toronto.edu/~graves/phd.pdf`). Now, before we start creating the network, first let's define the required hyperparameters such as the number of input/hidden/output nodes (that is, neurons):

```
// Network hyperparameters: Truncate reviews with length greater than this
static int truncateReviewsToLength = 30;
static int numEpochs = 10; // number of training epochs
static int batchSize = 64; //Number of examples in each minibatch
static int vectorSize = 300; //Size of word vectors in Google Word2Vec
static int seed = 12345; //Seed for reproducibility
static int numClasses = 2; // number of classes to be predicted
static int numHiddenNodes = 256;
```

We will now create a network configuration and conduct network training. With DL4J, you add a layer by calling a layer on the `NeuralNetConfiguration.Builder()`, specifying its place in the order of layers (the zero-indexed layer in the following code is the input layer):

```
MultiLayerConfiguration LSTMconf = new NeuralNetConfiguration.Builder()
    .seed(seed)
    .updater(new Adam(1e-8)) // Gradient updater with Adam
    .l2(1e-5) // L2 regularization coefficient for weights
    .optimizationAlgo(OptimizationAlgorithm.STOCHASTIC_GRADIENT_DESCENT)
    .weightInit(WeightInit.XAVIER)
.gradientNormalization(GradientNormalization.ClipElementWiseAbsoluteValue)
    .gradientNormalizationThreshold(1.0)
.trainingWorkspaceMode(WorkspaceMode.SEPARATE).inferenceWorkspaceMode(WorkspaceMode.SEPARATE)
```

```
.list()
.layer(0, new LSTM.Builder()
        .nIn(vectorSize)
        .nOut(numHiddenNodes)
        .activation(Activation.TANH)
        .build())
.layer(1, new LSTM.Builder()
        .nIn(numHiddenNodes)
        .nOut(numHiddenNodes)
        .activation(Activation.TANH)
        .build())
.layer(2, new RnnOutputLayer.Builder()
        .activation(Activation.SOFTMAX)
        .lossFunction(LossFunction.XENT)
        .nIn(numHiddenNodes)
        .nOut(numClasses)
        .build())
.pretrain(false).backprop(true).build();
```

Finally, we also specify that we do not need to do any pre-training (which is typically needed in a deep belief network or stacked auto-encoders). Then, we initialize the network and start the training on the training set:

```
MultiLayerNetwork model = new MultiLayerNetwork(LSTMconf);
model.init();
```

Typically, this type of network has lots of hyperparameters. Let's print the number of parameters in the network (and for each layer):

```
Layer[] layers = model.getLayers();
int totalNumParams = 0;
for(int i=0; i<layers.length; i++ ){
  int nParams = layers[i].numParams();
  System.out.println("Number of parameters in layer " + i + ": " +
nParams);
  totalNumParams += nParams;
}
System.out.println("Total number of network parameters: " +
totalNumParams);
```

>>
Number of parameters in layer 0: 570,368
Number of parameters in layer 1: 525,312
Number of parameters in layer 2: 514
Total number of network parameters: 1,096,194

As I said, our network has 1 million parameters, which is huge. This also imposes a great challenge while tuning hyperparameters. However, we will see some tricks in the FAQ section.

```
MultiLayerNetwork net = new MultiLayerNetwork(LSTMconf);
net.init();
net.setListeners(new ScoreIterationListener(1));
for (int i = 0; i < numEpochs; i++) {
  net.fit(train);
  train.reset();
  System.out.println("Epoch " + (i+1) + " finished ...");
}
System.out.println("Training has been completed");
```

Once the training has been completed, we can save the trained model for model persistence and subsequent reuse. For that, DL4J provides support for the trained model sterilization using the writeModel() method from the ModelSerializer class. Additionally, it provides the functionality for restoring the saved model using the restoreMultiLayerNetwork() method.

We will see more in the following step. Nevertheless, we can also save the network updater too, that is, the state for momentum, RMSProp, Adagrad, and so on:

```
File locationToSave = new File(modelPath); //location and file format
boolean saveUpdater = true; // we save the network updater too
ModelSerializer.writeModel(net, locationToSave, saveUpdater);
```

Restoring the trained model and evaluating it on the test set

Once the training has been completed, the next task will be to evaluate the model. We will evaluate the model's performance on the test set. For the evaluation, we will be using Evaluation(), which creates an evaluation object with two possible classes.

First, let's iterate the evaluation on every test sample and get the network's prediction from the trained model. Finally, the eval() method checks the prediction against the true class:

```
public static void networkEvaluator() throws Exception {
        System.out.println("Starting the evaluation ...");
        boolean saveUpdater = true;

        //Load the model
        MultiLayerNetwork restoredModel =
```

```
ModelSerializer.restoreMultiLayerNetwork(modelPath, saveUpdater);
    //WordVectors wordVectors = getWord2Vec();
    SentimentDatasetIterator test = new
SentimentDatasetIterator(DATA_PATH, wordVectors, batchSize,
truncateReviewsToLength, false);
    Evaluation evaluation = restoredModel.evaluate(test);
    System.out.println(evaluation.stats());
    System.out.println("----- Evaluation completed! -----");
}
```

>>>

```
=======================Scores=======================
# of classes: 2
Accuracy: 0.8632
Precision: 0.8632
Recall: 0.8632
F1 Score: 0.8634
Precision, recall, and F1: Reported for positive class (class 1 -"negative") only
=====================================================
```

The predictive accuracy for the sentiment analysis using LSTM is about 87%, which is good considering that we have not focused on hyperparameter tuning! Now, let's see how the classifier predicts across each class:

Predictions labeled as positive classified by model as positive: 10,777 times
Predictions labeled as positive classified by model as negative: 1,723 times
Predictions labeled as negative classified by model as positive: 1,696 times
Predictions labeled as negative classified by model as negative: 10,804 times

Similar to `Chapter 2`, *Cancer Types Prediction Using Recurrent Type Networks*, we will now compute another metric called Matthews's correlation coefficient for this binary classification problem:

```
// Compute Matthews correlation coefficient
EvaluationAveraging averaging = EvaluationAveraging.Macro;
double MCC = eval.matthewsCorrelation(averaging);
System.out.println("Matthews correlation coefficient: "+ MCC);
```

>>

Matthews's correlation coefficient: 0.22308172619187497

This shows a weakly positive relationship, showing that our model performs quite well. Up next, we will use the trained model for inferencing, that is, we will perform predictions on sample review texts.

Making predictions on sample review texts

Now, let's take a look at how our trained model generalizes, that is, how it performs on unseen review texts from the sentiment labeled sentences dataset. First, we need to restore the trained model from the disk:

```
System.out.println("Starting the evaluation on sample texts ...");
boolean saveUpdater = true;

MultiLayerNetwork restoredModel =
ModelSerializer.restoreMultiLayerNetwork(modelPath, saveUpdater);
SentimentDatasetIterator test = new SentimentDatasetIterator(DATA_PATH,
wordvectors, batchSize,
truncateReviewsToLength, false);
```

Now, we can randomly extract two review texts from IMDb, Amazon, and Yelp, where the first one expresses a positive sentiment, and the second one expresses a negative sentiment (according to the known labels). Then, we can create a HashMap containing both the review strings and labels:

```
String IMDb_PositiveReview = "Not only did it only confirm that the film
would be unfunny and generic, but
                            it also managed to give away the ENTIRE
movie; and I'm not exaggerating -
                            every moment, every plot point, every joke is
told in the trailer";

String IMDb_NegativeReview = "One character is totally annoying with a
voice that gives me the feeling of
                            fingernails on a chalkboard.";

String Amazon_PositiveReview = "This phone is very fast with sending any
kind of messages and web browsing
                            is significantly faster than previous
phones i have used";

String Amazon_NegativeReview = "The one big drawback of the MP3 player is
that the buttons on the phone's
                            front cover that let you pause and skip songs
lock out after a few seconds.";

String Yelp_PositiveReview = "My side Greek salad with the Greek dressing
was so tasty, and the pita and
                            hummus was very refreshing.";

String Yelp_NegativeReview = "Hard to judge whether these sides were good
because we were grossed out by
```

```
                                the melted styrofoam and didn't want to eat
it for fear of getting sick.";
```

Then, we create an array of the preceding strings:

```
String[] reviews = {IMDb_PositiveReview, IMDb_NegativeReview,
Amazon_PositiveReview,
                    Amazon_NegativeReview, Yelp_PositiveReview,
Yelp_NegativeReview};

String[] sentiments = {"Positive", "Negative", "Positive", "Negative",
"Positive", "Negative"};
Map<String, String> reviewMap = new HashMap<String, String>();

reviewMap.put(reviews[0], sentiments[0]);
reviewMap.put(reviews[1], sentiments[1]);
reviewMap.put(reviews[2], sentiments[2]);
reviewMap.put(reviews[3], sentiments[3]);
```

Then, we iterate over the map and do the sample evaluation using the pre-trained model as follows:

```
System.out.println("Starting the evaluation on sample texts ...");
for (Map.Entry<String, String> entry : reviewMap.entrySet()) {
        String text = entry.getKey();
        String label = entry.getValue();
        INDArray features = test.loadFeaturesFromString(text,
truncateReviewsToLength);
        INDArray networkOutput = restoredModel.output(features);
        int timeSeriesLength = networkOutput.size(2);
        INDArray probabilitiesAtLastWord =
networkOutput.get(NDArrayIndex.point(0),
                        NDArrayIndex.all(),
NDArrayIndex.point(timeSeriesLength - 1));

        System.out.println("-------------------------------");
        System.out.println("\n\nProbabilities at last time step: ");
        System.out.println("p(positive): " +
probabilitiesAtLastWord.getDouble(0));
        System.out.println("p(negative): " +
probabilitiesAtLastWord.getDouble(1));

        Boolean flag = false;
        if(probabilitiesAtLastWord.getDouble(0) >
probabilitiesAtLastWord.getDouble(1))
            flag = true;
        else
            flag = false;
```

```
            if (flag == true) {
                System.out.println("The text express a positive sentiment,
        actually it is " + label);
            } else {
                System.out.println("The text express a negative sentiment,
        actually it is " + label);
            }
        }
        System.out.println("----- Sample evaluation completed! -----");
    }
```

If you look at the preceding code block carefully, you can see that we converted each review text as a time series by extracting features. Then, we computed the network output (that is, probability). Then, we compare the probability, that is, if the probability is that of it being a positive sentiment, we set a flag as true, or false otherwise. This way, we then take a decision on the final class prediction.

We have also utilized the `loadFeaturesFromString()` method in the preceding code block, which converts a review string to features in `INDArray` format. It takes two parameters, `reviewContents`, which is the content of the review to vectorize, and `maxLength`, which is the maximum length of the review text. Finally, it returns a `features` array for the given input string:

```
public INDArray loadFeaturesFromString(String reviewContents, int
maxLength){
        List<String> tokens =
tokenizerFactory.create(reviewContents).getTokens();
        List<String> tokensFiltered = new ArrayList<>();
        for(String t : tokens ){
            if(wordVectors.hasWord(t)) tokensFiltered.add(t);
        }
        int outputLength = Math.max(maxLength,tokensFiltered.size());
        INDArray features = Nd4j.create(1, vectorSize, outputLength);

        for(int j=0; j<tokens.size() && j<maxLength; j++ ){
            String token = tokens.get(j);
            INDArray vector = wordVectors.getWordVectorMatrix(token);
            features.put(new INDArrayIndex[]{NDArrayIndex.point(0),
                    NDArrayIndex.all(), NDArrayIndex.point(j)},
vector);
        }
        return features;
    }
```

If you don't want to truncate, simply use `Integer.MAX_VALUE`.

Now, let's go back to our original discussion. Hilariously, we made it more human, that is, without utilizing an activation function. Finally, we print the result for each review text and its associated label:

```
>
Probabilities at last time step:
 p(positive): 0.003569001331925392
 p(negative): 0.9964309930801392
 The text express a negative sentiment, actually, it is Positive

p(positive): 0.003569058608263731
 p(negative): 0.9964308738708496
 The text express a negative sentiment, actually, it is Negative
 --------------------------------
 Probabilities at last time step:
 p(positive): 0.003569077467545867
 p(negative): 0.9964308738708496
 The text express a negative sentiment, actually, it is Negative

p(positive): 0.003569045104086399
 p(negative): 0.9964308738708496
 The text express a negative sentiment, actually, it is Positive
 --------------------------------
 Probabilities at last time step:
 p(positive): 0.003570008557289839
 p(negative): 0.996429979801178
 The text express a negative sentiment, actually, it is Positive

p(positive): 0.0035690285731106997
 p(negative): 0.9964309930801392
 The text express a negative sentiment, actually, it is Negative

----- Sample evaluation completed! -----
```

So, our trained model has made 50% incorrect predictions, especially since it always predicts a positive review as a negative. In short, it is not that good at generalizing to unknown texts, which can be seen with an accuracy of 50%.

Now, a stupid question might come to mind. Did our network underfit? Is there any way to observe how the training went? In other words, the question would be: Why didn't our LSTM net neural show higher accuracy? We will try to answer these questions in the next section. So stay with me!

Frequently asked questions (FAQs)

Now that we have solved the sentiment analysis problem with an acceptable level of accuracy, there are other practical aspects of this problem and overall deep learning phenomena that need to be considered too. In this section, we will see some frequently asked questions that might already be on your mind. Answers to these questions can be found in Appendix A:

1. I understand that the predictive accuracy of sentiment analysis using LSTM is still reasonable. However, it does not perform well on the Sentiment labeled dataset. Did our network overfit? Is there any way to observe how the training went?
2. Considering a huge number of review texts, can we perform the training on the GPU?
3. In relation to question 2, can we even undertake the whole process using Spark?
4. Where can I get more training datasets for sentiment analysis?
5. Instead of downloading the training data in `.zip` format manually, can we use the `extractTarGz()` method?
6. My machine has limited memory. Give me a clue as to how memory management and garbage collection work in DL4J.

Summary

In this chapter, we have seen how to implement and deploy a hands-on deep learning project that classifies review texts as either positive or negative based on the words they contain. We have used a large-scale movie review dataset that contains 50,000 reviews (training plus testing). A combined approach using Word2Vec (that is, a widely used word embedding technique in NLP) and the LSTM network for modeling was applied: the pre-trained Google news vector model was used as the neural word embeddings.

Then, the training vectors, along with the labels, were fed into the LSTM network, which successfully classified them as negative or positive sentiments. Then, it evaluated the trained model on the test set. Additionally, we have also seen how to apply text-based preprocessing techniques such as tokenizer, stop words removal and TF-IDF, as well as word-embedding operations in DL4J.

In the next chapter, we will see a complete example of how to develop a deep learning project to classify images using the DL4J transfer learning API. Through this application, users will be able to modify the architecture of an existing model, fine-tune learning configurations of an existing model, and hold parameters of a specified layer constantly during training, which is also referred to as frozen.

Answers to questions

Answer to question 1: We have seen that our trained model performs pretty well on the test set with an accuracy of 87%. Now, if we see the model versus iteration score and other parameters from the following graph, then we can see that our model was not overfitted:

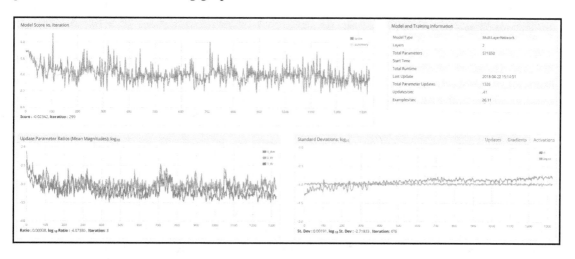

Model versus iteration score and other parameters of the LSTM sentiment analyzer

Now, for the sentiment labeled sentences, the trained model did not perform well. There could be several reasons for that. For example, our model is trained with only the movie review dataset, but here, we try to force our model to perform on different types of datasets too, for example, Amazon and Yelp. Nevertheless, we have not tuned the hyperparameters carefully.

Answer to question 2: Yes, in fact, this will be very helpful. For this, we have to make sure that our programming environment is ready. In other words, first, we have to configure CUDA and cuDNN on our machine.

However, make sure that your machine has a NVIDIA GPU installed and configured with sufficient memory and CUDA compute capability. If you do not know how to configure such prerequisites, refer to this URL at `https://docs.nvidia.com/deeplearning/sdk/cudnn-install/`. Once your machine has CUDA/cuDNN installed, in the `pom.xml` file, you have to add two entries:

- Backend in the project properties
- CUDA as the platform dependency

For step 1, the properties should now look as follows:

```
<properties>
        <project.build.sourceEncoding>UTF-8</project.build.sourceEncoding>
        <java.version>1.8</java.version>
        <nd4j.backend>nd4j-cuda-9.0-platform</nd4j.backend>
        <nd4j.version>1.0.0-alpha</nd4j.version>
        <dl4j.version>1.0.0-alpha</dl4j.version>
        <datavec.version>1.0.0-alpha</datavec.version>
        <arbiter.version>1.0.0-alpha</arbiter.version>
        <logback.version>1.2.3</logback.version>
</properties>
```

Now, for step 2, add the following dependency in the `pop.xml` file (that is, inside the dependencies tag):

```
<dependency>
        <groupId>org.nd4j</groupId>
        <artifactId>nd4j-cuda-9.0-platform</artifactId>
        <version>${nd4j.version}</version>
</dependency>
```

Then, update the Maven project, and the required dependencies will be downloaded automatically. Now, unless we perform the training on multiple GPUs, we do not need to make any changes. However, just run the same script again to perform the training. Then, you will experience the following logs on the console:

```
17:03:55.317 [main] INFO org.nd4j.linalg.factory.Nd4jBackend - Loaded
[JCublasBackend] backend
 17:03:55.360 [main] WARN org.reflections.Reflections - given scan urls are
empty. set urls in the configuration
 17:04:06.410 [main] INFO org.nd4j.nativeblas.NativeOpsHolder - Number of
threads used for NativeOps: 32
```

```
17:04:08.118 [main] DEBUG org.nd4j.jita.concurrency.CudaAffinityManager -
Manually mapping thread [18] to device [0], out of [1] devices...
17:04:08.119 [main] DEBUG org.nd4j.jita.concurrency.CudaAffinityManager -
Manually mapping thread [19] to device [0], out of [1] devices...
17:04:08.119 [main] DEBUG org.nd4j.jita.concurrency.CudaAffinityManager -
Manually mapping thread [20] to device [0], out of [1] devices...
17:04:08.119 [main] DEBUG org.nd4j.jita.concurrency.CudaAffinityManager -
Manually mapping thread [21] to device [0], out of [1] devices...
17:04:08.119 [main] DEBUG org.nd4j.jita.concurrency.CudaAffinityManager -
Manually mapping thread [22] to device [0], out of [1] devices...
17:04:08.119 [main] DEBUG org.nd4j.jita.concurrency.CudaAffinityManager -
Manually mapping thread [23] to device [0], out of [1] devices...
17:04:08.123 [main] INFO org.nd4j.nativeblas.Nd4jBlas - Number of threads
used for BLAS: 0
17:04:08.127 [main] INFO
org.nd4j.linalg.api.ops.executioner.DefaultOpExecutioner - Backend used:
[CUDA]; OS: [Windows 10]
17:04:08.127 [main] INFO
org.nd4j.linalg.api.ops.executioner.DefaultOpExecutioner - Cores: [8];
Memory: [7.0GB];
17:04:08.127 [main] INFO
org.nd4j.linalg.api.ops.executioner.DefaultOpExecutioner - Blas vendor:
[CUBLAS]
17:04:08.127 [main] INFO
org.nd4j.linalg.jcublas.ops.executioner.CudaExecutioner - Device opName:
[GeForce GTX 1050]; CC: [6.1]; Total/free memory: [4294967296]
```

Nevertheless, in Chapter 8, *Distributed Deep Learning – Video Classification Using Convolutional LSTM Networks*, we will see how to make everything faster and scalable overall on multiple GPUs.

Aswer to question 3: Yes, in fact, this will be very helpful. For this, we have to make sure that our programming environment is ready. In other words, first, we have to configure Spark on our machine. Once your machine has CUDA/cuDNN installed, we just want to configure Spark. In the pom.xml file, you have to add two entries:

- Backend in the project properties
- Spark dependency

For step 1, the properties should now look as follows:

```
<properties>
        <project.build.sourceEncoding>UTF-8</project.build.sourceEncoding>
        <java.version>1.8</java.version>
        <nd4j.backend>nd4j-cuda-9.0-platform</nd4j.backend>
        <nd4j.version>1.0.0-alpha</nd4j.version>
        <dl4j.version>1.0.0-alpha</dl4j.version>
        <datavec.version>1.0.0-alpha</datavec.version>
        <arbiter.version>1.0.0-alpha</arbiter.version>
        <dl4j.spark.version>1.0.0-alpha_spark_2</dl4j.spark.version>
        <logback.version>1.2.3</logback.version>
</properties>
```

Now, for step 2, add the following dependency in the pop.xml file (that is, inside the dependencies tag):

```
<dependency>
        <groupId>org.deeplearning4j</groupId>
        <artifactId>dl4j-spark_2.11</artifactId>
        <version>1.0.0-alpha_spark_2</version>
</dependency>
```

Then, update the Maven project, and the required dependencies will be downloaded automatically. Now, unless we perform the training on multiple GPUs, we do not need to make any changes. However, we need to convert the training/testing dataset into a Spark-compatible JavaRDD.

I have written all of the steps in the SentimentAnalyzerSparkGPU.java file that can be used to see how the overall steps work. A general warning is that if you perform the training on Spark, the DL4J UI will not work because of cross-dependencies on the Jackson library. For that, we must first create the JavaSparkContext using the sparkSession() method as follows:

```
public static JavaSparkContext spark;
static int batchSizePerWorker = 16;

public static JavaSparkContext getJavaSparkContext () {
                SparkConf sparkConf = new SparkConf();
                sparkConf.set ("spark.locality.wait", "0");
                sparkConf.setMaster ("local[*]").setAppName ("DL4J
Spark");

                spak = new JavaSparkContext (sparkConf);
                return spark;
}
```

Then, we have to convert the sentiment training dataset iterator to JavaRDD of the dataset. First, we create a list of datasets and then add each training sample to the list as follows:

```
List<DataSet> trainDataList = new ArrayList<>();
while(train.hasNext()) {
        trainDataList.add(train.next());
    }
```

Then, we create a `JavaSparkContext` by invoking the `sparkSession()` method as follows:

```
spark = createJavaSparkContext();
```

Finally, we utilize the `parallelize()` method of Spark to create the JavaRDD of the dataset, which can then be used to perform the training using Spark:

```
JavaRDD<DataSet> trainData = spark.parallelize(trainDataList);
```

Then, the Spark `TrainingMaster` uses the `ParameterAveragingTrainingMaster`, which helps perform the training using Spark. Please refer to Chapter 8, *Distributed Deep Learning – Video Classification Using Convolutional LSTM Networks*, for more details:

```
TrainingMaster<?, ?> tm = (TrainingMaster<?, ?>) new
ParameterAveragingTrainingMaster
            .Builder(batchSizePerWorker)
            .averagingFrequency(5).workerPrefetchNumBatches(2)
            .batchSizePerWorker(batchSizePerWorker).build();
```

Then, we create the `SparkDl4jMultiLayer` instead of just the `MultilayerNetwork` as we did previously:

```
SparkDl4jMultiLayer sparkNet = new SparkDl4jMultiLayer(spark, LSTMconf,
tm);
```

Then, we create a training listener that records the score of each iteration as follows:

```
sparkNet.setListeners(Collections.<IterationListener>singletonList(new
ScoreIterationListener(1)));
sparkNet.setListeners(new ScoreIterationListener(1));
```

Finally, we start the training as follows:

```
for (int i = 0; i < numEpochs; i++) {
        sparkNet.fit(trainData);
        System.out.println("Epoch " + (i+1) + " has been finished ...");
    }
```

However, using this approach, there is a drawback, that is, we cannot save the trained model directly like this but first, we have to fit the network using the training data and collect the output as the `MultiLayerNetwork` as follows:

```
MultiLayerNetwork outputNetwork = sparkNet.fit(trainData);

//Save the model
File locationToSave = new File(modelPath);

boolean saveUpdater = true;
ModelSerializer.writeModel(outputNetwork, locationToSave, saveUpdater);
```

Answer to question 4: There are many sources where you can get a sentiment analysis dataset. A few of them are listed here:

- The huge n-grams dataset from Google:
  storage.googleapis.com/books/ngrams/books/datasetsv2.html
- Twitter sentiment: http://www.sananalytics.com/lab/twitter-sentiment/
- UMICH SI650—sentiment classification dataset on Kaggle: http://inclass.kaggle.com/c/si650winter11/data
- Multi-domain sentiment dataset: http://www.cs.jhu.edu/~mdredze/datasets/sentiment/

Answer to question 5: The answer is no, but with a little effort we can make it work. For that, we can use the `ZipArchiveInputStream` and `GzipCompressorInputStream` classes from Apache commons as follows:

```
public static void extractZipFile(String inputPath, String outputPath)
            throws IOException {
            if (inputPath == null || outputPath == null)
                    return;
            final int bufferSize = 4096;
            if (!outputPath.endsWith("" + File.separatorChar))
                    outputPath = outputPath + File.separatorChar;
            try (ZipArchiveInputStream tais = new
ZipArchiveInputStream(new
                    GzipCompressorInputStream(
                    new BufferedInputStream(new
FileInputStream(inputPath))))) {
                    ZipArchiveEntry entry;
                    while ((entry = (ZipArchiveEntry)
tais.getNextEntry()) != null) {
                            if (entry.isDirectory()) {
                                    new File(outputPath +
entry.getName()).mkdirs();
```

```
                              } else {
                              int count;
                              byte data[] = newbyte[bufferSize];
                              FileOutputStream fos = new
FileOutputStream(outputPath + entry.getName());
                              BufferedOutputStream dest = new
BufferedOutputStream(fos, bufferSize);
                              while ((count = tais.read(data, 0,
bufferSize)) != -1) {
                                      dest.write(data, 0, count);
                                      }
                              dest.close();
                          }
                      }
                  }
      }
```

Answer to question 6: Well, this is really only a concern if your machine doesn't have enough memory. For this application, I did not face any OOP type issue while running this project as my laptop has 32 GB of RAM.

Apart from this step, we can also choose DL4J garbage collection, especially because memory is constrained on your end. DL4J provides a method called getMemoryManager() that returns a backend-specific MemoryManager implementation for low-level memory management. Additionally, we have to enable the periodic System.gc() calls with the windowsills minimal time in milliseconds between calls. Let's see an example:

```
Nd4j.getMemoryManager().setAutoGcWindow(10000); // min 10s between calls
```

However, simply set windowMillis to 0 to disable this option.

Transfer Learning for Image Classification

5

In Chapter 3, *Multi-Label Image Classification using Convolutional Neural Networks*, we saw how to develop an end-to-end project for handling multi-label image classification problems using CNN based on Java and the **Deeplearning4J** (**DL4J**) framework on real Yelp image datasets. For that purpose, we developed a CNN model from scratch.

Unfortunately, developing such a model from scratch is very time consuming and requires a significant amount of computational resources. Secondly, sometimes, we may not even have enough data to train such deep networks. For example, ImageNet is one of the largest image datasets at the moment and has millions of labeled images.

Therefore, we will develop an end-to-end project to solve dog versus cat image classification using a pretrained VGG-16 model, which is already trained with ImageNet. In the end, we will wrap up everything in a Java JFrame and JPanel application to make the overall pipeline understandable. Concisely, we will learn the following topics throughout an end-to-end project:

- Transfer learning for image classification
- Developing an image classifier using transfer learning
- Dataset collection and description
- Developing a dog versus cat detector UI
- **Frequently Asked Questions** (**FAQs**)

Image classification with pretrained VGG16

One of the most useful and emerging applications in the ML domain nowadays is using the transfer learning technique; it provides high portability between different frameworks and platforms.

Once you've trained a neural network, what you get is a set of trained hyperparameters' values. For example, **LeNet-5** has 60k parameter values, **AlexNet** has 60 million, and **VGG-16** has about 138 million parameters. These architectures are trained using anything from 1,000 to millions of images and typically have very deep architectures, having hundreds of layers that contribute toward so many hyperparameters.

There are many open source community guys or even tech giants who have made those pretrained models publicly available for research (and also industry) so that they can be restored and reused to solve similar problems. For example, suppose we want to classify new images into one of 1,000 classes in the case of AlexNet and 10 for LeNet-5. We typically do not need to deal with so many parameters but only a few selected ones (we will see an example soon).

In short, we do not need to train such a deep network from scratch, but we reuse the existing pre-trained model; still, we manage to achieve acceptable classification accuracy. More technically, we can use the weights of that pre-trained model as a feature extractor, or we can just initialize our architecture with it and then fine-tune them to our new task.

In this regard, while using the TL technique to solve your own problem, there might be three options available:

- **Use a Deep CNN as a fixed feature extractor**: We can reuse a pre-trained ImageNet having a fully connected layer by removing the output layer if we are no longer interested in the 1,000 categories it has. This way, we can treat all other layers, as a feature extractor. Even once you have extracted the features using the pre-trained model, you can feed these features to any linear classifier, such as the softmax classifier, or even linear SVM!
- **Fine-tune the Deep CNN**: Trying to fine-tune the whole network, or even most of the layers, may result in overfitting. Therefore, with some extra effort to fine-tune the pre-trained weights on your new task using backpropagation.
- **Reuse pre-trained models with checkpointing**: The third widely used scenario is to download checkpoints that people have made available on the internet. You may go for this scenario if you do not have big computational power to train the model from scratch, so you just initialize the model with the released checkpoints and then do a little fine-tuning.

Now at this point, you may have an interesting question come to mind: what is the difference between traditional ML and ML using transfer learning? Well, in traditional ML, you do not transfer any knowledge or representations to any other task, which is not the case in transfer learning.

Unlike traditional machine learning, the source and target task or domains do not have to come from the same distribution, but they have to be similar. Moreover, you can use transfer learning in case of fewer training samples or if you do not have the necessary computational power.

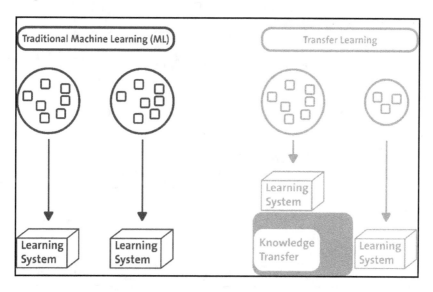

Traditional machine learning versus transfer learning

DL4J and transfer learning

Now, let's take a look how the DL4J provides us with these functionalities through the transfer learning API it has. The DL4J transfer learning API enables users to (see more at `https://deeplearning4j.org/transfer-learning`):

- Modify the architecture of an existing model
- Fine-tune learning configurations of an existing model
- Hold parameters of a specified layer (also called a **frozen layer**) constant during training

These functionalities are depicted in the following diagram, where we solve task B (similar to task A) using the transfer learning technique:

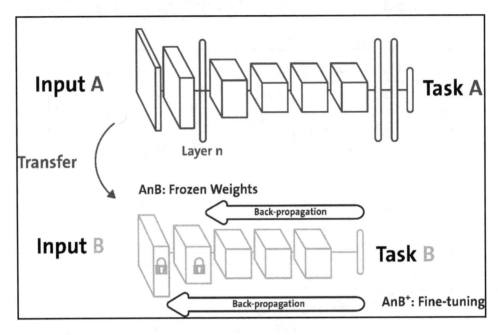

Working principle of transfer learning

In the next section, we will provide more insights into how to use such a pretrained model with DL4J to help us in transfer learning.

Developing an image classifier using transfer learning

In the next section, we will see how to distinguish between dogs and cats based on their raw images. We will also see how to implement our first CNN model to deal with the raw and color image having three channels.

This project is highly inspired (but extended significantly) by the "Java Image Cat&Dog Recognition with Deep Neural Networks" article by Klevis Ramo (http://ramok.tech/).

The `code` folder has three packages with a few Java files in each. Their functionalities are outlined as follows:

- `com.packt.JavaDL.DogvCatClassification.Train`:
  - `TrainCatvsDogVG16.java`: It is used to train the network and the trained model is saved to a user specific location. Finally, it prints the results.
  - `PetType.java`: Contains an `enum` type that specifies pet types (that is, cat, dog, and unknown).
  - `VG16CatvDogEvaluator.java`: Restores the trained model saved in a specified location by the `TrainCatvsDogVG16.java` class. Then it evaluates on both test and validation sets. Finally, it prints the results.
- `com.packt.JavaDL.DogvCatClassification.Classifier`:
  - `PetClassfier.java`: Gives the user the opportunity to upload a sample image (that is, either dog or cat). Then, the user can make the detection from a high-level UI.
- `com.packt.JavaDL.DogvCatClassification.UI`:
  - `ImagePanel.java`: Acts as the image panel by extending the Java JPanel
  - `UI.java`: Creates the user interface for uploading the image and shows the result
  - `ProgressBar.java`: Shows the progress bar

We will explore them step by step. First, let us look at the dataset description.

Dataset collection and description

For this end-to-end project, we will use the dog versus cat dataset from Microsoft that was provided for the infamous dogs versus cats classification problem as a playground competition. The dataset can be downloaded from `https://www.microsoft.com/en-us/download/details.aspx?id=54765`.

The train folder contains 25k images of both dogs and cats, where the labels are part of the filename. However, the test folder contains 12.5k images named according to numeric IDs. Now let's take a look at some sample snaps from the 25k images:

Showing the true labels of images that are randomly selected

For each image in the test set, we have to predict whether an image contains a dog (*1 = dog, 0 = cat*). In short, this is a binary classification problem.

Architecture choice and adoption

As mentioned earlier, we will be reusing the VGG-16 pretrained model, which is already trained with different images of cat and dog breeds from ImageNet (see the list here at `http://www.image-net.org/challenges/LSVRC/2014/results#clsloc`). The original VGG-16 model had 1,000 classes of images to be predicted as outlined in the following diagram:

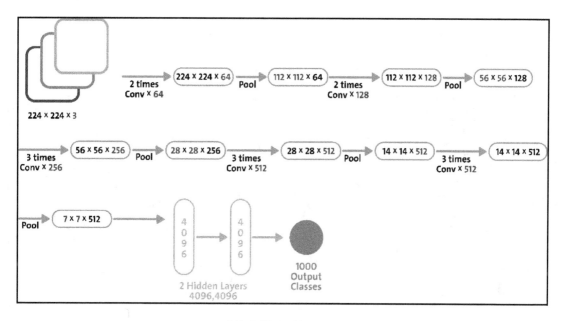

Original VGG-16 model architecture

Fortunately, the trained model and network weights are already available on the DL4J website (see `http://blob.deeplearning4j.org/models/vgg16_dl4j_inference.zip`) and the size is about 500 MB.

You can manually download and restore, or a better way is to do it the DL4J way, where you just need to specify the pretrained type (up to DL4J 1.0.0 alpha, there were only four pretrained types available, such as ImageNet, CIFAR, MNIST, and VGG-Face).

The latter is very straightforward; just use the following lines of code and the trained model will be downloaded automatically (it will take a while depending on Internet speed though):

```
ZooModel zooModel = new VGG16();
LOGGER.info(" VGG16 model is getting downloaded...");
ComputationGraph preTrainedNet = (ComputationGraph)
zooModel.initPretrained(PretrainedType.IMAGENET);
```

In the preceding code snippet, the ComputationGraph class is used to instantiate a computation graph, which is a neural network with an arbitrary (that is, a directed, acyclic graph) connection structure. This graph structure may also have an arbitrary number of inputs and outputs.

```
LOGGER.info(preTrainedNet.summary());
```

Now, let's take a look at the network architecture including the number of neurons in/out, the parameter shape, and the number of parameters:

```
===================================================================================================
VertexName (VertexType)              nIn,nOut  TotalParams ParamsShape                    Vertex Inputs
===================================================================================================
input_1 (InputVertex)                -,-          -        -                              -
block1_conv1 (ConvolutionLayer)      3,64         1792     W:{64,3,3,3}, b:{1,64}         [input_1]
block1_conv2 (ConvolutionLayer)      64,64        36928    W:{64,64,3,3}, b:{1,64}        [block1_conv1]
block1_pool (SubsamplingLayer)       -,-          0        -                              [block1_conv2]
block2_conv1 (ConvolutionLayer)      64,128       73856    W:{128,64,3,3}, b:{1,128}      [block1_pool]
block2_conv2 (ConvolutionLayer)      128,128      147584   W:{128,128,3,3}, b:{1,128}     [block2_conv1]
block2_pool (SubsamplingLayer)       -,-          0        -                              [block2_conv2]
block3_conv1 (ConvolutionLayer)      128,256      295168   W:{256,128,3,3}, b:{1,256}     [block2_pool]
block3_conv2 (ConvolutionLayer)      256,256      590080   W:{256,256,3,3}, b:{1,256}     [block3_conv1]
block3_conv3 (ConvolutionLayer)      256,256      590080   W:{256,256,3,3}, b:{1,256}     [block3_conv2]
block3_pool (SubsamplingLayer)       -,-          0        -                              [block3_conv3]
block4_conv1 (ConvolutionLayer)      256,512      1180160  W:{512,256,3,3}, b:{1,512}     [block3_pool]
block4_conv2 (ConvolutionLayer)      512,512      2359808  W:{512,512,3,3}, b:{1,512}     [block4_conv1]
block4_conv3 (ConvolutionLayer)      512,512      2359808  W:{512,512,3,3}, b:{1,512}     [block4_conv2]
block4_pool (SubsamplingLayer)       -,-          0        -                              [block4_conv3]
block5_conv1 (ConvolutionLayer)      512,512      2359808  W:{512,512,3,3}, b:{1,512}     [block4_pool]
block5_conv2 (ConvolutionLayer)      512,512      2359808  W:{512,512,3,3}, b:{1,512}     [block5_conv1]
block5_conv3 (ConvolutionLayer)      512,512      2359808  W:{512,512,3,3}, b:{1,512}     [block5_conv2]
block5_pool (SubsamplingLayer)       -,-          0        -                              [block5_conv3]
flatten (PreprocessorVertex)         -,-          -        -                              [block5_pool]
fc1 (DenseLayer)                     25088,4096 102764544  W:{25088,4096}, b:{1,4096}     [flatten]
fc2 (DenseLayer)                     4096,4096  16781312   W:{4096,4096}, b:{1,4096}      [fc1]
predictions (DenseLayer)             4096,1000  4097000    W:{4096,1000}, b:{1,1000}      [fc2]
---------------------------------------------------------------------------------------------------
          Total Parameters:  138357544
      Trainable Parameters:  138357544
         Frozen Parameters:  0
===================================================================================================
```

VGG-16 model architecture as a computational graph

Now that we have the pretrained model, using this, we will predict as many as 1,000 classes. And the trainable parameters are equal to total parameters: 138 million. It is a difficult job to train so many parameters.

Nevertheless, since we need only two classes to be predicted, we need to modify the model architecture slightly such that it outputs only two classes instead of 1,000. So we leave everything unchanged. The modified VGG-16 network will then look like this:

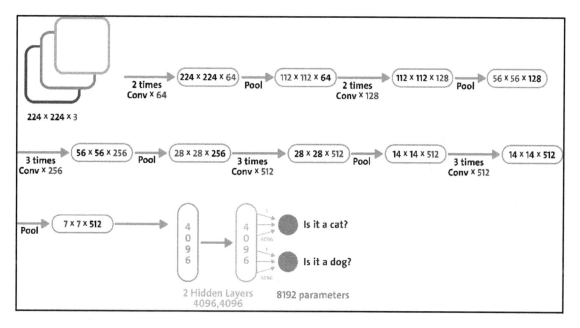

From the input to the last fully connected layer (that is, fc2) is freeze

In the preceding diagram, we freeze until the last pooling layer and use initial weights. The green part is the topic of interest that we want to train, so we are going to train only the last layer for the two classes. In other words, in our case, we are going to freeze from the input to the last fully connected layer, which is `fc2`. That is, the `featurizeExtractionLayer` variable value would be `fc2`.

However, before that, let us define some properties such as seed, the number of classes, and up to which layer we want to freeze:

```
private static final long seed = 12345;
private static final String FREEZE_UNTIL_LAYER = "fc2";
private static final int NUM_CLASS = 2;
```

Then we instantiate the configuration for fine-tuning, which will override the values for all non-frozen layers with the values set here:

```
FineTuneConfiguration fineTuneConf = new FineTuneConfiguration.Builder()
.optimizationAlgo(OptimizationAlgorithm.STOCHASTIC_GRADIENT_DESCENT)
        .updater(new Adam(0.001))
        .seed(seed)
        .build();
```

 FineTuneConfiguration is the configuration for fine-tuning. Values set in this configuration will override the values in each non-frozen layer. Interested readers can take a look at `https://deeplearning4j.org/doc/ org/deeplearning4j/nn/transferlearning/FineTuneConfiguration. html`.

Then we create a configuration graph that will do the trick: it will work as the transfer learner using pretrained VGG-16 model:

```
ComputationGraph vgg16Transfer = new
TransferLearning.GraphBuilder(preTrainedNet)
        .fineTuneConfiguration(fineTuneConf)
        .setFeatureExtractor(FREEZE_UNTIL_LAYER)
        .removeVertexKeepConnections("predictions")
        .setWorkspaceMode(WorkspaceMode.SEPARATE)
        .addLayer("predictions", new OutputLayer
.Builder(LossFunctions.LossFunction.NEGATIVELOGLIKELIHOOD)
                .nIn(4096).nOut(NUM_CLASS)
                .weightInit(WeightInit.XAVIER)
                .activation(Activation.SOFTMAX).build(),
FREEZE_UNTIL_LAYER)
        .build();
vgg16Transfer.setListeners(new ScoreIterationListener(5));
LOGGER.info(vgg16Transfer.summary());
```

The following screenshot shows the output of the previous code snippet:

```
==================================================================================================
VertexName (VertexType)                  nIn,nOut    TotalParams ParamsShape              Vertex Inputs
==================================================================================================
input_1 (InputVertex)                    -,-         -           -                        -
block1_conv1 (Frozen ConvolutionLayer)   3,64        1792        W:{64,3,3,3}, b:{1,64}   [input_1]
block1_conv2 (Frozen ConvolutionLayer)   64,64       36928       W:{64,64,3,3}, b:{1,64}  [block1_conv1]
block1_pool (Frozen SubsamplingLayer)    -,-         0           -                        [block1_conv2]
block2_conv1 (Frozen ConvolutionLayer)   64,128      73856       W:{128,64,3,3}, b:{1,128}  [block1_pool]
block2_conv2 (Frozen ConvolutionLayer)   128,128     147584      W:{128,128,3,3}, b:{1,128} [block2_conv1]
block2_pool (Frozen SubsamplingLayer)    -,-         0           -                        [block2_conv2]
block3_conv1 (Frozen ConvolutionLayer)   128,256     295168      W:{256,128,3,3}, b:{1,256} [block2_pool]
block3_conv2 (Frozen ConvolutionLayer)   256,256     590080      W:{256,256,3,3}, b:{1,256} [block3_conv1]
block3_conv3 (Frozen ConvolutionLayer)   256,256     590080      W:{256,256,3,3}, b:{1,256} [block3_conv2]
block3_pool (Frozen SubsamplingLayer)    -,-         0           -                        [block3_conv3]
block4_conv1 (Frozen ConvolutionLayer)   256,512     1180160     W:{512,256,3,3}, b:{1,512} [block3_pool]
block4_conv2 (Frozen ConvolutionLayer)   512,512     2359808     W:{512,512,3,3}, b:{1,512} [block4_conv1]
block4_conv3 (Frozen ConvolutionLayer)   512,512     2359808     W:{512,512,3,3}, b:{1,512} [block4_conv2]
block4_pool (Frozen SubsamplingLayer)    -,-         0           -                        [block4_conv3]
block5_conv1 (Frozen ConvolutionLayer)   512,512     2359808     W:{512,512,3,3}, b:{1,512} [block4_pool]
block5_conv2 (Frozen ConvolutionLayer)   512,512     2359808     W:{512,512,3,3}, b:{1,512} [block5_conv1]
block5_conv3 (Frozen ConvolutionLayer)   512,512     2359808     W:{512,512,3,3}, b:{1,512} [block5_conv2]
block5_pool (Frozen SubsamplingLayer)    -,-         0           -                        [block5_conv3]
flatten (PreprocessorVertex)             -,-         -           -                        [block5_pool]
fc1 (Frozen DenseLayer)                  25088,4096  102764544   W:{25088,4096}, b:{1,4096}  [flatten]
fc2 (Frozen DenseLayer)                  4096,4096   16781312    W:{4096,4096}, b:{1,4096}   [fc1]
predictions (OutputLayer)                4096,2      8194        W:{4096,2}, b:{1,2}      [fc2]
--------------------------------------------------------------------------------------------------
        Total Parameters:   134268738
    Trainable Parameters:   8194
       Frozen Parameters:   134260544
==================================================================================================
```

The frozen network has only 8,194 trainable parameters

In the preceding code, we removed previously computed predictions and instead used our way so that the modified network predicts only two classes by re-adding a new predictions layer.

In addition, the `setFeatureExtractor` method freezes the weights by specifying a layer vertex to set as a feature extractor. Then, the specified layer vertex and the layers on the path from an input vertex to it will be frozen, with the parameters staying constant.

Thus, we are going to train only 8,192 parameters (out of 138 million parameters) from the last layer to the two outputs; two extra parameters are for the biases for two classes. In short, by freezing until the fc2 layer, now the trainable parameters are drastically reduced from 138 million to 8,194 (that is *8,192 network params + 2 bias params*).

Train and test set preparation

Now that we have created a **ComputationGraph**, we need to prepare the training and test sets for the fine-tuning stage. But even before that, we define some parameters, such as allowable format and data paths:

```
public static final Random RAND_NUM_GEN = new Random(seed);
public static final String[] ALLOWED_FORMATS =
BaseImageLoader.ALLOWED_FORMATS;
public static ParentPathLabelGenerator LABEL_GENERATOR_MAKER = new
ParentPathLabelGenerator();
public static BalancedPathFilter PATH_FILTER = new
BalancedPathFilter(RAND_NUM_GEN, ALLOWED_FORMATS, LABEL_GENERATOR_MAKER);
```

Let's briefly discuss the difference between MultiLayerNetwork and ComputationGraph. In DL4J, there are two types of network composed of multiple layers:

- **MultiLayerNetwork**: A stack of neural network layers we've used so far.
- **ComputationGraph**: This allows networks to be built with the following features: multiple network input arrays and multiple network outputs (for both classification and regression). In this network type, layers connected with each other using a directed acyclic graph connection structure.

Anyway, let's come to the point. Once the params are set, the next task is defining the file paths. Readers should follow this path or show an accurate path during training:

```
public static String DATA_PATH = "data/DoG_CaT/data";
public static final String TRAIN_FOLDER = DATA_PATH + "/train";
public static final String TEST_FOLDER = DATA_PATH + "/test";
File trainData = new File(TRAIN_FOLDER);
```

Then we will use the NativeImageLoader class based on the JavaCV library for loading images, where the allowed formats are .bmp, .gif, .jpg, .jpeg, .jp2, .pbm, .pgm, .ppm, .pnm, .png, .tif, .tiff, .exr, and .webp:

 JavaCV uses wrappers from the JavaCPP presets of several libraries for computer vision (for example, OpenCV and FFmpeg). More details can be found at https://github.com/bytedeco/javacv.

```
FileSplit train = new FileSplit(trainData,
NativeImageLoader.ALLOWED_FORMATS, RAND_NUM_GEN);
```

Once the features are extracted from images, we randomly split the features space into 80% for training and the remaining 20% for validating the training itself to prevent overfitting:

```
private static final int TRAIN_SIZE = 80;
InputSplit[] sample = train.sample(PATH_FILTER, TRAIN_SIZE, 100 -
TRAIN_SIZE);
```

In addition, our DL4J network will not be able to consume the data in this format, but we need to convert it to DataSetIterator format:

```
DataSetIterator trainIterator = getDataSetIterator(sample[0]);
DataSetIterator devIterator = getDataSetIterator(sample[1]);
```

In the preceding lines, we converted both training and validation sets into DataSetIterator through the getDataSetIterator() method. The signature of this method can be seen as follows:

```
public static DataSetIterator getDataSetIterator(InputSplit sample) throws
IOException {
    ImageRecordReader imageRecordReader = new ImageRecordReader(224, 224,
3, LABEL_GENERATOR_MAKER);
    imageRecordReader.initialize(sample);

    DataSetIterator iterator = new
RecordReaderDataSetIterator(imageRecordReader,
                        BATCH_SIZE, 1, NUM_CLASS);
    iterator.setPreProcessor(new VGG16ImagePreProcessor());
    return iterator;
}
```

Fantastic! Up to this point, we have managed to prepare the training sets. Nevertheless, remember that this will take a while since it has to process 12,500 images.

Now we can start the training. However, you might be wondering why we did not talk about the test set. Well, yes! Definitely we will need the test set, too. However, let's discuss this in the network evaluation step.

Network training and evaluation

Now that training and test sets are prepared, we can start the training. However, before that, we define some hyperparameters for the dataset preparation:

```
private static final int EPOCH = 100;
private static final int BATCH_SIZE = 128;
private static final int SAVING_INTERVAL = 100;
```

Additionally, we specify the path where the trained model will be saved for future reuse:

```
private static final String SAVING_PATH =
"bin/CatvsDog_VG16_TrainedModel_Epoch100_v1.zip";
```

Now we can start training the network. We will do the training combined such that training is carried out with the training set and validation is effected by using the validation set. Finally, the network will evaluate the network performance using the test set. Therefore, for this, we need to prepare the test set too:

```
File testData = new File(TEST_FOLDER);
FileSplit test = new FileSplit(testData, NativeImageLoader.ALLOWED_FORMATS,
RAND_NUM_GEN);
DataSetIterator testIterator = getDataSetIterator(test.sample(PATH_FILTER,
1, 0)[0]);
```

Then we start the training; we used a batch size of 128 and 100 epochs. Therefore, the first while loop will be executed 100 times. Then, the second inner `while` loop will be executed 196 times (25,000 cat and dog images/128):

```
int iEpoch = 0;
int i = 0;
while (iEpoch < EPOCH) {
    while (trainIterator.hasNext()) {
        DataSet trained = trainIterator.next();
        vgg16Transfer.fit(trained);
        if (i % SAVING_INTERVAL == 0 && i != 0) {
            ModelSerializer.writeModel(vgg16Transfer, new
File(SAVING_PATH), false);
            evaluateOn(vgg16Transfer, devIterator, i);
        }
        i++;
    }
    trainIterator.reset();
    iEpoch++;
    evaluateOn(vgg16Transfer, testIterator, iEpoch);
}
```

This way, we've already tried to make the training faster, but still it might take several hours or even days depending on a number of an epoch that is set. And, if the training is carried out on a CPU rather than GPU, it might take several days. For me, it took 48 hours for 100 epochs. By the way, my machine has a Core i7 processor, 32 GB of RAM, and GeForce GTX 1050 GPU.

Epoch versus iteration
An epoch is a full traversal through the data, and one iteration is one
forward and one back propagation on the batch size specified.

Anyway, once the training is complete, the trained model will be saved in the location
specified previously. Now let us take a look at how the training went. For this, we will see
the performance on the validation set (as stated earlier, we used 15% of the total training set
as a validation set, that is, 5,000 images):

```
>>>
Cat classified by model as cat: 2444 times
Cat classified by model as dog: 56 times
Dog classified by model as cat: 42 times
Dog classified by model as dog: 2458 times
==========================Scores===========================
# of classes: 2
Accuracy: 0.9800
Precision: 0.9804
Recall: 0.9806
F1 Score: 0.9800
===========================================================
```

Then, when we evaluated our model on a full test set (that is, 12,500 images), I experienced
the following performance metrics:

```
>>>
Cat classified by model as cat: 6178 times
Cat classified by model as dog: 72 times
Dog classified by model as cat: 261 times
Dog classified by model as dog: 5989 times
==========================Scores====================
# of classes: 2
Accuracy: 0.9693
Precision: 0.9700
Recall: 0.9693
F1 Score: 0.9688
====================================================
```

Restoring the trained model and inferencing

Now that we have seen how our model performed, it would be worth exploring the feasibility of restoring the already trained model. In other words, we will restore the trained model and evaluate the network performance on both validation and test sets:

```
private static final String TRAINED_PATH_MODEL =
"bin/CatvsDog_VG16_TrainedModel_Epoch100_v1.zip";
ComputationGraph computationGraph =
ModelSerializer.restoreComputationGraph(new File(TRAINED_PATH_MODEL));

VG16CatvDogEvaluator().runOnTestSet(computationGraph);
VG16CatvDogEvaluator().runOnValidationSet(computationGraph);
```

In the previous line, of code, first, we restored the trained model from the disk; then we performed the evaluation on both the test set (full test set) and validation set (on 20% of the training set).

Now, let's take a look at the signature of the runOnTestSet() method, which is straightforward, in the sense that we already described a similar workflow in the previous subsection:

```
private void runOnTestSet(ComputationGraph computationGraph) throws
IOException {
        File trainData = new File(TrainCatvsDogVG16.TEST_FOLDER);
        FileSplit test = new FileSplit(trainData,
NativeImageLoader.ALLOWED_FORMATS,
                                    TrainCatvsDogVG16.RAND_NUM_GEN);

        InputSplit inputSplit = test.sample(TrainCatvsDogVG16.PATH_FILTER,
100, 0)[0];
        DataSetIterator dataSetIterator =
TrainCatvsDogVG16.getDataSetIterator(inputSplit);
        TrainCatvsDogVG16.evaluateOn(computationGraph, dataSetIterator, 1);
}
```

Now, let's take a look at the signature of the runOnValidationSet method:

```
private void runOnValidationSet(ComputationGraph computationGraph) throws
IOException {
        File trainData = new File(TrainCatvsDogVG16.TRAIN_FOLDER);
        FileSplit test = new FileSplit(trainData,
NativeImageLoader.ALLOWED_FORMATS,
                                    TrainCatvsDogVG16.RAND_NUM_GEN);

        InputSplit inputSplit = test.sample(TrainCatvsDogVG16.PATH_FILTER,
```

```
15, 80)[0];
        DataSetIterator dataSetIterator =
TrainCatvsDogVG16.getDataSetIterator(inputSplit);
        TrainCatvsDogVG16.evaluateOn(computationGraph, dataSetIterator, 1);
}
```

Making simple inferencing

Now we have seen that our trained model shows outstanding accuracy on both test and validation sets. So why don't we develop a UI that would help us make the thing easier? As outlined previously, we will develop a simple UI that will allow us to unload a sample image, and then we should be able to detect it through a simple button press. This part is pure Java, so I'm not going to discuss the details here.

If we run the `PetClassifier.java` class, it first loads our trained model and acts as the backend deployed the model. Then it calls the `UI.java` class to load the user interface, which looks as follows:

UI for the cat versus dog recognizer

In the console, you should experience the following logs/messages:

```
19:54:52.496 [pool-1-thread-1] INFO org.nd4j.linalg.factory.Nd4jBackend -
Loaded [CpuBackend] backend
19:54:52.534 [pool-1-thread-1] WARN org.reflections.Reflections - given
scan urls are empty. set urls in the configuration
19:54:52.865 [pool-1-thread-1] INFO org.nd4j.nativeblas.NativeOpsHolder -
Number of threads used for NativeOps: 4
19:54:53.249 [pool-1-thread-1] INFO org.nd4j.nativeblas.Nd4jBlas - Number
of threads used for BLAS: 4
19:54:53.252 [pool-1-thread-1] INFO
org.nd4j.linalg.api.ops.executioner.DefaultOpExecutioner - Backend used:
[CPU]; OS: [Windows 10]
19:54:53.252 [pool-1-thread-1] INFO
org.nd4j.linalg.api.ops.executioner.DefaultOpExecutioner - Cores: [8];
Memory: [7.0GB];
19:54:53.252 [pool-1-thread-1] INFO
org.nd4j.linalg.api.ops.executioner.DefaultOpExecutioner - Blas vendor:
[OPENBLAS]
19:55:09.015 [pool-1-thread-1] DEBUG org.reflections.Reflections - going to
scan these urls:
 . . .
9:55:13.394 [pool-1-thread-1] INFO
org.deeplearning4j.nn.graph.ComputationGraph - Starting ComputationGraph
with WorkspaceModes set to [training: NONE; inference: SEPARATE]
19:55:13.394 [pool-1-thread-1] DEBUG org.reflections.Reflections - going to
scan these urls:
19:55:13.779 [pool-1-thread-1] INFO
com.packt.JavaDL.DogvCatClassification.UI.UI - Model loaded successfully!
```

Now, let's upload a few photos from the test set (it makes more sense since we are reusing the trained model, which is trained to recognize only the training set, so the test set is still unseen):

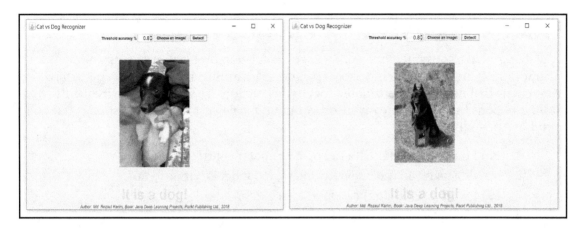

Our cat versus dog recognizer recognizes dogs from the images having dogs of different shapes and colors

Therefore, our trained model has been able to recognize dogs having a different shape, size, and color in terms of images. Now, let us try to upload a few cat images and see if it works:

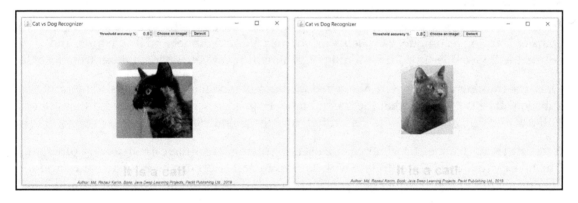

Our cat versus dog recognizer recognizes cats from the images having cats of different shape and colors

Frequently asked questions (FAQs)

Now that we have solved the dog versus cat classification problem with outstanding accuracy, there are other practical aspects of transfer learning and overall deep learning phenomena that need to be considered too. In this section, we will see some frequently asked questions that might already be on your mind. Answers to these questions can be found in Appendix A.

1. Can I train the model with my own animal images?
2. Training using all the images is taking too long. What can I do?
3. Can I wrap up this application as a web app?
4. Can I use VGG-19 for this task?
5. How many hyperparameters do we have? I also want to see for each layer.

Summary

In this chapter, we solved an interesting dog versus cat classification problem using the transfer learning technique. We used a pre-trained VGG16 model and its weights, and subsequently we fine-tuned the training with a real-life cat versus dog dataset from Kaggle.

Once the training was complete, we saved the trained model for model persistence and subsequent reuse. We saw that the trained model can successfully detect and differentiate both cat and dog images having very different sizes, qualities, and shapes.

Even the trained model/classifier can be used in solving a real-life cat versus dog problem. The takeaway is that this technique with some minimal effort can be extended and used for solving similar image classification problems, which applies to both binary and multiclass classification problems.

In the next chapter, we will see how to develop an end-to-end project that will detect objects from video frames when a video clip plays continuously. We will also see how to utilize a pre-trained `TinyYOLO` model, which is a smaller variant of the original YOLOv2 model.

Furthermore, some typical challenges in object detection from both still images and videos will be discussed. Then we will demonstrate how to solve them using bounding box and non-max suppression techniques. Nevertheless, we will see how to process a video clip using the JavaCV library on top of DL4J. Finally, we will see some frequently asked questions that should be useful for adopting and extending this project.

Answers to questions

Answer to question 1: Yes, of course, you can. However, please note that you have to provide a sufficient number of images, preferably at least a few thousand images for each animal type. Otherwise, the model will not be trained well.

Answer to question 2: A possible reason could be you are trying to feed all the images at once or you are training on CPU (and your machine does not have a good configuration). The former can be addressed easily; we can undertake the training in batch mode, which is recommended for the era of deep learning.

The latter case can be addressed by migrating your training from CPU to GPU. However, if your machine does not have a GPU, you can try migrating to Amazon GPU instance to get the support for a single (p2.xlarge) or multiple GPUs (for example, p2.8xlarge).

Answer to question 3: The application provided should be enough to understand the effectiveness of the application. However, this application can still be wrapped up as a web application where the trained model can be served at the backend.

I often use Spring Boot Framework (see more at `https://projects.spring.io/spring-boot/`) for this purpose. Apart from this, Java CUBA studio can be used too (see `https://www.cuba-platform.com/`).

As mentioned earlier in this chapter, VGG-16 is a small variant of VGG-19. Unfortunately, there is no way to use VGG-19 directly. However, readers can try to load VGG-19 can be imported with Keras import.

Answer to question 6: Just use the following code immediately after the network initialization:

```
//Print the number of parameters in the network (and for each layer)
Layer[] layers = model.getLayers();
int totalNumParams = 0;

for( int i=0; i<layers.length; i++ ){
        int nParams = layers[i].numParams();
        System.out.println("Number of parameters in layer " + i + ": " +
nParams);
        totalNumParams += nParams;
}
System.out.println("Total number of network parameters: " +
totalNumParams);

>>>
 Number of parameters in layer 0: 1792
```

```
Number of parameters in layer 1: 36928
Number of parameters in layer 2: 0
Number of parameters in layer 3: 73856
Number of parameters in layer 4: 147584
Number of parameters in layer 5: 0
Number of parameters in layer 6: 295168
Number of parameters in layer 7: 590080
Number of parameters in layer 8: 590080
Number of parameters in layer 9: 0
Number of parameters in layer 10: 1180160
Number of parameters in layer 11: 2359808
Number of parameters in layer 12: 2359808
Number of parameters in layer 13: 0
Number of parameters in layer 14: 2359808
Number of parameters in layer 15: 2359808
Number of parameters in layer 16: 2359808
Number of parameters in layer 17: 0
Number of parameters in layer 18: 102764544
Number of parameters in layer 19: 16781312
Number of parameters in layer 20: 8194
Total number of network parameters: 134268738
```

6
Real-Time Object Detection using YOLO, JavaCV, and DL4J

Deep Convolutional Neural Networks (**DCNN**) have been used in computer vision—for example, image classification, image feature extraction, object detection, and semantic segmentation. Despite such successes of state-of-the-art approaches for object detection from still images, detecting objects in a video is not an easy job.

Considering this drawback, in this chapter, we will develop an end-to-end project that will detect objects from video frames when a video clip plays continuously. We will be utilizing a trained YOLO model for transfer learning and JavaCV techniques on top of **Deeplearning4j** (**DL4J**) to do this. In short, the following topics will be covered throughout this end-to-end project:

- Object detection
- Challenges in object detection from videos
- Using YOLO with DL4J
- Frequently asked questions (FAQs)

Object detection from images and videos

Deep learning has been widely applied to various computer vision tasks such as image classification, object detection, semantic segmentation, and human pose estimation. When we intend to solve the object detection problem from images, the whole process starts from object classification. Then we perform object localization and finally, we perform the object detection.

This project is highly inspired by the Java Autonomous driving – Car detection article by Klevis Ramo (http://ramok.tech/). Also, some theoretical concepts are used (but significantly extended for this need) with due permission from the author.

Object classification, localization, and detection

In an object classification problem, from a given image (or video clip), we're interested to know if it contains a region of interest (ROI) or object. More formally, "the image contains a car" versus "the image does not contain any car." To solve this problem, over the last few years, ImageNet and PASCAL VOC (see more at http://host.robots.ox.ac.uk/pascal/voc/) have been in use and are based on deep CNN architectures .

Moreover, of course, the latest technological advances (that is, both software and hardware) have contributed to boosting the performance to the next level. Despite such success of state-of-the-art approaches for still images, detecting objects in videos is not easy. However, object detection from videos brings up new questions, possibilities, and challenges on how to solve the object detection problem for videos effectively and robustly.

Answering this question is not an easy job. First, let's try to solve the problem step by step. First let's try to answer for an still image. Well, when we want to use a CNN to predict if an image contains a particular object or not, we need to localize the object position in the image. To do that, we need to specify the position of the object in the image along with the classification task. This is usually done by marking the object with a rectangular box commonly known as a bounding box.

Now, the idea of a bounding box is that at each frame of a video, the algorithm is required to annotate bounding boxes and confidence scores on objects of each class. To grab the idea clearly, take a look at what a bounding box is. A bounding box is usually represented by the center (b^x, b^y), rectangle height (b^h), and rectangle width (b^w), as shown in the following diagram:

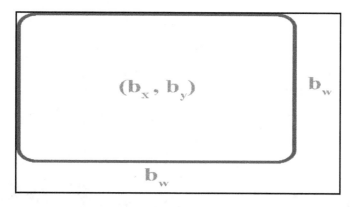

A bounding box representation

Now that we know how to represent such a bounding box, we can perceive what we need to define these things in our training data for each of the objects in the images too. Only then will the network be able to output the following:

- The probability of an image's class number (for example, 20% probability of being a car, 60% probability of being a bus, 10% probability of being a truck, or 10% probability of being a train)
- Also, the four variables defining the bounding box of the object

Knowing only this information is not enough. Interestingly, with this minimum contextual information about bounding box points (that is, center, width, and height), our model is still able to predict and give us a more detailed view of the content. In other words, using this approach, we can solve the object localization problem, but still it is applicable only for a single object.

Therefore, we can even go a step further by localizing not just a single object but multiple or all objects in the image, which will help us move toward the object detection problem. Although the structure of the original image remains the same, we need to deal with multiple bounding boxes in a single image.

Now to crack this problem, a state-of-the-art technique is dividing the image into smaller rectangles. And we have the same additional five variables we have already seen (P^c, b^x, b^y, b^h, b^w) and, of course, the normal prediction probabilities at each bounding box.

The idea sounds easy, but how would it work in practice? If we just need to deal with a static image classification problem, things become easier. Using a Naïve approach would be cropping each car image from a collection of thousands of car images and then we training a convolution neural network (for example, VGG-19) to train the model with all these images (although, each image might have a different size).

Typical highway traffic

Now, to handle this scenario, we can scan the image with a sliding rectangle window and each time let our model predict if there is a car in it or not. As we can see by using different sizes of rectangles, we can figure out quite a different shape for cars and their positions.

Albeit, this works quite well in detecting only cars, but imagine a more practical problem such as developing an autonomous driving application. On a typical highway, in a city even in a suburb, there will be many cars, buses, trucks, motorbikes, bicycles, and other vehicles. Moreover, there will be other objects, such as pedestrians, traffic signs, bridges, dividers, and lamp-posts. These will make the scenario more complicated. Nevertheless, the size of real images will very different (that is, much bigger) compared to cropped ones. Also, in the front, many cars might be approaching, so manual resizing, feature extraction and then handcraft training would be necessary.

Another issue would be the slowness of the training algorithm, so it would not be used for real-time video object detection. This application will be built so that you folks can learn something useful so that the same knowledge can be extended and applied to emerging applications, such as autonomous driving.

Anyway, let's come to the original discussion. When moving the rectangle (right, left, up and down), many shared pixels may not be reused but they are just recalculated repeatedly. Even with very accurate and different bounding box sizes, this approach will fail to mark the object with a bounding box very precisely.

Consequently, the model may not output the class of the vehicle very accurately as if the box may include only a part of the object. This might lead an autonomous driving car to be accident-prone—that is, may collide with other vehicles or objects. Now to get rid of this limitation, one of the state-of-the-art approaches is using the **Convolutional Sliding Window** (**CSW**) solution, which is pretty much utilized in YOLO (we will see this later on).

Convolutional Sliding Window (CSW)

In the previous subsection, we have seen that the Naïve sliding window-based approach has severe performance drawbacks since this type of approach is not able to reuse many of the values already computed.

Nevertheless, when each individual window moves, we need to execute millions of hyperparameters for all pixels in order to get a prediction. In reality, most of the computation could be reused by introducing convolution (refer to Chapter 5, *Image Classification using Transfer Learning*, to get to know more on transfer learning using pre-trained DCNN architecture for image classification). This can be achieved in two incremental ways:

- By turning full-connected CNN layers into convolution
- Using CSW

We have seen that whatever DCNN architectures people are using (for example, DarkNet, VGG-16, AlexNet, ImageNet, ResNet, and Inception), regardless of their size and configuration, in the end, they were used to feed fully connected neural nets with a different number of layers and output several predictions depending on classes.

In addition, these deep architectures typically have so many layers that it is difficult to interpret them well. Therefore, taking a smaller network sounds a reasonable choice. In the following diagram, the network takes a colored image (that is, RGB) of size 32 x 32 x 3 as input. It then uses the same convolution, which leaves the first two dimensions (that is, width x height) unchanged at 3 x 3 x 64 in order to get an output 32 x 32 x 64. This way, the 3rd dimension (that is, 64) remains the same as conv matrix.

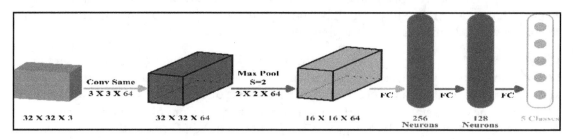

Then, a maximum pooling layer is placed to reduce the width and height but leaving the 3rd dimension unchanged at 16 x 16 x 64. After that, the reduced layer is fed into a dense layer having 2 hidden layers with 256 and 128 neurons each. In the end, the network outputs the probabilities of five classes using a Softmax layer.

Now, let's see how we can replace **fully connected** (**FC**) layers with conv layers while leaving the linear function of the input at 16 x 16 x 64, as illustrated by the following diagram:

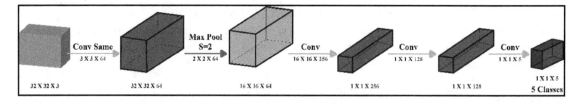

In the preceding diagram, we just replaced the FC layers with conv filters. In reality, a 16 x 16 x 256 conv filter is equivalent to a 16 x 16 x 64 x 256 matrix. In that case, the third dimension, 64, is always the same as the third dimension input 16 x 16 x 64. Therefore, it can be written as a 16 x 16 x 256 conv filter by omitting the 64, which is actually equivalent to the corresponding FC layer. The following math provides the answer as to why:

Out: 1 x 1 x 256 = in: [16 x 16 x 64] * conv: [16 x 16 x 64 x 256]

The preceding math signifies that every element of the output 1 x 1 x 256 is a linear function of a corresponding element of the input 16 x 16 x 64. The reason why we bothered to convert FC layers to convolution layers is that it will give us more flexibility in the way output is generated by the network: with an FC layer, we will always have the same output size, which is a number of classes.

Now, in order to see the effectiveness of replacing the FC layers with a convolution filter, we have to take an input image having a bigger size, say 36 x 36 x 3. Now, if we use the Naïve sliding window technique, where stride is 2 and we have FC, we need to move the original image size nine times to cover all, therefore, executing the model nine times as well. Hence, it definitely does not make sense to adopt that approach. Instead, let us try now to apply this new bigger matrix as input for our new model with convolution layers only.

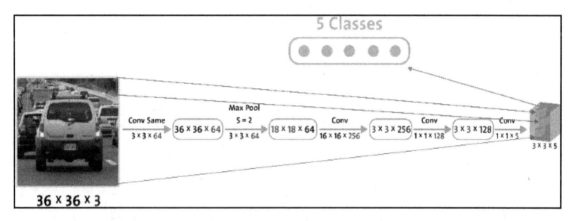

Now, we can see that the output has changed from 1 x 1 x 5 to 3 x 3 x 5, which is in comparison to FC. Again, if we recall the CSW-based approach, where we had to move the sliding window nine times to cover all images, which is interestingly equal to the 3 x 3 output of conv, nonetheless, each 3 x 3 cell represents the probability prediction results of a sliding window of 1 x 1 x 5 class! Therefore, instead of having only one 1 x 1 x 5 with 9 lots of sliding window moves, the output now with one shot is 3 x 3 x 5.

Now, using the CSW-based approach, we have been able to solve the object detection problem from images. Yet, this approach is not so accurate but still, will produce an acceptable result with marginal accuracy. Nevertheless, when it comes to real-time video, things get much more complicated. We will see how YOLO has solved the remaining limitation later in this chapter. For the time being, let's try to understand the underlying complexity in detecting objects from video clips.

Object detection from videos

Let's think of a simple scenario before digging down deeper. Suppose we have a video clip containing the movement of a cat or wolf in a forest. Now we want to detect this animal but while on the move at each timestep.

The following graph shows the challenges in such a scenario. The red boxes are ground truth annotations. The upper part of the figure (that is **a**) shows still-image object detection methods have large temporal fluctuations across frames, even on ground truth bounding boxes. The fluctuations may result from motion blur, video defocus, part occlusion and bad pose. Information from boxes of the same object on adjacent frames needs to be utilized for object detection in video.

On the other hand, (**b**) shows tracking is able to relate boxes of the same object. However, due to occlusions, appearance changes and pose variations, the tracked boxes may drift to non-target objects. Object detectors should be incorporated into tracking algorithms to constantly start new tracks when drifting occurs.

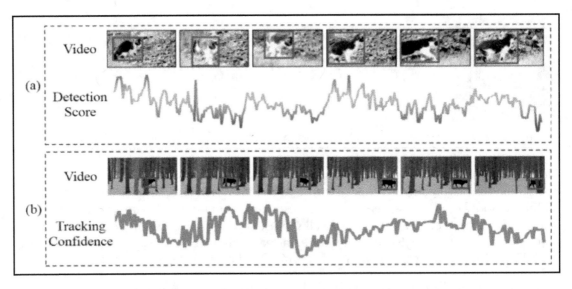

Challenges in object detection from the video (source: Kai Kang et al, Object Detection from Video Tubelets with Convolutional Neural Networks)

There are methods to tackle this problem. However, most of them focus on detecting one specific class of objects, such as pedestrians, cars, or humans with actions.

Fortunately, similar to object detection in still images being able to assist tasks including image classification, localization, and object detection, accurately detecting objects in videos could possibly boost the performance of video classification as well. By locating objects in the videos, the semantic meaning of a video could also be described more clearly, which results in more robust performance for video-based tasks.

In other words, existing methods for general object detection cannot be applied to solve this problem effectively. Their performance may suffer from large appearance changes of objects in videos. For instance, in the preceding graph (**a**), if the cat faces the camera at first and then turns back, it's back image cannot be effectively recognized as a cat because it contains little texture information and is not likely to be included in the training. Nevertheless, this is a simpler scenario where we have to detect a single object (that is, an animal).

When we want to develop an application for an autonomous driving car, we will have to deal with so many objects and considerations. Anyway, since we cannot cover all the aspects through this chapter, let's move to solving the problem with only a modicum of knowledge.

Furthermore, implementing and training these types of applications from scratch is time consuming and challenging too. Therefore, nowadays, transfer learning techniques are becoming popular and viable options. By utilizing a trained model, we can develop much more easily. One such trained object detection framework is YOLO, which is one of the state-of-the-art real-time object detection systems. These challenges and YOLO like frameworks have motivated me to develop this project with a minimum of effort.

You Only Look Once (YOLO)

Although we already addressed issues in object detection from static images by introducing convolution-sliding windows, our model still may not output very accurate bounding boxes, even with several bounding box sizes. Let's see how YOLO solves that problem well:

Using the bounding box specification, we go to each image and mark the objects we want to detect

We need to label our training data in some specific way so that the YOLO algorithm will work correctly. YOLO V2 format requires bounding box dimensions of b^x, b^y and b^h, b^w in order to be relative to the original image width and height.

First, we normally go to each image and mark the objects we want to detect. After that, each image is split into a smaller number of rectangles (boxes), usually, 13 x 13 rectangles, but here, for simplicity, we have 8 x 9. Both the bounding box (blue) and the object can be part of several boxes (green), so we can assign the object and the bounding box only to the box owning the centre of the object (yellow boxes).

This way, we train our model with four additional (besides identifying the object as a car) variables (b^x, b^y, b^h, and b^w) and assign those to the box owning the center b^x, b^y. Since the neural network is trained with this labeled data, it also predicts this four variables (besides what object is) values or bounding boxes.

Instead of scanning with predefined bounding box sizes and trying to fit the object, we let the model learn how to mark objects with bounding boxes. Therefore, bounding boxes are now flexible. This is definitely a better approach and the accuracy of the bounding boxes is much higher and more flexible.

Let us see how we can represent the output now that we have added four variables (b^x, b^y, b^h, and b^w) beside classes like 1-car, 2-pedestrian. In reality, another variable, P^c, is also added, which simply tells if the image has any of the objects we want to detect at all.

- **P^c =1(red)**: This means there is at least one of the objects, so it is worth looking at probabilities and bounding boxes
- **P^c =0(red)**: The image has none of the objects we want so we do not care about probabilities or bounding box specifications

The resultant predictions, b_w, and b_h, are normalized by the height and width of the image. (Training labels are chosen this way.) So, if the predictions b_x and b_y for the box containing the car are (0.3, 0.8), then the actual width and height on 13 x 13 feature maps are (13 x 0.3, 13 x 0.8).

A bounding box predicted by YOLO is defined relative to the box that owns the center of the object (yellow). The upper left corner of the box starts from (0, 0) and the bottom right (1, 1). Since the point is inside the box, in such a scenario, the sigmoid activation function makes sure that the center (b_x, b_y) is in the range 0-1, as outlined in the following diagram:

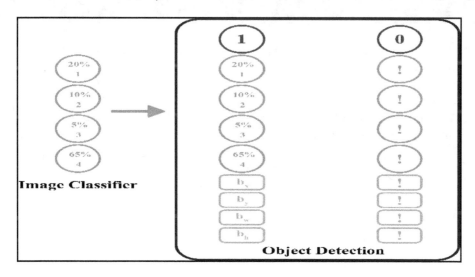

Sigmoid activation function makes sure that the center (b_x, b_y) is in the range 0-1

While b_h, b_w are calculated in proportion to w and h values (yellow) of the box, values can be greater than 1 (exponential used for positive values). In the picture, we can see that the width b_w of the bounding box is almost 1.8 times the size of the box width w. Similarly, b_h is approximately 1.6 times the size of box height h, as outlined in the following diagram:

Now, the question would be what is the probability that an object is contained in the bounding box? Well, to answer this question, we need to know the object score, which represents the probability that an object is contained inside a bounding box. It should be nearly 1 for the red and the neighboring grids, while almost 0 for, say, the grid at the corners. The following formulas describe how the network output is transformed so as to obtain bounding box predictions:

$$b_x = \sigma(t_x) + c_x$$
$$b_y = \sigma(t_y) + c_y$$
$$b_w = p_w e^{t_w}$$
$$b_h = p_h e^{t_h}$$

In the preceding formulas, b_x, b_y, b_w, and b_h are the x, y center coordinates, width and height, respectively, of our prediction. On the other hand, t_x, t_y, t_w, and t_h are what the network outputs. Furthermore, c_x and c_y are the top-left coordinates of the grid. Finally, p_w and p_h are anchor dimensions for the box.

The abjectness score is also passed through a sigmoid, as it is to be interpreted as a probability. Then, the class confidences are used that represent the probabilities of the detected object belonging to a particular class. After prediction, we see how much the predicted box intersects with the real bounding box labeled at the beginning. We try to maximize the intersection between them so ideally, the predicted bounding box is fully intersecting to the labelled bounding box.

In short, we provide enough labeled data with bounding boxes (b^x, b^y, b^h, b^w), then we split the image and assign it to the box containing the center, train using CSW network and predict the object and its position. So first, we classify, and then localize the object and detect it.

Up to this point, we can see that we have been able to overcome most of the obstacles using YOLO. However, in reality, there are further two small problems to solve. Firstly, even though if the object is assigned to one box (one containing the center of the object) in the training time, during inferencing, the trained model assumes several boxes (that is, yellow) have the center of the object (with red). Therefore, this confusion introduces its own bounding boxes for the same object.

Fortunately, the non-max suppression algorithm can solve this: first, the algorithm chooses a prediction box with a maximum P^c probability so that it has a value between 0 and 1 instead of binary 0 or 1 values. Then, every intersecting box above a certain threshold with respect to that box is removed. The same logic is repeated until there are no more bounding boxes left. Secondly, since we are predicting multiple objects (car, train, bus, and so on), the center of two or more objects may lie in a single box. This issue can be solved by introducing anchor boxes:

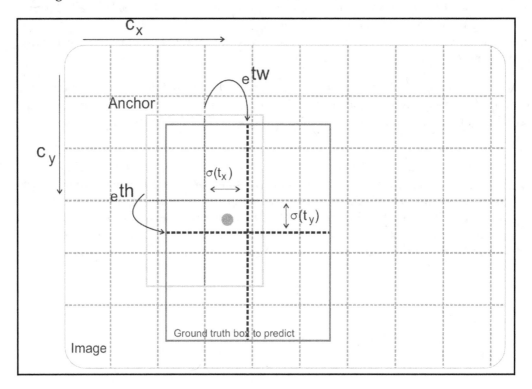

An anchor box specification

With anchor boxes, we choose several shapes of bounding boxes we find frequently used for the object we want to detect. Then, the dimensions of the bounding box are predicted by applying a log-space transform to the output and then multiplying them by an anchor.

Developing a real-time object detection project

In this section, we will be developing a video object classification application using pre-trained YOLO models (that is, transfer learning), DL4J, and OpenCV that can detect labels such as cars, and trees inside the video frame. To be frank, this application is also about extending an image detection problem to video detection. So let's get started.

Step 1 – Loading a pre-trained YOLO model

Since Alpha release 1.0.0, DL4J provides a Tiny YOLO model via ZOO. For this, we need to add a dependency to your Maven friendly `pom.xml` file:

```
<dependency>
  <groupId>org.deeplearning4j</groupId>
  <artifactId>deeplearning4j-zoo</artifactId>
  <version>${dl4j.version}</version>
</dependency>
```

Apart from this, if possible, make sure you utilize the CUDA and cuDNN by adding the following dependencies (see `Chapter 2`, *Cancer Types Prediction Using Recurrent Type Networks*, for more details):

```
<dependency>
  <groupId>org.nd4j</groupId>
  <artifactId>nd4j-cuda-9.0-platform</artifactId>
  <version>${nd4j.version}</version>
</dependency>
<dependency>
  <groupId>org.deeplearning4j</groupId>
  <artifactId>deeplearning4j-cuda-9.0</artifactId>
  <version>${dl4j.version}</version>
</dependency>
```

Then, we are ready to load the pre-trained Tiny YOLO model as a `ComputationGraph` with the following lines of code:

```
private ComputationGraph model;
private TinyYoloModel() {
        try {
            model = (ComputationGraph) new TinyYOLO().initPretrained();
            createObjectLabels();
        } catch (IOException e) {
```

```
            throw new RuntimeException(e);
        }
    }
```

In the preceding code segment, the createObjectLabels() method is referring to the labels from the PASCAL Visual Object Classes (PASCAL VOC) dataset that was used to train the YOLO 2 model. The signature of the method can be seen as follows:

```
private HashMap<Integer, String> labels;
void createObjectLabels() {
        if (labels == null) {
            String label = "aeroplanen" + "bicyclen" + "birdn" + "boatn" +
"bottlen" + "busn" + "carn" +
                    "catn" + "chairn" + "cown" + "diningtablen" + "dogn" +
"horsen" + "motorbiken" +
                    "personn" + "pottedplantn" + "sheepn" + "sofan" +
"trainn" + "tvmonitor";
            String[] split = label.split("\n");
            int i = 0;
            labels = new HashMap<>();
            for(String label1 : split) {
                labels.put(i++, label1);
            }
        }
    }
```

Now, let's create a Tiny YOLO model instance:

```
        static final TinyYoloModel yolo = new TinyYoloModel();
        public static TinyYoloModel getPretrainedModel() {
            return yolo;
        }
```

Now, out of curiosity, let's take a look at the model architecture and the number of hyperparameters in each layer:

```
TinyYoloModel model = TinyYoloModel.getPretrainedModel();
System.out.println(TinyYoloModel.getSummary());
```

```
===============================================================================================================
VertexName (VertexType)                  nIn,nOut  TotalParams ParamsShape                          Vertex Inputs
===============================================================================================================
input_1 (InputVertex)                    -,-        -          -                                    -
conv2d_1 (ConvolutionLayer)              3,16       432        W:{16,3,3,3}                         [input_1]
batch_normalization_1 (BatchNormalization)16,16     64           gamma:{1,16}, beta:{1,16}, mean:{1,16}, var:{1,16}[conv2d_1]
leaky_re_lu_1 (ActivationLayer)          -,-        0          -                                    [batch_normalization_1]
max_pooling2d_1 (SubsamplingLayer)       -,-        0          -                                    [leaky_re_lu_1]
conv2d_2 (ConvolutionLayer)              16,32      4608       W:{32,16,3,3}                        [max_pooling2d_1]
batch_normalization_2 (BatchNormalization)32,32     128          gamma:{1,32}, beta:{1,32}, mean:{1,32}, var:{1,32}[conv2d_2]
leaky_re_lu_2 (ActivationLayer)          -,-        0          -                                    [batch_normalization_2]
max_pooling2d_2 (SubsamplingLayer)       -,-        0          -                                    [leaky_re_lu_2]
conv2d_3 (ConvolutionLayer)              32,64      18432      W:{64,32,3,3}                        [max_pooling2d_2]
batch_normalization_3 (BatchNormalization)64,64     256          gamma:{1,64}, beta:{1,64}, mean:{1,64}, var:{1,64}[conv2d_3]
leaky_re_lu_3 (ActivationLayer)          -,-        0          -                                    [batch_normalization_3]
max_pooling2d_3 (SubsamplingLayer)       -,-        0          -                                    [leaky_re_lu_3]
conv2d_4 (ConvolutionLayer)              64,128     73728      W:{128,64,3,3}                       [max_pooling2d_3]
batch_normalization_4 (BatchNormalization)128,128   512          gamma:{1,128}, beta:{1,128}, mean:{1,128}, var:{1,128}[conv2d_4]
leaky_re_lu_4 (ActivationLayer)          -,-        0          -                                    [batch_normalization_4]
max_pooling2d_4 (SubsamplingLayer)       -,-        0          -                                    [leaky_re_lu_4]
conv2d_5 (ConvolutionLayer)              128,256    294912     W:{256,128,3,3}                      [max_pooling2d_4]
batch_normalization_5 (BatchNormalization)256,256   1024         gamma:{1,256}, beta:{1,256}, mean:{1,256}, var:{1,256}[conv2d_5]
leaky_re_lu_5 (ActivationLayer)          -,-        0          -                                    [batch_normalization_5]
max_pooling2d_5 (SubsamplingLayer)       -,-        0          -                                    [leaky_re_lu_5]
conv2d_6 (ConvolutionLayer)              256,512    1179648    W:{512,256,3,3}                      [max_pooling2d_5]
batch_normalization_6 (BatchNormalization)512,512   2048         gamma:{1,512}, beta:{1,512}, mean:{1,512}, var:{1,512}[conv2d_6]
leaky_re_lu_6 (ActivationLayer)          -,-        0          -                                    [batch_normalization_6]
max_pooling2d_6 (SubsamplingLayer)       -,-        0          -                                    [leaky_re_lu_6]
conv2d_7 (ConvolutionLayer)              512,1024   4718592    W:{1024,512,3,3}                     [max_pooling2d_6]
batch_normalization_7 (BatchNormalization)1024,1024 4096         gamma:{1,1024}, beta:{1,1024}, mean:{1,1024}, var:{1,1024}[conv2d_7]
leaky_re_lu_7 (ActivationLayer)          -,-        0          -                                    [batch_normalization_7]
conv2d_8 (ConvolutionLayer)              1024,1024  9437184    W:{1024,1024,3,3}                    [leaky_re_lu_7]
batch_normalization_8 (BatchNormalization)1024,1024 4096         gamma:{1,1024}, beta:{1,1024}, mean:{1,1024}, var:{1,1024}[conv2d_8]
leaky_re_lu_8 (ActivationLayer)          -,-        0          -                                    [batch_normalization_8]
conv2d_9 (ConvolutionLayer)              1024,125   128125     W:{125,1024,1,1}, b:{1,125}          [leaky_re_lu_8]
outputs (Yolo2OutputLayer)               -,-        0          -                                    [conv2d_9]
---------------------------------------------------------------------------------------------------------------
        Total Parameters:   15867885
        Trainable Parameters: 15867885
        Frozen Parameters:  0
===============================================================================================================
```

Network summary and layer structure of a pre-trained Tiny YOLO model

Therefore, our Tiny YOLO model has around 1.6 million parameters across its 29-layer network. However, the original YOLO 2 model has more layers. Interested readers can look at the original YOLO 2 at `https://github.com/yhcc/yolo2/blob/master/model_data/model.png`.

Step 2 – Generating frames from video clips

Now, to deal with real-time video, we can use video processing tools or frameworks such as JavaCV frameworks that can split a video into individual frames, and we take the image height and width. For this, we have to include the following dependency in the `pom.xml` file:

```xml
<dependency>
    <groupId>org.bytedeco</groupId>
    <artifactId>javacv-platform</artifactId>
    <version>1.4.1</version>
</dependency>
```

JavaCV uses wrappers from the JavaCPP presets of libraries commonly used by researchers in the field of computer vision (for example, OpenCV and FFmpeg), and provides utility classes to make their functionality easier to use on the Java platform, including Android. More details can be found at `https://github.com/bytedeco/javacv`.

For this project, I have collected two video clips (each 1 minute long) that should give you a glimpse into an autonomous driving car. I have downloaded the dataset from YouTube from the following links:

- *Building Self Driving Car - Local Dataset - Day*: `https://www.youtube.com/watch?v=7BjNbkONCFw`
- *Building Self Driving Car - Local Dataset - Night*: `https://www.youtube.com/watch?v=ev5nddpQQ9I`

After downloading them from YouTube downloader (or so), I renamed them as follows:

- `SelfDrivingCar_Night.mp4`
- `SelfDrivingCar_Day.mp4`

Now, if you play these clips, you will see how German people drive cars at 160 km/h or even faster. Now, let us parse the video (first we use day 1) and see some properties to get an idea of video quality hardware requirements:

```java
String videoPath = "data/SelfDrivingCar_Day.mp4";
FFmpegFrameGrabber frameGrabber = new FFmpegFrameGrabber(videoPath);
frameGrabber.start();

Frame frame;
double frameRate = frameGrabber.getFrameRate();
System.out.println("The inputted video clip has " +
frameGrabber.getLengthInFrames() + " frames");
System.out.println("Frame rate " + framerate + "fps");
```

```
>>>
   The inputted video clip has 1802 frames.
   The inputted video clip has frame rate of 29.97002997002997.
```

We then grab each frame and use `Java2DFrameConverter`; it helps us to convert frames to JPEG images:

```java
Java2DFrameConverter converter = new Java2DFrameConverter();
// grab the first frame
frameGrabber.setFrameNumber(1);
frame = frameGrabber.grab();
BufferedImage bufferedImage = converter.convert(frame);
```

```
System.out.println("First Frame" + ", Width: " + bufferedImage.getWidth() +
", Height: " + bufferedImage.getHeight());

// grab the second frame
frameGrabber.setFrameNumber(2);
frame = frameGrabber.grab();
bufferedImage = converter.convert(frame);
System.out.println("Second Frame" + ", Width: " + bufferedImage.getWidth()
+ ", Height: " + bufferedImage.getHeight());

>>>
 First Frame: Width-640, Height-360
 Second Frame: Width-640, Height-360
```

In this way, the preceding code will generate 1,802 JPEG images against an equal number of frames. Let's take a look at the generated images:

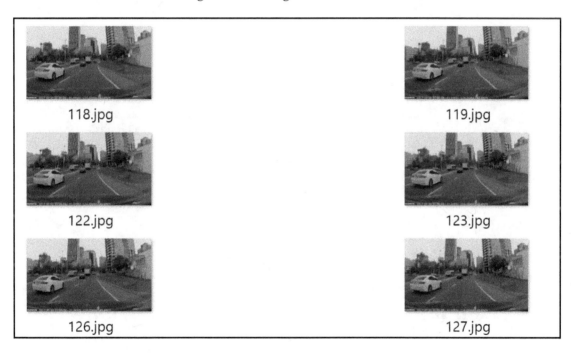

From video clip to video frame to image

Thus, the 1-minute long video clip has a fair number (that is, 1,800) of frames and is 30 frames per second. In short, this video clip has 720p video quality. So you can understand that processing this video should require good hardware; in particular, having a GPU configured should help.

Step 3 – Feeding generated frames into Tiny YOLO model

Now that we know some properties of the clip, we can start generating the frames to be passed to the Tiny YOLO pre-trained model. First, let's look at a less important but transparent approach:

```
private volatile Mat[] v = new Mat[1];
private String windowName = "Object Detection from Video";
try {
    for(int i = 1; i < frameGrabber.getLengthInFrames();
    i+ = (int)frameRate) {
            frameGrabber.setFrameNumber(i);
            frame = frameGrabber.grab();
            v[0] = new OpenCVFrameConverter.ToMat().convert(frame);
            model.markObjectWithBoundingBox(v[0], frame.imageWidth,
                                    frame.imageHeight, true,
windowName);
            imshow(windowName, v[0]);

            char key = (char) waitKey(20);
            // Exit on escape:
            if (key == 27) {
                destroyAllWindows();
                break;
            }
        }
    } catch (IOException e) {
        e.printStackTrace();
    } finally {
        frameGrabber.stop();
    }
    frameGrabber.close();
```

In the preceding code block, we send each frame to the model. Then we use the Mat class to represent each frame in an n-dimensional, dense, numerical multi-channel (that is, RGB) array.

To know more, visit https://docs.opencv.org/trunk/d3/d63/classcv_
1_1Mat.html#details.

In other words, we split the video clip into multiple frames and pass into the Tiny YOLO
model to process them one by one. This way, we apply a single neural network to the full
image.

Step 4 – Object detection from image frames

Tiny YOLO extracts the features from each frame as an n-dimensional, dense, numerical
multi-channel array. Then each image is split into a smaller number of rectangles (boxes):

```java
public void markObjectWithBoundingBox(Mat file, int imageWidth, int
imageHeight, boolean newBoundingBOx,
                                      String winName) throws Exception {
    // parameters matching the pretrained TinyYOLO model
    int W = 416; // width of the video frame
    int H = 416; // Height of the video frame
    int gW = 13; // Grid width
    int gH = 13; // Grid Height
    double dT = 0.5; // Detection threshold

    Yolo2OutputLayer outputLayer = (Yolo2OutputLayer)
model.getOutputLayer(0);
    if (newBoundingBOx) {
        INDArray indArray = prepareImage(file, W, H);
        INDArray results = model.outputSingle(indArray);
        predictedObjects = outputLayer.getPredictedObjects(results,
dT);

        System.out.println("results = " + predictedObjects);
        markWithBoundingBox(file, gW, gH, imageWidth, imageHeight);
    } else {
        markWithBoundingBox(file, gW, gH, imageWidth, imageHeight);
    }
    imshow(winName, file);
}
```

In the preceding code, the `prepareImage()` method takes video frames as images, parses them using the `NativeImageLoader class`, does the necessary preprocessing, and extracts image features that are further converted into `INDArray` format, consumable by the model:

```
INDArray prepareImage(Mat file, int width, int height) throws IOException {
        NativeImageLoader loader = new NativeImageLoader(height, width, 3);
        ImagePreProcessingScaler imagePreProcessingScaler = new
ImagePreProcessingScaler(0, 1);
        INDArray indArray = loader.asMatrix(file);
        imagePreProcessingScaler.transform(indArray);
        return indArray;
    }
```

Then, the `markWithBoundingBox()` method is used for non-max suppression in the case of more than one bounding box.

Step 5 – Non-max suppression in case of more than one bounding box

As YOLO predicts more than one bounding box per object, non-max suppression is implemented; it merges all detections that belong to the same object. Therefore, instead of using b^x, b^y, b^h, and b^w, we can use the top-left and bottom-right points. `gridWidth` and `gridHeight` are the number of small boxes we split our image into. In our case, this is 13 x 13, where w and h are the original image frame dimensions:

```
void markObjectWithBoundingBox(Mat file, int gridWidth, int gridHeight, int
w, int h, DetectedObject obj) {
        double[] xy1 = obj.getTopLeftXY();
        double[] xy2 = obj.getBottomRightXY();
        int predictedClass = obj.getPredictedClass();
        int x1 = (int) Math.round(w * xy1[0] / gridWidth);
        int y1 = (int) Math.round(h * xy1[1] / gridHeight);
        int x2 = (int) Math.round(w * xy2[0] / gridWidth);
        int y2 = (int) Math.round(h * xy2[1] / gridHeight);
        rectangle(file, new Point(x1, y1), new Point(x2, y2), Scalar.RED);
        putText(file, labels.get(predictedClass), new Point(x1 + 2, y2 -
2),
                        FONT_HERSHEY_DUPLEX, 1, Scalar.GREEN);
    }
```

Finally, we remove those objects that intersect with the max suppression, as follows:

```
static void removeObjectsIntersectingWithMax(ArrayList<DetectedObject>
detectedObjects,
                                        DetectedObject
maxObjectDetect) {
        double[] bottomRightXY1 = maxObjectDetect.getBottomRightXY();
        double[] topLeftXY1 = maxObjectDetect.getTopLeftXY();
        List<DetectedObject> removeIntersectingObjects = new ArrayList<>();
        for(DetectedObject detectedObject : detectedObjects) {
            double[] topLeftXY = detectedObject.getTopLeftXY();
            double[] bottomRightXY = detectedObject.getBottomRightXY();
            double iox1 = Math.max(topLeftXY[0], topLeftXY1[0]);
            double ioy1 = Math.max(topLeftXY[1], topLeftXY1[1]);

            double iox2 = Math.min(bottomRightXY[0], bottomRightXY1[0]);
            double ioy2 = Math.min(bottomRightXY[1], bottomRightXY1[1]);

            double inter_area = (ioy2 - ioy1) * (iox2 - iox1);

            double box1_area = (bottomRightXY1[1] - topLeftXY1[1]) *
(bottomRightXY1[0] - topLeftXY1[0]);
            double box2_area = (bottomRightXY[1] - topLeftXY[1]) *
(bottomRightXY[0] - topLeftXY[0]);

            double union_area = box1_area + box2_area - inter_area;
            double iou = inter_area / union_area;

            if(iou > 0.5) {
                removeIntersectingObjects.add(detectedObject);
            }
        }
        detectedObjects.removeAll(removeIntersectingObjects);
    }
```

In the second block, we scaled each image into 416 x 416 x 3 (that is, W x H x 3 RGB channels). This scaled image is then passed to Tiny YOLO for predicting and marking the bounding boxes as follows:

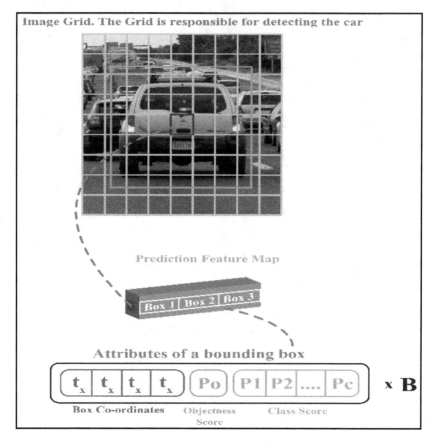

Our Tiny YOLO model predicts the class of an object detected in a bounding box

Once the `markObjectWithBoundingBox()` method is executed, the following logs containing the predicted class, b^x, b^y, b^h, b^w, and confidence (that is, the detection threshold) will be generated and shown on the console:

```
[4.6233e-11]], predictedClass=6),
DetectedObject(exampleNumber=0,
centerX=3.5445247292518616, centerY=7.621537864208221,
width=2.2568163871765137, height=1.9423424005508423,
confidence=0.7954192161560059,
classPredictions=[[ 1.5034e-7], [ 3.3064e-9]...
```

Step 6 – wrapping up everything and running the application

Since, up to this point, we know the overall workflow of our approach, we can now wrap up everything and see whether it really works. However, before that, let's take a look at the functionalities of different Java classes:

- `FramerGrabber_ExplorartoryAnalysis.java`: This shows how to grab frames from the video clip and save each frame as a JPEG image. Besides, it also shows some exploratory properties of the video clip.
- `TinyYoloModel.java`: This instantiates the Tiny YOLO model and generates the label. It also creates and marks the object with the bounding box. Nonetheless, it shows how to handle non-max suppression for more than one bounding box per object.
- `ObjectDetectorFromVideo.java`: The main class. It continuously grabs the frames and feeds them to the Tiny YOLO model (that is, until the user presses the *Esc* key). Then it predicts the corresponding class of each object successfully detected inside the normal or overlapped bounding boxes with non-max suppression (if required).

In short, first, we create and instantiate the Tiny YOLO model. Then we grab the frames and treat each frame as a separate JPEG image. Next, we pass all the images to the model and the model does its trick as outlined previously. The whole workflow can now be depicted with some Java code as follows:

```
// ObjectDetectorFromVideo.java
public class ObjectDetectorFromVideo{
    private volatile Mat[] v = new Mat[1];
    private String windowName;

    public static void main(String[] args) throws java.lang.Exception {
        String videoPath = "data/SelfDrivingCar_Day.mp4";
        TinyYoloModel model = TinyYoloModel.getPretrainedModel();
        System.out.println(TinyYoloModel.getSummary());
        new
ObjectDetectionFromVideo().startRealTimeVideoDetection(videoPath, model);
    }

    public void startRealTimeVideoDetection(String videoFileName,
TinyYoloModel model)
            throws java.lang.Exception {
        windowName = "Object Detection from Video";
        FFmpegFrameGrabber frameGrabber = new
```

```
FFmpegFrameGrabber(videoFileName);
        frameGrabber.start();

        Frame frame;
        double frameRate = frameGrabber.getFrameRate();
        System.out.println("The inputted video clip has " +
frameGrabber.getLengthInFrames() + " frames");
        System.out.println("The inputted video clip has frame rate of " +
frameRate);

        try {
            for(int i = 1; i < frameGrabber.getLengthInFrames(); i+ =
(int)frameRate) {
                frameGrabber.setFrameNumber(i);
                frame = frameGrabber.grab();
                v[0] = new OpenCVFrameConverter.ToMat().convert(frame);
                model.markObjectWithBoundingBox(v[0], frame.imageWidth,
frame.imageHeight,
                                                        true, windowName);
                imshow(windowName, v[0]);

                char key = (char) waitKey(20);
                // Exit on escape:
                if(key == 27) {
                    destroyAllWindows();
                    break;
                }
            }
        } catch (IOException e) {
            e.printStackTrace();
        } finally {
            frameGrabber.stop();
        }
        frameGrabber.close();
    }
}
```

Once the preceding class is executed, the application should load the pretrained model and the UI should be loaded, showing each object being classified:

Our Tiny YOLO model can predict multiple cars simultaneously from a video clip (day)

Now, to see the effectiveness of our model even in night mode, we can perform a second experiment on the night dataset. To do this, just change one line in the `main()` method, as follows:

```
String videoPath = "data/SelfDrivingCar_Night.mp4";
```

Once the preceding class is executed using this clip, the application should load the pretrained model and the UI should be loaded, showing each object being classified:

Our Tiny YOLO model can predict multiple cars simultaneously from a video clip (night)

Furthermore, to see the real-time output, execute the given screen recording clips showing the output of the application.

Frequently asked questions (FAQs)

In this section, we will see some frequently asked questions that might already be on your mind. Answers to these questions can be found in Appendix A.

1. Can't we train YOLO from scratch?
2. I was wondering whether we could use the YOLO v3 model.

3. What changes to the code do I need to make it work for my own video clip?
4. The application provided can detect cars and another vehicle in the video clip. However, the processing is not smooth. It seems to halt. How can I solve this issue?
5. Can I extend this app and make it work for a real-time video from a webcam?

Summary

In this chapter, we saw how to develop an end-to-end project that will detect objects from video frames when video clips play continuously. We saw how to utilize the pre-trained Tiny YOLO model, which is a smaller variant of the original YOLO v2 model.

Furthermore, we covered some typical challenges in object detection from both still images and videos, and how to solve them using bounding box and non-max suppression techniques. We learned how to process a video clip using the JavaCV library on top of DL4J. Finally, we saw some frequently asked questions that should be useful in implementing and extending this project.

In the next chapter, we will see how to develop anomaly detection, which is useful in fraud analytics in finance companies such as banks, and insurance and credit unions. It is an important task to grow the business. We will use unsupervised learning algorithms such as variational autoencoders and reconstructing probability.

Answers to questions

Answer to question 1: We can train a YOLO network from scratch, but that would take a lot of work (and costly GPU hours). As engineers and data scientists, we want to leverage as many prebuilt libraries and machine learning models as we can, so we are going to use a pre-trained YOLO model to get our application into production faster and more cheaply.

Answer to question 2: Perhaps yes, but the latest DL4J release provides only YOLO v2. However, when I talked to their Gitter (see `https://deeplearning4j.org/`), they informed me that with some additional effort, you can make it work. I mean you can import YOLO v3 with Keras import. Unfortunately, I tried but could not make it workfullly.

Answer to question 3: You should be able to directly feed your own video. However, if it does not work, or throws any unwanted exception, then video properties such as frame rate, width, and the height of each frame should be the same as the bounding box specifications.

Answer to question 4: Well, I've already stated that your machine should have good hardware specifications and processing should not cause any delays. For example, my machine has 32 GB of RAM, a core i7 processor, and GeForce GTX 1050 GPU with 4 GB of main memory, and the apps run very smoothly.

Answer to question 5: Perhaps, yes. In that case, the main source of the video should be from the webcam directly. According to the documentation provided at `https://github.com/bytedeco/javacv`, JavaCV also comes with a hardware-accelerated full-screen image display, easy-to-use methods to execute code in parallel on multiple cores, user-friendly geometric and color calibration of cameras, projectors, and so on.

Stock Price Prediction Using LSTM Network

7

Stock market price prediction is one of the most challenging tasks. One of the major reasons is noise and the volatile features of this type of dataset. Therefore, how to predict stock price movement accurately is still an open question for the modern trading world. However classical machine learning algorithms, such as Support vector machines, decision trees, and tree ensembles (for example, random forest and gradient-boosted trees), have been used in the last decade.

However, stock market prices have severe volatility and a historical perspective, which make them suited for time series analysis. This also challenges those classical algorithms, since long-term dependencies cannot be availed using those algorithms. Considering these challenges and the limitations of existing algorithms, in this chapter, we will see how to develop a real-life plain stock open or close price prediction using, LSTM on top of DL4J library.

A time series dataset generated from a real-life stock dataset will be used to train the LSTM model, which will be used to predict only one day ahead at a time. Briefly, we will learn the following topics throughout this end-to-end project:

- Stock price prediction and online trading
- Data collection and description
- Stock price prediction with LSTM
- FAQs.

State-of-the-art automated stock trading

Usually, in a security exchange, exchanges maintain order book lists of all buy and sell orders with their quantity and prices, and they execute them when a match is found between somebody buying and selling. In addition, exchanges keep and provide statistics about state trading, often captured as **OHCL** (short for, **open-high-close-low**) and volume for both currencies of a trader pair.

By the way, bar charts are used, showing open, high, low, and closing prices. Unlike line charts, OHLC charts enable technical analysts to evaluate intra-day volatility and see where prices opened and closed. Take a look at this diagram:

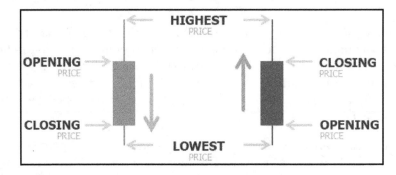

OHLC pricing model showing the open, high, low, and close prices of a certain time period (source: http://en.tradimo.com/tradipedia/ohlc-chart/)

This data is being presented as aggregated in some periods, from seconds to days, and even months. There are dedicated servers working on collecting this data for professional traders and institutions. Although you cannot expect to have all the order data available for free, some of it is accessible to the public and can be used. The first set is historical stock trading data (OHLC), and the second contains the technical indicators of stock trading.

For example, Bitcoin, which is one of the first cryptocurrencies, has attracted the interest of investors and traders. This is because of the following:

- With Bitcoin, is possible to start trading
- Bitcoin allows you to stay pseudo-anonymous
- There has been, dramatic growth during Bitcoin's history (see the following graph for some statistics), which lures long-term investors
- There is high volatility, which attracts daytraders

It is hard to predict the value of Bitcoin in the long term, as the value behind Bitcoin is less tangible, and its price mostly reflects market perception and is highly dependent on news, regulations, collaboration of governments and banks, technical issues of platform, such as transactions fees and size of block, interest of institutional investors in including Bitcoin into their portfolio and so on. Take a look at this screenshot:

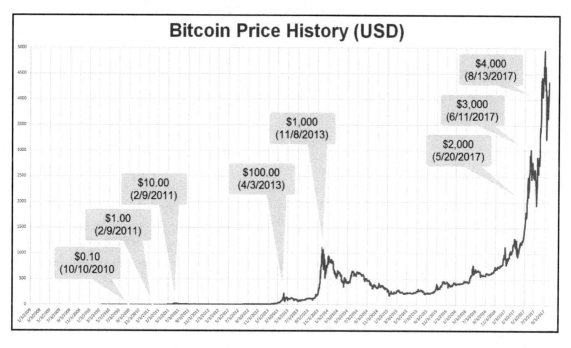

Bitcoin and its dramatic price increases until September 2017 (source: http://www.bitcoin2040.com/bitcoin-price-history/)

Now the question would be how to analyze this dataset in an automated way to help an investor or an online currency trader. Well, in the world of traditional securities, such as company's stocks, it used to be humans who would do the analytics, predict stock prices, and make the trades. Currently, the volume of Bitcoin trading is relatively low compared to traditional exchanges. Two of the reasons for this are high volatility in the stock market and regulations of cryptocurrencies. Take a look at this diagram:

Sell Orders		Total BTC available: 1389.60434169	Buy Orders		Total USD available: 7169835.14
Price per BTC	BTC Amount	Total: (USD)	Price per BTC	BTC Amount	Total: (USD)
6721.0	฿ 0.02010571	$ 135.14	6720.4	฿ 0.05000000	$ 336.02
6737.9	฿ 0.60000000	$ 4042.74	6720.3	฿ 0.08851000	$ 594.82
6738.1	฿ 0.60000000	$ 4042.86	6720.2	฿ 0.60000000	$ 4032.12
6746.0	฿ 0.03300000	$ 222.62	6720.0	฿ 0.03385000	$ 227.48
6746.1	฿ 0.00373000	$ 25.17	6717.0	฿ 0.01200000	$ 80.61
6750.5	฿ 0.25000000	$ 1687.63	6716.1	฿ 0.10000000	$ 671.61
6752.8	฿ 0.06569999	$ 443.66	6713.4	฿ 0.25000000	$ 1678.35
6755.9	฿ 0.42262157	$ 2855.19	6712.0	฿ 0.01472736	$ 98.86
6756.0	฿ 2.41686827	$ 16328.37	6709.6	฿ 0.07018430	$ 470.91
6757.1	฿ 0.25000000	$ 1689.28	6709.3	฿ 0.25000000	$ 1677.33

Bitcoin buy and sell orders for the BTC/USD pair (until June 18th, 2018, source: https://cex.io/trade#)

So, today, people mostly buy and sell Bitcoins with all the consequences of irrational behavior connected to that, but some attempts to automate Bitcoin trading have been made. The most famous one was a paper by MIT and another one by Stanford researchers, published in 2014.

Many things have changed, and taking into account the massive Bitcoin price increase during the last three years, anyone who would just buy and hold would be satisfied enough with the results. Definitely, some traders use **machine learning** (**ML**) for trading, and such applications look promising. Up to now, a few best possible approaches.

For the training, use order-book data instead of derived *OHLC + volume data*. Therefore, for training and prediction, use data in the following way:

- Split the data into a time series of a certain size (where size is a parameter to adjust).
- Cluster the time series data into K clusters, where K is the only parameter to tune. It is assumed that clusters with some natural trends will appear (sharp drop/rise in price and so on).
- For each cluster, train the regression/classifier to predict the price and the price change, respectively.

For the inferencing and evaluation, this approach considers the most recent time series with the size of a specific window and trains the model. Then it classifies the data as follows:

- It takes the most-recent time series with window size used for training and classifies it—which of the clusters does it belong to?
- It uses the ML model to predict the clusters for the price and the price change

This solution comes from 2014, but, still, it gives a certain level of robustness. By having many parameters to identify, and not having order-book historical data available, in this project, we use a simpler approach and dataset.

Developing a stock price predictive model

As stated earlier, the stock market price has severe volatility and historical perspective, which make it suited for time analysis. This also challenges those classical algorithms, since long-term dependencies cannot be availed using those algorithms.

As outlined in following diagram, first we collect historical financial data. The data is then converted into a time series after the necessary preprocessing and feature engineering. The resultant time series data is then fed into the LSTM to carry out the training. The following diagram illustrates this:

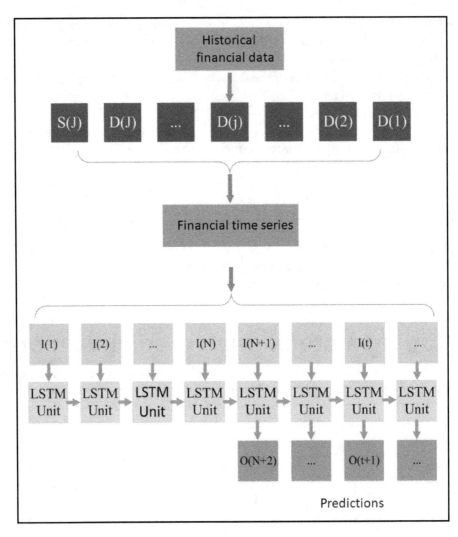

High-level data pipeline of the prototype used for this project

Therefore, we will be using LSTM not only because it outperforms classical algorithms but also because we can solve long-term dependencies with it. Consequently, our project will have the following steps:

1. Load and preprocess the data, and split it into train-and-test sets
2. Train the `LSTM` model with the data
3. Evaluate the model on test data
4. Visualize the model's performance

We will go into the details of each step. However, before that, knowing about the dataset is mandatory.

Data collection and exploratory analysis

As stated earlier, we will utilize historical stock data for training our LSTM network. The dataset has one minute OHLC data from 506 different securities for the period of January 2016 to December 2016. Let's take a look at the data we'll be using:

```java
//DataPreview.java
SparkSession spark =
SparkSession.builder().master("local").appName("StockPricePredictor").getOr
Create();
spark.conf().set("spark.sql.crossJoin.enabled", "true");//enables cross
joining across Spark DataFrames

// load data from csv file
String filename = "data/prices-split-adjusted.csv";
Dataset<Row> data = spark.read().option("inferSchema",
false).option("header", true)
        .format("csv").load(filename)
            .withColumn("openPrice",
functions.col("open").cast("double")).drop("open")
            .withColumn("closePrice",
functions.col("close").cast("double")).drop("close")
            .withColumn("lowPrice",
functions.col("low").cast("double")).drop("low")
            .withColumn("highPrice",
functions.col("high").cast("double")).drop("high")
            .withColumn("volumeTmp",
functions.col("volume").cast("double")).drop("volume")
            .toDF("date", "symbol", "open", "close", "low", "high",
"volume");
data.show(10);
```

The following snapshot shows the output from this code:

```
+----------+------+----------+----------+----------+----------+---------+
|      date|symbol|      open|     close|       low|      high|   volume|
+----------+------+----------+----------+----------+----------+---------+
|2016-01-05|  WLTW|    123.43|125.839996|122.309998|    126.25|2163600.0|
|2016-01-06|  WLTW|125.239998|119.980003|119.940002|125.540001|2386400.0|
|2016-01-07|  WLTW|116.379997|114.949997|    114.93|119.739998|2489500.0|
|2016-01-08|  WLTW|115.480003|116.620003|     113.5|117.440002|2006300.0|
|2016-01-11|  WLTW|117.010002|114.970001|114.089996|117.330002|1408600.0|
|2016-01-12|  WLTW|115.510002|115.550003|     114.5|116.059998|1098000.0|
|2016-01-13|  WLTW|116.459999|112.849998|112.589996|    117.07| 949600.0|
|2016-01-14|  WLTW|113.510002|114.379997|110.050003|115.029999| 785300.0|
|2016-01-15|  WLTW|113.330002|112.529999|111.919998|114.879997|1093700.0|
|2016-01-19|  WLTW|113.660004|110.379997|109.870003|115.870003|1523500.0|
+----------+------+----------+----------+----------+----------+---------+
only showing top 10 rows
```

A snapshot of the historical dataset used in this project

As shown in the preceding screenshot, our dataset has seven features. They're described as follows:

- `date`: Time elapsed between January 2016 and December 2016
- `symbol`: Ticker symbols for 506 different securities
- `open`: The price at the opening of the time interval
- `close`: The price at the closing of the time interval
- `high`: The highest price from all orders executed during the interval
- `low`: Same, but the lowest price
- `volume`: The sum of all stocks that were transferred during the time interval

Now let's take a look at some ticker symbols (see more in the `securities.csv` file):

```
data.createOrReplaceTempView("stock");
spark.sql("SELECT DISTINCT symbol FROM stock GROUP BY symbol").show(10);
```

The is snapshot shows the output from the previous code:

```
+------+
|symbol|
+------+
|  ALXN|
|   GIS|
|     K|
|   LEN|
|  SPGI|
|   AVY|
|   AIV|
|  MMM||
|   PKI|
|   PPG|
+------+
only showing top 10 rows
```

Some symbols whose stock price data is used in this project

If we need to learn about securities, the following table gives us some insight into this:

	Ticker symbol	Security	SEC filings	GICS Sector	GICS Sub Industry	Address of Headquarte
2	MMM	3M Company	reports	Industrials	Industrial Conglomerates	St. Paul, Minnesota
3	ABT	Abbott Laboratories	reports	Health Care	Health Care Equipment	North Chicago, Illinois
4	ABBV	AbbVie	reports	Health Care	Pharmaceuticals	North Chicago, Illinois
5	ACN	Accenture plc	reports	Information Technology	IT Consulting & Other Services	Dublin, Ireland
6	ATVI	Activision Blizzard	reports	Information Technology	Home Entertainment Software	Santa Monica, California
7	AYI	Acuity Brands Inc	reports	Industrials	Electrical Components & Equipment	Atlanta, Georgia
8	ADBE	Adobe Systems Inc	reports	Information Technology	Application Software	San Jose, California
9	AAP	Advance Auto Parts	reports	Consumer Discretionary	Automotive Retail	Roanoke, Virginia
10	AES	AES Corp	reports	Utilities	Independent Power Producers & Energy Traders	Arlington, Virginia

Some securities and their details, whose stock price data is used in this project

Then we decide to see the average price of four categories—open, close, low, and high—for all individual securities. Take a look at this code:

```
spark.sql("SELECT symbol, avg(open) as avg_open, "
          + "avg(close) as avg_close, "
          + "avg(low) as avg_low, "
          + "avg(high) as avg_high "
          + "FROM stock GROUP BY symbol")
          .show(10);
```

This snapshot shows the output from the previous code:

```
+------+-------------------+-------------------+-------------------+-------------------+
|symbol|           avg_open|          avg_close|            avg_low|           avg_high|
+------+-------------------+-------------------+-------------------+-------------------+
|  ALXN|108.80929055675361|108.80724465210005|107.01665432179338| 110.4220716129398|
|   GIS|  47.50769861662885|  47.53702609988646|  47.20578890436999|  47.81829174035188|
|     K|  60.7798750891033|60.812451743473225|60.396668640181694|  61.18173103064723|
|   LEN|  33.70927924404085|  33.69652100794552|  33.21101586038595|  34.17997733144158|
|  SPGI|   67.3407944982973|   67.3793473399546|  66.71868329568667|  67.96350737741204|
|   AVY|  46.31455735584563|  46.33024974460847|  45.88852444948926|  46.74310443303073|
|   AIV|30.436407484676547|30.45744606526678|30.130329164585707|  30.74774691770716|
|   MMM|120.07449489443817|120.14518169636774| 119.2890012593643|120.88434149375733|
|   PKI|  36.43588534619753|  36.45435866685586|  36.103569880363221|  36.76804199318962|
|   PPG|  73.98004543104427|  74.0137713237798|  73.34484397985231|  74.61900109335991|
+------+-------------------+-------------------+-------------------+-------------------+
only showing top 10 rows
```

Average prices for the open, close, low, and high categories

The preceding table, however, did not provide much insight, except when it came to the average prices. Therefore, knowing the minimum and maximum prices gives us an idea whether the stock market really has very high volatility. Take a look at this code:

```
spark.sql("SELECT symbol, "
        + "MIN(open) as min_open, MAX(open) as max_open, "
        + "MIN(close) as min_close, MAX(close) as max_close, "
        + "MIN(low) as min_low, MAX(low) as max_low, "
        + "MIN(high) as min_high, MAX(high) as max_high "
        + "FROM stock GROUP BY symbol")
        .show(10);
```

This snapshot shows the code's output:

```
+------+---------+----------+---------+----------+---------+----------+---------+----------+
|symbol| min_open|  max_open|min_close| max_close|  min_low|   max_low| min_high|  max_high|
+------+---------+----------+---------+----------+---------+----------+---------+----------+
|  ALXN|22.7250005|206.660004|    22.75|207.839996|22.4300005|205.509995|22.8999995|208.880005|
|   GIS|33.419998| 72.650002|    33.57| 72.639999|33.110001|      72.0|    33.73| 72.949997|
|     K|46.549999| 86.900002|46.509998| 86.980003|46.330002| 85.400002|    46.84| 87.160004|
|   LEN|     12.4| 55.360001|    12.71|     55.59|    11.93| 54.810001|    12.82| 56.040001|
|  SPGI|27.049999|127.900002|    27.02|127.559998|26.950001|126.559998|27.809999|128.399994|
|   AVY|    23.59| 78.839996|23.969999| 78.839996|    23.52| 78.480003|    24.66| 79.269997|
|   AIV|    15.38|     47.82|    15.21|     47.59|    15.01| 47.080002|    15.56|     47.91|
|   MMM|70.129997|181.729996|    70.93|181.419998|68.629997|181.320007|    72.18|182.270004|
|   PKI|     17.5| 56.869999|    17.49| 56.919998|17.450001| 56.599998|17.719999| 57.279999|
|   PPG|28.8199995|118.480003|    28.84|118.8499985|28.4799995|117.900002|    29.25|118.949997|
+------+---------+----------+---------+----------+---------+----------+---------+----------+
only showing top 10 rows
```

Average max and min prices for the open, close, low, and high categories

This table shows, for example, that the minimum opening and closing prices are not significantly different. However, the maximum opening price or even the closing price is very different. This is the nature of time series data, and it motivated me to choose LSTM by converting the data into a time series.

Preparing the training and test sets

One of the most important parts of the data science pipeline, after data collection (which was in a sense outsourced—we use data collected by others) is data preprocessing, that is, clearing the dataset and transforming it to suit our needs.

So, our goal is to predict the direction of price change from the actual price in dollars over time. To do that, we define variables such as file, symbol, batchSize, splitRatio, and epochs. You can see the explanation of each variable in the inline comments within this code:

```java
// StockPricePrediction.java
String file = "data/prices-split-adjusted.csv";
String symbol = "GRMN"; // stock name
int batchSize = 128; // mini-batch size
double splitRatio = 0.8; // 80% for training, 20% for testing
int epochs = 100; // training epochs
```

We use the StockDataSetIterator constructor variable to prepare the dataset for the model. Here, we prepare the input dataset for the model as a sequence format for category = PriceCategory.ALL, which means we will predict all five price categories (open, close, low, high, and volume). Take a look at this code:

```java
//StockPricePrediction.java
System.out.println("Creating dataSet iterator...");
PriceCategory category = PriceCategory.ALL; // CLOSE: predict close price

iterator = new StockDataSetIterator(file, symbol, batchSize, exampleLength,
splitRatio, category);
System.out.println("Loading test dataset...");
List<Pair<INDArray, INDArray>> test = iterator.getTestDataSet();
```

In the preceding code block, the PriceCategory constructor that we used has the following signature:

```java
public enum PriceCategory {
    OPEN, CLOSE, LOW, HIGH, VOLUME, ALL
}
```

In the same line, the following options are valid too:

```
PriceCategory category = PriceCategory.OPEN; // OPEN: predict open price
PriceCategory category = PriceCategory.CLOSE; // CLOSE: predict close price
PriceCategory category = PriceCategory.LOW; // LOW: predict low price
PriceCategory category = PriceCategory.HIGH; // HIGH: predict high price.
```

Whereas, inside, the constructor function of the `StockDataSetIterator` class has the following functionalities:

- We read the stock data from the file, and for each symbol we create a list
- We set the `miniBatchSize`, `exampleLength`, and `category` variables to class properties
- Then the `split` variable is computed based on the `splitRation` variable
- We separate the `stockDataList` into two parts: train and test
- Then the stock data is split into training and test sets
- We call the function `initializeOffsets()` to initial value for the array `exampleStartOffsets`

Following this, the `StockDataSetIterator()` constructor has the following signature, which generates the test dataset as a `List<Pair<INDArray, INDArray>>`:

```
//StockDataSetIterator.java
/** stock dataset for training */
private List<StockData> train;
```

In the following code, `StockData` is a case class that provides the structure of the dataset to be extracted or prepared from the input CSV file:

```
//StockData.java
private String date; // date
private String symbol; // stock name

private double open; // open price
private double close; // close price
private double low; // low price
private double high; // high price
private double volume; // volume

public StockData () {}

public StockData (String date, String symbol, double open, double close,
double low, double high, double volume) {
        this.date = date;
        this.symbol = symbol;
```

```
    this.open = open;
    this.close = close;
    this.low = low;
    this.high = high;
    this.volume = volume;
}
```

Then we have the following getter and setter methods for the aforementioned variable, which are as follows:

```
public String getDate() { return date; }
public void setDate(String date) { this.date = date; }

public String getSymbol() { return symbol; }
public void setSymbol(String symbol) { this.symbol = symbol; }

public double getOpen() { return open; }
public void setOpen(double open) { this.open = open; }

public double getClose() { return close; }
public void setClose(double close) { this.close = close; }

public double getLow() { return low; }
public void setLow(double low) { this.low = low; }

public double getHigh() { return high; }
public void setHigh(double high) { this.high = high; }

public double getVolume() { return volume; }
public void setVolume(double volume) { this.volume = volume; }
```

Now that we have seen the signature for the StockData.java class, it's time to create the test dataset as StockDataSetIterator:

```
/** adjusted stock dataset for testing */
private List<Pair<INDArray, INDArray>> test;

public StockDataSetIterator (String filename, String symbol, int
miniBatchSize, int exampleLength,
        double splitRatio, PriceCategory category) {
        List<StockData> stockDataList = readStockDataFromFile(filename,
symbol);

        this.miniBatchSize = miniBatchSize;
        this.exampleLength = exampleLength;
        this.category = category;
```

```
        int split = (int) Math.round(stockDataList.size() * splitRatio);
        train = stockDataList.subList(0, split);
        test = generateTestDataSet(stockDataList.subList(split,
stockDataList.size()));
        initializeOffsets();
    }
```

In the preceding method, the `initializeOffsets()` method is invoked to initialize the mini-batch offsets:

```
private void initializeOffsets() {
        exampleStartOffsets.clear();
        int window = exampleLength + predictLength;
        for(int i = 0; i < train.size() - window; i++) {
            exampleStartOffsets.add(i);
                }
    }
```

The actual reading is done using the `readStockDataFromFile()` method. Inside the constructor, first, we call the function `readStockDataFromFile()` to read data from the file and load it to the `stockDataList`. Then we initialize the `StockDataList` list to contain data read from the `csv` file.

Next, we initialize max in min arrays with `Double.MIN_VALUE` and `Double.MAX_VALUE`. Then the `CSV` file is read line by line for five values. The values are inserted subsequently into the constructor of the `StockData` object, and we add this object to `StockDataList`. Additionally, we throw if we have any exception. Finally, the method returns `StockDataList`. The signature of the method is as follows:

```
private List<StockData> readStockDataFromFile (String filename, String
symbol) {
        List<StockData> stockDataList = new ArrayList<>();
        try {
            for(int i = 0; i < maxArray.length; i++) { // initialize max
and min arrays
                maxArray[i] = Double.MIN_VALUE;
                minArray[i] = Double.MAX_VALUE;
            }
            List<String[]> list = new CSVReader(new
FileReader(filename)).readAll();//load as a list
            for(String[] arr : list) {
                if(!arr[1].equals(symbol)) continue;
                double[] nums = new double[VECTOR_SIZE];

                for(int i = 0; i < arr.length - 2; i++) {
                    nums[i] = Double.valueOf(arr[i + 2]);
```

```
                    if(nums[i] > maxArray[i]) maxArray[i] = nums[i];
                    if(nums[i] < minArray[i]) minArray[i] = nums[i];
                }
                stockDataList.add(new StockData(arr[0], arr[1], nums[0],
    nums[1],
                                    nums[2], nums[3], nums[4]));
            }
        } catch (IOException e) {
            e.printStackTrace();
        }
        return stockDataList;
    }
```

Then the `generateTestDataSet()` method actually generates the features only consumable by the LSTM model as `List<Pair<INDArray, INDArray>>`, where the ordering is set as `f` for faster construct:

```
private List<Pair<INDArray, INDArray>> generateTestDataSet (List<StockData>
stockDataList) {
        int window = exampleLength + predictLength;
        List<Pair<INDArray, INDArray>> test = new ArrayList<>();

        for (int i = 0; i < stockDataList.size() - window; i++) {
            INDArray input = Nd4j.create(new int[] {exampleLength,
VECTOR_SIZE}, 'f');

            for (int j = i; j < i + exampleLength; j++) {
                StockData stock = stockDataList.get(j);
                input.putScalar(new int[] {j - i, 0}, (stock.getOpen() -
minArray[0]) / (maxArray[0] -
                    minArray[0]));
                input.putScalar(new int[] {j - i, 1}, (stock.getClose() -
minArray[1]) / (maxArray[1] -
                    minArray[1]));
                input.putScalar(new int[] {j - i, 2}, (stock.getLow() -
minArray[2]) / (maxArray[2] -
                    minArray[2]));
                input.putScalar(new int[] {j - i, 3}, (stock.getHigh() -
minArray[3]) / (maxArray[3] -
                    minArray[3]));
                input.putScalar(new int[] {j - i, 4}, (stock.getVolume() -
minArray[4]) / (maxArray[4] -
                    minArray[4]));
            }
            StockData stock = stockDataList.get(i + exampleLength);
            INDArray label;
```

```
                    if (category.equals(PriceCategory.ALL)) {
                        label = Nd4j.create(new int[]{VECTOR_SIZE}, 'f'); //
ordering is set faster construct
                        label.putScalar(new int[] {0}, stock.getOpen());
                        label.putScalar(new int[] {1}, stock.getClose());
                        label.putScalar(new int[] {2}, stock.getLow());
                        label.putScalar(new int[] {3}, stock.getHigh());
                        label.putScalar(new int[] {4}, stock.getVolume());
                    } else {
                        label = Nd4j.create(new int[] {1}, 'f');
                        switch (category) {
                            case OPEN: label.putScalar(new int[] {0},
stock.getOpen()); break;
                            case CLOSE: label.putScalar(new int[] {0},
stock.getClose()); break;
                            case LOW: label.putScalar(new int[] {0},
stock.getLow()); break;
                            case HIGH: label.putScalar(new int[] {0},
stock.getHigh()); break;
                            case VOLUME: label.putScalar(new int[] {0},
stock.getVolume()); break;
                            default: throw new NoSuchElementException();
                        }
                    }
                    test.add(new Pair<>(input, label));
                }
            return test;
        }
```

In the previous code block, we save the `miniBatchSize`, `exampleLength`, and `category` variables as class properties. Then we compute the `split` variable based on the `splitRation` variable. We then separate the `stockDataList` into two parts:

- Indices starting from the beginning to `split` belong to train set
- Indices starting from split+1 to the end of the list belong to test set.

The test data generated is quite different from the train dataset. Call the function
`generatedTestDataSet()` to set up the test dataset. First, we set a window variable by
the example length and the prediction length. Then we loop through from 0 to test the data
length minus the window. Consider the following::

- Read five input variables: open price, close price, low price, high price, and
  volume.
- Base on the value of `category`, read the label value. If `category` is equal to `ALL`,
  then read five variables such as input variables. Otherwise, read only one
  variable via the value of `category`.

In the preceding code block, the labels are being fed using the `feedLabel()` method,
which goes as follows:

```
private double feedLabel(StockData data) {
        double value;

        switch(category) {
            case OPEN: value = (data.getOpen() - minArray[0]) /
(maxArray[0] - minArray[0]); break;
            case CLOSE: value = (data.getClose() - minArray[1]) /
(maxArray[1] - minArray[1]); break;
            case LOW: value = (data.getLow() - minArray[2]) / (maxArray[2]
- minArray[2]); break;
            case HIGH: value = (data.getHigh() - minArray[3]) /
(maxArray[3] - minArray[3]); break;
            case VOLUME: value = (data.getVolume() - minArray[4]) /
(maxArray[4] - minArray[4]); break;
            default: throw new NoSuchElementException();
        }
        return value;
    }
```

In the preceding code block, we initialize variable `value`. We then check the value of
variable `category`, and the computed value of variable `value` can be seen using math
notation as follows:

```
value = (data.getOpen() - minArray[0]) / (maxArray[0] - minArray[0])
```

Then both the features and labels are used to prepare the dataset. Take a look at this code:

```
public DataSet next(int num) {
        if(exampleStartOffsets.size() == 0) throw new
NoSuchElementException();
        int actualMiniBatchSize = Math.min(num,
```

```
exampleStartOffsets.size());

        INDArray input = Nd4j.create(new int[] {actualMiniBatchSize,
VECTOR_SIZE, exampleLength}, 'f');
        INDArray label;
        if(category.equals(PriceCategory.ALL))
            label = Nd4j.create(new int[] {actualMiniBatchSize,
VECTOR_SIZE, exampleLength}, 'f');
        else
            label = Nd4j.create(new int[] {actualMiniBatchSize,
predictLength, exampleLength}, 'f');
        for(int index = 0; index < actualMiniBatchSize; index++) {
            int startIdx = exampleStartOffsets.removeFirst();
            int endIdx = startIdx + exampleLength;

            StockData curData = train.get(startIdx);
            StockData nextData;

            for(int i = startIdx; i < endIdx; i++) {
                int c = i - startIdx;
                input.putScalar(new int[] {index, 0, c}, (curData.getOpen()
- minArray[0])
                                / (maxArray[0] - minArray[0]));
                input.putScalar(new int[] {index, 1, c},
(curData.getClose() - minArray[1])
                                / (maxArray[1] - minArray[1]));
                input.putScalar(new int[] {index, 2, c}, (curData.getLow()
- minArray[2])
                                / (maxArray[2] - minArray[2]));
                input.putScalar(new int[] {index, 3, c}, (curData.getHigh()
- minArray[3])
                                / (maxArray[3] - minArray[3]));
                input.putScalar(new int[] {index, 4, c},
(curData.getVolume() - minArray[4])
                                / (maxArray[4] - minArray[4]));
                nextData = train.get(i + 1);

                if(category.equals(PriceCategory.ALL)) {
                    label.putScalar(new int[] {index, 0, c},
(nextData.getOpen() - minArray[1])
                                    / (maxArray[1] - minArray[1]));
                    label.putScalar(new int[] {index, 1, c},
(nextData.getClose() - minArray[1])
                                    / (maxArray[1] - minArray[1]));
                    label.putScalar(new int[] {index, 2, c},
(nextData.getLow() - minArray[2])
                                    / (maxArray[2] - minArray[2]));
                    label.putScalar(new int[] {index, 3, c},
```

```
(nextData.getHigh() - minArray[3])
                                / (maxArray[3] - minArray[3]));
                    label.putScalar(new int[] {index, 4, c},
(nextData.getVolume() - minArray[4])
                                / (maxArray[4] - minArray[4]));
                } else {
                    label.putScalar(new int[]{index, 0, c},
feedLabel(nextData));
                }
                curData = nextData;
            }
            if(exampleStartOffsets.size() == 0) break;
        }
        return new DataSet(input, label);
    }
```

In the preceding code block, we loop through the epochs time, and for each time we loop until we have the data, fitting the network with a data get in function iterator.next(). Consider the following:

- We initialize two variables: input using actualMinibatchSize and label with category.
- We then loop from 0 to actualMiniBatchSize. Each time, we create two additional variables: curData, which is a StockData point of current time. Then we put their value into the input list. Similarly thenextData variable is also a StockData point of the day, which is after the day of curData. Finally, we put the value of nextData to label list.

LSTM network construction

As stated earlier, I wrote a class called RecurrentNets.java to build an LSTM network. We create a MultilayerNetwork LSTM network that consists of an input layer, four LSTM layers, three dense layers, and an output layer. The input consists of sequences of genetic variants.

We use the BuildBuildLstmNetworks() method with two parameters—number of input for input layers and number of output for output layers, as shown here:

```
private static final int lstmLayer1Size = 128;
private static final int lstmLayer2Size = 128;
private static final int denseLayerSize = 32;
private static final double dropoutRatio = 0.5;
private static final int truncatedBPTTLength = 22;
```

Now, before we start creating and building the network, let's see what our model would look like:

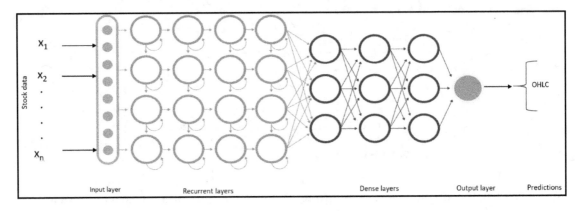

The stock price LSTM network

Then, the `createAndBuildLstmNetworks()` method is used to create and build the network with the preceding parameter setting:

```
public static MultiLayerNetwork createAndBuildLstmNetworks(int nIn, int
nOut) {
        // Creating MultiLayerConfiguration
        MultiLayerConfiguration conf = new NeuralNetConfiguration.Builder()
                .seed(123456)// for the reproducibility
.optimizationAlgo(OptimizationAlgorithm.STOCHASTIC_GRADIENT_DESCENT)//optim
izer
                .updater(new Adam(0.001)) // Adam updater with SGD
                .l2(1e-4)// l2 regularization
                .weightInit(WeightInit.XAVIER)// network weight
initialization
                .activation(Activation.RELU)// ReLU as activation
                .list()
                .layer(0, new LSTM.Builder()//LSTM layer 1
                        .nIn(nIn)
                        .nOut(lstmLayer1Size)
                        .activation(Activation.TANH)
                        .gateActivationFunction(Activation.HARDSIGMOID)//
Segment-wise linear
                                                                      //
approximation of sigmoid
                        .dropOut(dropoutRatio)// keeping drop-out ratio
                        .build())
                .layer(1, new LSTM.Builder()// LSTM layer 2
                        .nIn(lstmLayer1Size)
```

```
                            .nOut(lstmLayer2Size)
                            .activation(Activation.TANH)
                            .gateActivationFunction(Activation.HARDSIGMOID)
                            .dropOut(dropoutRatio)//kee drop-out ratio
                            .build())
                    .layer(2, new LSTM.Builder()//LSTM layer 3
                            .nIn(lstmLayer1Size)
                            .nOut(lstmLayer2Size)
                            .activation(Activation.TANH)
                            .gateActivationFunction(Activation.HARDSIGMOID)
                            .dropOut(dropoutRatio)// keep drop-out ratio
                            .build())
                    .layer(3, new DenseLayer.Builder()// FC layer 1
                            .nIn(lstmLayer2Size)
                            .nOut(denseLayerSize)
                            .activation(Activation.RELU)
                            .build())
                    .layer(4, new DenseLayer.Builder()//FC layer 2
                            .nIn(denseLayerSize)
                            .nOut(denseLayerSize)
                            .activation(Activation.RELU)
                            .build())
                    .layer(5, new DenseLayer.Builder()//FC layer 3
                            .nIn(denseLayerSize)
                            .nOut(denseLayerSize)
                            .activation(Activation.RELU)
                            .build())
                    .layer(6, new RnnOutputLayer.Builder() // RNN output layer
                            .nIn(denseLayerSize)
                            .nOut(nOut)
                            .activation(Activation.IDENTITY)// Regression with
MSE as the loss function
                            .lossFunction(LossFunctions.LossFunction.MSE)
                            .build())
                    .backpropType(BackpropType.TruncatedBPTT)// Back
propagation with time
                    .tBPTTForwardLength(truncatedBPTTLength)
                    .tBPTTBackwardLength(truncatedBPTTLength)
                    .pretrain(false).backprop(true)//no pretraining necessary
                    .build();

        // Creating MultiLayerNetwork using the above MultiLayerConfig
        MultiLayerNetwork net = new MultiLayerNetwork(conf);
        net.init(); // initilize the MultiLayerNetwork
        net.setListeners(new ScoreIterationListener(100));// shows score in
each 100th iteration/epoch
        return net; // return the MultiLayerNetwork
    }
```

Since we created and used an LSTM net several times in this chapter, I decided not to discuss its details. However, one important thing here is the use of the IDENTITY activation with Root Means Square Errors (RMSE), which is used for regression problems.

In short, to perform regression with a neural network in DL4J, you would set up a multilayer neural network and add an output layer at the end with the following properties, as shown previously:

```
//Create output layer
    .layer()
    .nIn($NumberOfInputFeatures)
    .nOut(1)// regression hence, only a single output
    .activation(Activation.IDENTITY)//Regression with RMSE as the loss
function
    .lossFunction(LossFunctions.LossFunction.RMSE)
```

 For more information on regression analysis using DL4j, interested readers can visit https://deeplearning4j.org/evaluation#Regression.

Network training, and saving the trained model

Now that our network as well as the training and test sets are ready, we can start training the network. For this, again we use the DL4J-provided fit() method. We loop through epochs times, for each time looping until we have the data. We fit the network with a miniBatchSize amount of data at each time step, as shown here:

```
// StockPricePrediction.java
System.out.println("Training LSTM network...");
for(int i = 0; i < epochs; i++) {
        while(iterator.hasNext()) net.fit(iterator.next()); // fit
model using mini-batch data
        iterator.reset(); // reset iterator
        net.rnnClearPreviousState(); // clear previous state
    }
```

```
>>
  Creating dataSet iterator...
  Loading test dataset...
  Building LSTM networks...
  Training LSTM network...
```

Once the training is completed, we save the trained model to disk (in directory `data`). Here I specified a sample name `StockPriceLSTM_+ category name + .zip` as shown here:

```
# StockPricePrediction.java
System.out.println("Saving model...");
File locationToSave = new
File("data/StockPriceLSTM_".concat(String.valueOf(category)).concat(".zip")
);

// saveUpdater: i.e., state for Momentum, RMSProp, Adagrad etc. Save this
to train your network in future
ModelSerializer.writeModel(net, locationToSave, true);
```

Now let's take a look at the number of parameters at each layer:

```
//Print the  number of parameters in the network (and for each layer)
Layer[] layers_before_saving = net.getLayers();
            int totalNumParams_before_saving = 0;

            for(int i=0; i<layers_before_saving.length; i++ ){
                int nParams = layers_before_saving[i].numParams();
                System.out.println("Number of parameters in layer " + i +
": " + nParams);
                totalNumParams_before_saving += nParams;
            }
System.out.println("Total number of network parameters: " +
totalNumParams_before_saving);

>>>
  Saving model...
  Number of parameters in layer 0: 68608
  Number of parameters in layer 1: 131584
  Number of parameters in layer 2: 131584
  Number of parameters in layer 3: 4128
  Number of parameters in layer 4: 1056
  Number of parameters in layer 5: 1056
  Number of parameters in layer 6: 165
  Total number of network parameters: 338181
```

Nevertheless, we enable the DL4J UI to view the training progress and params, as shown here:

```
//Initialize the user interface backend
UIServer uiServer = UIServer.getInstance();

//Configure where the network information (gradients, activations, score
vs. time etc) is to be stored. //Then add the StatsListener to collect this
```

```
information from the network, as it trains:
StatsStorage statsStorage = new InMemoryStatsStorage();

//Alternative: new FileStatsStorage(File) - see UIStorageExample. Attach
the StatsStorage instance to the //UI: this allows the contents of the
StatsStorage to be visualized:
uiServer.attach(statsStorage);

int listenerFrequency = 1;
net.setListeners(new StatsListener(statsStorage, listenerFrequency));
```

The following screenshot shows the output:

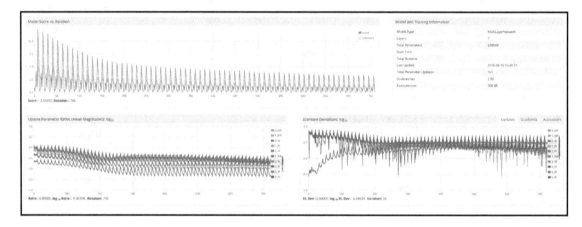

Network parameters on the UI

The graphs look as though they are not regularized, probably because we do not have enough training data.

Restoring the saved model for inferencing

Now that we have finished the training, and the trained model is at hand, we can either directly use that trained one on the fly as well as restore the saved model from disk, or start the inferencing. Take a look at this code:

```
System.out.println("Restoring model...");
net = ModelSerializer.restoreMultiLayerNetwork(locationToSave);

//print the score with every 1 iteration
net.setListeners(new ScoreIterationListener(1));
```

```
//Print the number of parameters in the network (and for each layer)
Layer[] layers = net.getLayers();

int totalNumParams = 0;
for( int i=0; i<layers.length; i++ ){
        int nParams = layers[i].numParams();
        System.out.println("Number of parameters in layer " + i + ": " +
nParams);
        totalNumParams += nParams;
}
System.out.println("Total number of network parameters: " +
totalNumParams);
```

```
>>>
 Restoring model...
 Number of parameters in layer 0: 68608
 Number of parameters in layer 1: 131584
 Number of parameters in layer 2: 131584
 Number of parameters in layer 3: 4128
 Number of parameters in layer 4: 1056
 Number of parameters in layer 5: 1056
 Number of parameters in layer 6: 165
 Total number of network parameters: 338181
```

Evaluating the model

The number of parameters is the same as the one we saved on disk. This means our trained model is not contaminated, so we are safe. Next up, we start evaluating the model on the test set. But, as stated earlier, we will perform a two-way evaluation of the model. First, we predict one feature of a stock, one day ahead, as shown here:

```
/** Predict one feature of a stock one-day ahead */
private static void predictPriceOneAhead (MultiLayerNetwork net,
List<Pair<INDArray, INDArray>> testData, double max, double min,
PriceCategory category) {
        double[] predicts = new double[testData.size()];
        double[] actuals = new double[testData.size()];
        for (int i = 0; i < testData.size(); i++) {
            predicts[i] =
net.rnnTimeStep(testData.get(i).getKey()).getDouble(exampleLength - 1)
                        * (max - min) + min;
            actuals[i] = testData.get(i).getValue().getDouble(0);
        }
        RegressionEvaluation eval = net.evaluateRegression(iterator);
        System.out.println(eval.stats());
        System.out.println("Printing predicted and actual values...");
```

```
        System.out.println("Predict, Actual");
        for (int i = 0; i < predicts.length; i++)
            System.out.println(predicts[i] + "," + actuals[i]);
        System.out.println("Plottig...");
        PlotUtil.plot(predicts, actuals, String.valueOf(category));
    }
```

In the preceding code block, we perform the training for a single category, for example, by setting any one of the following options:

```
PriceCategory category = PriceCategory.OPEN; // OPEN: predict open price
PriceCategory category = PriceCategory.CLOSE; // CLOSE: predict close price
PriceCategory category = PriceCategory.LOW; // LOW: predict low price
PriceCategory category = PriceCategory.HIGH; // HIGH: predict high price
```

We can do the evaluation simultaneously for all the categories by setting `PriceCategory category = PriceCategory.ALL; // ALL: predict close price`.

Thus, we predict all the features (open, close, low, high prices, and volume) of a stock, one day ahead. The process of evaluation on a category is the same within case all categories. There is only one thing different: We need to loop through a number of categories using `PlotUtil` for the draw XY line chart, as shown here:

```
/** Predict all the features (open, close, low, high prices and volume) of
a stock one-day ahead */
private static void predictAllCategories (MultiLayerNetwork net,
List<Pair<INDArray, INDArray>> testData, INDArray max, INDArray min) {
        INDArray[] predicts = new INDArray[testData.size()];
        INDArray[] actuals = new INDArray[testData.size()];
        for(int i = 0; i < testData.size(); i++) {
            predicts[i] =
net.rnnTimeStep(testData.get(i).getKey()).getRow(exampleLength - 1)
                        .mul(max.sub(min)).add(min);
            actuals[i] = testData.get(i).getValue();
        }
        System.out.println("Printing predicted and actual values...");
        System.out.println("Predict, Actual");

        for(int i = 0; i < predicts.length; i++)
            System.out.println(predicts[i] + "\t" + actuals[i]);
        System.out.println("Plottig...");
        RegressionEvaluation eval = net.evaluateRegression(iterator);
        System.out.println(eval.stats());
        for(int n = 0; n < 5; n++) {
            double[] pred = new double[predicts.length];
            double[] actu = new double[actuals.length];
```

```
        for(int i = 0; i < predicts.length; i++) {
            pred[i] = predicts[i].getDouble(n);
            actu[i] = actuals[i].getDouble(n);
        }
        String name;
        switch(n) {
            case 0: name = "Stock OPEN Price"; break;
            case 1: name = "Stock CLOSE Price"; break;
            case 2: name = "Stock LOW Price"; break;
            case 3: name = "Stock HIGH Price"; break;
            case 4: name = "Stock VOLUME Amount"; break;
            default: throw new NoSuchElementException();
        }
        PlotUtil.plot(pred, actu, name);
    }
}
```

In the preceding code block, we go to the function `predictAllCategories()` to see how evaluation goes on in all categories. Next, we create two arrays, `predicts` and `actuals`, to store the predicted result and the actual result. Then we loop over the test data. Then we do the following:

- Call the function `net.rnnTimeStep()` with parameter as the key of row i-th and append the result to the `predicts` list
- Actual value gets from the value of test data row i^{th}
- Print the predicted value and actual values

Finally, we loop through five categories; we're using the `PlotUtil.java` to draw an *XY* line chart between predicted and actual values. Consider the following:

- The initial two double arrays are named `pred` and `actu` with size equal to the size of the predicted length.
- Loop through the `predicts` and `actuals` arrays and, get the double value of each element in each list.
- With each value of *n* has four values from 0 to 4. Set the variable `name` to the ledge of the *Y* column.
- Call the function `PlotUtil` to draw the *XY* line.

By the way, the `PlotUtil.java` class is used to draw an *XY* line for predicted versus actual values, which goes as follows:

```java
public static void plot(double[] predicts, double[] actuals, String name) {
        double[] index = new double[predicts.length];
        for(int i = 0; i < predicts.length; i++)
            index[i] = i;
        int min = minValue(predicts, actuals);
        int max = maxValue(predicts, actuals);
        final XYSeriesCollection dataSet = new XYSeriesCollection();
        addSeries(dataSet, index, predicts, "Predicted");
        addSeries(dataSet, index, actuals, "Actual");
        final JFreeChart chart = ChartFactory.createXYLineChart(
                "Predicted vs Actual", // chart title
                "Index", // x axis label
                name, // y axis label
                dataSet, // data
                PlotOrientation.VERTICAL,
                true, // include legend
                true, // tooltips
                false // urls
            );
        XYPlot xyPlot = chart.getXYPlot();
        // X-axis
        final NumberAxis domainAxis = (NumberAxis) xyPlot.getDomainAxis();
        domainAxis.setRange((int) index[0], (int) (index[index.length - 1]
 + 2));
        domainAxis.setTickUnit(new NumberTickUnit(20));
        domainAxis.setVerticalTickLabels(true);
        // Y-axis
        final NumberAxis rangeAxis = (NumberAxis) xyPlot.getRangeAxis();
        rangeAxis.setRange(min, max);
        rangeAxis.setTickUnit(new NumberTickUnit(50));
        final ChartPanel panel = new ChartPanel(chart);
        final JFrame f = new JFrame();
        f.add(panel);
        f.setDefaultCloseOperation(WindowConstants.EXIT_ON_CLOSE);
        f.pack();
        f.setVisible(true);
    }
```

In the preceding code block, the `addSeries()` method is used to add the *XY* series, which is as follows:

```
private static void addSeries (final XYSeriesCollection dataSet, double[]
x, double[] y, final String label){
        final XYSeries s = new XYSeries(label);
        for(int j = 0; j < x.length; j++ ) s.add(x[j], y[j]);
        dataSet.addSeries(s);
    }
```

Apart from these, finding the min, max values of `predicted` and `actual` values that we used in the preceding code happen as follows:

- **Finding min:** First, we set variable `min` as `MAX_VALUE`. Then we loop through the `predicted` and `actual` arrays, such that if `min` is greater than any element, then we reset `min` as the current element. Then we take the integer closest lower bound of value of min:

```
private static int minValue (double[] predicts, double[] actuals) {
        double min = Integer.MAX_VALUE;

        for(int i = 0; i < predicts.length; i++) {
            if(min > predicts[i]) min = predicts[i];
            if(min > actuals[i]) min = actuals[i];
        }
        return (int) (min * 0.98);
    }
```

- **Finding max:** First, we set the variable `max` as `MIN_VALUE`. Then we loop through the `predicts` and `actual` arrays such that if `max <` any element, we reset `max` as this element. Then we take the integer closest to the upper bound of the value of max as shown here:

```
private static int maxValue (double[] predicts, double[] actuals) {
        double max = Integer.MIN_VALUE;

        for(int i = 0; i < predicts.length; i++) {
            if(max < predicts[i]) max = predicts[i];
            if(max < actuals[i]) max = actuals[i];
        }
        return (int) (max * 1.02);
    }
```

Finally, we use the `addSeries()` method to add a series to dataSet while plotting the graph. Nevertheless, since the task is a regression, we perform the evaluation showing regression metrics too, such as MSE, MAE, R2, and so on.

Now, based on the preceding plans and based on the value of variable `category`, we have two methods to evaluate the model. If the category is ALL, then the network will predict all categories; otherwise, the network will work only on one category. First, for only a single category, say OPEN. Take a look at this code:

```
System.out.println("Evaluating...");
if(category.equals(PriceCategory.OPEN)) {
        INDArray max = Nd4j.create(iterator.getMaxArray());
        INDArray min = Nd4j.create(iterator.getMinArray());
        predictAllCategories(net, test, max, min);
} else {
        double max = iterator.getMaxNum(category);
        double min = iterator.getMinNum(category);
        predictPriceOneAhead(net, test, max, min, category);
}
System.out.println("Done...");
```

```
>>>
Evaluating...
Printing predicted and actual values...
Predict, Actual
----------------------------------------
29.175033326034814,35.61000061035156
29.920153324534823,35.70000076293945
30.84457991629533,35.9900016784668
31.954761620513793,36.150001525878906
33.171770076832885,36.79999923706055
34.42622247035372,36.150001525878906
35.63831635695636,36.41999816894531
36.79695794284552,36.04999923706055
37.79222186089784,35.9900016784668
38.45504267616927,35.470001220703125
38.837315702846766,35.66999816894531
```

Then the regression metrics will be printed as follows (you may experience slightly different result, though):

Column MSE MAE RMSE RSE PC R^2
----
col_0 3.27134e-02 1.14001e-01 1.80868e-01 5.53901e-01 7.17285e-01 4.46100e-01

Finally, we observe the following screenshot showing predicted versus actual OPEN prices:

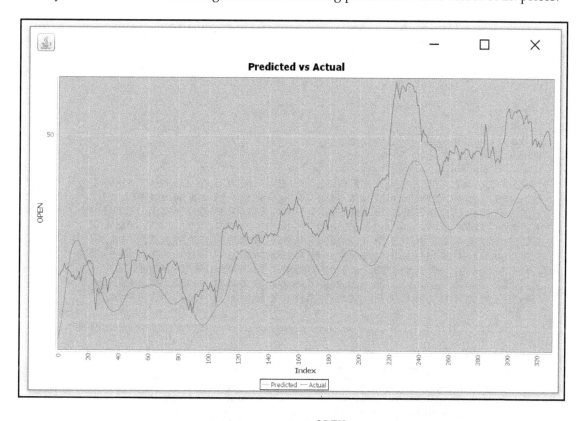

Predicted versus actual prices for OPEN category

Then, for only the **ALL** category, we run a similar code, except that `PriceCategory.ALL` is used as follows:

```
System.out.println("Evaluating...");
if(category.equals(PriceCategory.ALL)) {
        INDArray max = Nd4j.create(iterator.getMaxArray());
        INDArray min = Nd4j.create(iterator.getMinArray());
        predictAllCategories(net, test, max, min);
} else {
        double max = iterator.getMaxNum(category);
        double min = iterator.getMinNum(category);
        predictPriceOneAhead(net, test, max, min, category);
   }
System.out.println("Done...");
```

>>>
 Evaluating...
Printing predicted and actual values...
Predict, Actual

---------- --
[[27.8678,27.1462,27.0535,27.9431, 9.7079e5]] [[35.6100,35.8900,35.5500,36.1100, 1.5156e6]]
[[28.3925,27.2648,27.2769,28.4423, 1.2579e6]] [[35.7000,35.8100,35.6500,36.1000,8.623e5]]
[[29.0413,27.4402,27.6015,29.1540, 1.6014e6]] [[35.9900,36.1400,35.9000,36.3200, 1.0829e6]]
[[29.9264,27.6811,28.0419,30.1133, 2.0673e6]] [[36.1500,36.7100,36.0700,36.7600, 1.0635e6]]
[[30.9201,27.9385,28.5584,31.2908, 2.5381e6]] [[36.8000,36.5700,36.4600,37.1600, 1.0191e6]]
[[32.0080,28.2469,29.1343,32.6514, 3.0186e6]] [[36.1500,36.2300,35.9300,36.7600, 1.8299e6]]
[[33.1358,28.5809,29.7641,34.1525, 3.4644e6]] [[36.4200,36.5400,36.1800,36.8900,8.774e5]]
[[45.2637,31.2634,39.5828,53.1128, 5.0282e6]] [[50.3600,49.2200,49.1700,50.4500,9.415e5]]
[[45.1651,31.2336,39.5284,52.9815, 4.9879e6]] [[49.1700,49.0100,48.8100,49.4400,9.517e5]]

Then the regression metrics will be printed as follows (you may experience slightly different result, though):

Column MSE MAE RMSE RSE PC R^2

----
col_0 4.52917e-02 1.35709e-01 2.12819e-01 7.49715e-01 6.60401e-01 2.50287e-01
col_1 1.52875e-01 3.27669e-01 3.90993e-01 2.54384e+00 6.61151e-01 -1.54384e+00
col_2 8.46744e-02 2.19064e-01 2.90989e-01 1.41381e+00 6.01910e-01 -4.13806e-01
col_3 6.05071e-02 1.93558e-01 2.45982e-01 9.98581e-01 5.95618e-01 1.41977e-03
col_4 2.34488e-02 1.17289e-01 1.53130e-01 9.97561e+00 5.59983e-03 -8.97561e+00

Now take a look at the following graph, showing predicted versus actual ALL prices:

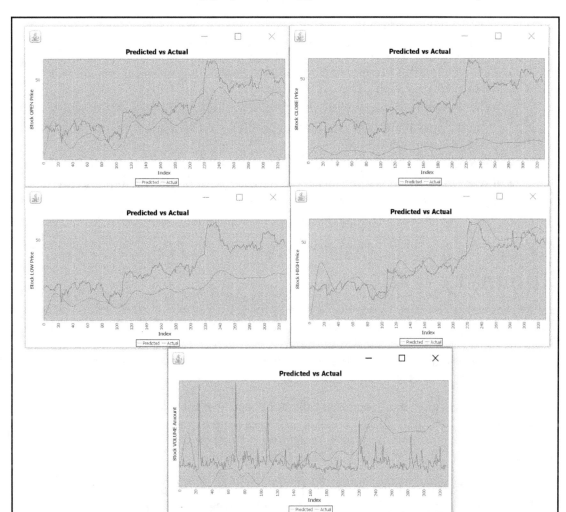

Predicted versus actual prices for ALL categories

From the graph, we can see that the price for OPEN and HIGH shows a good fit, whereas LOW shows a somewhat good fit. Unfortunately, CLOSE and VOLUME show a very disappointing fit (see the preceding regression result table). One possible reason could be lack of data. And also, the hyperparameters used are not hypertuned at all. Nevertheless, most of the hyperparameters were chosen naively.

Frequently asked questions (FAQs)

In this section, we will see some frequently asked questions that may be already on your mind. Answers to these questions can be found in Appendix A:

1. Can I extend this project for Bitcoin price prediction purposes? If so, how and where can I get such datasets?
2. What happens if you take predicted values as input for the next prediction?
3. I understand that this is a regression problem, but how can I predict whether a price will go up or down?
4. I would like to extend this app and deploy a web application. How can I do that?
5. I want to extend this application not only for price prediction, but also for anomaly detection in prices. How can I do that?
6. Can I use similar technique for stock price recommendation?

Summary

In this chapter,we saw how to develop a demo project for predicting stock prices for five categories: OPEN, CLOSE, LOW, HIGH, and VOLUME. However, our approach cannot generate an actual signal. Still, it gives some idea of how to use LSTM. I know there are some serious drawbacks of this approach. Nevertheless, we did not use enough data, which potentially limits the performance of such a model.

In the next chapter, we will see how to apply deep learning approaches to a video dataset. We will describe how to process and extract features from a large collection of video clips. Then we will make the overall pipeline scalable and faster by distributing the training on multiple devices (CPUs and GPUs), and run them in parallel.

We will see a complete example of how to develop a deep learning application that accurately classifies a large collection of a video dataset, such as UCF101, using a combined CNN-LSTM network with DL4J. It overcomes the limitations of standalone CNN or LSTM networks. The training will be carried out on an Amazon EC2 GPU compute cluster. Eventually, this end-to-end project can be treated as a primer for human activity recognition from video or so.

Answers to questions

Answer to question 1: Some historical Bitcoin data can be downloaded from Kaggle, for example, `https://www.kaggle.com/mczielinski/bitcoin-historical-data/data`.

Once you've downloaded the dataset, try to extract the most important features and convert the dataset into a time series so that it can be fed into an LSTM model. Then the model can be trained with the time series for each time step.

Answer to question 2: Our sample project only calculates the stock price of those stocks whose actual stock price is given, and not the next day's stock price. It shows `actual` and `predicted`, but the next day's stock price should only contain `predicted`. This is what is happening if we take predicted values as input for the next prediction:

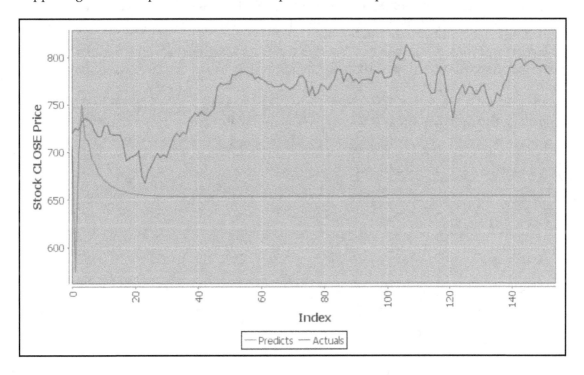

Predicted versus actual prices for $\mathbb{ALL}$ categories, where predicted values are input for the next prediction

Answer to question 3: Well, then the task would be a binary classification problem. To make this happen, you need to make two changes:

- Convert the dataset such that there will be two labels
- Replace the `IDENTITY` activation function and `RMSE` loss with cross-entropy loss

Answer to question 4: That is a great idea. You can try improving the modeling by following questions 1 and 2. Then you can save the model on disk for later stage inferencing. Finally, you can serve this model as a web application, as suggested in previous chapters.

Answer to question 5: Applying anomaly detection in such a dataset is very challenging, and I am not sure whether it is feasible, since the market has very high volatility. Therefore, the time series will have very many vicissitudes sometimes, which is the nature of the stock market. This helps the trained model to identify that abnormal volatility.

Answer **to question 6:** Yes, you can. You can try using **Machine Learning based ZZAlpha Ltd. Stock Recommendations 2012-2014 Data Set.** This dataset can be downloaded from `UCI ML repository` at `https://archive.ics.uci.edu/ml/datasets/` `Machine+Learning+based+ZZAlpha+Ltd.+Stock+Recommendations+2012-2014`. The repository also describes the problem as well as the dataset.

8
Distributed Deep Learning – Video Classification Using Convolutional LSTM Networks

So far, we have seen how to develop deep-learning-based projects on numerals and images. However, applying similar techniques to video clips, for example, for human activity recognition from video, is not straightforward.

In this chapter, we will see how to apply deep learning approaches to a video dataset. We will describe how to process and extract features from a large collection of video clips. Then we will make the overall pipeline scalable and faster by distributing the training on multiple devices (CPUs and GPUs), and run them in parallel.

We will see a complete example of how to develop a deep learning application that accurately classifies a large collection of a video dataset, such as UCF101 dataset, using a combined CNN and LSTM network with **Deeplearning4j** (**DL4J**). This overcomes the limitation of standalone CNN or RNN **Long Short-Term Memory** (**LSTM**) networks.

The training will be carried out on an Amazon EC2 GPU compute cluster. Eventually, this end-to-end project can be treated as a primer for human activity recognition from a video or so. Concisely, we will learn the following topics throughout an end-to-end project:

- Distributed deep learning across multiple GPUs
- Dataset collection and description
- Developing a video classifier using a convolutional-LSTM network
- Frequently asked questions (FAQs)

Distributed deep learning across multiple GPUs

As stated earlier, we will see a systematic example for classifying a large collection of video clips from the `UCF101` dataset using a convolutional-LSTM network. However, first we need to know how to distribute the training across multiple GPUs. In previous chapters, we discussed several advanced techniques such as network weight initialization, batch normalization, faster optimizers, proper activation functions, etc. these certainly help the network to converge faster. However, still, training a large neural network on a single machine can take days or even weeks. Therefore, this is not a viable way for working with large-scale datasets.

Theoretically, there are two main methods for the distributed training of neural networks: data parallelism and model parallelism. DL4J relies on data parallelism called distributed deep learning with parameter averaging. Nevertheless, multimedia analytics typically makes things even more complicated, since, from a single video clip, we can see thousands of frames and images, and so on. To get rid of this issue, we will first distribute computations across multiple devices on just one machine, and then do it on multiple devices across multiple machines as follows:

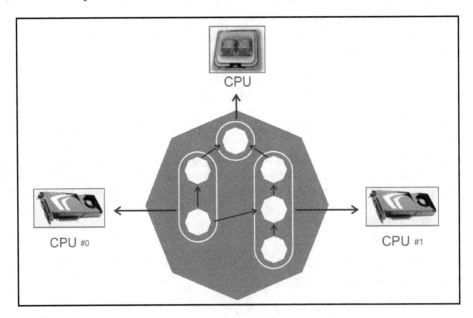

Executing a DL4J Java application across multiple devices in parallel

For example, you can typically train a neural network just as fast using eight GPUs on a single machine rather than 16 GPUs across multiple machines. The reason is simple—the extra delay imposed by network communications in a multi-machine setup. The following diagram shows how to configure DL4J that uses CUDA and cuDNN to control GPUs and boost DNNs:

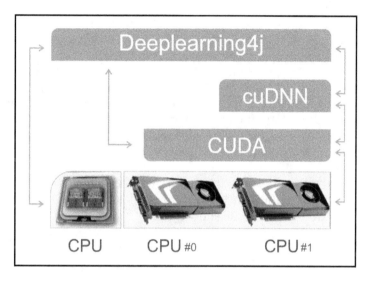

DL4J uses CUDA and cuDNN to control GPUs and boost DNNs

Distributed training on GPUs with DL4J

DL4J works on distributed GPUs as well as on native (that is, ones with CPU backend). It allows users to run locally on a single GPU, such as the Nvidia Tesla, Titan, or GeForce GTX, and in the cloud on Nvidia GRID GPUs. We can also perform the training on an Amazon AWS EC2 GPU cluster,by having multiple GPUs installed.

To train a neural network on GPUs, you need to make some changes to the pom.xml file in your root directory, such as properties and dependency management for pulling down the required dependencies provided by the DL4j team. First, we take care of the project properties, as follows:

```
<properties>
        <project.build.sourceEncoding>UTF-8</project.build.sourceEncoding>
        <java.version>1.8</java.version>
        <jdk.version>1.8</jdk.version>
        <nd4j.backend>nd4j-cuda-9.0-platform</nd4j.backend>
```

```
<nd4j.version>1.0.0-alpha</nd4j.version>
<dl4j.version>1.0.0-alpha</dl4j.version>
<datavec.version>1.0.0-alpha</datavec.version>
<arbiter.version>1.0.0-alpha</arbiter.version>
<logback.version>1.2.3</logback.version>
</properties>
```

In the preceding `<properties>` tag, as the entries explain, we will be using DL4J 1.0.0-alpha version with CUDA 9.0 platform as the backend. In addition, we plan to use Java 8. Nonetheless, an additional property for `logback` is defined.

Logback is intended as a successor to the popular log4j project, picking up where log4j left off. Logback's architecture is sufficiently generic so as to apply under different circumstances. Presently, logback is divided into three modules, logback-core, logback-classic and logback-access. For more information, readers should refer to `https://logback.qos.ch/`.

I am assuming you have already configured CUDA and cuDNN and set the path accordingly. Once we have defined the project properties, the next important task would be to define GPU-related dependencies, as shown here:

```
<dependency>
    <groupId>org.nd4j</groupId>
    <artifactId>nd4j-cuda-9.0-platform</artifactId>
    <version>${nd4j.version}</version>
</dependency>
<dependency>
    <groupId>org.deeplearning4j</groupId>
    <artifactId>deeplearning4j-cuda-9.0</artifactId>
    <version>${dl4j.version}</version>
</dependency>
```

Where ND4J is the numerical computing engine that powers DL4J and acts as the backends, or different types of hardware that it works on. If your system has multiple GPUs installed, you can train your model in data-parallel mode, which is called **multi-GPU data parallelism**. DL4J provides a simple wrapper that can be instantiated, something like this:

```
// ParallelWrapper will take care of load balancing between GPUs.
ParallelWrapper wrapper = new ParallelWrapper.Builder(YourExistingModel)
    .prefetchBuffer(24)
    .workers(8)
    .averagingFrequency(1)
    .reportScoreAfterAveraging(true)
    .useLegacyAveraging(false)
    .build();
```

A more concrete example can be seen as follows:

```
ParallelWrapper wrapper = new ParallelWrapper.Builder(net)
            .prefetchBuffer(8)// DataSets prefetching options. Set to
number of actual devices
            .workers(8)// set number of workers equal to number of
available devices
            .averagingFrequency(3)// rare averaging improves performance,
but reduce accuracy
            .reportScoreAfterAveraging(true) // if set TRUE, on every
averaging model's score reported
            .build();
```

`ParallelWrapper` takes your existing model as the primary argument and does training in parallel by keeping the number of workers equal to or higher than the number of GPUs on your machine.

Within `ParallelWrapper`, the initial model will be duplicated, and each worker will be training its own model. After every N iterations in `averagingFrequency(X)`, all models will be averaged, and training continues. Now, to use this functionality, use the following dependency in the `pom.xml` file:

```xml
<dependency>
        <groupId>org.deeplearning4j</groupId>
        <artifactId>deeplearning4j-parallel-wrapper_2.11</artifactId>
        <version>${dl4j.version}</version>
</dependency>
```

For more up-to-date documentation, interested readers can check out the following link: `https://deeplearning4j.org/gpu`.

Now we have a theoretical understanding of how to distribute DL-based training across multiple GPUs. We will see a hands-on example soon in the next section.

Video classification using convolutional – LSTM

In this section, we will start combining convolutional, max pooling, dense, and recurrent layers to classify each frame of a video clip. Specifically, each video contains several human activities, which persist for multiple frames (though they move between frames) and may leave the frame. First, let's get a more detailed description of the dataset we will be using for this project.

UCF101 – action recognition dataset

UCF101 is an action recognition dataset of realistic action videos, collected from YouTube and having 101 action categories covering 13,320 videos. The videos are collected with variations in camera motion, object appearance and pose, object scale, viewpoint, cluttered background, and illumination condition.

The videos in 101 action categories are further clustered into 25 groups (clips in each group have common features, for example, background and viewpoint) having four to seven videos of an action in each group. There are five action categories: human-object interaction, body-motion only, human-human interaction, playing musical instruments, and dports.

A few more facts about this dataset:

- UCF101 videos contain different frame lengths, ranging between 100 and 300 frames per video clip
- UCF101 uses the XVID compression standard (that is, .avi format)
- The UCF101 dataset has picture size of 320 x 240
- The UCF101 dataset contains different classes in different video files

A high-level glimpse of the dataset can be as follows:

Some random clips from the UCF50 dataset (source: http://crcv.ucf.edu/data/UCF50.php)

Preprocessing and feature engineering

Processing video files is a very challenging task. Especially when it comes to reading video clips by handling and interoperating different encodings; this is a tedious job. Also, video clips may contain distorted frames, which is an obstacle when extracting high-quality features.

Considering these, in this subsection, we will see how to preprocess video clips by dealing with the video encoding problem, and then we will describe the feature extraction process in detail.

Solving the encoding problem

Dealing with video data in Java is a troublesome job (given that we don't have many libraries like Python), especially if the videos come in old `.avi` or such formats. I have seen some blogs and examples on GitHub using JCodec Java library Version 0.1.5 (or 0.2.3) to read and parse `UCF101` video clips in an MP4 format.

Even DL4J depends on datavec-data-codec, which depends on old JCodec API and is incompatible with the new version. Unfortunately, even this newer version of JCodec cannot read `UCF101` videos. Therefore, I decided to use the FFmpeg to process the video in MP4 format. This comes under the JavaCV library, which I've discussed already in an earlier chapter. Anyway, to use this library, just include the following dependency in the `pom.xml` file:

```
<dependency>
        <groupId>org.bytedeco</groupId>
        <artifactId>javacv-platform</artifactId>
        <version>1.4.1</version>
</dependency>
```

As the `UCF101` comes in `.avi` format, I had a hard time processing them with either JCodec or FFfmpeg libraries in Java. Therefore, I converted the video to MP4 format in a handcrafted way.

For this, I wrote a Python script (named `prepare.py`, which can be found under this chapter's code repository). This Python does download, extract, and decode the full `UCF101` dataset, but it may take several hours, depending upon the hardware config and Internet speed. Although putting Python code is not relevant to this book, I still put it so that folks can get some idea of how the thing works, so take a look at this code:

```python
import os

ROOT = os.path.dirname(os.path.abspath(__file__))
DATA = os.path.join(ROOT, 'VideoData')
UCF_RAW = os.path.join(ROOT, 'VideoData', 'UCF101')
UCF_MP4 = os.path.join(ROOT, 'VideoData', 'UCF101_MP4')

if not os.path.isdir(UCF_MP4):
    print("Start converting UCF101 dataset to MP4...")
    filepaths = []

    for label_dir in os.listdir(os.path.join(UCF_RAW)):
        for file in os.listdir(os.path.join(UCF_RAW, label_dir)):
            filepath = (UCF_RAW, label_dir, file)
            filepaths.append(filepath)
    files_len = len(filepaths)
    os.mkdir(UCF_MP4)

    for i, (_, label_dir, file_avi) in enumerate(filepaths):
        if file_avi.endswith('.avi'):
            file_mp4 = file_avi.rstrip('.avi') + '.mp4'
            input_filepath = os.path.join(UCF_RAW, label_dir, file_avi)
            output_filepath = os.path.join(UCF_MP4, label_dir, file_mp4)

            if not os.path.isfile(output_filepath):
                output_dir = os.path.join(UCF_MP4, label_dir)
                if not os.path.isdir(output_dir):
                    os.mkdir(output_dir)
                os.system('ffmpeg -v error -i %s -strict -2 %s' %
(input_filepath, output_filepath))
            print("%d of %d files converted" % (i+1, files_len))
    print("Dataset ready")
```

As this code shows, you just need to download the `UCF101` dataset from `http://crcv.ucf.edu/data/UCF101.php` and put it in the `VideoData/UCF101` folder. Then Python uses the built-in FFmpeg package to convert all the `.avi` files to `.mp4` format, and saves in the `VideoData/UCF101_MP4` directory once it is executed using the `$ python3 prepare.py` command.

Data processing workflow

Once the files are in MP4 format, we can start extracting the features. Now, in order to process the UCF101 dataset and extract the features, I wrote three more Java classes, outlined as follows:

- UCF101Reader.java: This is the main entry point for video file reading, decoding, and conversion to ND4J vectors. It receives the full path to the dataset and creates the DataSetIterator required for the neural network. In addition, it generates a list of all classes, and it assigns sequential integers for them.
- UCF101ReaderIterable.java: This reads all the clips and decodes using JCodec.
- RecordReaderMultiDataSetIterator.java: This is similar to the one provided by DL4J but an improved version, which works pretty well on the new version of JCodec.

Then, to prepare the train and test split, the UCF101Reader.getDataSetIterator() method has been used. The method reads each video clip, but, first, it decides on how many examples (video files) to read based on parameters and offset value. These parameters are then passed to UCF101ReaderIterable. The signature of this method is as follows:

```
public UCF101Reader(String dataDirectory) {
        this.dataDirectory = dataDirectory.endsWith("/") ? dataDirectory :
dataDirectory + "/";
            }

public DataSetIterator getDataSetIterator(int startIdx, int nExamples, int
miniBatchSize) throws Exception {
    ExistingDataSetIterator iter = new
ExistingDataSetIterator(createDataSetIterable(startIdx,
                                                nExamples,
miniBatchSize));
        return new AsyncDataSetIterator(iter,1);
    }
```

In this method, `ExistingDataSetIterator` acts as a wrapper that provides
a `DataSetIterator` interface to the existing Java `Iterable<DataSet>` and
`Iterator<DataSet>`. Then the `UCF101Reader.UCF101ReaderIterable()` method is
used to create the label map (class name to int index) and inverse label map, as shown here:

```
private UCF101RecordIterable createDataSetIterable(int startIdx, int
nExamples, int miniBatchSize)
                                                    throws IOException {
        return new UCF101RecordIterable(dataDirectory, labelMap(), V_WIDTH,
V_HEIGHT, startIdx, nExamples);
                }
```

As you can see from the following, `dataDirectory` is the directory of the video in MP4
format, (`V_WIDTH`, `V_HEIGHT`) signifies the size of the video frame, and `labelMap()`
provides the mapping for each video clip:

```
public static final int V_WIDTH = 320;
public static final int V_HEIGHT = 240;
public static final int V_NFRAMES = 100;
private final String dataDirectory;
private volatile Map<Integer, String> _labelMap;
```

So, the signature of `labelMap()` is as follows:

```
public Map<Integer, String> labelMap() throws IOException {
        if (_labelMap == null) {
            synchronized (this) {
                if (_labelMap == null) {
                    File root = new File(dataDirectory);
                    _labelMap = Files.list(root.toPath()).map(f ->
f.getFileName().toString())
                                .sorted().collect(HashMap::new, (h, f) ->
h.put(h.size(), f), (h, o) -> {});
                }
            }
        }
        return _labelMap;
    }
```

Then, `UCF101ReaderIterable.iterator()` is used to create an iterator of `DataSet`
required by the network. This iterator is transmitted to the `ExistingDataSetIterator` to
be in a form required by the neural net API, `DataSetIterator`, as shown here:

```
// The @NotNull Annotation ensures iterator() method des not return null.
@NotNull
@Override
```

```
public Iterator<DataSet> iterator() {
        return
rowsStream(dataDirectory).skip(this.skip).limit(this.limit).flatMap(p ->
            dataSetsStreamFromFile(p.getKey(),
p.getValue())).iterator();
    }
```

In addition, `AsyncDataSetIterator` is used to do all data processing in a separated thread. Whereas `UCF101ReaderIterable.rowStream()` lists all dataset files and creates a sequence of files and corresponding class labels, as shown here:

```
public static Stream<Pair<Path, String>> rowsStream(String dataDirectory) {
        try {
            List<Pair<Path, String>> files =
Files.list(Paths.get(dataDirectory)).flatMap(dir -> {
                try {
                    return Files.list(dir).map(p -> Pair.of(p,
dir.getFileName().toString())));
                } catch (IOException e) {
                    e.printStackTrace();
                    return Stream.empty();
                }
            }).collect(Collectors.toList());
            Collections.shuffle(files, new Random(43));
            return files.stream();
        } catch (IOException e) {
            e.printStackTrace();
            return Stream.empty();
        }
    }
}
```

Then, the `UCF101ReaderIterable.dataSetStreamFromFile()` method is used to convert the underlying iterator to java streams. It is just a technical step to convert iterators to streams. Because it is more convenient in Java to filter some elements and limit the number of elements in the stream. Take a look at this code!

```
private Stream<DataSet> dataSetsStreamFromFile(Path path, String label) {
        return
StreamSupport.stream(Spliterators.spliteratorUnknownSize(dataSetsIteratorFr
omFile(path,
                                label), Spliterator.ORDERED), false);
    }
```

The `UCF101ReaderIterable.dataSetIteratorFromFile()` method receives the video file path and then creates frame reader (`FrameGrab`—JCodec class). Finally, it passes the frame reader to `RecordReaderMultiDataSetIterator.nextDataSet`, as shown here:

```
private Iterator<DataSet> dataSetsIteratorFromFile(Path path, String label)
{
        FileChannelWrapper _in = null;
        try {
            _in = NIOUtils.readableChannel(path.toFile());
            MP4Demuxer d1 = MP4Demuxer.createMP4Demuxer(_in);
            SeekableDemuxerTrack videoTrack_ =
(SeekableDemuxerTrack)d1.getVideoTrack();
            FrameGrab fg = new FrameGrab(videoTrack_, new
AVCMP4Adaptor(videoTrack_.getMeta()));

            final int framesTotal = videoTrack_.getMeta().getTotalFrames();
            return
Collections.singleton(recordReaderMultiDataSetIterator.nextDataSet(_in,
framesTotal,
                    fg, labelMapInversed.get(label),
labelMap.size())).iterator();
        } catch(IOException | JCodecException e) {
            e.printStackTrace();
            return Collections.emptyIterator();
        }
    }
}
```

In the preceding code block, the `RecordReaderMultiDataSetIterator.nextDataSet()` method is used to convert each video frame to dataSet, compatible with DL4J. In its turn, DataSet is an association of the features vector generated from the frame and the labels vector generated from frame the label using one-hot encoding.

Well, this logic is based on the `RecordReaderMultiDataSetIterator` class of DL4J but necessary support comes from the latest JCodec API. Then we used the `UCF101RecordIterable.labelToNdArray()` method to encode labels in ND4J `INDArray` format:

```
private INDArray labelToNdArray(String label) {
        int maxTSLength = 1; // frames per dataset
        int labelVal = labelMapInversed.get(label);
        INDArray arr = Nd4j.create(new int[]{1, classesCount}, 'f');
        arr.put(0, labelVal, 1f);
        return arr;
}
```

The previously mentioned workflow steps can be depicted in the following diagram:

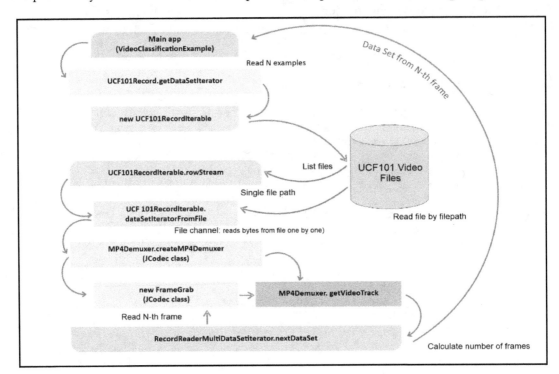

Data flow in the feature extraction process

Simple UI for checking video frames

I developed a simple UI application, using Java Swing to test whether the code correctly handles frames. This UI reads an input video file in MP4 format and shows frames to the reader one by one like a simple video player. The UI application is named `JCodecTest.java`.

In the `JCodecTest.java` class, the `testReadFrame()` method utilizes the `getFrameFromFile()` method from the `FrameGrab` class (that is, from the JavaCV library) and checks whether the frame extraction process from each video clip works correctly. Here is the signature:

```
private void testReadFrame(Consumer<Picture> consumer) throws IOException,
JCodecException {
        // Read the clip sequentially one by one
        next:
```

```
        for(Iterator<Pair<Path, String>> iter = rowsStream().iterator();
iter.hasNext(); ) {
            Pair<Path, String> pair = iter.next();
            Path path = pair.getKey();
            pair.getValue();

            for(int i = 0; i < 100; i++) {
                try {
                    // Hold video frames as pictures
                    Picture picture =
FrameGrab.getFrameFromFile(path.toFile(), i);
                    consumer.accept(picture);
                } catch (Throwable ex) {
                    System.out.println(ex.toString() + " frame " + i + " "
+ path.toString());
                    continue next;
                }
            }
            System.out.println("OK " + path.toString());
        }
    }
```

In the preceding code block, the rowsStream() method is as follows:

```
private Stream<Pair<Path, String>> rowsStream() {
        try {
            return Files.list(Paths.get(dataDirectory)).flatMap(dir -> {
                try {
                    return Files.list(dir).map(p -> Pair.of(p,
dir.getFileName().toString())));
                } catch (IOException e) {
                    e.printStackTrace();
                    return Stream.empty();
                }
            });
        } catch (IOException e) {
            e.printStackTrace();
            return Stream.empty();
        }
    }
```

To see the effectiveness of this approach, readers can execute the `JCodecTest.java` class containing the `main()` method, as follows:

```
private String dataDirectory = "VideoData/UCF101_MP4/";
public static void main(String[] args) throws IOException, JCodecException
{
        JCodecTest test = new JCodecTest();
        test.testReadFrame(new FxShow());
}
```

Once it is executed, you will experience the following output, as shown in this screenshot:

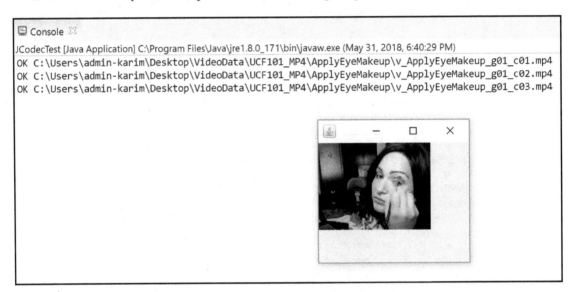

The JCodecTest.java class checks whether the frame extraction from each video clip works correctly

Preparing training and test sets

As described earlier, the `UCF101Reader.java` class is used to extract the features and prepare the training and test sets. First, we set and show Java the MP4 file's path, as shown here:

```
String dataDirectory = "VideoData/UCF101_MP4/";// Paths to video dataset
```

It is to be noted that training the network with the video clips took about 45 hours for me on the EC2 `p2.8xlarge` machine. However, I did not have that patience for a second time; therefore, I performed the training by utilizing only these video categories having 1,112 video clips:

/home/karim/VideoData/UCF101_MP4/				
Name	S...	Changed	Rights	Owner
..		5/6/2018 11:19:24 AM	rwxrwxr-x	karim
ApplyEyeMakeup		5/6/2018 11:22:26 AM	rwxrwxr-x	karim
ApplyLipstick		5/6/2018 11:24:45 AM	rwxrwxr-x	karim
Archery		5/6/2018 11:23:20 AM	rwxrwxr-x	karim
BabyCrawling		5/6/2018 11:21:36 AM	rwxrwxr-x	karim
BalanceBeam		5/6/2018 11:19:59 AM	rwxrwxr-x	karim
BandMarching		5/6/2018 11:26:18 AM	rwxrwxr-x	karim
BaseballPitch		5/6/2018 11:24:05 AM	rwxrwxr-x	karim
Basketball		5/6/2018 11:20:40 AM	rwxrwxr-x	karim
BasketballDunk		5/6/2018 11:23:28 AM	rwxrwxr-x	karim

The UCF101 dataset directory structure (MP4 version)

Then we define the minibatch size to be used for preparing the training and test sets. For our case, I put 128, as you can see:

```
private static int miniBatchSize = 128;
private static int NUM_EXAMPLE = 10;
UCF101Reader reader = new UCF101Reader(dataDirectory);
```

We define the offset from which file the extraction process will start taking place:

```
int examplesOffset = 0; // start from N-th file
```

Then we decide how many sample video clips are to be used for training the network, whereas the `UCF101Reader.fileCount()` method returns the number of video clips in the `UCF101_MP4` directory. Take a look at this code line:

```
int nExamples = Math.min(NUM_EXAMPLE, reader.fileCount());
```

Next, we compute the test set start index. We use 80% for training and the other 20% for testing . Let's see the code:

```
int testStartIdx = examplesOffset + Math.max(2, (int) (0.8 * nExamples));
//80% in train, 20% in test
int nTest = nExamples - testStartIdx + examplesOffset;
System.out.println("Dataset consist of " + reader.fileCount() + " video
clips, use "
                    + nExamples + " of them");
```

Now we prepare the training set. For this, the `getDataSetIterator()` method does the trick by returning the `DataSetIterator` for all video clips except the ones that are planned to be used for the test set. Take a look at this code:

```
System.out.println("Starting training...");
DataSetIterator trainData = reader.getDataSetIterator(examplesOffset,
nExamples - nTest, miniBatchSize);
```

Then we prepare the test set. For this, again the `getDataSetIterator()` method does the trick by returning the `DataSetIterator` for all video clips except those planned to be used for the test set. Take a look at this code:

```
System.out.println("Use " + String.valueOf(nTest) + " video clips for
test");
DataSetIterator testData = reader.getDataSetIterator(testStartIdx,
nExamples, miniBatchSize);
```

Fantastic! Up to this point, we have been able to prepare both training and test sets. Now the next step would be to create the network and perform the training.

Network creation and training

Now we start creating the network by combining convolutional, max pooling, dense (feedforward), and recurrent (LSTM) layers to classify each frame of a video clip. First, we need to define some hyperparameters and the necessary instantiation, as shown here:

```
private static MultiLayerConfiguration conf;
private static MultiLayerNetwork net;
private static String modelPath = "bin/ConvLSTM_Model.zip";
private static int NUM_CLASSES;
private static int nTrainEpochs = 100;
```

Here, `NUM_CLASSES` is the number of classes from `UCF101` calculated as the quantity of directories in the dataset base directory:

```
NUM_CLASSES = reader.labelMap().size();
```

Then we start the training by calling the `networkTrainer()` method. Well, as I stated earlier, we will be combining convolutional, max pooling, dense (feedforward), and recurrent (LSTM) layers to classify each frame of a video clip. The training data is first fed to the convolutional layer (layer 0), which then gets subsampled (layer 1) before being inputted into the second convolutional layer (layer 2). Then the second convolutional layer feeds the fully connected layer (layer 3).

It is to be noted that for the first CNN layer we have CNN preprocessor input width/height 13 x 18, which reflects a picture size of 320 x 240. This way, the dense layer acts as the input layer for the LSTM layer (layer 4, but feel free to use regular LSTM too). However, it is important to note that dense layer inputs have a size of 2,340 (that is, 13 * 18 * 10).

Then the recurrent feedback is connected to RNN output layer, which has a softmax activation function for probability distribution over the classes. We also use gradient normalization to deal with the vanishing and exploding gradient problem, and the backpropagation in the last layer is truncated BPTT. Apart from these, we use some other hyperparameters; those are self-explanatory. The following diagram shows this network setting:

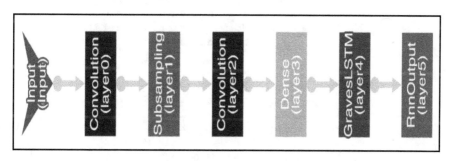

Network architecture

Now, from the coding point of view, the `networkTrainer()` method has the following network configuration:

```
//Set up network architecture:
conf = new NeuralNetConfiguration.Builder()
                .seed(12345)
                .l2(0.001) //l2 regularization on all layers
                .updater(new Adam(0.001)) // we use Adam as updater
```

```
                        .list()
                        .layer(0, new ConvolutionLayer.Builder(10, 10)
                                .nIn(3) //3 channels: RGB
                                .nOut(30)
                                .stride(4, 4)
                                .activation(Activation.RELU)
                                .weightInit(WeightInit.RELU)
                                .build()) //Output: (130-10+0)/4+1 = 31 -> 31*31*30
                        .layer(1, new
    SubsamplingLayer.Builder(SubsamplingLayer.PoolingType.MAX)
                                .kernelSize(3, 3)
                                .stride(2, 2).build()) //(31-3+0)/2+1 = 15
                        .layer(2, new ConvolutionLayer.Builder(3, 3)
                                .nIn(30)
                                .nOut(10)
                                .stride(2, 2)
                                .activation(Activation.RELU)
                                .weightInit(WeightInit.RELU)
                                .build()) //Output: (15-3+0)/2+1 = 7 -> 7*7*10 =
    490
                        .layer(3, new DenseLayer.Builder()
                                .activation(Activation.RELU)
                                .nIn(2340) // 13 * 18 * 10 = 2340, see CNN layer
    width x height
                                .nOut(50)
                                .weightInit(WeightInit.RELU)
    .gradientNormalization(GradientNormalization.ClipElementWiseAbsoluteValue)
                                .gradientNormalizationThreshold(10)
                                .updater(new AdaGrad(0.01))// for faster
    convergence
                                .build())
                        .layer(4, new LSTM.Builder()
                                .activation(Activation.SOFTSIGN)
                                .nIn(50)
                                .nOut(50)
                                .weightInit(WeightInit.XAVIER)
                                .updater(new AdaGrad(0.008))
    .gradientNormalization(GradientNormalization.ClipElementWiseAbsoluteValue)
                                .gradientNormalizationThreshold(10)
                                .build())
                        .layer(5, new
    RnnOutputLayer.Builder(LossFunctions.LossFunction.MCXENT)
                                .activation(Activation.SOFTMAX)
                                .nIn(50)
                                .nOut(NUM_CLASSES)
                                .weightInit(WeightInit.XAVIER)
    .gradientNormalization(GradientNormalization.ClipElementWiseAbsoluteValue)
                                .gradientNormalizationThreshold(10)
```

```
                        .build())
                .inputPreProcessor(0, new
RnnToCnnPreProcessor(UCF101Reader.V_HEIGHT,
                                UCF101Reader.V_WIDTH, 3))
                .inputPreProcessor(3, new CnnToFeedForwardPreProcessor(13,
18, 10))
                .inputPreProcessor(4, new FeedForwardToRnnPreProcessor())
                .pretrain(false).backprop(true)
                .backpropType(BackpropType.TruncatedBPTT)
                .tBPTTForwardLength(UCF101Reader.V_NFRAMES / 5)
                .tBPTTBackwardLength(UCF101Reader.V_NFRAMES / 5)
                .build();
```

Next, based on the preceding network configuration setting, we create a `MultiLayerNetwork` and initialize it, as shown here:

```
net = new MultiLayerNetwork(conf);
net.init();
net.setListeners(new ScoreIterationListener(1));
```

Then we can observe the number of parameters across each layer, as shown here:

```
System.out.println("Number of parameters in network: " + net.numParams());
for(int i=0; i<net.getnLayers(); i++){
    System.out.println("Layer " + i + " nParams = " +
net.getLayer(i).numParams());
}
```

>>>
Number of parameters in network: 149599
Layer 0 nParams = 9030
Layer 1 nParams = 0
Layer 2 nParams = 2710
Layer 3 nParams = 117050
Layer 4 nParams = 20350
Layer 5 nParams = 459

Finally, we start the training using this training set:

```
for (int i = 0; i < nTrainEpochs; i++) {
        int j = 0;
        while(trainData.hasNext()) {
                long start = System.nanoTime();
                DataSet example = trainData.next();
                net.fit(example);
                System.out.println(" Example " + j + " processed in "
                        + ((System.nanoTime() - start) / 1000000)
```

```
+ " ms");
                    j++;
            }
        System.out.println("Epoch " + i + " complete");
    }
```

We save the trained network and video configuration using the `saveConfigs()` method, and the signature of this method is pretty straightforward, as you can see:

```
private static void saveConfigs() throws IOException {
        Nd4j.saveBinary(net.params(),new File("bin/videomodel.bin"));
        FileUtils.writeStringToFile(new File("bin/videoconf.json"),
conf.toJson());
    }
```

Then we save the trained model for later inferencing purposes using the `saveNetwork()` method; it is as follows:

```
privates tatic void saveNetwork() throws IOException {
        File locationToSave = new File(modelPath);
        boolean saveUpdater = true;
        ModelSerializer.writeModel(net, locationToSave, saveUpdater);
    }
```

Performance evaluation

To evaluate the network performance, I wrote the `evaluateClassificationPerformance()` method, which takes the test set and `evalTimeSeries` evaluation, as shown here:

```
private static void evaluateClassificationPerformance(MultiLayerNetwork
net, int testStartIdx,
                        int nExamples, DataSetIterator testData) throws
Exception {
        Evaluation evaluation = new Evaluation(NUM_CLASSES);
        while(testData.hasNext()) {
            DataSet dsTest = testData.next();
            INDArray predicted = net.output(dsTest.getFeatureMatrix(),
false);
            INDArray actual = dsTest.getLabels();
            evaluation.evalTimeSeries(actual, predicted);
            }
        System.out.println(evaluation.stats());
    }
```

>>>
Predictions labeled as 0 classified by model as 0: 493 times
Predictions labeled as 0 classified by model as 7: 3 times
Predictions labeled as 1 classified by model as 6: 287 times
Predictions labeled as 1 classified by model as 7: 1 times
Predictions labeled as 2 classified by model as 6: 758 times
Predictions labeled as 2 classified by model as 7: 3 times
Predictions labeled as 3 classified by model as 6: 111 times
Predictions labeled as 3 classified by model as 7: 1 times
Predictions labeled as 4 classified by model as 6: 214 times
Predictions labeled as 4 classified by model as 7: 2 times
Predictions labeled as 5 classified by model as 6: 698 times
Predictions labeled as 5 classified by model as 7: 3 times
Predictions labeled as 6 classified by model as 6: 128 times
Predictions labeled as 6 classified by model as 5: 1 times
Predictions labeled as 7 classified by model as 7: 335 times
Predictions labeled as 8 classified by model as 8: 209 times
Predictions labeled as 8 classified by model as 7: 2 times
=======================Scores==================
# of classes: 9
Accuracy: 0.4000
Precision: 0.39754
Recall: 0.4109
F1 Score: 0.4037
Precision, recall & F1: macro-averaged (equally weighted avg. of 9 classes)
==

Now, to follow the aforementioned steps more clearly, here is the main() method
containing the steps:

```
public static void main(String[] args) throws Exception {
        String dataDirectory = "VideoData/UCF101_MP4/";
        UCF101Reader reader = new UCF101Reader(dataDirectory);
        NUM_CLASSES = reader.labelMap().size();
        int examplesOffset = 0; // start from N-th file
        int nExamples = Math.min(NUM_EXAMPLE, reader.fileCount()); // use
only "nExamples" for train/test
        int testStartIdx = examplesOffset + Math.max(2, (int) (0.9 *
nExamples)); //90% train, 10% in test
        int nTest = nExamples - testStartIdx + examplesOffset;
        System.out.println("Dataset consist of " + reader.fileCount() + "
images, use "
                        + nExamples + " of them");

        //Conduct learning
        System.out.println("Starting training...");
        DataSetIterator trainData =
```

```
reader.getDataSetIterator(examplesOffset,
                              nExamples - nTest, miniBatchSize);
        networkTrainer(reader, trainData);
        //Save network and video configuration
        saveConfigs();
        //Save the trained model
        saveNetwork();

        //Evaluate classification performance:
        System.out.println("Use " + String.valueOf(nTest) + " images for
validation");
        DataSetIterator testData = reader.getDataSetIterator(testStartIdx,
nExamples, miniBatchSize);
        evaluateClassificationPerformance(net,testStartIdx,nTest,
testData);
    }
```

We have not achieved higher accuracy. There could be many reasons for this. For example, we have used only a few categories (that is, only 9 out of 101). Therefore, our model did not get enough training data to learn. Also, most of the hyperparameters were set naively.

Distributed training on AWS deep learning AMI 9.0

So far, we have seen how to perform training and inferencing on a single GPU. However, to make the training even faster in a parallel and distributed way, having a machine or server with multiple GPUs is a viable option. An easy way to achieve this is by using AMAZON EC2 GPU compute instances.

For example, P2 is well suited for distributed deep learning frameworks that come with the latest binaries of deep learning frameworks (MXNet, TensorFlow, Caffe, Caffe2, PyTorch, Keras, Chainer, Theano, and CNTK) pre-installed in separate virtual environments.

An even bigger advantage is that they are fully configured with NVidia CUDA and cuDNN. Interested readers can take a look at https://aws.amazon.com/ec2/instance-types/p2/. A short glimpse of P2 instances configuration and pricing is as follows:

P2 Instance Details

Name	GPUs	vCPUs	RAM (GiB)	Network Bandwidth	Price/Hour*	RI Price / Hour**
p2.xlarge	1	4	61	High	$0.900	$0.425
p2.8xlarge	8	32	488	10 Gbps	$7.200	$3.400
p2.16xlarge	16	64	732	20 Gbps	$14.400	$6.800

P2 instance details

For this project, I decided to use `p2.8xlarge`. You can create it too, but make sure that you have already submitted an increased limit to at least one instance, which may take as long as three days. However, if you do not know how to do that, just create an account on AWS and finish the verification; then go to the EC2 management console. On the left panel, click on the **Limits** tab, which will take you a page where you can submit an increase limit request by clicking on the **Request limit increase** link.

Anyway, I assume that you know this simple stuff, so I'll move forward to creating an instance of type `p2.8xlarge`. On the left panel, click on the **Instances** menu, which should take you to the following page:

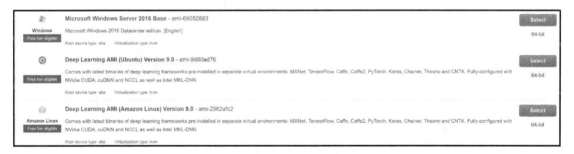

Selecting a deep learning AMI

An easy option would be creating a deep learning AMI (Ubuntu) Version 9.0, which has already configured CUDA and cuDNN, which can be used across eight GPUs. Another good thing is that it has 32 computing cores and 488 GB of RAM; this would be sufficient for our dataset too. Therefore, instead of using video clips of only nine categories, we can perform the training with the full dataset.

However, note that, since we will be using DL4J, which is based on JVM, Java has to be installed and configured (`JAVA_HOME` has to be set). First, connect with your instance from SSH or using an SFTP client. Then on Ubuntu, we can do this with a few commands, as shown here:

```
$ sudo apt-get install python-software-properties
$ sudo apt-get update
$ sudo add-apt-repository ppa:webupd8team/java
$ sudo apt-get update
```

Then, depending on the version you want to install, execute one of the following commands:

```
$ sudo apt-get install oracle-java8-installer
```

After installing, do not forget to set Java home. Just apply the following commands (we assume Java is installed at `/usr/lib/jvm/java-8-oracle`):

```
$ echo "export JAVA_HOME=/usr/lib/jvm/java-8-oracle" >> ~/.bashrc
$ echo "export PATH=$PATH:$JAVA_HOME/bin" >> ~/.bashrc
$ source ~/.bashrc
```

Now let's see the `Java_HOME`, as follows:

```
$ echo $JAVA_HOME
```

Now you should observe the following result on the Terminal:

```
/usr/lib/jvm/java-8-oracle
```

Finally, let's check to make sure that Java has been installed successfully by issuing this command (you may see the latest version!):

```
$ java -version

>>>
java version "1.8.0_121"
Java(TM) SE Runtime Environment (build 1.8.0_121-b15)
Java HotSpot(TM) 64-Bit Server VM (build 25.121-b15, mixed mode)
```

Fantastic! We have been able to set up and configure Java on our instance. Then let's see whether the GPUs drivers are configured by issuing the `nvidia-smi` command on the Terminal:

```
ubuntu@ip-172-31-40-27:~$ nvidia-smi
Sat Jun  2 18:29:31 2018
+-----------------------------------------------------------------------------+
| NVIDIA-SMI 384.111                 Driver Version: 384.111                  |
|-------------------------------+----------------------+----------------------+
| GPU  Name        Persistence-M| Bus-Id        Disp.A | Volatile Uncorr. ECC |
| Fan  Temp  Perf  Pwr:Usage/Cap|         Memory-Usage | GPU-Util  Compute M. |
|===============================+======================+======================|
|   0  Tesla K80            On  | 00000000:00:17.0 Off |                    0 |
| N/A   41C    P8    26W / 149W |      1MiB / 11439MiB |      0%      Default |
+-------------------------------+----------------------+----------------------+
|   1  Tesla K80            On  | 00000000:00:18.0 Off |                    0 |
| N/A   35C    P8    30W / 149W |      1MiB / 11439MiB |      0%      Default |
+-------------------------------+----------------------+----------------------+
|   2  Tesla K80            On  | 00000000:00:19.0 Off |                    0 |
| N/A   44C    P8    26W / 149W |      1MiB / 11439MiB |      0%      Default |
+-------------------------------+----------------------+----------------------+
|   3  Tesla K80            On  | 00000000:00:1A.0 Off |                    0 |
| N/A   39C    P8    29W / 149W |      1MiB / 11439MiB |      0%      Default |
+-------------------------------+----------------------+----------------------+
|   4  Tesla K80            On  | 00000000:00:1B.0 Off |                    0 |
| N/A   44C    P8    27W / 149W |      1MiB / 11439MiB |      0%      Default |
+-------------------------------+----------------------+----------------------+
|   5  Tesla K80            On  | 00000000:00:1C.0 Off |                    0 |
| N/A   34C    P8    28W / 149W |      1MiB / 11439MiB |      0%      Default |
+-------------------------------+----------------------+----------------------+
|   6  Tesla K80            On  | 00000000:00:1D.0 Off |                    0 |
| N/A   43C    P8    27W / 149W |      1MiB / 11439MiB |      0%      Default |
+-------------------------------+----------------------+----------------------+
|   7  Tesla K80            On  | 00000000:00:1E.0 Off |                    0 |
| N/A   36C    P8    29W / 149W |      1MiB / 11439MiB |      0%      Default |
+-------------------------------+----------------------+----------------------+

+-----------------------------------------------------------------------------+
| Processes:                                                       GPU Memory |
|  GPU       PID   Type   Process name                             Usage      |
|=============================================================================|
|  No running processes found                                                 |
+-----------------------------------------------------------------------------+
ubuntu@ip-172-31-40-27:~$
```

Showing Tesla K80 GPUs on a p2.8 xlarge instance

As we can see, initially, there's no usage of GPUs, but it clearly says that, on the instance, there are eight Tesla K80 GPUs installed and configured. Now that our GPUs and machine are fully configured, we can focus on the project. We are going to use more or less the same code that we used previously but with some minimal modifications. The very first change we need to make is to add the following line at the beginning of our `main()` method:

```
CudaEnvironment.getInstance().getConfiguration()
        .allowMultiGPU(true) // key option enabled
        .setMaximumDeviceCache(2L * 1024L * 1024L * 1024L) // large cache
        .allowCrossDeviceAccess(true); // cross-device access for faster
model averaging over a piece
```

Then we perform the training across eight GPUs, using ParallelWrapper, which take cares of load balancing between GPUs. The network construction is the same as before, as shown here:

```
net = new MultiLayerNetwork(conf);
net.init();

ParallelWrapper wrapper = new ParallelWrapper.Builder(net)
        .prefetchBuffer(8)// DataSets prefetching options. Set this with
respect to number of devices
        .workers(8)// set number of workers equal to number of available
devices -i.e. 8 for p2.8xlarge
        .averagingFrequency(3)// rare averaging improves performance, but
might reduce model accuracy
        .reportScoreAfterAveraging(true) // if set TRUE, on every avg. model
score will be reported
        .build();
```

Now we start the training by fitting the full test set, as shown here:

```
for (int i = 0; i < nTrainEpochs; i++) {
    wrapper.fit(trainData);
    System.out.println("Epoch " + i + " complete");
}
```

That is all we need to make. However, make sure you import the following at the beginning of the `VideoClassificationExample.java` file for the `CudaEnvironment` and `ParallelWrapper`, as shown here:

```
import org.nd4j.jita.conf.CudaEnvironment;
import org.deeplearning4j.parallelism.ParallelWrapper;
```

Nonetheless, I still believe that showing the code for the `main()` method and the
`networkTrainer()` methods would be helpful. In addition, to avoid possible confusion, I
have written two Java classes for single and multiple GPUs:

- `VideoClassificationExample.java`: For a single GPU or CPU
- `VideoClassificationExample_MUltipleGPU.java`: For multiple GPUs on
  an AWS EC2 instance

So, the latter class has a method, `networkTrainer()`, which is used to create a network for
distributed training, as follows:

```
private static void networkTrainer(UCF101Reader reader, DataSetIterator
trainData) throws Exception {
    //Set up network architecture:
    conf = new NeuralNetConfiguration.Builder()
                    .seed(12345)
                    .l2(0.001) //l2 regularization on all layers
                    .updater(new Adam(0.001))
                    .list()
                    .layer(0, new ConvolutionLayer.Builder(10, 10)
                            .nIn(3) //3 channels: RGB
                            .nOut(30)
                            .stride(4, 4)
                            .activation(Activation.RELU)
                            .weightInit(WeightInit.RELU)
                            .build())   //Output: (130-10+0)/4+1 = 31 ->
31*31*30
                    .layer(1, new
SubsamplingLayer.Builder(SubsamplingLayer.PoolingType.MAX)
                            .kernelSize(3, 3)
                            .stride(2, 2).build())    //(31-3+0)/2+1 = 15
                    .layer(2, new ConvolutionLayer.Builder(3, 3)
                            .nIn(30)
                            .nOut(10)
                            .stride(2, 2)
                            .activation(Activation.RELU)
                            .weightInit(WeightInit.RELU)
                            .build())    //Output: (15-3+0)/2+1 = 7 -> 7*7*10 =
490
                    .layer(3, new DenseLayer.Builder()
                            .activation(Activation.RELU)
                            .nIn(2340) // 13 * 18 * 10 = 2340, see CNN layer
width x height
                            .nOut(50)
                            .weightInit(WeightInit.RELU)
    .gradientNormalization(GradientNormalization.ClipElementWiseAbsoluteValue)
```

```
                        .gradientNormalizationThreshold(10)
                        .updater(new AdaGrad(0.01))
                        .build())
                .layer(4, new LSTM.Builder()
                        .activation(Activation.SOFTSIGN)
                        .nIn(50)
                        .nOut(50)
                        .weightInit(WeightInit.XAVIER)
                        .updater(new AdaGrad(0.008))
.gradientNormalization(GradientNormalization.ClipElementWiseAbsoluteValue)
                        .gradientNormalizationThreshold(10)
                        .build())
                .layer(5, new
RnnOutputLayer.Builder(LossFunctions.LossFunction.MCXENT)
                        .activation(Activation.SOFTMAX)
                        .nIn(50)
                        .nOut(NUM_CLASSES)
                        .weightInit(WeightInit.XAVIER)
.gradientNormalization(GradientNormalization.ClipElementWiseAbsoluteValue)
                        .gradientNormalizationThreshold(10)
                        .build())
                .inputPreProcessor(0, new
RnnToCnnPreProcessor(UCF101Reader.V_HEIGHT,
                                UCF101Reader.V_WIDTH, 3))
                .inputPreProcessor(3, new CnnToFeedForwardPreProcessor(13,
18, 10))
                .inputPreProcessor(4, new FeedForwardToRnnPreProcessor())
                .pretrain(false).backprop(true)
                .backpropType(BackpropType.TruncatedBPTT)
                .tBPTTForwardLength(UCF101Reader.V_NFRAMES / 5)
                .tBPTTBackwardLength(UCF101Reader.V_NFRAMES / 5)
                .build();

        net = new MultiLayerNetwork(conf);
        net.init();
        net.setListeners(new ScoreIterationListener(1));

        System.out.println("Number of parameters in network: " +
net.numParams());
        for( int i=0; i<net.getnLayers(); i++ ){
                System.out.println("Layer " + i + " nParams = " +
net.getLayer(i).numParams());
        }

    // ParallelWrapper will take care of load balancing between GPUs.
    ParallelWrapper wrapper = new ParallelWrapper.Builder(net)
            .prefetchBuffer(8)// DataSets prefetching options. Set value
with respect to number of devices
```

```
                    .workers(8)// set number of workers equal to number of
available devices
                    .averagingFrequency(3)// rare avg improves performance, but
might reduce accuracy
                    .reportScoreAfterAveraging(true) // if set TRUE, on every avg.
model score will be reported
                    .build();
        for (int i = 0; i < nTrainEpochs; i++) {
                    wrapper.fit(trainData);
                    System.out.println("Epoch " + i + " complete");
            }
        }
```

Now the `main()` method is as follows:

```
public static void main(String[] args) throws Exception {
        // Workaround for CUDA backend initialization
        CudaEnvironment.getInstance()
                .getConfiguration()
                .allowMultiGPU(true)
                .setMaximumDeviceCache(2L * 1024L * 1024L * 1024L)
                .allowCrossDeviceAccess(true);
        String dataDirectory = "/home/ubuntu/UCF101_MP4/";
        UCF101Reader reader = new UCF101Reader(dataDirectory);
        NUM_CLASSES = reader.labelMap().size();
        int examplesOffset = 0; // start from N-th file
        int nExamples = Math.min(NUM_EXAMPLE, reader.fileCount()); // use
only "nExamples" for train/test
        int testStartIdx = examplesOffset + Math.max(2, (int) (0.9 *
nExamples)); //90% train, 10% in test
        int nTest = nExamples - testStartIdx + examplesOffset;

        System.out.println("Dataset consist of " + reader.fileCount() + "
images, use "
                            + nExamples + " of them");

        //Conduct learning
        System.out.println("Starting training...");
        DataSetIterator trainData =
reader.getDataSetIterator(examplesOffset,
                            nExamples - nTest, miniBatchSize);
        networkTrainer(reader, trainData);
        //Save network and video configuration
        saveConfigs();
        //Save the trained model
        saveNetwork();

        //Evaluate classification performance:
```

```
        System.out.println("Use " + String.valueOf(nTest) + " images for
    validation");
        DataSetIterator testData = reader.getDataSetIterator(testStartIdx,
    nExamples, 10);
        evaluateClassificationPerformance(net,testStartIdx,nTest,
    testData);
    }
```

That's all we need before executing the
`VideoClassificationExample_MUltipleGPU.java` class. It should also be noted that
running a standalone Java class is not a good idea from the terminal. Therefore, I would
suggest creating a `fat` `.jar` and including all the dependencies. To do that, move your
code to the instance using any SFTP client. Then install `maven`:

```
$sudo apt-get install maven
```

Once the maven is installed, we can start creating the fat JAR file containing all the
dependencies, like so:

```
$ sudo mvn clean install
```

Then, after a while, a fat JAR file will be generated in the target directory. We move to that
directory and execute the JAR file, as shown here:

```
$ cd target/
$ java -Xmx30g -jar VideoClassifier-0.0.1-SNAPSHOT-jar-with-
dependencies.jar
```

At this point, please make sure that you have set all the paths properly and have the
necessary permissions. Well, I assume everything is set properly. Then, executing the
preceding command will force DL4J to pick BLAS, CUDA, and cuDNN and perform the
training and other steps. Roughly, you should see the following logs on the Terminal:

```
ubuntu@ip-172-31-40-27:~/JavaDeepLearningDL4J/target$ java -Xmx30g -jar
VideoClassifier-0.0.1-SNAPSHOT-jar-with-dependencies.jar
```

The preceding command should start the training and you should observe the following
logs on the Terminal/command line:

```
Dataset consist of 1112 images, use 20 of them
Starting training...
18:57:34.815 [main] INFO org.nd4j.linalg.factory.Nd4jBackend - Loaded
[JCublasBackend] backend
18:57:34.844 [main] WARN org.reflections.Reflections - given scan urls are
empty. set urls in the configuration
18:57:47.447 [main] INFO org.nd4j.nativeblas.NativeOpsHolder - Number of
```

```
threads used for NativeOps: 32
18:57:51.433 [main] DEBUG org.nd4j.jita.concurrency.CudaAffinityManager -
Manually mapping thread [28] to device [0], out of [8] devices...
18:57:51.441 [main] INFO org.nd4j.nativeblas.Nd4jBlas - Number of threads
used for BLAS: 0
18:57:51.447 [main] INFO
org.nd4j.linalg.api.ops.executioner.DefaultOpExecutioner - Backend used:
[CUDA]; OS: [Linux]
18:57:51.447 [main] INFO
org.nd4j.linalg.api.ops.executioner.DefaultOpExecutioner - Cores: [32];
Memory: [26.7GB];
18:57:51.447 [main] INFO
org.nd4j.linalg.api.ops.executioner.DefaultOpExecutioner - Blas vendor:
[CUBLAS]
18:57:51.452 [main] INFO
org.nd4j.linalg.jcublas.ops.executioner.CudaExecutioner - Device opName:
[Tesla K80]; CC: [3.7]; Total/free memory: [11995578368]
18:57:51.452 [main] INFO
org.nd4j.linalg.jcublas.ops.executioner.CudaExecutioner - Device opName:
[Tesla K80]; CC: [3.7]; Total/free memory: [11995578368]
18:57:51.452 [main] INFO
org.nd4j.linalg.jcublas.ops.executioner.CudaExecutioner - Device opName:
[Tesla K80]; CC: [3.7]; Total/free memory: [11995578368]
 18:57:51.452 [main] INFO
org.nd4j.linalg.jcublas.ops.executioner.CudaExecutioner - Device opName:
[Tesla K80]; CC: [3.7]; Total/free memory: [11995578368]
18:57:51.452 [main] INFO
org.nd4j.linalg.jcublas.ops.executioner.CudaExecutioner - Device opName:
[Tesla K80]; CC: [3.7]; Total/free memory: [11995578368]
18:57:51.452 [main] INFO
org.nd4j.linalg.jcublas.ops.executioner.CudaExecutioner - Device opName:
[Tesla K80]; CC: [3.7]; Total/free memory: [11995578368]
18:57:51.452 [main] INFO
org.nd4j.linalg.jcublas.ops.executioner.CudaExecutioner - Device opName:
[Tesla K80]; CC: [3.7]; Total/free memory: [11995578368]
18:57:51.452 [main] INFO
org.nd4j.linalg.jcublas.ops.executioner.CudaExecutioner - Device opName:
[Tesla K80]; CC: [3.7]; Total/free memory: [11995578368]
18:57:51.697 [main] DEBUG org.nd4j.jita.handler.impl.CudaZeroHandler -
Creating bucketID: 1
18:57:51.706 [main] DEBUG org.nd4j.jita.handler.impl.CudaZeroHandler -
Creating bucketID: 2
18:57:51.711 [main] DEBUG org.reflections.Reflections - going to scan these
urls:
jar:file:/home/ubuntu/JavaDeepLearningDL4J/target/VideoClassifier-0.0.1-
SNAPSHOT-jar-with-dependencies.jar!/.
...
```

Then the training should start. Now let's check whether DL4J is utilizing all the GPUs. To know this, again execute the `nvidia-smi` command on the Terminal, which should show the following:

```
ubuntu@ip-172-31-40-27:~$ nvidia-smi
Sat Jun  2 13:50:01 2018
+-----------------------------------------------------------------------------+
| NVIDIA-SMI 384.111                   Driver Version: 384.111                |
|-------------------------------+----------------------+----------------------+
| GPU  Name            Persistence-M| Bus-Id        Disp.A | Volatile Uncorr. ECC |
| Fan  Temp  Perf  Pwr:Usage/Cap|         Memory-Usage | GPU-Util  Compute M. |
|===============================+======================+======================|
|   0  Tesla K80             On  | 00000000:00:17.0 Off |                    0 |
| N/A   67C    P0    61W / 149W |   1244MiB / 11439MiB |      0%      Default |
+-------------------------------+----------------------+----------------------+
|   1  Tesla K80             On  | 00000000:00:18.0 Off |                    0 |
| N/A   56C    P0    73W / 149W |    666MiB / 11439MiB |      0%      Default |
+-------------------------------+----------------------+----------------------+
|   2  Tesla K80             On  | 00000000:00:19.0 Off |                    0 |
| N/A   67C    P0    61W / 149W |    666MiB / 11439MiB |      0%      Default |
+-------------------------------+----------------------+----------------------+
|   3  Tesla K80             On  | 00000000:00:1A.0 Off |                    0 |
| N/A   55C    P0    71W / 149W |    666MiB / 11439MiB |      0%      Default |
+-------------------------------+----------------------+----------------------+
|   4  Tesla K80             On  | 00000000:00:1B.0 Off |                    0 |
| N/A   69C    P0    61W / 149W |    666MiB / 11439MiB |      0%      Default |
+-------------------------------+----------------------+----------------------+
|   5  Tesla K80             On  | 00000000:00:1C.0 Off |                    0 |
| N/A   52C    P0    70W / 149W |    666MiB / 11439MiB |      0%      Default |
+-------------------------------+----------------------+----------------------+
|   6  Tesla K80             On  | 00000000:00:1D.0 Off |                    0 |
| N/A   68C    P0    62W / 149W |    666MiB / 11439MiB |      0%      Default |
+-------------------------------+----------------------+----------------------+
|   7  Tesla K80             On  | 00000000:00:1E.0 Off |                    0 |
| N/A   55C    P0    71W / 149W |    666MiB / 11439MiB |      0%      Default |
+-------------------------------+----------------------+----------------------+

+-----------------------------------------------------------------------------+
| Processes:                                                       GPU Memory |
|  GPU       PID   Type   Process name                             Usage      |
|=============================================================================|
|    0     26536      C   java                                      1229MiB |
|    1     26536      C   java                                       651MiB |
|    2     26536      C   java                                       651MiB |
|    3     26536      C   java                                       651MiB |
|    4     26536      C   java                                       651MiB |
|    5     26536      C   java                                       651MiB |
|    6     26536      C   java                                       651MiB |
|    7     26536      C   java                                       651MiB |
+-----------------------------------------------------------------------------+
ubuntu@ip-172-31-40-27:~$
```

Showing resource usage on Tesla K80 GPUs on the p2.8 xlarge instance

Since there are many video clips, training will take a few hours. Once the training is completed, the code should provide similar or slightly better classification accuracy.

Frequently asked questions (FAQs)

Now that we have solved the video classification problem, but with low accuracy, there are other practical aspects of this problem and overall deep learning phenomena that need to be considered too. In this section, we will see some frequently asked questions that may be on your mind. Answers to these questions can be found in Appendix A.

1. My machine has multiple GPUs installed (for example, two), but DL4J is using only one. How do I fix this problem?
2. I have configured a p2.8 xlarge EC2 GPU compute instance on AWS. However, it is showing low disk space while installing and configuring CUDA and cuDNN. How to fix this issue?
3. I understand how the distributed training happens on AWS EC2 AMI instance. However, my machine has a low-end GPU, and often I get OOP on the GPU. How can solve the issue?
4. Can I treat this application as a human activity recognition from a video?

Summary

In this chapter, we developed a complete deep learning application that classifies a large collection of video datasets from the `UCF101` dataset. We applied a combined CNN-LSTM network with DL4J that overcome the limitation of standalone CNN or RNN LSTM networks.

Finally, we saw how to perform training in parallel and distributed ways across multiple devices (CPUs and GPUs). In summary, this end-to-end project can be treated as a primer for human activity recognition from a video. Although we did not achieve high accuracy after training, in the network with a full video dataset and hyperparameter tuning, the accuracy will definitely be increased.

The next chapter is all about designing a machine learning system driven by criticisms and rewards. We will see how to develop a demo GridWorld game using DL4J, RL4J, and neural Q-learning, which acts as the Q-function. We will start from reinforcement learning and its theoretical background so that the concepts are easier to grasp.

Answers to questions

Answer to question 1: This means the training is not being distributed, which also means that your system is forcing you to use just one GPU. Now to solve this issue, just add the following line at the beginning of your `main()` method:

```
CudaEnvironment.getInstance().getConfiguration().allowMultiGPU(true);
```

Answer to question 2: Well, this is certainly an AWS EC2-related question. However, I will provide a short explanation. If you see the default boot device, it allocates only 7.7 GB of space, but about 85% is allocated for the udev device, as shown here:

```
ubuntu@ip-172-31-38-158:~$ df -h
Filesystem      Size  Used Avail Use% Mounted on
udev            241G     0  241G   0% /dev
tmpfs            49G  8.6M   49G   1% /run
/dev/xvda1      7.7G  856M  6.9G  11% /
tmpfs           241G     0  241G   0% /dev/shm
tmpfs           5.0M     0  5.0M   0% /run/lock
tmpfs           241G     0  241G   0% /sys/fs/cgroup
tmpfs            49G     0   49G   0% /run/user/1000
ubuntu@ip-172-31-38-158:~$
```

Showing storage on a p2.8xlarge instance

Now, to get rid of this issue, you can specify sufficient storage in the boot device while creating the instance, as follows:

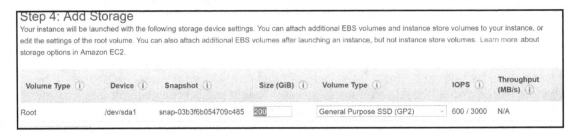

Step 4: Add Storage

Your instance will be launched with the following storage device settings. You can attach additional EBS volumes and instance store volumes to your instance, or edit the settings of the root volume. You can also attach additional EBS volumes after launching an instance, but not instance store volumes. Learn more about storage options in Amazon EC2.

Volume Type ⓘ	Device ⓘ	Snapshot ⓘ	Size (GiB) ⓘ	Volume Type ⓘ	IOPS ⓘ	Throughput (MB/s) ⓘ
Root	/dev/sda1	snap-03b3f6b054709c485	200	General Purpose SSD (GP2)	600 / 3000	N/A

Increasing storage on the default boot device the on p2.8xlarge instance

Answer to question 3: Well, if this is the case, you can probably do the training on CPU instead of GPU. However, if performing training on a GPU is mandatory, I recommend using the HALF datatype.

If your machine and code can afford using half-precision math, you can enable this as the data type. It will then ensure 2x less GPU memory usage by DL4J. To enable this, just add the following line of code to the beginning of the main() method (even before the multi-GPU allows one):

```
DataTypeUtil.setDTypeForContext(DataBuffer.Type.HALF);
```

 Using the HALF datatype will force your network to squash less precision compared to float or double types. Nonetheless, tuning your network may be harder.

Answer to question 4: We have not managed to achieve good accuracy. This is the main objective of this end-to-end chapter. Therefore, after training the network with the full video dataset and hyperparameter tuning, the accuracy will definitely increase.

Finally, and to be honest, Java is not the perfect choice if you want to take an application to production. I am saying this because so many advanced feature-extraction libraries from video clips are in Python, and those can be used too.

Playing GridWorld Game Using Deep Reinforcement Learning

9

As human beings, we learn from experiences. We have not become so charming overnight or by accident. Years of compliments as well as criticism have all helped shape who we are today. We learn how to ride a bike by trying out different muscle movements until it just clicks. When you perform actions, you are sometimes rewarded immediately, and this is known as **reinforcement learning (RL).**

This chapter is all about designing a machine learning system driven by criticisms and rewards. We will see how to develop a demo GridWorld game using **Deeplearning4j (DL4J)**, **reinforcement learning 4j (RL4J)**, and Neural Q-learning that acts as the Q function. We will start from reinforcement learning and its theoretical background so that the concept is easier to grasp. In summary, the following topics will be covered in this chapter:

- Notation, policy, and utility in reinforcement learning
- Deep Q-learning algorithm
- Developing a GridWorld game using deep Q-learning
- Frequently asked questions (FAQs)

Notation, policy, and utility for RL

Whereas supervised and unsupervised learning appear at opposite ends of the spectrum, RL exists somewhere in the middle. It is not supervised learning, because the training data comes from the algorithm deciding between exploration and exploitation.

In addition, it is not unsupervised, because the algorithm receives feedback from the environment. As long as you are in a situation where performing an action in a state produces a reward, you can use reinforcement learning to discover a good sequence of actions to take the maximum expected rewards. The goal of an RL agent will be to maximize the total reward that it receives in the end. The third main sub-element is the value function.

While rewards determine an immediate desirability of states, values indicate the long-term desirability of states, taking into account the states that may follow and the available rewards in those states. The value function is specified with respect to the chosen policy. During the learning phase, an agent tries actions that determine the states with the highest value, because these actions will get the best amount of reward in the end.

Reinforcement learning techniques are being used in many areas. A general idea that is being pursued right now is creating an algorithm that does not need anything apart from a description of its task. When this kind of performance is achieved, it will be applied virtually everywhere.

Notations in reinforcement learning

You may notice that reinforcement learning jargon involves incarnating the algorithm into taking actions in situations to receive rewards. In fact, the algorithm is often referred to as an agent that acts with the environment.

You can just think it is an intelligent hardware agent sensing with sensors and interact with the environment using its actuators. Therefore, it should not be a surprise that much of RL theory is applied in robotics. Now, to prolong our discussion further, we need to know a few terminologies:

- **Environment**: This is the system having multiple states and mechanisms to transition in between states. For example, for a GridWorld game playing agent's the environment is the grid space itself that defines the states and the way the agent gets rewarded to reach the goal.
- **Agent**: This is an autonomus system that interacts with the environment. For example, in our GridWorld game, an agent is the player.
- **State**: A state in an environment is a set of variables that fully describe the environment.

- **Goal**: It is also a state, which provides a higher discounted cumulative reward than any other state. For our GridWorld game, the goal is the state where the player wants to reach ultimately, but by accumulating the highest possible rewards.
- **Action**: Actions define the transition between different states. Thus, upon execution of an action, an agent can be rewarded or punished from the environment.
- **Policy**: This defines a set of rules based on actions to be performed and executed for a given state in the environment.
- **Reward**: This is a positive or negative quantity (that is score) for good and bad action/move respectively. Ultimately, the learning goal is reaching the goal with maximum score (reward). This way, rewards are essentially the training set for an agent.
- **Episode (also known as trials)**: This is the number of steps necessary to reach the goal state from the initial state (that is, position of an agent).

We will discuss more on policy and utility later in this section. The following diagram demonstrates the interplay between states, actions, and rewards. If you start at state s_1, you can perform action a_1 to obtain a reward $r\ (s_1, a_1)$. Arrows represent actions, and states are represented by circles:

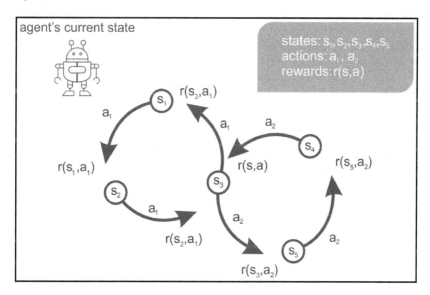

When an agent performs an action, the state produces a reward

A robot performs actions to change between different states. But how does it decide which action to take? Well, it is all about using a different or a concrete policy.

Policy

In reinforcement learning, a policy is a set of rules or a strategy. Therefore, one of the learning outcomes is to discover a good strategy that observes the long-term consequences of actions in each state. So, technically, a policy defines an action to be taken in a given state. The following diagram shows the optimal action given any state:

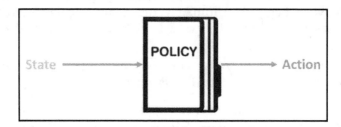

A policy defines an action to be taken in a given state

The short-term consequence is easy to calculate:It is just the reward. Although performing an action yields an immediate reward, it is not always a good idea to choose the action greedily with the best reward. There may be different types of policies dependeing upon your RL problem formulation, as outlined here:

- When an agent always try to achieve the highest immediate reward by performing an action, we call this **greedy policy**.
- If an action is performed arbitrarily, the policy is called **random policy**.
- When a neural network learns a policy for picking actions by updating weights through backpropopagation and explicit feedback from the environment, we call this **policy gradients**.

If we want to come up with a robust a policy to solve an RL problem, we have to find the optimal one that performs better than that of random and greedy policies. In this chapter, we will see why policy gradient is more direct and optimistic.

Utility

The long-term reward is the **utility**. To decide which action to take, an agent can the action that produces the highest utility in a greedy way. The utility of performing an action *a* at a state *s* is written as a function *Q(s, a)*, called the utility function. The utility function predicts the immediate and final rewards based on an optimal policy generated by the input consisting of state and action, as shown in the following diagram:

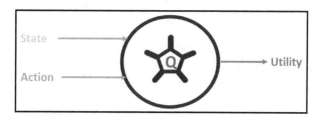

Using a utility function

Neural Q-learning

Most reinforcement learning algorithms boil down to just three main steps: infer, do, and learn. During the first step, the algorithm selects the best action *a* in a given state *s* using the knowledge it has so far. Next, it performs an action to find the reward *r* as well as the next state *s'*.

Then it improves its understanding of the world using the newly acquired knowledge *(s, r, a, s')*. These steps can be formulated even better using QLearning algorithms, which is more or less at the core of Deep Reinforcement Learning.

Introduction to QLearning

Computing the acquired knowledge using *(s, r, a, s')* is just a naive way to calculate the utility. So, we need to find a more robust way to compute it in such that we calculate the utility of a particular state-action pair *(s, a)* by recursively considering the utilities of future actions. The utility of your current action is influenced by not only the immediate reward but also the next best action, as shown in the following formula, called **Q-function**:

$$Q(s, a) = r(s, a) + \gamma \, max \, Q(s', a')$$

In the previous formula, s' denotes the next state, a' denotes the next action, and the reward of taking action a in state s is denoted by $r(s, a)$. Whereas, γ is a hyperparameter called the **discount factor**. If γ is 0, then the agent chooses a particular action that maximizes the immediate reward. Higher values of γ will make the agent put more importance on considering long-term consequences.

In practice, we have more such hyperparameters to be considered. For example, if a vacuum cleaner robot is expected to learn to solve tasks quickly but not necessarily optimally, we may want to set a faster learning rate.

Alternatively, if a robot is allowed more time to explore and exploit, we might tune down the learning rate. Let us call the learning rate α, and change our utility function as follows (note that when $\alpha = 1$, both the equations are identical):

$$Q\left(s_t, a_t\right) \leftarrow (1-\alpha) \cdot \underbrace{Q\left(s_t, a_t\right)}_{\text{old value}} + \underbrace{\alpha}_{\text{learning rate}} \cdot \Bigg(\underbrace{r_t}_{\text{reward}} + \underbrace{\gamma}_{\text{discount factor}} \cdot \overbrace{\underbrace{\max_a Q\left(s_{t+1}, a\right)}_{\text{estimate of optimal future value}}}^{\text{learned value}} \Bigg)$$

In summary, an RL problem can be solved if we know this $Q(s, a)$ function. This motivates researchers to propose a more advanced **QLearning** algorithm called **neural QLearning**, which is a type of algorithm used to calculate state-action values. It falls under the class of **temporal difference** (**TD**) algorithms, which suggests that time differences between actions taken and rewards received are involved.

Neural networks as a Q-function

Now we know the state and the action to perform. However, the QLearning agent needs to know the search space of the form (states x actions). The next step consists of creating the graph or search space, which is the container responsible for any sequence of states. The QLSpace class defines the search space (states x actions) for the QLearning algorithm, as shown in the following diagram:

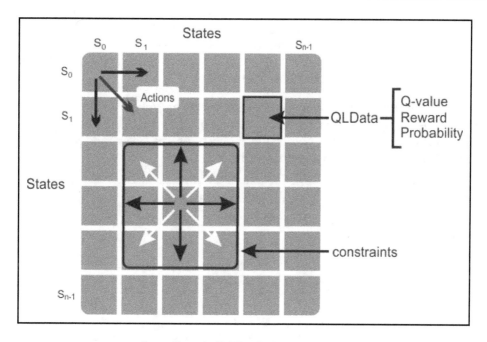

State transition matrix with QLData (Q-value, reward, probability)

The end user with a list of states and actions can provide the search space. Alternatively, it is automatically created by providing the number of states, by taking the following parameters:

- **States**: The sequence of all possible states defined in the Q-learning search space
- **Goals**: A list of identifiers of states that are goals

However, classical notation of such a search space (or lookup table) is sometimes not efficient; as in most interesting problems, our state-action space is much too large to store in a table, for example, the *Pac-Man* game. Rather we need to generalize and pattern-match between states anyway. In other words, we need our Q-learning algorithm to say, *The value of this kind of state is X* instead of saying, *the value of this exact, super-specific state is X*.

Here neural-network-based Q-learning can be used instead of a lookup table as our $Q(s, a)$ such that it accepts a state s and an action a and spits out the value of that state-action. However, as I alluded to earlier, an NN sometimes has millions of parameters associated with it. These are the weights. Therefore, our Q function actually looks like $Q(s, a, \theta)$, where θ is a vector of parameters.

Instead of iteratively updating values in a table, we will iteratively update the θ parameters of our neural network so that it learns to provide us with better estimates of state-action values. By the way, we can use gradient descent (backpropagation) to train such a deep Q-learning network just like any other neural networks.

For example, if the state (search space) is represented by an image, a neural network can rank the possible actions made by the agent such that it can predict the possible reward. For example, running left returns five points, jumping up returns seven, and jumping down returns two points, but running left returns none.

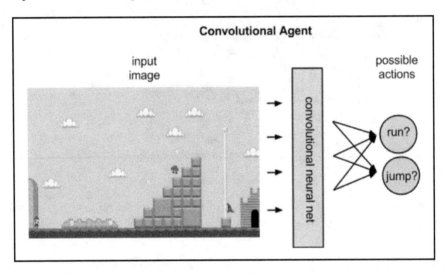

Using a neural network for reinforcement learning-based gaming

To make this happen, instead of having to run our network forward for every action, we can run it forward once we just need to get the *max Q(s',a')*, that is, *max Q* values for every possible action in the new state *s'*.

We will see how to create a deep Q-learning network like this with `MultiLayerNetwork` and the `MultiLayerConfiguration` configuration of DL4J. Therefore, the neural network will serve as our Q-function. Now that we have minimal theoretical knowing about RL and Q-learning, it is time to get to coding.

Developing a GridWorld game using a deep Q-network

We will now start diving into **Deep Q-Network** (**DQN**) to train an agent to play GridWorld, which is a simple text-based game. There is a 4 x 4 grid of tiles and four objects are placed. There is an agent (a player), a pit, a goal, and a wall.

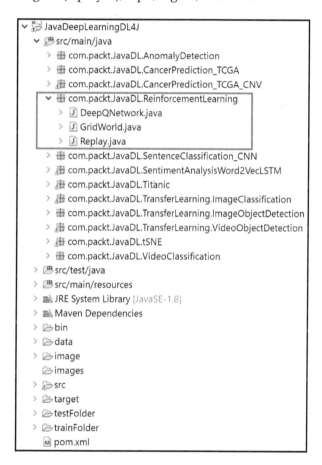

GridWorld project structure

The project has the following structure:

- `DeepQNetwork.java`: Provides the reference architecture for the DQN
- `Replay.java`: Generates replay memory for the DQN to ensure that the gradients of the deep network are stable and do not diverge across episodes
- `GridWorld.java`: The main class used for training the DQN and playing the game.

By the way, we perform the training on GPU and cuDNN for faster convergence. However, feel free to use the CPU backend as well if your machine does not have a GPU.

Generating the grid

We will be developing a simple game by initializing a grid in exactly the same way each time. The game starts with the agent (*A*), goal (+), pit (-), and wall (*W*). All elements are randomly placed on the grid in each game. This is such that the Q-learning just needs to learn how to move the agent from a known starting position to a known goal without hitting the pit, which gives negative rewards. Take a look at this screenshot:

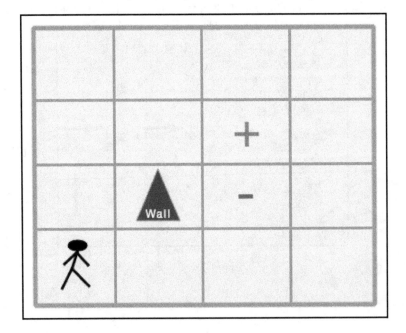

A grid for the GridWorld game showing the elements (that is, agent, goal, pit, and wall)

In short, the target of the game is to reach the goal, where the agent will receive a numerical reward. For simplicity, we will avoid a pit; if the agent lands on the pit, it gets penalized with a negative reward.

The wall can block the agent's path too, but it offers no reward or penalty, so we're safe. Since this is a simple way of defining the state, the agent can make the following moves (that is, actions):

- Up
- Down
- Left
- Right

This way, an action *a* can be defined as follows: a ∈ A {up, down, left, right}. Now let's see, based on the preceding assumption, how the grid would look:

```java
// Generate the GridMap
int size = 4;
float[][] generateGridMap() {
        int agent = rand.nextInt(size * size);
        int goal = rand.nextInt(size * size);

        while(goal == agent)
            goal = rand.nextInt(size * size);
        float[][] map = new float[size][size];

        for(int i = 0; i < size * size; i++)
            map[i / size][i % size] = 0;
        map[goal / size][goal % size] = -1;
        map[agent / size][agent % size] = 1;

        return map;
    }
```

Once the grid is constructed, it can be printed as follows:

```java
void printGrid(float[][] Map) {
        for(int x = 0; x < size; x++) {
            for(int y = 0; y < size; y++) {
                System.out.print((int) Map[x][y]);
            }
            System.out.println(" ");
        }
        System.out.println(" ");
    }
```

Calculating agent and goal positions

Now the search space for the agent is ready. So let's calculate the initial position of the agent and the goal. First, we compute the initial position of the agent in the grid, as follows:

```
// Calculate the position of agent
int calcAgentPos(float[][] Map) {
        int x = -1;
        for(int i = 0; i < size * size; i++) {
            if(Map[i / size][i % size] == 1)
                return i;
        }
        return x;
    }
```

Then we calculate the position of the goal, as follows:

```
// Calculate the position of goal. The method takes the grid space as input
int calcGoalPos(float[][] Map) {
        int x = -1;// start from the initial position

        // Then we loop over the grid size say 4x4 times
        for(int i = 0; i < size * size; i++) {
            // If the mapped position is the initial position, we update
    the position
            if(Map[i / size][i % size] == -1)
                return i;
        }
        return x; // agent cannot move to any other cell
    }
```

Now the generated grid can be considered as four separate grid planes, where each plane represents the position of each element. In the following diagram, the agent's current grid position is (3, 0), the wall is at (0, 0), the pit is at (0, 1), and the goal is at (1, 0), which also means that all other elements are 0s:

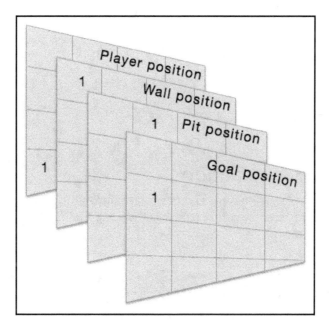

A generated grid can be considered as four separate grid planes

Thus, we developed the grid such that some of the objects contain a *1* at the same *x*, *y* position (but different *z* positions), which indicates they're at the same position on the grid.

Calculating the action mask

Here, we set all the outputs to 0, except the one for the action we actually saw, such that the network multiplies its outputs by a mask corresponding to the one-hot encoded action. We can then pass 0 as the target for all unknown actions, and our neural network should thus perform fine. When we want to predict all actions, we can simply pass a mask of all 1s:

```
// Get action mask
int[] getActionMask(float[][] CurrMap) {
        int retVal[] = { 1, 1, 1, 1 };

        int agent = calcAgentPos(CurrMap); //agent current position
        if(agent < size) // if agent's current pos is less than 4, action
mask is set to 0
            retVal[0] = 0;
        if(agent >= (size * size - size)) // if agent's current pos is 12,
we set action mask to 0 too
            retVal[1] = 0;
        if(agent % size == 0) // if agent's current pos is 0 or 4, we set
```

```
action mask to 0 too
        retVal[2] = 0;
    if(agent % size == (size - 1))// if agent's current pos is 7/11/15,
we set action mask to 0 too
        retVal[3] = 0;

    return retVal; // finally, we return the updated action mask.
}
```

Providing guidance action

Now the agent's action plan is known. The next task is providing some guidance to the agent moving from the current position towards the goal. For example, not all the action is accurate, that is, a bad move:

```
// Show guidance move to agent
float[][] doMove(float[][] CurrMap, int action) {
    float nextMap[][] = new float[size][size];
    for(int i = 0; i < size * size; i++)
        nextMap[i / size][i % size] = CurrMap[i / size][i % size];

    int agent = calcAgentPos(CurrMap);
    nextMap[agent / size][agent % size] = 0;
    if(action == 0) {
        if(agent - size >= 0)
            nextMap[(agent - size) / size][agent % size] = 1;
        else {
            System.out.println("Bad Move");
            System.exit(0);
        }
    } else if(action == 1) {
        if(agent + size < size * size)
            nextMap[(agent + size) / size][agent % size] = 1;
        else {
            System.out.println("Bad Move");
            System.exit(0);
        }
    } else if (action == 2) {
        if((agent % size) - 1 >= 0)
            nextMap[agent / size][(agent % size) - 1] = 1;
        else {
            System.out.println("Bad Move");
            System.exit(0);
        }
    } else if(action == 3) {
        if((agent % size) + 1 < size)
```

```
                nextMap[agent / size][(agent % size) + 1] = 1;
        else {
            System.out.println("Bad Move");
            System.exit(0);
        }
    }
    return nextMap;
}
```

In the previous code block, we encoded the action as follows: 0 is up, 1 is down, 2 is left, and 3 is right. Otherwise, we treat the action as a bad move, and so the agent gets penalized.

Calculating the reward

Now that the agent is provided with some guidance—reinforcement—the next task is to calculate the reward for each action the agent makes. Take a look at this code:

```
// Compute reward for an action
float calcReward(float[][] CurrMap, float[][] NextMap) {
        int newGoal = calcGoalPos(NextMap);// first, we calculate goal
position for each map
        if(newGoal == -1) // if goal position is the initial position (i.e.
no move)
                return (size * size + 1); // we reward the agent to 4*4+ 1 = 17
(i.e. maximum reward)
        return -1f; // else we reward -1.0 for each bad move
    }
```

Flattening input for the input layer

Then we need to convert the output of the network into a 1D-feature vector, to be used by the DQN. This flattening gets the output of the network; it flattens all its structure to create a single long-feature vector to be used by the dense layer. Take a look at this code:

```
INDArray flattenInput(int TimeStep) {
        float flattenedInput[] = new float[size * size * 2 + 1];

        for(int a = 0; a < size; a++) {
            for(int b = 0; b < size; b++) {
                if(FrameBuffer[a][b] == -1)
                    flattenedInput[a * size + b] = 1;
                else
                    flattenedInput[a * size + b] = 0;
```

```
        if (FrameBuffer[a][b] == 1)
            flattenedInput[size * size + a * size + b] = 1;
        else
            flattenedInput[size * size + a * size + b] = 0;
    }
}
flattenedInput[size * size * 2] = TimeStep;
return Nd4j.create(flattenedInput);
}
```

Up to this point, we just created the logical skeleton for the GridWorld. Thus, we create the DQN before we start playing the game.

Network construction and training

As I stated, we will create a DQN network using MultiLayerNetwork and the MultiLayerConfiguration configuration of DL4J, which will serve as our Q-function. Therefore, the first step is to create a MultiLayerNetwork by defining MultiLayerConfiguration. Since the state has 64 elements—4 x 4 x 4—our network has to have an input layer of 64 units, two hidden layers of 164 and 150 units each, and an output layer of 4, for four possible actions (up, down, left, and right). This is outlined here:

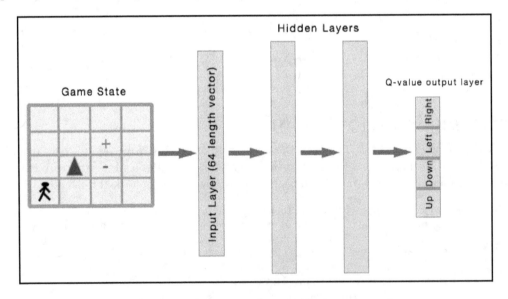

The structure of the DQN network, showing an input layer, two hidden layers, and an output layer

Nevertheless, we will be using experience replay memory for training our DQN, which will help us store the transitions observed by the agent. This will allow the DQN to reuse this data later. By sampling from it randomly, the transitions that build up a batch are de-correlated. It has been shown that this greatly stabilizes and improves the DQN training procedure. Following the preceding config, the following code can be used to create such a MultiLayerConfiguration:

```
int InputLength = size * size * 2 + 1;
int HiddenLayerCount = 150;

MultiLayerConfiguration conf = new NeuralNetConfiguration.Builder()
                .seed(12345)      //Random number generator seed for improved
repeatability. Optional.
.optimizationAlgo(OptimizationAlgorithm.STOCHASTIC_GRADIENT_DESCENT)
                .weightInit(WeightInit.XAVIER)
                .updater(new Adam(0.001))
                .l2(0.001) // l2 regularization on all layers
                .list()
                .layer(0, new DenseLayer.Builder()
                        .nIn(InputLength)
                        .nOut(HiddenLayerCount)
                        .weightInit(WeightInit.XAVIER)
                        .activation(Activation.RELU)
                        .build())
                .layer(1, new DenseLayer.Builder()
                        .nIn(HiddenLayerCount)
                        .nOut(HiddenLayerCount)
                        .weightInit(WeightInit.XAVIER)
                        .activation(Activation.RELU)
                        .build())
                .layer(2,new OutputLayer.Builder(LossFunction.MSE)
                        .nIn(HiddenLayerCount)
                        .nOut(4) // for 4 possible actions
                        .weightInit(WeightInit.XAVIER)
                        .activation(Activation.IDENTITY)
                        .weightInit(WeightInit.XAVIER)
                        .build())
                .pretrain(false).backprop(true).build();
```

Then we use this configuration to create a DQN:

```
DeepQNetwork RLNet = new DeepQNetwork(conf, 100000, .99f, 1d, 1024, 500,
1024, InputLength, 4);
```

We will discuss the parameters shortly, but, before that, we'll look at how to create such a deep architecture. First, we define some parameters:

```java
int ReplayMemoryCapacity;
List<Replay> ReplayMemory;
double Epsilon;
float Discount;
MultiLayerNetwork DeepQ; // Initial DeepQNet
MultiLayerNetwork TargetDeepQ; // Target DeepQNet
int BatchSize;
int UpdateFreq;
int UpdateCounter;
int ReplayStartSize;
Random r;
int InputLength;
int NumActions;
INDArray LastInput;
int LastAction;
```

Then we define the constructor to initialize these parameters:

```java
DeepQNetwork(MultiLayerConfiguration conf, int replayMemoryCapacity, float
discount, double epsilon, int batchSize, int updateFreq, int
replayStartSize, int inputLength, int numActions){
        // First, we initialize both the DeepQNets
        DeepQ = new MultiLayerNetwork(conf);
        DeepQ.init();
        TargetDeepQ = new MultiLayerNetwork(conf);
        TargetDeepQ.init();

        // Then we initialize the target DeepQNet's params
        TargetDeepQ.setParams(DeepQ.params());
        ReplayMemoryCapacity = replayMemoryCapacity;
        Epsilon = epsilon;
        Discount = discount;
        r = new Random();
        BatchSize = batchSize;
        UpdateFreq = updateFreq;
        UpdateCounter = 0;
        ReplayMemory = new ArrayList<Replay>();
        ReplayStartSize = replayStartSize;
        InputLength = inputLength;
        NumActions = numActions;
    }
```

The following is the implementation for the main loop of the algorithm:

1. We set up a `for` loop to the number of episodes while the game is in progress.
2. We run the Q-network forward.
3. We use an epsilon-greedy implementation, so at time *t* with probability ϵ, the *agent* chooses a random action. However, with probability 1–ϵ, the action associated with the highest Q-value from our neural network is performed.
4. Then the agent takes an action *a*, which is determined in the previous step; we observe a new state *s'* and reward r_{t+1}.
5. Then the Q-network forward pass is executed using *s'*, and the highest Q-value (maxQ) is stored.
6. The agent's target value is then computed as reward + (gamma * maxQ) to train the network, where gamma is a parameter ($0<=\gamma<=1$).
7. We aim to update the output associated with the action we just took for four possible outputs. Here, the agent's target output vector is the same as the output vector from the first execution, except the one output associated with an action to *reward + (gamma * maxQ)*.

The preceding steps are for one episode, and then the loop iterates for the defined episode by the user. In addition, the grid is first constructed, and then the next reward for each move is computed and saved. In short, the preceding steps can be represented as follows:

```
GridWorld grid = new GridWorld();
grid.networkConstruction();

// We iterate for 100 episodes
for(int m = 0; m < 100; m++) {
          System.out.println("Episode: " + m);
          float CurrMap[][] = grid.generateGridMap();

          grid.FrameBuffer = CurrMap;
          int t = 0;
          grid.printGrid(CurrMap);

          for(int i = 0; i < 2 * grid.size; i++) {
               int a = grid.RLNet.getAction(grid.flattenInput(t),
grid.getActionMask(CurrMap));
                 float NextMap[][] = grid.doMove(CurrMap, a);
                 float r = grid.calcReward(CurrMap, NextMap);
                 grid.addToBuffer(NextMap);
                 t++;

                 if(r == grid.size * grid.size + 1) {
```

```
                    grid.RLNet.observeReward(r, null,
    grid.getActionMask(NextMap));
                        break;
                }

                grid.RLNet.observeReward(r, grid.flattenInput(t),
    grid.getActionMask(NextMap));
                    CurrMap = NextMap;
            }
    }
```

In the preceding code block, network computes the observed reward for each mini batch of flattened input data. Take a look at this:

```
void observeReward(float Reward, INDArray NextInputs, int
NextActionMask[]){
        addReplay(Reward, NextInputs, NextActionMask);

        if(ReplayStartSize < ReplayMemory.size())
            networkTraining(BatchSize);
        UpdateCounter++;
        if(UpdateCounter == UpdateFreq){
            UpdateCounter = 0;
            System.out.println("Reconciling Networks");
            reconcileNetworks();
        }
    }
```

The preceding reward is calculated to estimate the optimal future value:

```
int getAction(INDArray Inputs , int ActionMask[]){
        LastInput = Inputs;
        INDArray outputs = DeepQ.output(Inputs);
        System.out.print(outputs + " ");
        if(Epsilon > r.nextDouble()) {
            LastAction = r.nextInt(outputs.size(1));
            while(ActionMask[LastAction] == 0)
                LastAction = r.nextInt(outputs.size(1));
            System.out.println(LastAction);
            return LastAction;
        }
        LastAction = findActionMax(outputs , ActionMask);
        System.out.println(LastAction);
        return LastAction;
    }
```

In the preceding code block, the future reward is computed by taking the maximum value of the neural network output. Take a look at this:

```
int findActionMax(INDArray NetOutputs , int ActionMask[]){
        int i = 0;
        while(ActionMask[i] == 0) i++;
        float maxVal = NetOutputs.getFloat(i);
        int maxValI = i;

        for(; i < NetOutputs.size(1) ; i++){
            if(NetOutputs.getFloat(i) > maxVal && ActionMask[i] == 1){
                maxVal = NetOutputs.getFloat(i);
                maxValI = i;
            }
        }
        return maxValI;
    }
```

As stated before, the observed reward is computed once the network training starts. The combined input is computed as follows:

```
INDArray combineInputs(Replay replays[]){
        INDArray retVal = Nd4j.create(replays.length , InputLength);
        for(int i = 0; i < replays.length ; i++){
            retVal.putRow(i, replays[i].Input);
        }
        return retVal;
    }
```

Then the network needs to compute the combined input for the next pass. Take a look at this code:

```
INDArray combineNextInputs(Replay replays[]){
        INDArray retVal = Nd4j.create(replays.length , InputLength);
        for(int i = 0; i < replays.length ; i++){
            if(replays[i].NextInput != null)
                retVal.putRow(i, replays[i].NextInput);
        }
        return retVal;
    }
```

In the previous code blocks, the map at each time step is saved with the addToBuffer() method, which is as follows:

```
void addToBuffer(float[][] nextFrame) {
        FrameBuffer = nextFrame;
    }
```

Then the DQNet takes the flattening input into batches for each episode, and the training starts. Then the current and target outputs by maximizing the reward are computed based on the current and target inputs. Take a look at this code block:

```
void networkTraining(int BatchSize){
        Replay replays[] = getMiniBatch(BatchSize);
        INDArray CurrInputs = combineInputs(replays);
        INDArray TargetInputs = combineNextInputs(replays);

        INDArray CurrOutputs = DeepQ.output(CurrInputs);
        INDArray TargetOutputs = TargetDeepQ.output(TargetInputs);
        float y[] = new float[replays.length];
        for(int i = 0 ; i < y.length ; i++){
            int ind[] = { i , replays[i].Action };
            float FutureReward = 0 ;
            if(replays[i].NextInput != null)
                FutureReward = findMax(TargetOutputs.getRow(i) ,
replays[i].NextActionMask);
            float TargetReward = replays[i].Reward + Discount *
FutureReward ;
            CurrOutputs.putScalar(ind , TargetReward ) ;
        }
        //System.out.println("Avgerage Error: " + (TotalError / y.length)
);
        DeepQ.fit(CurrInputs, CurrOutputs);
    }
```

In the preceding code block, future rewards are computed by maximizing the value of the neural network output, as shown here:

```
float findMax(INDArray NetOutputs , int ActionMask[]){
        int i = 0;
        while(ActionMask[i] == 0) i++;
        float maxVal = NetOutputs.getFloat(i);
        for(; i < NetOutputs.size(1) ; i++){
            if(NetOutputs.getFloat(i) > maxVal && ActionMask[i] == 1){
                maxVal = NetOutputs.getFloat(i);
            }
        }
        return maxVal;
    }
```

As I stated earlier, this is very simple game, and if the agent takes action 2 (that is, left), one step results in reaching the goal. Therefore, we just keep all other outputs the same as before and change the one for the action we took. So, implementing experience replay is a better idea, which gives us mini-batch updating in an online learning scheme.

It works such that we run the agent to collect enough transitions to fill up the replay memory, without training. For example, our memory may be of size 10,000. Then, at every step, the agent will obtain a transition; we'll add this to the end of the memory and pop off the earliest one. Take a look at this code:

```
void addReplay(float reward , INDArray NextInput , int NextActionMask[]){
        if(ReplayMemory.size() >= ReplayMemoryCapacity )
            ReplayMemory.remove( r.nextInt(ReplayMemory.size()) );
        ReplayMemory.add(new Replay(LastInput , LastAction , reward ,
NextInput , NextActionMask));
    }
```

Then, sample a mini batch of experiences from the memory randomly, and update our Q-function on that, similar to mini-batch gradient descent. Take a look at this code:

```
Replay[] getMiniBatch(int BatchSize){
        int size = ReplayMemory.size() < BatchSize ? ReplayMemory.size() :
BatchSize ;
        Replay[] retVal = new Replay[size];
        for(int i = 0 ; i < size ; i++){
            retVal[i] = ReplayMemory.get(r.nextInt(ReplayMemory.size()));
        }
        return retVal;
    }
```

Playing the GridWorld game

For this project, I haven't used any visualization to demonstrate the states and actions. Rather it is a text-based game, as I alluded to earlier. Then you can run the GridWorld.java class (containing the main method) using following invocation:

```
DeepQNetwork RLNet = new DeepQNetwork(conf, 100000, .99f, 1d, 1024, 500,
1024, InputLength, 4);
```

In this invocation, here's the parameter description outlined:

- conf: This is the MultiLayerConfiguration used to create the DQN
- 100000: This is the replay memory capacity
- .99f: The discount
- 1d: This is the epsilon

- `1024`: The batch size
- `500`: This is the update frequency; second 1,024 is the replay start size
- `InputLength`: This is the input length of size x size x 2 + 1= 33 (considering size=4)
- `4`: This is the number of possible actions that can be performed by the agent.

We initialize epsilon (*ϵ*-greedy action selection) to 1, which will decrease by a small amount on every episode. This way, it will eventually reach 0.1 and saturate. Based on the preceding setting, the training should be started, which will start generating a grid representing the map at each timestamp and the outputs of the DQN for the up/down/left/right order, followed by the index of the highest value.

We do not have any module for a graphical representation of the game. So in the previous result, 0, 1, -1, and so on,the grid represents the map at each timestamp for five episodes. The numbers in brackets are just the outputs of the DQN, followed by the index of the highest value. Take a look at this code block:

```
Scanner keyboard = new Scanner(System.in);
for(int m = 0; m < 10; m++) {
        grid.RLNet.SetEpsilon(0);
        float CurrMap[][] = grid.generateGridMap();
        grid.FrameBuffer = CurrMap;

        int t = 0;
        float tReward = 0;

        while(true) {
            grid.printGrid(CurrMap);
            keyboard.nextLine();

            int a = grid.RLNet.getAction(grid.flattenInput(t),
grid.getActionMask(CurrMap));
            float NextMap[][] = grid.doMove(CurrMap, a);
            float r = grid.calcReward(CurrMap, NextMap);

            tReward += r;
            grid.addToBuffer(NextMap);
            t++;
            grid.RLNet.observeReward(r, grid.flattenInput(t),
grid.getActionMask(NextMap));

            if(r == grid.size * grid.size + 1)
                break;
            CurrMap = NextMap;
        }
```

```
        System.out.println("Net Score: " + (tReward));
    }
    keyboard.close();
}
```

>>>
Episode: 0
0000
01-10
0000
0000
[[0.2146, 0.0337, -0.0444, -0.0311]] 2
[[0.1105, 0.2139, -0.0454, 0.0851]] 0
[[0.0678, 0.3976, -0.0027, 0.2667]] 1
[[0.0955, 0.3379, -0.1072, 0.2957]] 3
[[0.2498, 0.2510, -0.1891, 0.4132]] 0
[[0.2024, 0.4142, -0.1918, 0.6754]] 2
[[0.1141, 0.6838, -0.2850, 0.6557]] 1
[[0.1943, 0.6514, -0.3886, 0.6868]] 0
Episode: 1
0000
0000
1000
00-10
[[0.0342, 0.1792, -0.0991, 0.0369]] 0
[[0.0734, 0.2147, -0.1360, 0.0285]] 1
[[0.0044, 0.1295, -0.2472, 0.1816]] 3
[[0.0685, 0.0555, -0.2153, 0.2873]] 0
[[0.1479, 0.0558, -0.3495, 0.3527]] 3
[[0.0978, 0.3776, -0.4362, 0.4475]] 0
[[0.1010, 0.3509, -0.4134, 0.5363]] 2
[[0.1611, 0.3717, -0.4411, 0.7929]] 3

....
Episode: 9
0000
1-100
0000
0000
[[0.0483, 0.2899, -0.1125, 0.0281]] 3
0000
0000
0-101
0000
[[0.0534, 0.2587, -0.1539, 0.1711]] 1
Net Score: 10.0

Thus, the agent has been able to make a total score of 10 (that is, positive).

Frequently asked questions (FAQs)

Now that we have solved the GridWorld problem, there are other practical aspects in reinforcement learning and overall deep learning phenomena that need to be considered too. In this section, we will see some frequently asked questions that may be already on your mind. Answers to these questions can be found in Appendix.

1. What is Q in Q-learning?
2. I understand that we performed the training on GPU and cuDNN for faster convergence. However, there is no GPU on my machine. What can I do?
3. There is no visualization, so it is difficult to follow the moves made by the agent toward the target.
4. Give a few more examples of reinforcement learning.
5. How do I reconcile the results obtained for our mini-batch processing?
6. How would I reconcile the DQN?
7. I would like to save the trained network. Can I do that?
8. I would like to restore the saved (that is, trained) network. Can I do that?

Summary

In this chapter, we saw how to develop a demo GridWorld game using DL4J, RL4J, and neural Q-learning, which acts as the Q-function. We also provided some basic theoretical background necessary for developing a deep QLearning network for playing the GridWorld game. However, we did not develop any module for visualizing the moves of the agent for the entire episodes.

In the next chapter, we will develop a very common end-to-end movie recommendation system project, but with the neural **Factorization Machine** (**FM**) algorithm. The MovieLens 1 million dataset will be used for this project. We will be using RankSys and Java-based FM libraries for predicting both movie ratings and rankings from the users. Nevertheless, Spark ML will be used for exploratory analysis of the dataset.

Answers to questions

Answer to question 1: Do not confuse the Q in Q-learning with the Q-function we have discussed in the previous parts. The Q-function is always the name of the function that accepts states and actions and spits out the value of that state-action pair. RL methods involve a Q-function but are not necessarily Q-learning algorithms.

Answer to question 2: No worries as you can perform the training on a CPU backend too. In that case, just remove the entries for CUDA and cuDNN dependencies from the `pom.xml` file and replace them with the CPU ones. The properties would be:

```
<properties>
        <project.build.sourceEncoding>UTF-8</project.build.sourceEncoding>
        <java.version>1.8</java.version>
         <nd4j.version>1.0.0-alpha</nd4j.version>
        <dl4j.version>1.0.0-alpha</dl4j.version>
      <datavec.version>1.0.0-alpha</datavec.version>
       <arbiter.version>1.0.0-alpha</arbiter.version>
       <logback.version>1.2.3</logback.version>
</properties>
```

Don't use these two dependencies:

```
<dependency>
        <groupId>org.nd4j</groupId>
         <artifactId>nd4j-cuda-9.0-platform</artifactId>
         <version>${nd4j.version}</version>
</dependency>
<dependency>
        <groupId>org.deeplearning4j</groupId>
        <artifactId>deeplearning4j-cuda-9.0</artifactId>
        <version>${dl4j.version}</version>
</dependency>
```

Use only one, as follows:

```
<dependency>
        <groupId>org.nd4j</groupId>
        <artifactId>nd4j-native</artifactId>
        <version>${nd4j.version}</version>
</dependency>
```

Then you are ready to get going with the CPU backend.

Answer to question 3: As stated earlier, the initial target was to develop a simple text-based game. However, with some effort, all the moves can be visualized too. I want to leave this up to the readers. Nevertheless, the visualization module will be added to the GitHub repository very soon.

Answer to question 4: Well, there are some basic examples of RL4J on the DL4J GitHub repository at `https://github.com/deeplearning4j/dl4j-examples/`. Feel free to try to extend them to meet your needs.

Answer to question 5: Processing each mini-batch gives us the best weights/biases result for the input used in that mini-batch. This question evolves several subquestions related to this: i) How do we reconcile the results obtained for all mini-batches? ii) Do we take the average to come up with the final weights/biases for the trained network?

Therefore, each mini-batch contains the average of the gradients of individual errors. If you had two mini-batches, you could take the average of the gradient updates of both mini-batches to tweak the weights, to reduce the error for those samples.

Answer to question 6: Refer to question 5 to get the theoretical understanding. However, in our example, use the `setParams()` method from DL4J, which helps you reconcile network:

```
void reconcileNetworks(){
    TargetDeepQ.setParams(DeepQ.params());
    }
```

Now the question would be: Where do we use such reconciling? Well, the answer is while computing the reward (see the `observeReward()` method).

Answer to question 7: Saving the DQN is similar to saving another DL4J-based network. For this, I wrote a method called `saveNetwork()` that saves network parameters as a single ND4J object in JSON format. Take a look at this:

```
public boolean saveNetwork(String ParamFileName , String JSONFileName){
        //Write the network parameters for later use:
        try(DataOutputStream dos = new
DataOutputStream(Files.newOutputStream(Paths.get(ParamFileName)))){
            Nd4j.write(DeepQ.params(),dos);
        } catch(IOException e) {
            System.out.println("Failed to write params");
            return false;
        }
        //Write the network configuration:
        try{
```

```
        FileUtils.write(new File(JSONFileName),
DeepQ.getLayerWiseConfigurations().toJson());
        } catch (IOException e) {
            System.out.println("Failed to write json");
            return false;
        }
        return true;
    }
```

Answer to question 8: Restoring the DQN is similar to saving another DL4J-based network. For this, I wrote a method called `restoreNetwork()` that reconciles the params and reloads the saved network as `MultiLayerNetwork`. Here it is:

```
public boolean restoreNetwork(String ParamFileName , String JSONFileName){
        //Load network configuration from disk:
        MultiLayerConfiguration confFromJson;
        try{
            confFromJson =
MultiLayerConfiguration.fromJson(FileUtils.readFileToString(new
File(JSONFileName)));
        } catch(IOException e1) {
            System.out.println("Failed to load json");
            return false;
        }

        //Load parameters from disk:
        INDArray newParams;
        try(DataInputStream dis = new DataInputStream(new
FileInputStream(ParamFileName))){
            newParams = Nd4j.read(dis);
        } catch(FileNotFoundException e) {
            System.out.println("Failed to load parems");
            return false;
        } catch (IOException e) {
            System.out.println("Failed to load parems");
            return false;
        }
        //Create a MultiLayerNetwork from the saved configuration and
parameters
        DeepQ = new MultiLayerNetwork(confFromJson);
        DeepQ.init();
        DeepQ.setParameters(newParams);
        reconcileNetworks();
        return true;
    }
```

10
Developing Movie Recommendation Systems Using Factorization Machines

Factorization machines (**FM**) are a set of algorithms that enhance the performance of linear models by incorporating second-order feature interactions that are absent in **matrix factorization** (**MF**) algorithms in a supervised way. Therefore, FMs are very robust compared to their classical counterpart—**collaborative filtering** (**CF**)—and are gaining popularity in personalization and recommendation systems because they can be used to discover latent features underlying the interactions between two different kinds of entities.

In this chapter, we will develop a sample project for predicting both the rating and ranking to show their effectiveness. Nevertheless, we will see some theoretical background of recommendation systems using MF and CF before diving into the project's implementation using RankSys library-based FMs. In summary, the following topics will be covered in this chapter:

- Recommendation systems
- Matrix factorization and the collaborative filtering approach
- Developing FM-based move recommendation systems
- Frequently asked questions (FAQs).

Recommendation systems

Recommender techniques are nothing but information agents that try to predict items that users may be interested in and recommend the best ones to the target user. These techniques can be classified based on the information sources they use. For example, user features (age, gender, income, and location), item features (keywords, and genres), user-item ratings (explicit ratings, and transaction data), and other information about the user and item that are useful for the process of recommendation.

Thus, a recommendation system; otherwise known as a **recommendation engine** (**RE**) is a subclass of information filtering systems that help to predict the rating or preference based on the rating provided by users to an item. In recent years, recommendation systems have become increasingly popular.

Recommendation approaches

There are a couple of ways to develop REs to produce a list of recommendations, for example, collaborative and content-based filtering, knowledge-based, or the personality-based approach.

Collaborative filtering approaches

By using CF approaches, an RE can be built based on a user's past behavior. Numerical ratings are given on consumed items. Sometimes, it can be based on the decisions made by other users who also have purchased the same items using some widely used data mining algorithms such as Apriori or FP-growth. In the following diagram, you can get some idea of the different recommendation systems:

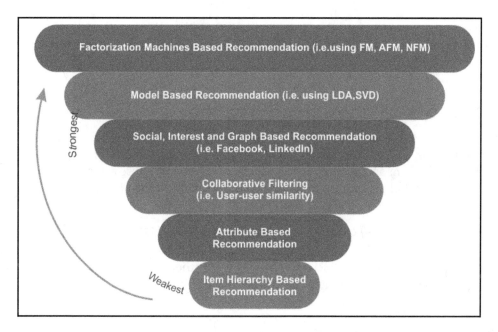

A comparative view of different recommendation systems

Even though these are successful recommendation systems, CF-based approaches often suffer from the following three problems:

- **Cold start:** Sometimes, they can become stuck when a large amount of data about users is required to make a more accurate recommendation system.
- **Scalability:** A large amount of computation power is often necessary to calculate recommendations using a dataset with millions of users and products.
- **Sparsity:** This often happens with crowdsourced datasets when a huge number of items are sold on major e-commerce sites. All recommendation datasets are crowd-sourced in some sense. This is a general problem for almost all recommendation systems that have a sufficiently large number of items to offer to a sufficiently large number of users and need not be confined to e-commerce sites only.

In this case, active users may rate only a small subset of the whole items sold, so even the most popular items have very few ratings. Accordingly, the user versus items matrix becomes very sparse. In other words, handling a large-scale sparse matrix is computationally very challenging.

To overcome these issues, a particular type of collaborative filtering algorithm uses matrix factorization, which is a low-rank matrix approximation technique. We will see an example of this later in this chapter.

Content-based filtering approaches

With content-based filtering approaches, a series of discrete characteristics of an item are utilized to recommend additional items with similar properties. Sometimes, it is based on a description of the item and a profile of the user's preferences. These approaches try to recommend items that are similar to those that a user liked in the past, or that are currently being used.

A key issue with content-based filtering is whether the system is able to learn user preferences from their actions regarding one content source and use them with other content types. When this type of RE is deployed, it can then be used to predict items or ratings for items that the user may have an interest in.

Hybrid recommender systems

As you have seen, there are several pros and cons of using collaborative filtering and content-based filtering approaches. Therefore, to overcome the limitations of these two approaches, recent trends have shown that a hybrid approach can be more effective and accurate. Sometimes, factorization approaches such as FM and **Singular Value Decomposition** (**SVD**) are used to make them robust.

Model-based collaborative filtering

Collaborative filtering methods are classified as memory-based, such as the user-based algorithm and model-based collaborative filtering (kernel mapping is recommended). In the model-based collaborative filtering technique, users and products are described by a small set of factors, also called **latent factors** (**LFs**). The LFs are then used to predict the missing entries. The **Alternating Least Squares** (**ALS**) algorithm is used to learn these latent factors.

Compared to a memory-based approach, a model-based approach can handle the sparsity of the original matrix better. This is also scalable, faster, and can avoid overfitting issues. However, it is not flexible and adaptable because it is difficult to add data to the model. Now, let's take a look at an important element in the collaborative filtering approach, called the utility matrix.

The utility matrix

In a collaborative filtering-based recommendation system, there are dimensions of entities: users and items (items refers to products, such as movies, games, and songs). As a user, you might have preferences for certain items. Therefore, these preferences must be motivated out of the data about items, users, or ratings. This data is often represented as a utility matrix, such as a user-item pair. This type of value can represent what is known about the degree of preference that the user has for a particular item.

The following table shows an example utility matrix that represents the rating users have given to movies on a 1-5 scale, with 5 being the highest rating. **HP1**, **HP2**, and **HP3** are acronyms for *Harry Potter I, II,* and *III*, **TW** stands for *Twilight*, and **SW1**, **SW2**, and **SW3** ;stands for *Star Wars episodes 1*, 2, and 3. The letters **A**, **B**, **C**, and **D** represent the users:

	HP 1	HP 2	HP 3	TW	SW 1	SW 2	SW 3
A	4			5	1		
B	5	5	4				
C				2	4	5	
D		3					3

Utility matrix (user versus movies matrix)

There are many blank entries for the user-movie pairs. This means that users have not rated those movies, which increases sparsity. Using this matrix, the goal is to predict the blanks in the utility matrix. Suppose we are curious to know whether user **A** would like **SW2**. This is difficult to predict since there is not much data in the matrix.

Therefore, other properties regarding movies, such as the producer, director, leading actors, or even the similarity of their names, can be used to compute the similarity of the movies **SW1** and **SW2**. This similarity would drive us to conclude that since **A** did not like **SW1**, they are unlikely to enjoy **SW2** either.

However, this might not work for a larger dataset. Therefore, with much more data, we might observe that the people who rated both **SW1** and **SW2** were inclined to give them similar ratings. Finally, we can conclude that A would also give **SW2** a low rating, similar to **A**'s rating of **SW1**. This approach, however, has a serious drawback called the ;**cold-start problem**.

The cold-start problem in collaborative-filtering approaches

The term cold-start problem sounds funny, but, as the name implies, it derives from cars. In recommendation engines, however, the term cold-start simply means a circumstance that is not yet optimal for the engine to provide the best possible results.

In collaborative filtering approaches, the recommender system would identify users who share preferences with the active user and propose items that like-minded users have favored. Due to the cold-start problem, this approach would fail to consider items that no-one in the community has rated.

Recommendation engines using CF-based approaches recommend each item based on user actions. The more user actions an item has, the easier it is to tell which user would be interested in it and what other items are similar to it. As time progresses, the system will be able to give more and more accurate recommendations. At a certain stage, when new items or users are added to the user-item matrix, the following problem occurs:

items \ users	1	2	3	4	5	6	7	8	9	10	...	n
1	1		1			1				1		
2							1	1	1			
3	1	1		1				1	1			1
4		1			1			1	1			
...			1				1					
m												

Users versus items matrices sometimes lead to the cold-start problem

In this case, the RE does not have enough knowledge about this new user or this new item yet. The content-based filtering approach, similar to FM, is a method that can be incorporated to alleviate the cold-start problem.

Factorization machines in recommender systems

In real life, most recommendation problems assume that we have a rating dataset formed by a collection of (user, item, and rating) tuples. However, in many applications, we have plenty of item metadata (tags, categories, and genres) that can be used to make better predictions.

This is one of the benefits of using FMs with feature-rich datasets, because there is a natural way in which extra features can be included in the model, and higher-order interactions can be modeled using the dimensionality parameter.

A few recent types of research show which feature-rich datasets give better predictions:

- Xiangnan He and Tat-Seng Chua, *Neural Factorization Machines for Sparse Predictive Analytics*. During proceedings of SIGIR '17, Shinjuku, Tokyo, Japan, August 07-11, 2017
- Jun Xiao, Hao Ye, Xiangnan He, Hanwang Zhang, Fei Wu and Tat-Seng Chua (2017). *Attentional Factorization Machines: Learning the Weight of Feature Interactions via Attention Networks* IJCAI, Melbourne, Australia, August 19-25, 2017

These papers explain how to make existing data into a feature-rich dataset and how FMs were implemented on the dataset. Therefore, researchers are trying to use FMs to develop more accurate and robust REs. In the next section, we will start developing our project for movie recommendations using FMs. For that, we will be using Apache Spark and RankSys libraries.

Existing recommendation algorithms require a consumption (product) or rating (movie) dataset in *(user, item, rating)* tuples. These types of dataset are mostly used by variations of CF algorithms. CF algorithms have been widely adopted and have proven to yield good results.

However, in many instances, we have plenty of item metadata (tags, categories, and genres) that can be used to make better predictions as well. Unfortunately, CF algorithms do not use these types of metadata.

FMs can make use of these feature-rich (meta) datasets. An FM can consume these extra features to model higher-order interactions specifying the dimensionality parameter d. Most importantly, FMs are also optimized for handling large-scale sparse datasets. Therefore, a second order FM model would suffice because there is not enough information to estimate interactions that are more complex:

	Feature vector x																			Target y	
x_1	1	0	0	...	1	0	0	0	...	0.3	0.3	0.3	0	...	13	0	0	0	0	...	5	y_1
x_2	1	0	0	...	0	1	0	0	...	0.3	0.3	0.3	0	...	14	1	0	0	0	...	3	y_2
x_3	1	0	0	...	0	0	1	0	...	0.3	0.3	0.3	0	...	16	0	1	0	0	...	1	y_3
x_4	0	1	0	...	0	0	1	0	...	0	0	0.5	0.5	...	5	0	0	0	0	...	4	y_4
x_5	0	1	0	...	0	0	0	1	...	0	0	0.5	0.5	...	8	0	0	1	0	...	5	y_5
x_6	0	0	1	...	1	0	0	0	...	0.5	0	0.5	0	...	9	0	0	0	0	...	1	y_6
x_7	0	0	1	...	0	0	1	0	...	0.5	0	0.5	0	...	12	1	0	0	0	...	5	y_7
	A	B	C	...	TI	NH	SW	ST	...	TI	NH	SW	ST	...	Time	TI	NH	SW	ST	...		
		User				Movie					Other Movie rated						Last Movie rated					

An example training dataset representing a personalization problem with the feature vectors x and the target y. Here, rows refer to movies, while columns include director, actor and genre info, and so on

Let's assume that the dataset of a prediction problem is described by a design matrix $X \in \mathbb{R}^{nxp}$,. In the preceding diagram, the ith row, $x_i \in \mathbb{R}^{p}$ of X, describes one case with p real-valued variables and where y_i is the prediction target of the ith case. Alternatively, we can describe this set as a set S of tuples (x,y), where (again) $x \in \mathbb{R}^{p}$ is a feature vector and y is its corresponding target or label.

In other words, in figure 7, every row represents a feature vector x_i with its corresponding target y_i. For easier interpretation, the features are grouped into indicators for the active user (blue), the active item (red), other movies rated by the same user (orange), the time in months (green), and the last movie rated (brown).

Then, the FM algorithm models all the nested interactions (up to order d) between p input variables in x using the following factorized interaction parameters:

$$\hat{y}(x) = w_0 + \sum_{i=1}^{n} w_i x_i + \sum_{i=1}^{n} \sum_{j=i+1}^{n} \langle v_i, v_j \rangle x_i x_j$$

In this equation, the vs represent k-dimensional latent vectors associated with each variable (the users and the items), and the bracket operator represents the inner product. This kind of representation with data matrices and feature vectors is common in many machine learning approaches, for example, in linear regression or support vector machines (SVM).

However, if you are familiar with the MF models, the preceding equation should look familiar: it contains a global bias as well as user/item-specific biases and includes user-item interactions. Now, if we assume that each $x(j)$ vector is only non-zero at positions u and i, we get the classic MF model:

$$\hat{y} = w_0 + w_i + w_u + \langle v_j v_j \rangle$$

Nevertheless, FMs can also be used for classification or regression and are much more computationally efficient on large, sparse datasets than traditional algorithms like linear regression. This property is why FM is widely used for recommendation: user count and item count are typically very large although the actual number of recommendations is very small (users do not rate all available items!).

Developing a movie recommender system using FMs

In this project, we will show you how to do ranking prediction from the MovieLens 1m dataset. First, we will prepare the dataset. Then, we will train the FM algorithm, which eventually predicts the rankings and ratings for movies. The project code has the following structure:

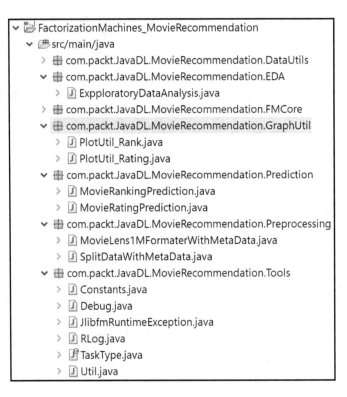

Movie rating and ranking prediction project structure

In summary, the project has the following structure:

- **EDA:** This package is used to do an exploratory analysis of the MovieLens 1M dataset.
- **Tools, FMCore, and DataUtils:** These are the core FM libraries. For the purpose of this probject, I used (but extended) the RankSys library (see the GitHub repository at https://github.com/RankSys/RankSys).

- **Preprocessing:** This package is used to convert the `MovieLens` 1M dataset into LibFM format.
- **Prediction:** This package is used for the movie rating and ranking prediction.
- **GraphUtil:** This package visualizes some performance metrics over iteration.

We will go through all of these packages step by step. Nevertheless, knowing the dataset is a mandate.

Dataset description and exploratory analysis

The MovieLens 1M small dataset was downloaded (and used with necessary permission) from the MovieLens website at `https://grouplens.org/datasets/movielens/`. I sincerely acknowledge and thank F. Maxwell Harper and Joseph A. Konstan for making the datasets available for use. The dataset was published in *MovieLens Dataset: History and Context*. ACM Transactions on Interactive Intelligent Systems (TiiS) 5, 4, Article 19 (December 2015), 19 pages.

There are three files in the dataset: `movies.dat`, `ratings.dat`, and `users.dat`, which are related to movies, ratings, and users, respectively. These files contain 1,000,209 anonymous ratings of approximately 3,900 movies made by 6,040 MovieLens users who joined MovieLens in 2000. All of the ratings are contained in the `ratings.dat` file and are in the following format:

```
UserID::MovieID::Rating::Timestamp
```

The description is as follows:

- `UserID`: This ranges between 1 and 6,040
- `MovieID`: This ranges between 1 and 3,952
- `Rating`: These are made on a 5-star scale
- `Timestamp`: This is represented in seconds

Note that each user has rated at least 20 movies. Movie information, on the other hand, is in the `movies.dat` file and is in the following format:

```
MovieID::Title::Genres
```

The description is as follows:

- `Title`: These are identical to titles provided by IMDb (with the release year)
- `Genres`: These are comma-separated (,), and each movie is categorized as action, adventure, animation, children's, comedy, crime, drama, war, documentary, fantasy, film-noir, horror, musical, mystery, romance, sci-fi, thriller, and western

Finally, user information is in the `users.dat` file and is in the following format:

```
UserID::Gender::Age::Occupation::Zip-code
```

All demographic information is provided voluntarily by the users and is not checked for accuracy. Only users who have provided some demographic information are included in this dataset. An M for male and F for female denote gender. Age is chosen from the following ranges:

- 1: Under 18
- 18: 18-24
- 25: 25-34
- 35: 35-44
- 45: 45-49
- 50: 50-55
- 56: 56+

Occupation is chosen from the following choices:

- 0: Other, or not specified
- 1: Academic/educator
- 2: Artist
- 3: Clerical/admin
- 4: College/grad student
- 5: Customer service
- 6: Doctor/healthcare
- 7: Executive/managerial
- 8: Farmer
- 9: Homemaker
- 10: K-12 student

- 11: Lawyer
- 12: Programmer
- 13: Retired
- 14: Sales/marketing
- 15: Scientist
- 16: Self-employed
- 17: Technician/engineer
- 18: Tradesman/craftsman
- 19: Unemployed
- 20: Writer

Now that we know the dataset, we can play with the datasets toward exploratory analysis. First, we will create a Spark session as the gateway to the Spark program:

```
SparkSession spark = new Builder()
                .master("local[*]")
                .config("spark.sql.warehouse.dir", "temp/")// change
accordingly
                .appName("MovieRecommendation")
                .getOrCreate();
```

Then, we will load and parse the `rating.dat` file to do some exploratory analysis. The following lines of code should return the DataFrame rating:

```
// Read RatingsFile
Dataset<Row> df1 = spark.read()
                .format("com.databricks.spark.csv")
                .option("inferSchemea", "true")
                .option("header", "true")
                .load(ratingsFile);

Dataset<Row> ratingsDF = df1.select(df1.col("userId"), df1.col("movieId"),
                df1.col("rating"), df1.col("timestamp"));
ratingsDF.show(10);
```

The output is as follows:

```
+------+-------+------+----------+
|userId|movieId|rating| timestamp|
+------+-------+------+----------+
|     1|     31|   2.5|1260759144|
|     1|   1029|   3.0|1260759179|
|     1|   1061|   3.0|1260759182|
|     1|   1129|   2.0|1260759185|
|     1|   1172|   4.0|1260759205|
|     1|   1263|   2.0|1260759151|
|     1|   1287|   2.0|1260759187|
|     1|   1293|   2.0|1260759148|
|     1|   1339|   3.5|1260759125|
|     1|   1343|   2.0|1260759131|
+------+-------+------+----------+
only showing top 10 rows
```

Next, we will load the `movies.dat` and prepare the movies DataFrame:

```
// Read MoviesFile
Dataset<Row> df2 = spark.read()
            .format("com.databricks.spark.csv")
            .option("inferSchema", "true")
            .option("header", "true")
            .load(movieFile);
Dataset<Row> moviesDF = df2.select(df2.col("movieId"), df2.col("title"),
df2.col("genres"));
moviesDF.show(10);
```

The output is as follows:

```
+-------+--------------------+--------------------+
|movieId|               title|              genres|
+-------+--------------------+--------------------+
|      1|    Toy Story (1995)|Adventure|Animati...|
|      2|      Jumanji (1995)|Adventure|Childre...|
|      3|Grumpier Old Men ...|      Comedy|Romance|
|      4|Waiting to Exhale...|Comedy|Drama|Romance|
|      5|Father of the Bri...|              Comedy|
|      6|         Heat (1995)|Action|Crime|Thri...|
|      7|      Sabrina (1995)|      Comedy|Romance|
|      8| Tom and Huck (1995)|  Adventure|Children|
|      9| Sudden Death (1995)|              Action|
|     10|    GoldenEye (1995)|Action|Adventure|...|
+-------+--------------------+--------------------+
only showing top 10 rows
```

Then, we will register both DataFrames as temporary tables to make querying easier. To register both Datasets, the following lines of code need to be used:

```
ratingsDF.createOrReplaceTempView("ratings");
moviesDF.createOrReplaceTempView("movies");
```

Note that this will help to make in-memory querying faster by creating a temporary view as a table in-memory. Then, we will opt to explore some rating and movie-related statistics:

```
long numberOfRatings = ratingsDF.count();
long numberOfUsers =
ratingsDF.select(ratingsDF.col("userId")).distinct().count();
long numberOfMovies =
ratingsDF.select(ratingsDF.col("movieId")).distinct().count();

String print = String.format("Got %d ratings from %d users on %d movies.",
numberOfRatings, numberOfUsers, numberOfMovies);
System.out.println(print);
```

The output is as follows:

```
Got 100004 ratings from 671 users on 9066 movies.
```

Now, let's get the maximum and minimum ratings along with the count of users who have rated a movie. However, you need to perform a SQL query on the rating table we just created in-memory in the previous step. Making a query here is simple, and it is similar to making a query from a MySQL database or RDBMS.

However, if you are not familiar with SQL-based queries, you are suggested to look at the SQL query specification to find out how to perform a selection using SELECT from a particular table, how to perform the ordering using ORDER, and how to perform a joining operation using the JOIN keyword.

Well, if you know the SQL query, you should get a new dataset by using a complex SQL query as follows:

```
// Get the max, min ratings along with the count of users who have rated a
movie.
Dataset<Row> sqlDF = spark.sql(
                "SELECT movies.title, movierates.maxr, movierates.minr,
movierates.cntu "
                        + "FROM (SELECT "
                        + "ratings.movieId, MAX(ratings.rating) AS maxr,"
                        + "MIN(ratings.rating) AS minr, COUNT(distinct
userId) AS cntu "
                        + "FROM ratings "
```

```
        + "GROUP BY ratings.movieId) movierates "
        + "JOIN movies ON movierates.movieId=movies.movieId
"
        + "ORDER BY movierates.cntu DESC");
sqlDF.show(10);
```

The output is as follows:

```
+--------------------+----+----+----+
|               title|maxr|minr|cntu|
+--------------------+----+----+----+
|  Forrest Gump (1994)| 5.0| 1.0| 341|
|  Pulp Fiction (1994)| 5.0| 0.5| 324|
|Shawshank Redempt...| 5.0| 1.0| 311|
|Silence of the La...| 5.0| 0.5| 304|
|Star Wars: Episod...| 5.0| 0.5| 291|
|Jurassic Park (1993)| 5.0| 0.5| 274|
|   Matrix, The (1999)| 5.0| 1.0| 259|
|    Toy Story (1995)| 5.0| 1.0| 247|
|Schindler's List ...| 5.0| 0.5| 244|
|Terminator 2: Jud...| 5.0| 1.0| 237|
+--------------------+----+----+----+
only showing top 10 rows
```

Now, to get an insight, we need to know more about the users and their ratings. Let's find the top 10 most active users and how many times they have rated a movie:

```
// Top 10 active users and how many times they rated a movie.
Dataset<Row> mostActiveUsersSchemaRDD = spark.sql(
        "SELECT ratings.userId, count(*) AS ct "
        + "FROM ratings "
        + "GROUP BY ratings.userId "
        + "ORDER BY ct DESC LIMIT 10");
mostActiveUsersSchemaRDD.show(10);
```

The output is as follows:

```
+------+----+
|userId|  ct|
+------+----+
|   547|2391|
|   564|1868|
|   624|1735|
|    15|1700|
|    73|1610|
|   452|1340|
|   468|1291|
|   380|1063|
|   311|1019|
|    30|1011|
+------+----+
```

Finally, let's have a look at a particular user and find the movies that, say, user 668, rated higher than 4:

```
// Movies that user 668 rated higher than 4
Dataset<Row> userRating = spark.sql(
            "SELECT ratings.userId, ratings.movieId, ratings.rating,
movies.title "
                    + "FROM ratings JOIN movies "
                    + "ON movies.movieId=ratings.movieId "
                    + "WHERE ratings.userId=668 AND ratings.rating >
4");
userRating.show(10);
```

The output is as follows:

```
+------+-------+------+--------------------+
|userId|movieId|rating|               title|
+------+-------+------+--------------------+
|   668|    296|   5.0| Pulp Fiction (1994)|
|   668|    593|   5.0|Silence of the La...|
|   668|    608|   5.0|         Fargo (1996)|
|   668|   1213|   5.0|    Goodfellas (1990)|
|   668|   1221|   5.0|Godfather: Part I...|
|   668|   2324|   5.0|Life Is Beautiful...|
|   668|   2908|   5.0|Boys Don't Cry (1...|
|   668|   2997|   5.0|Being John Malkov...|
+------+-------+------+--------------------+
```

Movie rating prediction

First, we perform the rating prediction using FM algorithms that learn using `PointWiseGradientDescent`. We start with preprocessing and converting data into the LibFM format. To run this rating prediction using the following order of execution:

1. First, execute `MovieLensFormaterWithMetaData.java` ;to generate the `MovieLens` data in the `LibFM` format.
2. Then, execute `SplitDataWithMetaData.java` to prepare the training, test, and validation sets.
3. Finally, execute ;`MovieRatingPrediction.java`, which is the main class.

Converting the dataset into LibFM format

The FM-based model that we are going to reuse can consume the training data only in LibFM format, which is more or less the same as LibSVM. Therefore, first, we must format the MovieLens 1M dataset sp that the training dataset contains both users, movies, and existing rating information.

> The LibFM format is similar to the LibSVM format but has some basic differences. For more information, interested readers can take a look at `http://www.libfm.org/libfm-1.42.manual.pdf`.

At the same time, new features will be generated by the user information and movie information. First, we will define the input (this will be updated according to users, movies, and ratings) and output file path as follows:

```
//MovieLensFormaterWithMetaData.java
private static String inputfilepath;
private static String outputfilepath;
```

Then, we define the data path and the output folder, where the generated data in LibFM format will be saved:

```
String foldername = "ml-1m";
String outFolder = "outFolder";
```

Then, we define the target column, which is to be predicted by the FM model. Additionally, we also delete the timestamp column:

```
private static int targetcolumn = 0;
private static String deletecolumns = "3";
```

Then, we set the separator as : : and offset:

```
private static String separator = "::";
private static int offset = 0;
```

Then, we read and parse the user's data (that is, `users.dat`) and create three
`Map<Integer, String>` for the user's genre, the user's age, and the user's occupation:

```
Set<Integer> deletecolumnsset = new HashSet<Integer>();
Map<String, Integer> valueidmap = new HashMap<String, Integer>();

targetcolumn = 2; // movielens format
String[] deletecolumnarr = deletecolumns.split(";");

for(String deletecolumn : deletecolumnarr) {
        deletecolumnsset.add(Integer.parseInt(deletecolumn));
    }
inputfilepath = foldername + File.separator + "users.dat";
Reader fr = new FileReader(inputfilepath);
BufferedReader br = new BufferedReader(fr);

Map<Integer, String> usergenemap = new HashMap<Integer, String>();
Map<Integer, String> useragemap = new HashMap<Integer, String>();
Map<Integer, String> useroccupationmap = new HashMap<Integer, String>();

String line;
while (br.ready()) {
        line = br.readLine();
        String[] arr = line.split(separator);
        usergenemap.put(Integer.parseInt(arr[0]), arr[1]);
        useragemap.put(Integer.parseInt(arr[0]), arr[2]);
        useroccupationmap.put(Integer.parseInt(arr[0]), arr[3]);
    }
br.close();
fr.close();
```

Then, we parse the movie dataset to create a `Map<Integer, String>` for movies:

```
inputfilepath = foldername + File.separator + "movies.dat";
fr = new FileReader(inputfilepath);
br = new BufferedReader(fr);

Map<Integer, String> moviemap = new HashMap<Integer, String>();

while (br.ready()) {
        line = br.readLine();
        String[] arr = line.split(separator);
```

```
            moviemap.put(Integer.parseInt(arr[0]), arr[2]);
    }
    br.close();
    fr.close();
```

Then, we parse the rating dataset to create a `Map<Integer, String>` for existing ratings. Additionally, we define the output filename where the rating data in the LibFM format will be saved:

```
inputfilepath = foldername + File.separator + "ratings.dat";
outputfilepath = outFolder + File.separator + "ratings.libfm";
BufferedWriter writer = new BufferedWriter(new OutputStreamWriter(new
FileOutputStream(outputfilepath)));

        fr = new FileReader(inputfilepath);
        br = new BufferedReader(fr);

        while(br.ready()) {
            line = br.readLine();
            String[] arr = line.split(separator);
            StringBuilder sb = new StringBuilder();
            sb.append(arr[targetcolumn]);
            int columnidx = 0;
            int userid = Integer.parseInt(arr[0]);
            int movieid = Integer.parseInt(arr[1]);
            for(int i = 0; i < arr.length; i++) {
                if(i != targetcolumn && !deletecolumnsset.contains(i)) {
                    String useroritemid = Integer.toString(columnidx) + " "
+ arr[i];
                    if(!valueidmap.containsKey(useroritemid)) {
                        valueidmap.put(useroritemid, offset++);
                    }
                    sb.append(" ");
                    sb.append(valueidmap.get(useroritemid));
                    sb.append(":1");

                    columnidx++;
                }
```

Then, we start adding attributes such as gender information, age, occupation, and movie class information:

```
// Add attributes
String gender = usergenemap.get(userid);
String attributeid = "The gender information " + gender;
 if(!valueidmap.containsKey(attributeid)) {
            valueidmap.put(attributeid, offset++);
```

```
        }

        sb.append(" ");
        sb.append(valueidmap.get(attributeid));
        sb.append(":1");

        String age = useragemap.get(userid);
        attributeid = "The age information " + age;
        if(!valueidmap.containsKey(attributeid)) {
            valueidmap.put(attributeid, offset++);
        }

        sb.append(" ");
        sb.append(valueidmap.get(attributeid));
        sb.append(":1");

        String occupation = useroccupationmap.get(userid);
        attributeid = "The occupation information " + occupation;
        if(!valueidmap.containsKey(attributeid)) {
            valueidmap.put(attributeid, offset++);
        }

        sb.append(" ");
        sb.append(valueidmap.get(attributeid));
        sb.append(":1");

        String movieclassdesc = moviemap.get(movieid);
        String[] movieclassarr = movieclassdesc.split("\\|");
        for(String movieclass : movieclassarr) {
            attributeid = "The movie class information " + movieclass;
            if(!valueidmap.containsKey(attributeid)) {
                valueidmap.put(attributeid, offset++);
            }

            sb.append(" ");
            sb.append(valueidmap.get(attributeid));
            sb.append(":1");
}
```

In the previous code block, `:1` ;stands for which movie the user has provided a rating for. Finally, we add the metadata information, `userid` and `movieid`:

```
//add metadata information, userid and movieid
sb.append("#");
sb.append(userid);
sb.append(" "+movieid);
writer.write(sb.toString());
writer.newLine();
```

Now, the resulting rating dataset (once `MovieLensFormaterWithMetaData.java` is executed) in LibFM format will be saved in the `formatted_data` directory as `ratings.libfm` ;having the following structure:

```
5 0:1 1:1 2:1 3:1 4:1 5:1#1 1193
3 0:1 6:1 2:1 3:1 4:1 7:1 8:1 9:1#1 661
3 0:1 10:1 2:1 3:1 4:1 9:1 11:1#1 914
4 0:1 12:1 2:1 3:1 4:1 5:1#1 3408
5 0:1 13:1 2:1 3:1 4:1 7:1 8:1 14:1#1 2355
3 0:1 15:1 2:1 3:1 4:1 16:1 17:1 14:1 11:1#1 1197
5 0:1 18:1 2:1 3:1 4:1 16:1 17:1 5:1#1 1287
5 0:1 19:1 2:1 3:1 4:1 14:1 5:1#1 2804
4 0:1 20:1 2:1 3:1 4:1 7:1 8:1 9:1#1 594
4 0:1 21:1 2:1 3:1 4:1 17:1 8:1 5:1 9:1#1 919
```

Training and test set preparation

Now that we have seen how to convert rating, movie, and metadata, we can now start creating training, test, and validation sets from the data in LibFM format. First, we set the path of the LibFM files to be used as follows:

```
//SplitDataWithMetaData.java
private static String ratinglibFM = formattedDataPath + "/" +
"ratings.libfm"; // input
private static String ratinglibFM_train = formattedDataPath + "/" +
"ratings_train.libfm"; // for traning
private static String ratinglibFM_test = formattedDataPath + "/" +
"ratings_test.libfm"; // for testing
private static String ratinglibFM_test_meta = formattedDataPath
+"/"+"ratings_test.libfm.meta";// metadata
private static String ratinglibFM_valid = formattedDataPath + "/" +
"ratings_valid.libfm"; // validation
```

Then, we show the output directory to write the split training, validation, and test sets:

```
private static String formattedDataPath = "outFolder";
```

Then, we instantiate the `BufferedWriter` that is going to be used for writing the split files:

```
Reader fr = new FileReader(ratinglibFM);
Random ra = new Random();

BufferedWriter trainwrite = new BufferedWriter(new OutputStreamWriter(new
FileOutputStream(ratinglibFM_train)));

BufferedWriter testwrite = new BufferedWriter(new OutputStreamWriter(new
FileOutputStream(ratinglibFM_test)));

BufferedWriter testmetawrite = new BufferedWriter(new
OutputStreamWriter(new
FileOutputStream(ratinglibFM_test_meta)));
BufferedWriter validwrite = new BufferedWriter(new OutputStreamWriter(new
FileOutputStream(ratinglibFM_valid)));

BufferedReader br = new BufferedReader(fr);
String line = null;
int testline = 0;
while(br.ready()) {
        line = br.readLine();
        String[] arr = line.split("#");
        String info = arr[0];
        double dvalue = ra.nextDouble();
        if(dvalue>0.9)
                {
                  validwrite.write(info);
                  validwrite.newLine();
                }
        else if(dvalue <= 0.9 && dvalue>0.1) {
                    trainwrite.write(info);
                    trainwrite.newLine();
          } else {
                    testwrite.write(info);
                    testwrite.newLine();
              if(arr.length==2)
                    {
                    testmetawrite.write(arr[1] + " " + testline);
                    testmetawrite.newLine();
                    testline++;
                }
            }
        }
    }
```

Finally, we close the file pointers to release the resources:

```
br.close();
fr.close();

trainwrite.flush();
trainwrite.close();
testwrite.flush();
testwrite.close();

validwrite.flush();
validwrite.close();
testmetawrite.flush();
testmetawrite.close();
```

Now, the resulting rating datasets (once `SplitDataWithMetaData.java` is executed) in LibFM format will be saved in the `formatted_data` directory having the following LibFM (similar to LibSVM) format:

```
5 0:1 1:1 2:1 3:1 4:1 5:1
3 0:1 6:1 2:1 3:1 4:1 7:1 8:1 9:1
3 0:1 10:1 2:1 3:1 4:1 9:1 11:1
3 0:1 15:1 2:1 3:1 4:1 16:1 17:1 14:1 11:1
5 0:1 18:1 2:1 3:1 4:1 16:1 17:1 5:1
5 0:1 19:1 2:1 3:1 4:1 14:1 5:1
4 0:1 20:1 2:1 3:1 4:1 7:1 8:1 9:1
4 0:1 21:1 2:1 3:1 4:1 17:1 8:1 5:1 9:1
5 0:1 22:1 2:1 3:1 4:1 7:1 8:1 9:1
4 0:1 23:1 2:1 3:1 4:1 9:1
4 0:1 24:1 2:1 3:1 4:1 5:1
```

Finally, the directory (that is, `formatted_data`) will have the following files in it:

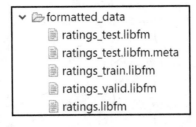

Fantastic! Now that our dataset is ready, we can now start making the movie rating prediction using the FM algorithm.

Movie rating prediction

Now that all of the datasets required for training, validating, and evaluating are ready, we can start training the FM model. We first start by showing the filename for the training data:

```
final String trainFile = formattedDataPath+ "/" + "ratings_train.libfm";
```

Then, we set the testing data file path:

```
final String testFile = formattedDataPath+ "/" + "ratings_test.libfm";
```

Then, we set the testing metadata file path:

```
final String testMetaFile = formattedDataPath+ "/" +
"ratings_test.libfm.meta";
```

Then, the filename for the final prediction output file:

```
final String outputFile = formattedDataPath+ "/" + "predict_output.txt";
```

Then, we set up the path for writing the logs, metrics, time, and so on for each iteration to a file (but don't worry, we will see them in graph form, too):

```
final String rLog = outPut + "/" + "metrics_logs.txt";
```

Then, we set up the dimension of k0, k1, and k2 so that k0 is use bias, k1 is the use of one-way interactions, and k2 is the dim of two-way interactions:

```
final String dimension = "1,1,8"; // tunable parameters
```

We will iterate the training for 100 times the number of iterations:

```
final String iterations = "100"; // tunable parameter
```

We then set the learning rate for SGD—the rate at which the optimizer tries to minimize the error:

```
final String learnRate = "0.01"; // tunable and learnable parameter
```

Now that the optimizer knows the learning rate, the next important parameter is setting up the regularization parameters to regularize the training against overfitting.

The Java-based FM library needs three-way regularization: bias, one-way, and two-way regularization. Therefore, the format accepted by the FM library is r0, r1, r2. Here, r0 is bias regularization, r1 is one-way regularization, and r2 is two-way regularization:

```
final String regularization = "0,0,0.1";
```

Then, we initialize the standard deviations for the initialization of two-way factors:

```
final String stdDeviation = "0.1";
```

Then, we use the ;LibSVMDataProvider() class for loading both training and test sets:

```
System.out.println("Loading train...t");
DataProvider train = new LibSVMDataProvider();
Properties trainproperties = new Properties();

trainproperties.put(Constants.FILENAME, trainFile);
train.load(trainproperties, false);

System.out.println("Loading test... t");
DataProvider test = new LibSVMDataProvider();
Properties testproperties = new Properties();

testproperties.put(Constants.FILENAME, testFile);
test.load(testproperties, false);
```

One the training and test sets are loaded, we start creating the user-item table (that is, the main table):

```
int num_all_attribute = Math.max(train.getFeaturenumber(),
test.getFeaturenumber());
DataMetaInfo meta = new DataMetaInfo(num_all_attribute);
meta.debug();
Debug.openConsole();
```

Then, we instantiate the factorization machine before we start the training:

```
FmModel fm = new FmModel();
```

Then, the init() method is used for initializing the parameters needed for instantiating and training the following FM model's parameters:

```
public FmModel()
    {
        num_factor = 0;
        initmean = 0;
        initstdev = 0.01;
        reg0 = 0.0;
```

```
        regw = 0.0;
        regv = 0.0;
        k0 = true;
        k1 = true;
    }
```

The signature of the `init()` method goes as follows:

```
public void init()
    {
        w0 = 0;
        w = new double[num_attribute];
        v = new DataPointMatrix(num_factor, num_attribute);
        Arrays.fill(w, 0);
        v.init(initmean, initstdev);
        m_sum = new double[num_factor];
        m_sum_sqr = new double[num_factor];
    }
```

Then, we set the number of attributes and standard deviations from the main class:

```
fm.num_attribute = num_all_attribute;
fm.initstdev = Double.parseDouble(stdDeviation);
```

Then, we set the number of dimensions in the factorization. In our case, we have 3-way interaction—user, movie, and rating:

```
Integer[] dim = getIntegerValues(dimension);
assert (dim.length == 3);
fm.k0 = dim[0] != 0;
fm.k1 = dim[1] != 0;
fm.num_factor = dim[2];
```

The preceding values are actually parsed using the `getIntegerValues()` method, which accepts the dimension as a string and split using `,`.

Finally, it returns only integer values for the dimension to be used by the model for making interactions. The following signature is used for this:

```
static public Integer[] getIntegerValues(String parameter) {
        Integer[] result = null;
        String[] strresult = Util.tokenize(parameter, ",");
        if(strresult!=null && strresult.length>0) {
            result = new Integer[strresult.length];
            for(int i=0;i<strresult.length;i++) {
                result[i] = Integer.parseInt(strresult[i]);
            }
```

```
        }
        return result;
    }
```

Then, we set up the learning method as **Stochastic Gradient Descent (SGD)**:

```
FmLearn fml = new FmLearnSgdElement();
((FmLearnSgd) fml).num_iter = Integer.parseInt(iterations);

fml.fm = fm;
fml.max_target = train.getMaxtarget();
fml.min_target = train.getMintarget();
fml.meta = meta;
```

Then, we define the task to be performed. In our case, it is regression. However, we are going to use ;TASK_CLASSIFICATION for classification:

```
fml.task = TaskType.TASK_REGRESSION
```

Then, we set the regularization:

```
Double[] reg = getDoubleValues(regularization);
assert ((reg.length == 3)); // should meet 3 way regularization

fm.reg0 = reg[0];
fm.regw = reg[1];
fm.regv = reg[2];
```

Then, when it comes to the learning rate, we have to set the learning rates (individual, per layer) unlike the DL4J library:

```
FmLearnSgd fmlsgd = (FmLearnSgd) (fml);

if (fmlsgd != null) {
        Double[] lr = getDoubleValues(learnRate);
        assert (lr.length == 1);
        fmlsgd.learn_rate = lr[0];
        Arrays.fill(fmlsgd.learn_rates, lr[0]);
}
```

The preceding values are actually parsed using the `getDoubleValues()` method, which accepts the learning rate as a string and split using `,`. Finally, it returns only a single value for the learning rate to be used by the model. The following signature is used for this:

```
static public Double[] getDoubleValues(String parameter) {
        Double[] result;
        String[] strresult = Util.tokenize(parameter, ",");
        if(strresult!=null && strresult.length>0) {
            result = new Double[strresult.length];
            for(int i=0; i<strresult.length; i++) {
                result[i] = Double.parseDouble(strresult[i]);
            }
        }
        else {
            result = new Double[0];
        }
        return result;
    }
```

Now that all the hyperparameters are set, we are ready to start the training. For this, unlike DL4J FM, it comes with a `;learn()` method for learning the model:

```
fml.learn(train, test);
```

The `learn()` method is an abstract method that takes both train and test sets:

```
//FmLearn.java
public abstract void learn(DataProvider train, DataProvider test) throws
Exception;
```

The concrete implementation of the `;learn()` method takes both the training and test sets. Then, it shuffles the training set to avoid the bias in training. Then, it performs the prediction operation using the `;predict()` method for the task type we defined at the beginning (that is, regression in our case).

Finally, it evaluates the model on the test set and computes the MSE for both the training and test set. The actual implementation of this method goes as follows:

```
//FmLearnSgdElement.java
public void learn(DataProvider train, DataProvider test)  throws Exception{
        super.learn(train, test);
        List<Double> iterationList=new ArrayList<Double>();
        List<Double> trainList=new ArrayList<Double>();
        List<Double> testList=new ArrayList<Double>();

        // SGD
```

```
        for(int i = 0; i < num_iter; i++) {
            try
            {
                double iteration_time = Util.getusertime();
                train.shuffle();
                for(train.getData().begin(); !train.getData().end();
train.getData().next()) {
                    double p = fm.predict(train.getData().getRow(), sum,
sum_sqr);
                    double mult = 0;

                    if(task == TaskType.TASK_REGRESSION) {
                        p = Math.min(max_target, p);
                        p = Math.max(min_target, p);
                        mult = -
(train.getTarget()[train.getData().getRowIndex()]-p);
                    } else if(task == TaskType.TASK_CLASSIFICATION) {
                        mult = -
train.getTarget()[train.getData().getRowIndex()]*
                                (1.0-1.0/(1.0+Math.exp(-
train.getTarget()[train.getData()
                                .getRowIndex()]*p)));
                    }
                    SGD(train.getData().getRow(), mult, sum);
                }
                iteration_time = (Util.getusertime() - iteration_time);
                double rmse_train = evaluate(train);
                double rmse_test = evaluate(test);
                iterationList.add((double)i);
                testList.add(rmse_test);
                trainList.add(rmse_train);
                String print = String.format("#Iterations=%2d::
                            Train_RMSE=%-10.5f   Test_RMSE=%-10.5f", i,
rmse_train, rmse_test);
                Debug.println(print);
                if(log != null) {
                    log.log("rmse_train", rmse_train);
                    log.log("time_learn", iteration_time);
                    log.newLine();
                }
            }
            catch(Exception e)
            {
                throw new JlibfmRuntimeException(e);// Exception library
for Java FM
            }
        }
PlotUtil_Rating.plot(convertobjectArraytoDouble(iterationList.toArray()),
```

```
            convertobjectArraytoDouble(testList.toArray()),
            convertobjectArraytoDouble(trainList.toArray())));

    }
```

In the preceding code block, the FM model performs the prediction operation, similar to any other regression algorithm, by considering three-way interaction and so on and computing the prediction as a probability:

```
// FmModel.java, we create a sparse matrix
public double predict(SparseRow x, double[] sum, double[] sum_sqr)
    {
        double result = 0;
        if(k0) {
            result += w0;
        }
        if(k1) {
            for(int i = 0; i < x.getSize(); i++) {
                result += w[x.getData()[i].getId()] *
x.getData()[i].getValue();
            }
        }
        for(int f = 0; f < num_factor; f++) {
            sum[f] = 0;
            sum_sqr[f] = 0;
            for(int i = 0; i < x.getSize(); i++) {
                double d = v.get(f,x.getData()[i].getId()) *
x.getData()[i].getValue();
                sum[f] = sum[f]+d;
                sum_sqr[f] = sum_sqr[f]+d*d;
            }
            result += 0.5 * (sum[f]*sum[f] - sum_sqr[f]);
        }

        return result;
    }
```

Nevertheless, at the end, the training and test MSE per iteration is visualized using the plot() method from the PlotUtil_Rating class. We'll discuss this class later on.

Additionally, we also initialize the logging so that the result and progress of the computations are printed on the console:

```
System.out.println("logging to " + rLog);
RLog rlog = new RLog(rLog);
fml.log = rlog;
fml.init();
rlog.init();
fm.debug();
fml.debug();
```

Finally, we evaluate the model on the test set. Since our task is a regression task, we compute the regression metric, such as RMSE, for each iteration:

```
String print = String.format("#Iterations=%s:: Train_RMSE=%-10.5f
Test_RMSE=%-10.5f", iterations, fml.evaluate(train), fml.evaluate(test));
System.out.println(print);
```

```
>>>
Loading train...
Loading test...
#attr=9794 #groups=1
#attr_in_group[0]=9794
logging to outFolder/output.txt
num_attributes=9794
use w0=true
use w1=true
dim v =8
reg_w0=0.0
reg_w=0.0
reg_v=0.0
init ~ N(0.0,0.1)
num_iter=100
task=TASK_REGRESSION
min_target=1.0
max_target=5.0
learnrate=0.01
learnrates=0.01,0.01,0.01
#iterations=100
#Iterations= 0:: Train_RMSE=0.92469 Test_RMSE=0.93231
#Iterations= 1:: Train_RMSE=0.91460 Test_RMSE=0.92358
#Iterations= 2:: Train_RMSE=0.91595 Test_RMSE=0.92535
#Iterations= 3:: Train_RMSE=0.91238 Test_RMSE=0.92313

...
#Iterations=98:: Train_RMSE=0.84275 Test_RMSE=0.88206
#Iterations=99:: Train_RMSE=0.84068 Test_RMSE=0.87832
```

Finally, we save the prediction and all associated metrics in a file:

```
// prediction at the end
String print = String.format("#Iterations=%s::  Train_RMSE=%-10.5f
Test_RMSE=%-10.5f", iterations, fml.evaluate(train), fml.evaluate(test));
System.out.println(print);

// save prediction
Map<Integer, String> ratingsMetaData = new HashMap<>();
if(Files.exists(Paths.get(testMetaFile))) {
        BufferedReader bufferedReader = new BufferedReader(new
FileReader(testMetaFile));
        String line;
        while((line = bufferedReader.readLine()) != null) {
            String[] splitLine = line.split("\\s+");
            if(splitLine.length > 0) {
                Integer indexKey = Integer.parseInt(splitLine[2]);
                String userIdmovieIdValue = splitLine[0] + " " +
splitLine[1];

                ratingsMetaData.put(indexKey, userIdmovieIdValue);
            }
        }
    }

double[] pred = new double[test.getRownumber()];
fml.predict(test, pred);
Util.save(ratingsMetaData, pred, outputFile);
String FILENAME = Constants.FILENAME;
// Save the trained FM model
fmlsgd.saveModel(FILENAME);
```

The preceding code block will generate two files called ;predict_output.txt and metrics_logs.txt for writing predicted results and logs, respectively. For example, a sample from the predicted_output.txt file shows that the second column is the movie ID and the third column is the predicted rating out of 5.0, as follows:

```
1 3408 4.40
1 2797 4.19
1 720 4.36
1 1207 4.66
2 1537 3.92
2 1792 3.39
2 1687 3.32
2 3107 3.55
2 3108 3.46
2 3255 3.65
```

On the other hand, `metrics_logs.txt` shows metrics such as RMSE, MAE, logs, as shown in the following diagram:

```
rmse      mae time_pred   time_learn  time_learn2 time_learn4 rmse_train
0.9275955978932888  0.7365065595728909  0.0559999942779541  0.621999979019165   NaN NaN 0.9198445445939268
0.9407647914787951  0.7294899596692839  0.03400015830993652 0.7159998416900635  NaN NaN 0.9319879497222021
0.9184153371129748  0.7253438212645523  0.03299999237060547 0.5260000228881836  NaN NaN 0.9070322657717291
0.9176294326054297  0.7242150425581235  0.03399991989135742 0.5379998683929443  NaN NaN 0.9056342946016255
0.9132507564794741  0.7134487812431016  0.03600001335144043 0.5269999504089355  NaN NaN 0.89951865257831
0.9137783879031901  0.7115911503494833  0.037999868392944336 0.7339999675750732  NaN NaN 0.8996410144580471
0.9103229305286898  0.7207182087788873  0.03399991989135742 0.8540000915527344  NaN NaN 0.8948129152871857
0.9112892202865233  0.72193143849607    0.03599977493286133 0.747999906539917   NaN NaN 0.8940408851122638
0.9158240594263269  0.7326954653664787  0.03399991989135742 0.7970001697540283  NaN NaN 0.8974186861344857
```

Nevertheless, since making some sense of the training status and prediction, it is difficult just seeing these values, therefore, I decided to plot them. The following graph shows the MSE for both the training and testing phase for each iteration:

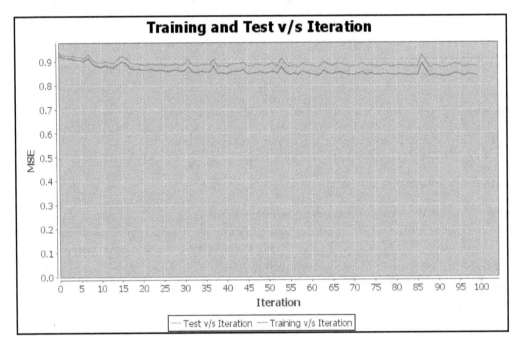

Training and test MSE per iteration (for 100 iterations)

The preceding graph shows that both training and test errors are consistent, which means the FM model was not overfitted. This graph also shows that the error count is still very high. Then, I iterated the training 1,000 times and found that errors had been reduced slightly, which is reported in the following graph:

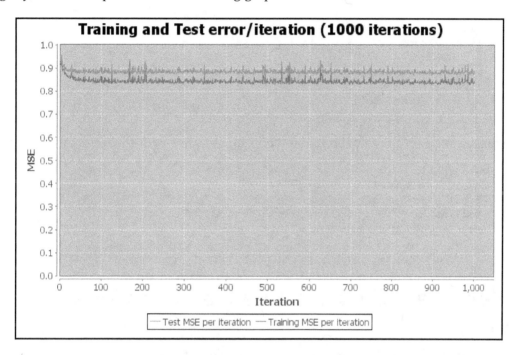

Training and test MSE per iteration for up to 1,000 iterations

Now, to plot the preceding graph, I wrote a ;plot() method in the PlotUtil_Rating.java class that uses the ;JFreeChart library for plotting the training and test error/iteration:

```
public static void plot(double[] iterationArray, double[] testArray,
double[] trainArray) {
    final XYSeriesCollection dataSet = new XYSeriesCollection();
    addSeries(dataSet, iterationArray, testArray, "Test MSE per
iteration");
    addSeries(dataSet, iterationArray, trainArray, "Training MSE per
iteration");
    final JFreeChart chart = ChartFactory.createXYLineChart(
            "Training and Test error/iteration (1000 iterations)", // chart
title
            "Iteration", // x axis label
            "MSE", // y axis label
```

```
            dataSet, // data
            PlotOrientation.VERTICAL,
            true, // include legend
            true, // tooltips
            false // urls
    );
    final ChartPanel panel = new ChartPanel(chart);
    final JFrame f = new JFrame();
    f.add(panel);
    f.setDefaultCloseOperation(WindowConstants.EXIT_ON_CLOSE);
    f.pack();
    f.setVisible(true);
}
```

Whereas the addSeries() method from the XYSeries class adds the series for the plot:

```
private static void addSeries (final XYSeriesCollection dataSet, double[]
x, double[] y, final String label){
    final XYSeries s = new XYSeries(label);
    for(int j = 0; j < x.length; j++ ) s.add(x[j], y[j]);
    dataSet.addSeries(s);
}
```

Which one makes more sense ;– ranking or rating?

Is a rating or ranking prediction more logical while developing a movie recommendation system? If the amount of ratings per user is high enough, factorizing the user-product matrix is the best thing, in my opinion. However, if the dataset is too sparse, the prediction can be extremely inaccurate.

Knowing this fact, I was exploring the RankSys library and found that one of the contributors is arguing that ranking is more logical. He did not provide any explanation, though. Later on, I talked to some recommender system developers and researchers and got to know that he probably meant ranking is less sensitive to the prediction error due to the gap between a number of ratings and items. The reason is that ranking preserves the hierarchy, independent of the absolute rating.

Based on this understanding, later on, I decided to go one step further toward ranking prediction. For this, I wrote a spate class called `RankingPrediction.java` for predicting movie ranking by each user in the test set, which has the following structure:

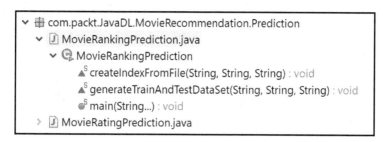

Movie ranking prediction subproject structure

This has three methods, which are as follows:

- `createIndexFromFile()`: This method is used for the creation of indexes from files that are passing as an argument in the method parameters itself.
- `generateTrainAndTestDataSet()`: This is used for separating data into training and testing sets, which is an important part of evaluating data mining models.
- `main()`: This is used for the creation of indexes, both for items and users, and is used for the following operations:
    - Index for a set of users
    - Index for a set of items
    - Stores the preferences/rating for users and items provided by `FastUserIndex` and `FastItemIndex`
    - Creates a recommender interface that will be used by `FMRecommender`
    - Uses a factorization machine that uses `RMSE-like loss` with a balanced sampling of negative instances

First, we set the path of the input data files:

```
final String folderPath = "ml-1m";
final String indexPath = "index";
final String userFileName = "users.dat";
final String moviesFileName = "movies.dat";
final String ratingsFileName = "ratings.dat";
final String encodingUTF8 = "UTF-8";

final String userDatPath = folderPath + "/" + userFileName;
final String movieDatPath = folderPath + "/" + moviesFileName;
```

Then, we set the path for the user and movie indexes stated previously:

```
final String indexPath = "index";
final String userIndexPath = indexPath + "/" + "userIndex";
final String movieIndexPath = indexPath + "/" + "movieIndex";
```

Then, we set the path for the resultant file, where the training and test set will be generated:

```
String trainDataPath = indexPath + "/ratings_train";
String testDataPath = indexPath + "/ratings_test";
final String ratingsDatPath = folderPath + "/" + ratingsFileName;
```

Then, we create the user index for all the users in the `users.dat` file. Here, the users are internally represented with numerical indices from 0 (inclusive) to the number of indexed users (exclusive):

```
FastUserIndex<Long> userIndex =
SimpleFastUserIndex.load(UsersReader.read(userIndexPath, lp));
```

In the preceding line of code, we used the `SimpleFastUserIndex` class from the RankSys library that helped in creating a simple implementation of `FastUserIndex` backed by a bi-map called ;IdxIndex.

Then, we create the item index for all of the items in the `movies.dat` file. This creates the index for a set of items. Here, the items are internally represented with numerical indices from 0 (inclusive) to the number of indexed items (exclusive):

```
FastItemIndex<Long> itemIndex =
SimpleFastItemIndex.load(ItemsReader.read(movieIndexPath, lp));
```

In the preceding line of code, we used the `SimpleFastItemIndex` class from the RankSys library, which helps us create a simple implementation of `FastItemIndex` backed by a bimap called `;IdxIndex`. Then, we store the preferences/rating for users and items provided by `FastUserIndex` and `FastItemIndex`:

```
FastPreferenceData<Long, Long> trainData =
SimpleFastPreferenceData.load(SimpleRatingPreferencesReader.get().read(trai
nDataPath, lp, lp), userIndex, itemIndex);

FastPreferenceData<Long, Long> testData =
SimpleFastPreferenceData.load(SimpleRatingPreferencesReader.get().read(test
DataPath, lp, lp), userIndex, itemIndex);
```

Then, we invoke these two methods for creating user and item indexes:

```
if (!Files.exists(Paths.get(userIndexPath))) {
    createIndexFromFile(userDatPath, encodingUTF8, userIndexPath);
}

if (!Files.exists(Paths.get(movieIndexPath))) {
    createIndexFromFile(movieDatPath, encodingUTF8, movieIndexPath);
}
```

In the preceding if statements, we generated indexes from file using the `createIndexFromFile()` method that goes as follows:

```
static void createIndexFromFile(String fileReadPath, String encodings,
String fileWritePath) throws IOException {
        BufferedReader bufferedReader = new BufferedReader(new
InputStreamReader(new FileInputStream(
                        fileReadPath), Charset.forName(encodings)));
        BufferedWriter writer = new BufferedWriter(new OutputStreamWriter(
                        new FileOutputStream(fileWritePath)));

        String line;
        while((line = bufferedReader.readLine()) != null) {
            StringBuilder builder = new StringBuilder();
            String[] lineArray = line.split("::");
            builder.append(lineArray[0]);
            writer.write(builder.toString());
            writer.newLine();
        }
        writer.flush();

        bufferedReader.close();
        writer.close();
    }
```

Once the index files are generated, we then start generating the training and test sets as follows:

```
if ( !Files.exists(Paths.get(trainDataPath))) {
    generateTrainAndTestDataSet(ratingsDatPath, trainDataPath,
testDataPath);
}
```

In this code block, we used the ;generateTrainAndTestDataSet() method for generating both training and test sets:

```
static void generateTrainAndTestDataSet(String ratingsDatPath, String
trainDataPath, String testDataPath) throws IOException {
        BufferedWriter writerTrain = new BufferedWriter(new
OutputStreamWriter(
                    new FileOutputStream(trainDataPath)));

        BufferedWriter writerTest = new BufferedWriter(new
OutputStreamWriter(
                    new FileOutputStream(testDataPath)));

        BufferedReader bufferedReader = new BufferedReader(new
FileReader(ratingsDatPath));
        List<String> dummyData = new ArrayList<>();
        String line;

        while((line = bufferedReader.readLine()) != null) {
            String removeDots = line.replaceAll("::", "\t");
            dummyData.add(removeDots);
        }
        bufferedReader.close();

        Random generator = new Random();
        int dataSize = dummyData.size();
        int trainDataSize = (int)(dataSize * (2.0 / 3.0));
        int i = 0;
        while(i < trainDataSize){
            int random = generator.nextInt(dummyData.size()-0) + 0;
            line = dummyData.get(random);
            dummyData.remove(random);
            writerTrain.write(line);
            writerTrain.newLine();
            i++;
        }

        int j = 0;
        while(j < (dataSize - trainDataSize)){
```

```
            writerTest.write(dummyData.get(j));
            writerTest.newLine();
            j++;
        }

    writerTrain.flush();
    writerTrain.close();

    writerTest.flush();
    writerTest.close();
    }
```

The preceding method divides up 2/3 as the training set and 1/3 as the test set. Finally, the file pointers are closed to release the resources. If the preceding three if statements executed successfully, you should see that two index files and two other files for the training and test sets have been generated:

Then, we create a recommender interface, which will be used by the `FMRecommender` class, which generates recommendations without any restriction on the items being recommended:

```
Map<String, Supplier<Recommender<Long, Long>>> recMap = new HashMap<>();
```

Finally, wrap up the preference factorization machine to work with RankSys user-preference pairs. Then, we train the model by setting the learning rate, regularization, and standard deviation, and iterate the training up to 100 times using `PointWiseGradientDescent`. FM then uses RMSE-like loss with a balanced sampling of negative instances:

```
// Use Factorisation machine that uses RMSE-like loss with balanced
sampling of negative instances:
String outFileName = "outFolder/Ranking_RMSE.txt";
recMap.put(outFileName, Unchecked.supplier(() -> {
        double negativeProp = 2.0D;
        FMData fmTrain = new OneClassPreferenceFMData(trainData,
negativeProp);
        FMData fmTest = new OneClassPreferenceFMData(testData,
```

```
negativeProp);
            double learnRate = 0.01D; // Learning Rate
            int numIter = 10; // Number of Iterations
            double sdev = 0.1D;
            double regB = 0.01D;
            double[] regW = new double[fmTrain.numFeatures()];
            Arrays.fill(regW, 0.01D);
            double[] regM = new double[fmTrain.numFeatures()];
            Arrays.fill(regM, 0.01D);
            int K = 100;
            // returns enclosed FM
            FM fm = new FM(fmTrain.numFeatures(), K, new Random(), sdev);
            (new PointWiseGradientDescent(learnRate, numIter,
PointWiseError.rmse(),
                                        regB, regW, regM)).learn(fm,
fmTrain, fmTest);
                // From general purpose factorization machines to preference
FM for user-preference
            PreferenceFM<Long, Long> prefFm = new PreferenceFM<Long,
Long>(userIndex, itemIndex, fm);
            return new FMRecommender<Long, Long>(prefFm);
        }));
```

In the preceding code block, the FM model is trained using the `learn()` method, which is pretty similar to the `learn()` method used for predicting rating in the previous section. Then, to evaluate the model, first, we set the target user and `SimpleRecommendationFormat`, which is in tab-separated, user-item score triplets (that is, present in the original dataset):

```
Set<Long> targetUsers =
testData.getUsersWithPreferences().collect(Collectors.toSet());
//Format of the recommendation generated by the FM recommender model as
<user, prediction)
RecommendationFormat<Long, Long> format = new
SimpleRecommendationFormat<>(lp, lp);
Function<Long, IntPredicate> filter = FastFilters.notInTrain(trainData);
int maxLength = 100;
```

Then, we invoke the `RecommenderRunner` interface to generate recommendations and print it based on the format:

```
// Generate recommendations and print it based on the format.
RecommenderRunner<Long, Long> runner = new
FastFilterRecommenderRunner<>(userIndex, itemIndex, targetUsers.stream(),
filter, maxLength);
 recMap.forEach(Unchecked.biConsumer((name, recommender) -> {
            System.out.println("Ranking prediction is ongoing...");
```

```
            System.out.println("Result will be saved at " + name);
            try(RecommendationFormat.Writer<Long, Long> writer =
format.getWriter(name)) {
                runner.run(recommender.get(), writer);
            }
        }));
```

The preceding code block will perform the evaluation on the test set and write the recommendation in the text file we specified previously:

>>
Ranking prediction is ongoing...
Result will be saved at outFolder/Ranking_RMSE.txt
INFO: iteration n = 1 t = 3.92s
INFO: iteration n = 2 t = 3.08s
INFO: iteration n = 3 t = 2.88s
INFO: iteration n = 4 t = 2.84s
INFO: iteration n = 5 t = 2.84s
INFO: iteration n = 6 t = 2.88s
INFO: iteration n = 7 t = 2.87s
INFO: iteration n = 8 t = 2.86s
INFO: iteration n = 9 t = 2.94s
...
INFO: iteration n = 100 t = 2.87s
Graph plotting...

The prediction has been saved at outFolder/Ranking_RMSE.txt

Now, let's take a look at the output file:

944 2396 0.9340957389234708
944 593 0.9299994477666256
944 1617 0.9207678675263278
944 50 0.9062805385053954
944 1265 0.8740234972054955
944 589 0.872143533435846
944 480 0.8659624750023733
944 2028 0.8649344355656503
944 1580 0.8620307480644472
944 2336 0.8576568651679782
944 1196 0.8570902991702303

This snapshot from the output file shows the predicted ranking by user 944 for different movies. Now that we can see that our FM model has predicted the user's ranking for movies, inspecting model performance in terms of accuracy and execution time would make sense.

For this, I wrote a class called `PlotUtil_Rank.java`. This class takes the metrics type and a number of iterations and generates the plot using the `plot()` method:

```java
public static void plot(double[] iterationArray, double[] timeArray, String
chart_type, int iter) {
        String series = null;
        String title = null;
        String x_axis = null;
        String y_axis = null;
        if(chart_type =="MSE"){
            series = "MSE per Iteration (" + iter + " iterations)";
            title = "MSE per Iteration (" + iter + " iterations)";
            x_axis = "Iteration";
            y_axis = "MSE";
        }else {
            series = "Time per Iteration (" + iter + " iterations)";
            title = "Time per Iteration (" + iter + " iterations)";
            x_axis = "Iteration";
            y_axis = "Time";
        }

        final XYSeriesCollection dataSet = new XYSeriesCollection();
        addSeries(dataSet, iterationArray, timeArray, series);
        final JFreeChart chart = ChartFactory.createXYLineChart(
                title, // chart title
                x_axis, // x axis label
                y_axis, // y axis label
                dataSet, // data
                PlotOrientation.VERTICAL,
                true, // include legend
                true, // tooltips
                false // urls
                );
        final ChartPanel panel = new ChartPanel(chart);
        final JFrame f = new JFrame();
        f.add(panel);
        f.setDefaultCloseOperation(WindowConstants.EXIT_ON_CLOSE);
        f.pack();
        f.setVisible(true);
    }
```

This method is further called from the `PointWiseGradientDescent.java` class. First, we create two `ArrayList` of `Double` to hold the execution time and MSE:

```
//PointWiseGradientDescent.java
List<Double> timeList = new ArrayList<Double>();
List<Double> errList = new ArrayList<Double>();
```

Then, for each iteration, the ;learn() method generates both the MSE error and time for each iteration and puts them in the list:

```
iter = t;
long time1 = System.nanoTime() - time0;
iterationList.add((double)iter);
timeList.add((double)time1 / 1_000_000_000.0);
errList.add(error(fm, test));
```

Finally, the `plot()` method is called as follows to plot the graph:

```
PlotUtil_Rank.plot(convertobjectArraytoDouble(iterationList.toArray()),
convertobjectArraytoDouble(errList.toArray()), "MSE", iter);

PlotUtil_Rank.plot(convertobjectArraytoDouble(iterationList.toArray()),
convertobjectArraytoDouble(timeList.toArray()), "TIME", iter);
```

By the way, `convertobjectArraytoDouble()`, which is shown in the following code, is used to convert the object array into doubles to act as data points for the plots:

```
public double [] convertobjectArraytoDouble(Object[] objectArray){
            double[] doubleArray = newdouble[objectArray.length];
            //Double[ ]doubleArray=new Double();
            for(int i = 0; i < objectArray.length; i++){
                Object object = objectArray[i];
                String string = object.toString(); double dub =
Double.valueOf(string).doubleValue();
                doubleArray[i] = dub;
                }
            return doubleArray;
    }
```

The preceding invocation should generate two graphs. First, we see the MSE per iteration, and the following graph reports the same for 100 iterations:

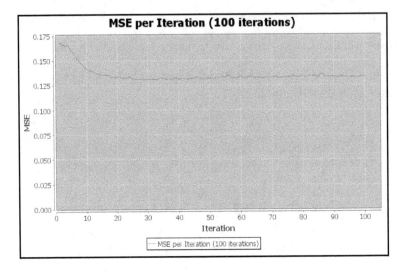

MSE per iteration (up to 100th)

Then, we see the time per iteration, and the following graph reports the same for the 100th iteration:

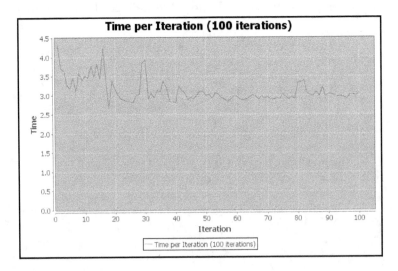

Time per iteration (up to 100th)

Finally, from the second graph, we cannot make important insights except that the execution time per iteration fluctuated a lot. However, on the 90th iteration, the time needed for each iteration was saturated.

On the other hand, the MSE drastically decreased after the 20th iteration from 0.16 to 0.13, but was saturated after the 25th iteration. This means increasing only a number of iterations, will not help us further reduce the MSE. Therefore, I would suggest that you try this after changing not only the number of iterations but also other hyperparameters.

Frequently asked questions (FAQs)

Now that we have seen how to develop a movie recommendation that predicts both the rating and ranking of movies by users, there are some issues that require our attention, too. Also, we couldn't cover/discuss the library in this chapter, so I suggest that you read the documentation more carefully.

However, we will still see some frequently asked questions that might already be on your mind in this section. Answers to these questions can be found in the Appendix.

1. How can I save a trained FM model?
2. How can I restore a saved FM model from disk?
3. Can I use the FM algorithm for solving a classification task?
4. Give me a few example use cases where FM algorithms have been used.
5. Can I use the FM algorithm for making top-N recommendations?

Summary

In this chapter, we saw how to develop a movie recommendation system using FMs, which are a set of algorithms that enhance the performance of linear models by incorporating second-order feature interactions that are absent in matrix factorization algorithms in a supervised way.

Nevertheless, we have seen some theoretical background of recommendation systems using matrix factorization and collaborative filtering before diving into the project's implementation using RankSys library-based FMs. Due to page limitation, I didn't discuss the library more extensively. However, readers are suggested to take a look athe API documentation on GitHub at `https://github.com/RankSys/RankSys`.

This project not only covers movie rating prediction by individual users but also discusses ranking prediction, too. Consequently, we also used FMs for predicting the ranking of movies.

This is more or less the end of our journey toward developing an end-to-end project with Java. However, we are not done yet! In the next chapter, we will discuss some recent trends of deep learning. Then, we will see some emerging use cases that can be implemented using DL4J library or least we'll see some pointers.

Answers to questions

Answer to question 1: For this, you can invoke the `saveModel()` method by providing the input model filename:

```
String FILENAME = Constants.FILENAME;
// Save the trained FM model
fmlsgd.saveModel(FILENAME);
```

The `saveModel()` method goes as follows:

```
public void saveModel(String FILENAME) throws Exception
    {
        FILENAME = Constants.FILENAME;
        FileOutputStream fos = null;
        DataOutputStream dos = null;
        try {
            fos = new FileOutputStream(FILENAME);
            dos = new DataOutputStream(fos);
            dos.writeBoolean(fm.k0);
            dos.writeBoolean(fm.k1);
            dos.writeDouble(fm.w0);
            dos.writeInt(fm.num_factor);
            dos.writeInt(fm.num_attribute);
            dos.writeInt(task.ordinal());
            dos.writeDouble(max_target);
            dos.writeDouble(min_target);
            for(int i=0;i<fm.num_attribute;i++)
            {
                dos.writeDouble(fm.w[i]);
            }
            for(int i=0;i<fm.num_factor;i++)
            {
                dos.writeDouble(fm.m_sum[i]);
            }
```

```
        for(int i=0;i<fm.num_factor;i++)
        {
            dos.writeDouble(fm.m_sum_sqr[i]);
        }
        for(int i_1 = 0; i_1 < fm.num_factor; i_1++) {
            for(int i_2 = 0; i_2 < fm.num_attribute; i_2++) {
                dos.writeDouble(fm.v.get(i_1,i_2));
            }
        }
        dos.flush();
    }
    catch(Exception e) {
        throw new JlibfmRuntimeException(e);
    } finally {
        if(dos!=null)
            dos.close();
        if(fos!=null)
            fos.close();
    }
}
```

Then, the method will save all the metadata (including dimension, rank, weight, and attribute information) of the trained model onto disk.

Answer to question 2: For this, you can invoke the ;therestoreModel() method by providing the input model filename:

```
public void restoreModel(String FILENAME) throws Exception
    {
        FILENAME = Constants.FILENAME;
        InputStream is = null;
        DataInputStream dis = null;
        try {
            is = new FileInputStream(FILENAME);
            dis = new DataInputStream(is);
            fm.k0 = dis.readBoolean();
            fm.k1 = dis.readBoolean();
            fm.w0 = dis.readDouble();
            fm.num_factor = dis.readInt();
            fm.num_attribute = dis.readInt();
            if(dis.readInt() == 0)
            {
                task = TaskType.TASK_REGRESSION;
            }
            else
            {
                task = TaskType.TASK_CLASSIFICATION;
```

```
            }
            max_target = dis.readDouble();
            min_target = dis.readDouble();
            fm.w = new double[fm.num_attribute];
            for(int i=0;i<fm.num_attribute;i++)
            {
                fm.w[i] = dis.readDouble();
            }
            fm.m_sum = new double[fm.num_factor];
            fm.m_sum_sqr = new double[fm.num_factor];
            for(int i=0;i<fm.num_factor;i++)
            {
                fm.m_sum[i] = dis.readDouble();
            }
            for(int i=0;i<fm.num_factor;i++)
            {
                fm.m_sum_sqr[i] = dis.readDouble();
            }
            fm.v = new DataPointMatrix(fm.num_factor, fm.num_attribute);
            for(int i_1 = 0; i_1 < fm.num_factor; i_1++) {
                for(int i_2 = 0; i_2 < fm.num_attribute; i_2++) {
                    fm.v.set(i_1,i_2, dis.readDouble());
                }
            }
        }
        catch(Exception e) {
            throw new JlibfmRuntimeException(e);
        } finally {
            if(dis!=null)
                dis.close();
            if(is!=null)
                is.close();
        }
    }
```

The invocation of this method will restore the saved model, including all the metadata (for example, dimension, rank, weight, and attribute information) of the trained model from the disk.

Answer to question 3: Yes, of course. This algorithm is very effective for very sparse datasets, too. All you need is to have the predicted labels in the integer and the task type classification, that is, `task == TaskType.TASK_CLASSIFICATION`.

Answer to question 4: There are several use cases where FM-based approaches have been applied. For example:

- Predicting whether the user is going to buy an item in a session from a given sequence of click events performed by users. Also, if he/she is buying, what would be the items he/she is going to buy? This problem is called the RecSys Challenge 2015 (see more at `http://2015.recsyschallenge.com/challenge.html`).

  To see a sample solution, interested readers can take a look at the following book titled *Deep Learning with TensorFlow - Second Edition* by Karim et al Packt Publishing, March 2018 (see more at `https://www.packtpub.com/big-data-and-business-intelligence/deep-learning-tensorflow-second-edition`).

- *Using Factorization Machines for Hybrid Recommendation Systems Based on Behavioral, Product, and Customer Data* (see more at `https://dl.acm.org/citation.cfm?id=2796542`).

Answer to question 5: Yes, you can extract it from implicit feedback (from reviews, events, transactions, and so on), since converting the rating prediction results to top-N lists is a trivial job. However, I don't think there's any open source implementations available, but you can of course try by modifying LibFM significantly to use pairwise ranking.

11
Discussion, Current Trends, and Outlook

Deep neural networks being at the core of **deep learning** (DL) allow computational models that are composed of multiple processing layers to learn representations of data with multiple levels of abstraction. These methods have dramatically improved the state-of-the-art stuff in speech recognition, multimedia (image/audio/video) analytics, NLP, image processing and segmentation, visual object recognition, object detection, and many other domains in life sciences, such as cancer genomics, drug discovery, personalized medicine, and biomedical imaging.

Throughout this book, we have seen how to use JVM-based DL libraries to develop some applications covering these areas. I confess that some projects were not so comprehensive and cannot be deployed commercially but need some extra effort. Nonetheless, showing how to deploy such models was not within the scope of this book. However, at least these should provide us with some core insights.

Now that we've come to the end of our little journey of deep learning with different Java libraries, it is time to wrap up everything. But before that, in this chapter, we'll discuss the completed projects and some abstract takeaways. Then we'll provide some suggestions for improvement. Additionally, we'll cover some extension guidelines for other real-life deep learning projects. In summary, the following topics will be covered in this chapter:

- Discussions on projects, outlook, future improvement, and extension
- Current trends on supervised and unsupervised deep learning algorithms
- Frequently asked questions (FAQs)

Discussion and outlook

Throughout this book, we have covered 10 end-to-end projects. We started our journey with an introduction to deep learning and finished at a factorization-machine based movie recommendation system project. In this section, we'll briefly review these projects, discuss potential limitations, and provide some future directions toward improvement and extension.

Discussion on the completed projects

In between, we tried to cover several real-life projects from diverse domains such as healthcare, sentiment analysis in NLP, transfer learning, image and video classification, distributed deep learning and training, reinforcement learning, online trading, and real-life object detection from video. These are outlined as follows:

- Titanic survival prediction using MLP and LSTM networks
- Cancer types prediction using recurrent type networks
- Multi-label Image classification using convolutional neural networks
- Sentiment analysis using Word2Vec and LSTM network
- Image classification using transfer learning
- Real-time object detection using YOLO, JavaCV, and DL4J
- Stock price prediction using the LSTM network
- Distributed deep learning for video classification using convolutional LSTM
- Using deep reinforcement learning for a GridWorld game
- Developing a movie recommendation system using factorization machines

Now we will discuss the pros, cons, and future directions for improving these projects for possible extension.

Titanic survival prediction using MLP and LSTM networks

In this project, our main goal was to get familiar with Apache Spark ML library, followed by a basic introduction to machine learning, deep learning their types, architectures, and frameworks.

We could not achieve higher accuracy. Then, in `Chapter 2`, *Cancer Types Prediction Using Recurrent Type Networks*, we revisited the same project but using a robust recurrent LSTM network, which shows higher accuracy. The takeaway was learning how to prepare the dataset by considering most of the features and feeding into Spark and a DL4J-based MLP classifier.

In addition, this dataset is not so high dimensional, so applying DL methods is not a good idea. Therefore, I would recommend using other tree ensembles such as random forest and gradient-boosted trees for modeling and deployment.

Cancer type prediction using recurrent type networks

We solved an interesting project, where we successfully classified cancer patients based on cancer types. For this, we used the LSTM network. We used a very high-dimensional gene expression dataset. We converted the dataset into sequence format and trained the LSTM net for each sample per time step.

This project also shows the robustness of deep architecture such as LSTM, demonstrating that even without applying dimensionality reduction, the model can handle a very high-dimensional dataset.

One of the potential limitations of this approach was that we considered only a gene expression dataset, so it cannot be deployed for a real-life prognosis and diagnosis, whereas other datasets such as **Copy Number Variation** (**CNV**), DNA methylation, and survival-related clinical outcomes, have to be considered as well. Nonetheless, domain expertise from biomedical engineers and doctors is needed to come up with an integrated solution.

Finally, the takeaway is that at least it shows how to handle at least one type of cancer genomics dataset. Therefore, the same techniques can be applied to other data types too. Then, a multimodal network has to be developed by taking the input from domain experts before deploying, such as an AI expert system.

Image classification using convolutional neural networks

In this project, we saw how to solve a multi-label image classification problem. We used real Yelp images. Then we trained a CNN to predict the classes for each tagged image. In this project, the most challenging part was feature engineering, as we had to deal with not only images but also different tags and metadata. Unfortunately, we could not achieve very high accuracy.

The takeaway would be that similar approaches can be applied to solve other image datasets having multi-labels. Yet, a multiclass classification problem can be solved with minimal effort as well. All you need is to prepare the dataset such that a CNN-based model can consume it. Apart from this outlook, the project in Chapter 5, *Image Classification using Transfer Learning,* can be extended to solve similar problems.

Sentiment analysis using Word2Vec and the LSTM network

In this project, we saw how to develop a sentiment analysis application using Word2Vec and LSTM. We also discussed how to convert unstructured texts into neural word embedding, and later on transform them into the sequence form required to train the LSTM network. Then we trained LSTM with the sequence of the corresponding texts at each time step.

This project also addressed a binary classification problem with very high accuracy. In the same line, this application can be extended for classifying other problems, such as spam versus ham for messages and email, and movie or product reviews. Finally, in the FAQ section, we discussed how to solve the same problem with CNN, which can achieve similar accuracy to LSTM.

Image classification using transfer learning

In this chapter, we solved an interesting dog versus cat classification problem using the transfer learning technique. We used a pre-trained VGG16 model and its weights, and subsequently we fine-tuned the training with a real-life cat versus dog dataset from Kaggle.

Once the training was completed, we saved the trained model for model persistence and later reuse. We saw that the trained model could successfully detect and differentiate between cat and dog images with very different sizes, quality, and shapes.

The trained model/classifier can be used to solve cat versus dog problems in real life. Finally, the lesson was that this similar technique with minimal efforts, can be extended and used to solve similar image classification problems; this applies for both binary and multiclass classification problems.

Real-time object detection using YOLO, JavaCV, and DL4J

In this project, we again used the transfer learning technique to solve another interesting problem, which is real-time object detection from video clips. We used a pre-trained YOLOv2 model, JavaCV, and DL4J libraries to solve this problem.

As stated in the chapter, we extended the image recognition idea to solve this problem. That is, our technique generates video frames as images and then recognizes objects from the frame using the bounding box approach. The takeaway is that although we used a video clip to show the evaluation, it still showed very good accuracy. And from the provided demo, anyone can observe that most of the objects in the clip were accurately identified. Thus, a similar technique, can be extended for real-time object detection.

In this regard, we saw some tips to collect real-time videos from a webcam or video camera (or even a mobile phone) and feed them into our YOLOv2 model using the JavaCV library.

Stock price prediction using LSTM network

In this project, we saw how to develop a demo project for predicting the stock prices for five categories: OPEN, CLOSE, LOW, HIGH, and VOLUME. However, this result also lacks the actual signal; all your network has to do is produce a value similar to the last input of the price.

If we took your prediction as the input for the next prediction, we saw that the results were quite bad. I know there are some serious drawbacks of this approach. Nevertheless, we had not used enough data, which potentially limits the performance of such a model.

Knowing the drawback of this project, the biggest takeaway is extending Bitcoin or another cryptocurrency price prediction. As suggested in the FAQ section, historical Bitcoin data can be downloaded from Kaggle. Then, similar feature engineering as we used in this project can be used to prepare the sequence dataset. Nevertheless, CNN-based approaches can be used too.

Distributed deep learning – video classification using a convolutional-LSTM network

In this project, we developed a complete deep learning application that classifies a large collection of a video dataset from the UCF101 dataset. We applied a combined CNN-LSTM network with **deeplearning4j (DL4J)** that overcame the limitations of standalone CNN or RNN **Long Short-Term Memory (LSTM)** networks.

Finally, we saw how to perform training in both a parallel and distributed manner across multiple devices (CPUs and GPUs) on AWS EC2 AMI 9.0. We performed parallel and distributed training on a `p2.8xlarge` instance with 8 GPUs, 32 computing cores, and 488 GB of RAM.

One of the greatest takeaways from this chapter was that this end-to-end project can be treated as a primer for human activity recognition from video. Secondly, we did not achieve high accuracy because we had not trained the model with all the available video clips.

Therefore, having the network trained with the a full video dataset and hyperparameter tuning definitely increases accuracy. In that case, deploying the improved model is commercially possible. Finally, if you want to make the training even faster, configuring a Hadoop cluster and distributing the training on both GPUs and Spark is possible.

Using deep reinforcement learning for GridWorld

In this project, we saw how to develop a demo GridWorld game using DL4J and Neural QLearning, which acts as the Q function. We also provided some basic theoretical background for developing DQN to play a GridWorld game. However, we did not develop a module for visualizing the moves of the agent for the entire episodes. I confess that it was the biggest drawback of this project. However, I discussed some improvements in the FAQ section.

The takeaway from this project is extending this application with a visualization model or even developing other RL-based games, such as Doom and ALE would be a good idea. Secondly and finally, we can also think of developing another interesting RL project for online trading.

Movie recommender system using factorization machines

In this project, we saw how to develop a movie recommendation system using factorization machines (FMs) that are a set of algorithms that enhance the performance of linear models by incorporating second-order feature interactions that are absent in matrix factorization algorithms in a supervised way.

Nevertheless, we saw some theoretical background of recommendation systems using matrix factorization and collaborative filtering before diving the project implementation using RankSys library-based FMs. This project not only covered movie-rating prediction by individual users but also discussed ranking predictions. Consequently, we used FM for predicting rankings for movies too.

However, the potential limitation is that this library is not scalable and well structured, I would say. Therefore, trying Python-based FM libraries would be a better idea. Finally, the biggest takeaway is extending this application with Python-based FM libraries for even larger movie datasets from MovieLens or IMDb, which is recommended.

Current trends and outlook

As a researcher, I work as a **Program Committee (PC)** member for conferences such as WWW'2018, ISWC'2018, ESWC'2017/2018, and ESWC SemDeep'2018 international workshops. Apart from these, I am also a guest editor for International Semantic Web Journal, Journal of Cloud Computing, and Briefings in Bioinformatics.

While reviewing numerous papers for these conferences and journals, I found that researchers have not limited themselves to developing emerging use cases and analytical solutions using original RNN, CNN, DBN or autoencoders. They are coming up with ideas across new architectures by combining them for diverse domains.

Current trends

As discussed in `Chapter 1`, *Getting Started with Deep Learning*, researchers have recently proposed so many emergent DL architectures. These include not only improving CNN/RNN and their variants but also some other special types of architecture: **Deep SpatioTemporal Neural Networks (DST-NNs)**, **Multi-Dimensional Recurrent Neural Networks (MD-RNNs)**, **Convolutional AutoEncoders (CAEs)**, deep embedding clustering, and so on.

Nevertheless, there are a few more emerging networks, such as CapsNets, which is an improved version of a CNN designed to remove the drawbacks of regular CNNs as proposed by Hinton et al. Then we have residual neural networks for image recognition and **Generative Adversarial Networks (GANs)** for simple image generation.

Apart from these trends and use cases, different deep and emerging architectures are being used in multimedia analytics; computer vision (especially semantic image segmentation); anomaly detection from IoT, image, and network traffic; neural machine translation for NLP; and integration of knowledge graphs with neural networks.

Outlook on emergent DL architectures

In this subsection, we'll discuss some emergent architectures and their variants, focusing on some use cases.

Residual neural networks

Because of the millions of billions of hyperparameters and other practical aspects associated with them, it is difficult to train deep neural networks. To overcome this limitation, Kaiming He et al. (see `https://arxiv.org/abs/1512.03385v1`) proposed a **residual learning framework (RNN)** to ease the training of networks that are substantially deeper than those used previously. Now, according to the original paper:

> *"In this network setting, instead of hoping each stack of layers directly fits a desired underlying mapping, we explicitly let these layers fit a residual mapping. The original mapping is recast into F(x)+x. We hypothesize that it is easier to optimize the residual mapping than to optimize the original, unreferenced mapping. To the extreme, if an identity mapping were optimal, it would be easier to push the residual to zero than to fit an identity mapping by a stack of nonlinear layers."*

This way, RNNs are easier to optimize and can gain accuracy from considerably increased depth compared to other DNN architectures. The downside is that building a network by simply stacking residual blocks inevitably limits its optimization ability. To overcome this limitation, Ke Zhang et al. also proposed using a multilevel residual networks (see at `https://arxiv.org/abs/1608.02908`).

Consequently, residual networks are in use to solve many emerging use cases, including:

- *Skeleton-Based Action Recognition with Spatial Reasoning and Temporal Stack Learning* (see more at `https://arxiv.org/pdf/1805.02335`).
- Recently, Yuan et al. proposed *Hyperspectral Image Denoising Employing a Spatial-Spectral Deep Residual Convolutional Neural Network* (see `https://arxiv.org/pdf/1806.00183`).
- *A Dynamic Model for Traffic Flow Prediction Using Improved DRN* (see more at `https://arxiv.org/pdf/1805.00868`)
- *Classification of simulated radio signals using Wide Residual Networks for use in the search for extra-terrestrial intelligence* (see more at `https://arxiv.org/pdf/1803.08624`)

GANs

GANs are deep neural net architectures that consist of two networks pitted against each other (hence the name adversarial). Ian Goodfellow et al. introduced GANs in a paper (see more at `https://arxiv.org/abs/1406.2661v1`). GAN is one of the best research outcomes in AI that can learn to mimic any distribution of data. This is such that a trained GAN can be deployed to create worlds similar to our own, especially for images, music, speech, or prose.

Although the original GAN paper targeted simple image generation such as DCGAN, BEGAN, and so on, people are extending the idea for font generation, anime character generation, interactive image generation, text-to-image generation, 2D object generation, human pose estimation, and so on. A few concrete research-oriented use cases as outlined as follows:

- For generating an image sequence from the description with LSTM (see more at `https://arxiv.org/pdf/1806.03027`)
- Generative adversarial networks for **electroencephalographic** (**EEG**) brain signals (see more at `https://arxiv.org/pdf/1806.01875`)
- For natural language generation for electronic health records (see more at `https://arxiv.org/pdf/1806.01353`)
- For chest X-ray segmentation (see more at `https://arxiv.org/pdf/1806.00600`)

Capsule networks (CapsNet)

As discussed in `Chapter 1`, *Getting Started with Deep Learning*, CNNs perform well at classifying good quality images. However, if the images have rotation, tilt, or any other different orientation, CNNs give very poor performance. Even the pooling operation in CNNs cannot help much with positional invariance.

To overcome the this limitation of CNN, Geoffrey Hinton et al. come up with a ground breaking idea called **CapsuleNetworks (CapsNet)** that are particularly good at handling different types of visual stimulus and encoding things such as pose (position, size, and orientation), deformation, velocity, albedo, hue, texture.

In a regular DNN, we keep on adding layers (more layers means a deeper network). In CapsNet, the idea is to add more layers inside a single layer. This way, a CapsNet is a nested set of neural layers. In CapsNet, the limitation of max-pooling layer is overcome and replaced with **routing by agreement (RBA)** to capture low-level visual information.

Unfortunately, the original paper is too theoretical. Therefore, researchers are trying to extend the idea of CapsNet for different AI and data science projects including image classification, GAN improvement and at improving RL-based gaming experience. A few example use cases are listed as follows:

- *Object Localization and Motion Transfer learning with Capsules* (see `https://arxiv.org/pdf/1805.07706`)
- *An attention-based Bi-GRU-CapsNet model for hypernymy detection between compound entities* (see more at `https://arxiv.org/pdf/1805.04827`)
- *Brain Tumor Type Classification via Capsule Networks* (see more at `https://arxiv.org/pdf/1802.10200`)
- *CapsuleGAN: Generative Adversarial Capsule Network* (see more at `https://arxiv.org/pdf/1802.06167`)
- *Deep Reinforcement Learning using Capsules in Advanced Game Environments* (see more at `https://arxiv.org/pdf/1801.09597`)

Apart from these emerging architectures, people are trying to use GAN architectures for image synthesis using CapsNet (see `https://arxiv.org/pdf/1806.03796`). Researchers have also used adversarial autoencoders for speech-based emotion recognition (see `https://arxiv.org/pdf/1806.02146`). Finally, I would suggest readers to know the recent trends in artificial intelligence, machine learning, and deep learning from `https://arxiv.org/list/cs.AI/recent`.

Semantic image segmentation

Image segmentation is the way to partition an image into several coherent parts, but *without* any attempt at understanding what these parts represent. Semantic segmentation, on the other hand, attempts to partition the image into semantically meaningful parts and to classify each part into one of the predetermined classes.

Such semantic segmentation of raw brain images into gray matter, white matter, and cerebrospinal fluid helps classify them based on the segmented areas. Deep-learning-based techniques are being in use and very successful such as **Stacked Denoising Autoencoders (SDAE)**.

Nevertheless, the recurrent-based fully convolutional network is being in use for semantic segmentation of high-resolution remote sensing images (see more at `https://arxiv.org/pdf/1805.02091`). This types of image segmentation are being in use in emerging use cases such as Pelvic MRImage analysis, object detection for self-driving cars, geospatial image classification (see `http://www.semantic-web-journal.net/system/files/swj1862.pdf`), and many more.

Deep learning for clustering analysis

Clustering analysis is one of the most widely used data-driven task. To date, existing clustering analysis techniques use classical clustering algorithms such as k-means, bisecting k-means, or the Gaussian mixture model. In particular, the k-means clustering algorithm and its several variants have been proposed to address issues with higher-dimensional input spaces.

However, they are fundamentally limited to linear embedding. Hence, they cannot model nonlinear relationships. Nevertheless, fine-tuning in these approaches is based on only cluster assignment hardening loss. Therefore, a fine-grained clustering accuracy cannot be achieved.

In short, relatively less research has focused on deep-learning-based representation learning and clustering analysis. However, the quality of k-means is dependent on the data distribution. Deep architecture can help the model learn a mapping from the data space to a lower-dimensional feature space in which it iteratively optimizes a clustering objective.

Considering these limitations and motivations, researchers have come up with deep-learning-based clustering techniques for clustering very-high-dimensional data and nonlinear objects. In these approaches, k-means is incorporated with deep architectures, where both the clustering-assignment-hardening loss (from k-means) and reconstruction loss (from DNN) are optimized simultaneously. These approaches include:

- *Unsupervised Deep Embedding for Clustering Analysis* by Xie et al. (see `https://arxiv.org/pdf/1511.06335.pdf`)
- *Neural Networks-based Clustering using Pairwise Constraints* by Hsu et al. (see more at `https://arxiv.org/abs/1511.06321`)
- *Discriminatively Boosted Clustering (DBC)* by Liu et al. (see more at `http://dataclustering.cse.msu.edu/papers/boost_cluster.pdf`)
- *Clustering with Deep Learning: Taxonomy and New Methods* by Elie et al. (see more at `https://arxiv.org/abs/1801.07648`)
- *Recurrent Deep Embedding Networks for Genotype Clustering and Ethnicity Prediction* by Karim et al. (see more at `https://arxiv.org/pdf/1805.12218.pdf`)

Frequently asked questions (FAQs)

We have analyzed the completed projects and looked at recent trends. Based on these, there might be several questions in your mind. In this section, I will try to devise some such questions and provide sample answers:

1. In this chapter, we argued that using GAN, we could solve many research problems. Is there any GAN implementation in DL4J?
2. In this chapter, we argued that using CapsNet is a better idea for handling images having different shapes and orientation. Is there any implementation for CapsNet in DL4J?
3. In `Chapter 1`, *Getting Started with Deep Learning*, we discussed DBNs and restricted Boltzmann machines as their basic building blocks. However, we have not used DBNs in any of the completed projects. What is the reason for this?
4. In this chapter, we argued that using unsupervised anomaly detection from IoT sensor data or images is an emerging research use case. Are there any examples of this in DL4J?
5. Are there any examples of developing recommendation engines with DL4J?

6. Considering the fact that smartphones nowadays are very powerful, can we develop image/object detection applications on a smartphone?
7. How could I wrap-up a deep learning application as a web app?
8. I am having issues while running the projects. In addition, I am experiencing issues while configuring the development environment (for example, on Eclipse/IntelliJ IDEA and configuring CUDA/CuDNN). What can I do?

Answers to questions

Answer to question 1: There is an inactive issue on this. Interested readers can look at `https://github.com/deeplearning4j/deeplearning4j/issues/1737` to know the current update. However, the discussion loop is not very active.

Answer to question 2: As far as I know, there is no CapsNet implementation in DL4J. Also, I didn't see any open discussion/issues on this topic. I asked in the DL4j Gitter channel but nobody replied.

Answer to question 3: Both unsupervised pre-training and supervised fine-tuning can be performed using DBN. That means this probabilistic network is an intelligent choice if we do not have enough labeled data but still want to perform NN-based training.

Answer to question 4: Yes, there is an example of anomaly detection using a variational autoencoder with reconstruction probability for MNIST data. Take a look at DL4J examples at `https://github.com/deeplearning4j/dl4j-examples/tree/master/dl4j-examples/src/main/java/org/deeplearning4j/examples/unsupervised/anomalydetection`. However, this example can be extended for other datasets too.

Answer to question 5: There is an example for well-dressed recommendation engine in this link `https://deeplearning4j.org/welldressed-recommendation-engine`.

Answer to question 6: Deep learning and neural networks can be deployed in Android devices too. For more information, refer to `https://deeplearning4j.org/android`.

Answer to question 7: Once the NN is trained, the network can be used for inference, or making predictions about the data it sees. Inference happens to be a much less compute-intensive process. Then, Spring Boot or another framework can be used to wrap up the application as a web app. See some guidelines at `https://deeplearning4j.org/build_vgg_webapp`.

Answer to question 8: You should follow the instructions I provided in the chapters. In addition, the code of this book is available on GitHub, so feel free to PR or create new issues and I will try to fix them as soon as possible. About any new issues, you can ask through the DL4J Gitter live channel at `https://gitter.im/deeplearning4j/deeplearning4j`.

Other Books You May Enjoy

If you enjoyed this book, you may be interested in these other books by Packt:

Mastering Java Machine Learning
Dr. Uday Kamath, Krishna Choppella

ISBN: 9781785880513

- Master key Java machine learning libraries, and what kind of problem each can solve, with theory and practical guidance.
- Explore powerful techniques in each major category of machine learning such as classification, clustering, anomaly detection, graph modeling, and text mining.
- Apply machine learning to real-world data with methodologies, processes, applications, and analysis.
- Techniques and experiments developed around the latest specializations in machine learning, such as deep learning, stream data mining, and active and semi-supervised learning.
- Build high-performing, real-time, adaptive predictive models for batch- and stream-based big data learning using the latest tools and methodologies.
- Get a deeper understanding of technologies leading towards a more powerful AI applicable in various domains such as Security, Financial Crime, Internet of Things, social networking, and so on.

Neural Network Programming with Java - Second Edition
Fabio M. Soares, Alan M. F. Souza

ISBN: 9781787126053

- Develop an understanding of neural networks and how they can be fitted
- Explore the learning process of neural networks
- Build neural network applications with Java using hands-on examples
- Discover the power of neural network's unsupervised learning process to extract the intrinsic knowledge hidden behind the data
- Apply the code generated in practical examples, including weather forecasting and pattern recognition
- Understand how to make the best choice of learning parameters to ensure you have a more effective application
- Select and split data sets into training, test, and validation, and explore validation strategies

Leave a review - let other readers know what you think

Please share your thoughts on this book with others by leaving a review on the site that you bought it from. If you purchased the book from Amazon, please leave us an honest review on this book's Amazon page. This is vital so that other potential readers can see and use your unbiased opinion to make purchasing decisions, we can understand what our customers think about our products, and our authors can see your feedback on the title that they have worked with Packt to create. It will only take a few minutes of your time, but is valuable to other potential customers, our authors, and Packt. Thank you!

Index

used, for video classification 404
Copy Number Variation (CNV) 401

D

datasets
  about 162
  large Movie Review dataset 162
  sentiment labeled dataset 164
Deep Belief Networks (DBN) 67
Deep Learning (DL)
  about 9, 17
  cloud-based platforms 39
  frameworks 37
  ML, taking to next level 17, 19
  Titanic survival prediction 40
Deep Neural Networks (DNNs)
  about 29
  Deep Belief Networks 30
  drawbacks 112
  hidden units 31
  image classification 112
  Multilayer Perceptron 30
deep Q-network
  used, for developing 325
deep reinforcement learning
  using, for GridWorld 404
Deep SpatioTemporal Neural Networks (DST-NNs) 405
Deeplearning4J (DL4J)
  about 9, 157, 279, 404
  and transfer learning 193
  ComputationGraph 202
  MultiLayerNetwork 202
  reference 96, 283
  transfer learning API, reference 193
  used, for distributed training on GPUs 281
  used, for real-time object detection 403
discount factor 322
distributed deep learning
  across multiple GPUs 280, 281

E

Elastic Compute Cloud (EC2) 39
electroencephalographic (EEG) 407

emergent DL architectures
  about 35, 406
  capsule networks (CapsNet) 36, 408
  deep learning, for clustering analysis 409, 410
  Generative Adversarial Networks (GANs) 36, 407
  Residual Neural Networks (RNN) 35, 406, 407
  semantic image segmentation 409
epoch 80
exploration
  versus exploitation 15
Extraction Transformation Load (ETL) 12

F

factorization machines (FM)
  about 347
  in recommender systems 355
  used, for developing movie recommender system 356
  used, in recommender systems 353
  using, in movie recommender system 405
feedforward neural network (FFNN) 28
FineTuneConfiguration 200
forward pass 23
fully connected (FC) layers 218

G

Gated Recurrent Units (GRUs) 35
Generative Adversarial Networks (GANs) 35, 406, 407
  references 407
GPUs
  distributed training, with DL4J 281, 283
Gradient Descent (GD) 26
greedy policy 320
grid, GridWorld game
  action mask, calculating 329
  agent position, calculating 328
  generating 327
  goal position, calculating 328
  guidance action, providing 330
  input, flattening for input layer 331
  reward, calculating 331
GridWorld game
  developing, with deep Q-network 325

www.ingramcontent.com/pod-product-compliance
Lightning Source LLC
La Vergne TN
LVHW081511050326
832903LV00025B/1441

* 9 7 8 1 7 8 8 9 9 7 4 5 4 *